CUPID'S
POISONED
ARROW

CUPID'S POISONED ARROW

FROM *Habit* TO *Harmony*
IN *Sexual Relationships*

MARNIA ROBINSON

Foreword by
DOUGLAS WILE, PhD

North Atlantic Books
Berkeley, California

Published by
North Atlantic Books
Huichin, unceded Ohlone land
Berkeley, California

Cover and book design © Ayelet Maida; cover source image © ImageDJ
Printed in the United States of America

Cupid's Poisoned Arrow: From Habit to Harmony in Sexual Relationships is sponsored and published by North Atlantic Books, an educational nonprofit based in the unceded Ohlone land Huichin (Berkeley, CA) that collaborates with partners to develop cross-cultural perspectives; nurture holistic views of art, science, the humanities, and healing; and seed personal and global transformation by publishing work on the relationship of body, spirit, and nature.

North Atlantic Books's publications are distributed to the US trade and internationally by Penguin Random House Publisher Services. For further information, visit our website at www.northatlanticbooks.com.

Although anyone may find the suggestions in this book useful and beneficial, they are not intended as a diagnosis, prescription, recommended treatment, or cure for any specific problem, whether medical, emotional, psychological, social, or spiritual. This book was written for educational purposes only and not designed to replace therapy or consultation with a qualified professional.

Library of Congress Cataloging-in-Publication Data
Robinson, Marnia, 1954–
   Cupid's poisoned arrow : from habit to harmony in sexual relationships / Marnia Robinson.
      p. cm.
   Includes index.
   ISBN 978-1-55643-809-7
   1. Sex.   2. Man-woman relationships.   3. Intimacy (Psychology)   I. Title.
HQ21 .R7513
306.7—dc22   2008041425

11 12 13 KPC 25 24

This book is lovingly dedicated to
Gary Bruce Wilson,
whose courage, insight, and open heart
brought it to life.

IN GRATITUDE

This book could not have been compiled or published without the generous and dedicated efforts of many people over a fifteen-year period. For some reason, most of them prefer to remain anonymous. Nevertheless, there are a few bold people I would like to thank by name. Mary Sharpe has contributed countless insights, bits of relevant research, and practical suggestions for many years. She even returned to university to obtain a second advanced degree, in theology, at Cambridge in order to study and write about sexuality and the sacred. Her work led to many intriguing discoveries, some of which are in this book. Steve Coffin and Jay Moller have both shared hours of their precious time critiquing the text and asking shrewd, and sometimes awkward, questions, which strengthened it a great deal. Mari Petersen's loyal encouragement and insights about attachment were invaluable. Augustin Masquilier voluntarily spent hours recreating, and teaching me how to manage, my Web site, which opened portals for some amazing bloggers. Their willingness to experiment with the concepts in this book and offer their own stories were precious gifts—and an enjoyable experiment in oneness.

I have also been blessed with some wonderful male and female mentors in the form of professors, bosses, and close relatives. Their strong centers of gravity, healthy boundaries, and shrewd grasp of human nature have supported and sustained me when the path seemed steep. Finally, my husband, Gary Wilson, contributed the hours of careful study and related insights that made this material's key concepts accessible for the science-drenched West. He also supplied the loving yang energy that fueled the writing.

I am deeply indebted to this chain of enthusiasts, loved ones, and guardians, which stretches around the globe, with special links in Australia, Belgium, Chile, England, Germany, Italy, Sweden, Taiwan, and the United States.

CONTENTS

FOREWORD

Marnia Robinson's book is the fulfillment of a dream I shared at the end of *Art of the Bedchamber:* that Asian sexual practices, developed under conditions of polygamy and proto-science, could be adapted for modern monogamy and gender equality. Asian male fantasies of achieving immortality by stealing female sexual essence and phobias of essence-stealing female fox fairies can now be explained by neurochemistry. But more than unraveling the mysteries of ancient Asian sexology, Robinson has employed a cinematographer's mastery of montage to craft a dazzling panorama of intimate personal experience, anecdote, ancient wisdom, philosophy, psychology, and medicine. The book's content richness will satisfy scholars and scientists in many fields, but its wit and style will rivet any thoughtful man or woman who has ever stopped to reflect upon the human sexual tragicomedy.

Like a thriller that reveals its climax at the beginning, Robinson's book leaves the reader intrigued by every twist and turn of autobiography and intellectual inquiry to discover what brought her to such a revolutionary conclusion. She does not bow down to the idols of "ancient wisdom" or mainstream scientific consensus, but stands courageously on the two feet of the truth of her own experience and the latest discoveries in neuroscience.

You may come to this book for advice on your sex life, but you will come away with something more like the Theory of Everything in human behavior. Robinson has brought so much humanity and humor to her quest that you may not even notice that she has skillfully used the most advanced scientific discoveries to salvage good old-fashioned romance.

Sex, avarice, and violence are the three two-edged swords of human evolution: how to tame sex without destroying love, how to tame avarice without destroying creativity, and how to tame violence without destroying courage have been the preoccupation of religion, politics, and philosophy from time immemorial. Somehow avarice and violence seem simple in comparison to sex, but Robinson has made, perhaps, the boldest and most thoroughgoing attempt to date. She aims to put your sex life on a diet, but like all good diets, it is not about eating less as much as eating smarter. The sciences and social sciences have polarized along a nature-nurture axis, but she has navigated a middle path between biological determinism and cultural construction to return to the Epicurean vision of using reason to refine pleasure.

—Douglas Wile, PhD, author of *Art of the Bedchamber: The Chinese Sexual Yoga Classics Including Women's Solo Meditation Texts*

PREFACE

My parents and my grandparents stayed married until death parted them. I, on the other hand, couldn't keep my relationships going for more than a few years, and I wasn't alone. The marriages of all three friends whose weddings I attended as bridesmaid *also* ended in divorce. Why? Sociologist Kelly Musick says it's due to women's financial independence. "What's keeping people together is their love and commitment for each other, and that's fragile."[1]

Why were love and commitment becoming so fragile? Exactly how could the fact that I earned my own living *cause* disharmony? That made no sense. I was too much of a romantic to consider the possibility that sexual unions had *always* been fragile, and that women's increased financial independence simply enabled partners to move on with greater ease.

Instead, I tried all the familiar recommendations for healing disharmony in intimate relationships: improved communication, finding a more "ideal" mate, more passion, loving my inner child, negotiation, and so forth. Yet these remedies did not arrest relationship deterioration when trouble started. Eventually I realized that they sometimes address only *symptoms* of a more fundamental problem. That problem is right under our noses. It has always been there, but now that we can dissolve our marriages with greater ease, it is even more glaring. Once we acknowledge the problem, the solution is evident.

The trouble begins with sex. Not exciting sex versus boring sex, or too little sex versus too much, as most of us conclude, but rather fertilization behavior itself. After all, platonic friendships between men and women work fairly well. The trouble generally erupts after we become lovers. And what else begins then? For everyone? The quest to have our sexual needs met *as thoroughly as possible.*

Passion seems like our best friend, often the one indisputably good thing about an otherwise dysfunctional relationship. However, sexual satiety—that "I'm done!" feeling after sex—turns out to be a subconscious, surprisingly persuasive, mammalian signal. It urges us toward habituation (feeling fed up with a mate). Because we're unaware of this signal, we ascribe the friction in our relationships to other causes.

The more dissatisfied we grow, the less likely we are to stumble upon the *other* way of easing sexual tension: relaxed, gentle intercourse that soothes sexual frustration entirely differently.

"WHO'S IN CHARGE?"

There's an optimistic belief that doing what your body is *inclined* to do will lead to well-being and contentment. Actually, given our unquenchable appetites, most of us would be healthier on a Paleolithic diet of whole foods (no refined starches and sugars). But a diet for our sex lives? Surely if our early ancestors pursued sexual satiety whenever opportunity knocked, we'll be just fine doing the same thing.

This logic assumes that you're programmed for your own benefit. In fact, evolution has wired you not for your individual welfare, but for your genes' success. What serves your genes? Two things. The first is lots of fertilization attempts. You experience this as the drive to exhaust yourself sexually when you can. The second is different parents for your offspring. You experience this as disenchantment with sexual exclusivity.

What serves *you* best? A solid emotional bond with a mate, harmony, lots of affectionate, generous touch, and a reliable way to ease sexual frustration. About thirteen percent of lucky couples find their way to this balance naturally,[1a] but most of us are no better "swans" than we are dieters.

So, how do our genes push us to exhaust our sexual desire for each other instead of promoting harmony? New advances in brain science (especially neuroendocrinology) are revealing that disillusionment between lovers may have less to do with communication or compatibility than we thought, and more to do with a primitive pathway that runs through our mammalian brains (limbic brains), known as our *reward circuitry*. This group of structures guarantees that we receive a powerful neurochemical "reward" when we pursue a new partner and engage in hot sex, or even think about either one.

The neurochemical payoff at the moment of orgasm feels like it promotes bonding. Yet such bonds are more fragile than we like to admit. At climax, a neurochemical blast triggers further events for approximately two weeks. These fluctuations deep in the brain drive us toward sexual satiety and subtle changes in mood, which often create emotional friction between lovers (Cupid's poison). Uneasiness also leaves us vulnerable to promises of quick relief—another potential mate (real or virtual) being one of the most alluring. Thus orgasm turns out to be related to making more babies *and* making them with more than one partner.

In essence, our scheming genes have subverted human will to their purposes. Once you understand the means they use, their unsuspected effects upon you and your unions, and a practical alternative for easing sexual tension and finding contentment, you will be in a better position to choose whether you wish to remain under their spell.

We humans are unique among mammals in that we have the capacity to comprehend our subconscious mating programming and choose to manage it consciously. This is a blessing, because we are better off in harmonious relationships with high levels of trust than we are in mindless mating dances orchestrated to propel sperm to egg, bond us long enough for two caregivers to attach to any offspring, and then urge us onward to new partners.

Most of us sense that the gains from caring deeply about another person we trust are profound. In fact, as pair-bonding mammals, we've evolved to find such connections highly beneficial. Not only do trusted companionship and loving touch change our outlook on life for the better, they also improve physical health and reduce stress.

Sexual intimacy that can do all this is truly great sex. And to experience it continuously all we have to do is stay in love. Indeed, if logic ruled, we *would* stay in love. The problem arises when our genes rule and the aftereffects from their incentive plan (unbridled passion) separate lovers by causing them to exhaust their desire for each other. As my husband, Will, put it, "Evolution doesn't give a rat's rump about happiness, fidelity, or lifelong companionship." This is why we inherit an uneasy tension between our *add-a-mate* program and our *pair-bonding* program.

To cope with this reality, ancient Chinese Taoists, among others, recommended learning to make love very calmly and *without orgasm,* unless conception is desired. This unfamiliar approach doesn't trigger our subconscious mating program with its add-a-mate subtext. The gift of this approach is not just that it allows lovers to have intercourse often without a buildup of sexual frustration. It also takes advantage of a second built-in mammalian program: attachment. Evolved to tie us to our children and parents, our bonding program can solidify and protect our romances, too. Using it is nearly effortless once we master (actually, recall) a set of simple cues. Results include greater harmony and well-being, and, remarkably, less sexual frustration.

ONWARD

The first part of this book explains why I chose to explore another way to make love, and recounts the discoveries that followed this decision. What began as a subjective, personal exploration of ancient wisdom about managing my love life unexpectedly expanded into the realm of objective scientific research once my husband and I began collaborating. I was astonished at how neatly recent research on the brain dovetailed with the observations and claims of ancient sages. This alignment of past wisdom, personal experience, and recent research has pushed me to share this information.

If you find that the material in this book brings your resistance and skepticism to the fore, you are not alone. You may even feel that you are being urged to try something against your will. I experienced these feelings myself—and more so during the two weeks after an orgasm. After all, this material confronts one of the most powerful programs in our brain: our mating program. Who wants to opt for generous, relaxed affection in the bedroom when our brain chemistry is all set up to "reward" us for being as driven as possible in that quarter?

On the other hand, the situation is not unlike driving a car with two pedals. Once we become aware of how our mating and bonding pedals operate, it's up to each of us to decide how we use them—depending upon our goals for a relationship. Should you decide you want to quiet the strident signals from your mating program for a few weeks to see what it yields, this book offers a way to make the experiment with a minimum of inner conflict. After all, other than passing up some orgasms, what have you got to lose?

Another goal of this book is to initiate a broader discussion of our subconscious mating and bonding programs and their unacknowledged roles in our lives. Armed with a deeper understanding of how sex actually bends our perceptions and priorities, we can start the process of steering consciously for better results. Like the sages of the past who carefully studied sex from the point of view of increased harmony and improved health, lovers can begin to make their own investigations with greater awareness. They can take into account what best keeps them making love contentedly throughout their unions. They can also address the natural potential of orgasm to become compulsive, and how best to cope.

Much of the text consists of real people's observations, although I've changed their names. I also could not resist peppering the pages with others' witticisms about the gender gap. Why not have a good laugh at the tricks our sneaky genes have played on us, and then get on with outsmarting *them*?

After all, probably ninety-nine percent of sexual encounters take place without the intention to fertilize an ovum. When we insist on engaging in sexual behavior that is fertilization-driven despite its drawbacks, it is like continuing to eat high-calorie desserts because one percent of the population wants to gain weight.

> I don't mind women leaving me, but they always have to tell you why.
> —Richard Pryor

Now that the planet is teeming with underfed, underloved human beings, it may be time to master this ancient alternative and add it to our lovemaking repertoire. Sex and intimate relationships are two of life's most valuable treasures. Whatever your economic woes, I hope the information here will help you protect, and so benefit more than ever from, these widely available riches as you chart your ideal course. At the very least you will know more about how Cupid poisons his arrow as you work toward creating the intimate relationship for which your soul yearns.

Those people are happy who relish love's pleasure
Enjoying Aphrodite's sensual embrace
As a ship riding easy on a calm sea,
Avoiding the obsession that leads to disgrace.
For sex, like a horsefly, can madden with its sting,
And Eros [Cupid] has two arrows to his string....
A mere scratch from the first brings lifelong joy,
But the second wounds to death, and breeds despair.
Goddess born in Cyprus [Aphrodite], keep my bedroom safe
From the mortal arrow, make love in my life
A steady, continuing delight,
Not obsessional or destructive. Let me serve
The great queen with ecstasy, as is her right,
But commit no crimes for her, nor become her slave.

—Euripides (ca. 480–406 BCE), *Iphegenia at Aulis*

CHAPTER ONE

BIOLOGY HAS PLANS
FOR YOUR LOVE LIFE

Having sex to the point of satiety (that "I'm done!" feeling) is a mammalian *mating* signal to lose interest in one mate, and find novel mates appealing.

Even though humans are pair-bonders, the habit of pursuing passion to the point of quenching desire can set off unsuspected mood swings, cause resentment toward a lover, and erode attraction (Cupid's poison).

There are two fundamentally different ways of making love: one for fertilization, and one for triggering closer bonding *(karezza)*.

Hit by Cupid's arrow! What an exhilarating, enviable state of affairs. Like everyone else, you want to believe that the key to lasting romantic bliss is a partner with whom you feel a passion so intense that it can never fade. Yet, have you ever fallen in love with total abandon, experienced wonderful lovemaking, been sure you wanted to stay together forever—and then noticed recurring emotional friction arising between you and your beloved? If you're married, do you have a sense that the honeymoon is over? Perhaps one of you sometimes becomes clingy and demanding while the other feels devoured and needs "space." Maybe you experience subtle, periodic irritation, or a sense of stagnation that is gradually extinguishing your former delight in each other. Perhaps you engage in spectacular fights interspersed with passionate reconciliation.

This subconscious alienation—which mates so often encounter despite their desire to remain in love—is the result of an unsuspected poison on Cupid's arrow. When we fall in love, a primitive part of our brain pierces us with a desire for great passion (Cupid's dart). An orgasm feels great, and if it were the end of the story, lovers would be able to do what comes naturally in the bedroom *and* live happily ever after. The problem is that sex—especially the kind with lots of orgasms all around, leading to that feeling of "I'm definitely done!" (sexual satiety)—isn't an isolated event. Orgasm is the peak of a much longer *cycle* of subsequent changes deep in the brain. These lingering effects, and the unwelcome feelings they evoke, can poison our relationship without our conscious awareness. Remarkably, such diverse symptoms as selfishness, unfulfilled needs, communication problems, infidelity, and sexless marriages can all originate in these hidden commands.

In some of us this "poison" takes effect so rapidly that we part after a single tryst. More often there is a period of relative relationship happiness, supported by a short-lived love potion. This honeymoon harmony (or lust) encourages us to bond for a while. On average it's long enough for mates to produce and attach to a child, even if they do not, in fact, procreate.

Creeping disillusionment, born of Cupid's poison, then motivates us to merge our genes with exciting new partners as well (even though we may choose to grit our teeth and resist temptation). Why? Our genes are programmed for their own immortality, and they don't politely wait for opportunity to knock. These little wisps of DNA urge us toward lots of pregnancies *and* a variety of partners. The more dissimilar our offspring, the better the odds that some of them will survive changed conditions or epidemics in order to procreate. Our willingness to shop for unfamiliar genes would once have helped protect small populations from the dangers of inbreeding.

Moreover, our genes do their best to keep us to a tight schedule. Anthropologist Helen Fisher estimates that we're molded to stay together for about four years. Across fifty-eight diverse cultures, she found that divorce rates peak then.[2] However, in Muslim countries where divorce was easy to arrange, marriages tended to end even sooner.

In short, both the sweet and sour phases of romance improve the chances that our genes will make it into the next generation—even if we are left cynical or brokenhearted. Our genetic mating program is working brilliantly. It just doesn't have *our* best interests in mind. As pair-bonding mammals, we benefit in surprising ways from trusted companionship with a mate, and when we sacrifice those benefits to our genetic success, it hurts.

Usually when Cupid's poison curdles a romance, we conclude that we either chose the wrong mate or that men and women are just hopelessly different. Yet it's not our differences that cause this distress. It is what we have in common: involuntary, biological responses that are as unconscious as blinking. We are *programmed* for this pain-

> Most of us tend to wear intellectual blinders, often failing to recognize something until we first have an explanation for it . . . or at least, an expectation of it. Believing is seeing.
> —Barash and Lipton,
> *The Myth of Monogamy*

ful unraveling just as surely as we are programmed to fall deliriously in love in the first place.

Of course, resentment and issues in intimate relationships can also come from other factors, such as money-management differences, childhood trauma, and personal eccentricities. Yet this hidden biological factor could prove the most reliable when it comes to churning up recurring relationship friction. At the very least, it can make other challenges more difficult to resolve.

One clue that emotional distance is programmed into our intimacy is that marital happiness typically erodes over time.[3] Mysteriously, however, friendships or other close family relationships are *immune* to this programmed deterioration.[4] Could this be because romantic relationships plunge us into passion to the point of "enough already!" while other close relationships do not? Sounds farfetched. Yet for most mammals *frenzied mating to the point of disinterest (surfeit) is the signal to become restless and move on* to another dance partner. Could our mammalian heritage have saddled us with similar subconscious responses to sexual satiety, which also make *us* restless? Are we wired to grow apart from a familiar mate—even though we're still programmed to seek the benefits of long-term companionship?

More important, what can we do if we wish to protect our relationships from Cupid's poison? We can manage our sexual encounters differently, so we're less susceptible to Cupid's maddening sting, and more inclined to find love a steady, continuing delight. Both ancient wisdom and modern scientific findings point to how we can achieve this end, but to benefit from this information we need to see clearly what we're up against.

THE COOLIDGE EFFECT

Consider what happens when you drop a male rat into a cage with a receptive female rat. First you'll see a frenzy of copulation. (Possibly it gets lonely in the lab, given experiments like this one.) After a while, the fireworks stop. Mr. Rat heads for the recliner, toting the remote. As a result of his changed body chemistry, Mrs. Rat now looks uninteresting to him.[5] However, if Miss Ratty (a new female) shows up, his exhaustion will miraculously fade long enough for him to gallantly attempt his fertilization duties.

A rodent's renewable virility is not indicative of an insatiable libido. Nor does it increase his well-being—although it may look (and temporarily feel to him) that way. His behavior correlates with surges of neurochemicals in his tiny brain, which command him to leave no willing female unfertilized.

Conniving genes can be slave drivers in this regard. Males of the furry little marsupial species (*Antechinus stuartii*) are so preoccupied with copulation that they destroy their own immune systems, and die of various diseases at the conclusion of mating season.[6] When scientists furnish the animals with some artificial will power by tempering their male sex hormones, their immune systems keep them in working order.

True love ends even more abruptly for the male praying mantis (at least for those unlucky enough to "get it on" in captivity). The female causes the male to deliver his sperm by chewing off his head. (Suggestion: Never "do lunch" with a female mantis.)

Animals that are less concerned about closure simply identify and reject those with which they have already sexually satiated themselves. Scientists know this reflex as the "Coolidge effect." It earned its name many years ago when President Coolidge and his wife were touring a farm. While the president was elsewhere, the farmer proudly showed Mrs. Coolidge a rooster that "could copulate with hens all day long, day after day." Mrs. Coolidge coyly suggested that the farmer share that impressive feat with Mr. Coolidge, which he did.

The president thought for a moment and then inquired, "With the same hen?"

"No, sir," replied the farmer.

"Tell that to Mrs. Coolidge," retorted the president.

The Coolidge effect has been widely observed among mammals, even in females. Some female rodents, for example, flirt a lot more—arching in inviting displays—with unfamiliar partners than with those with which they've already copulated.[7]

Does a variation of the Coolidge effect show up in human behavior? I recall a conversation I once had with a man who had grown up in Los Angeles. "I quit counting at 350 lovers," he confessed, "and I guess there must be something terribly wrong with me because I always lost interest in them sexually so quickly. Some of those women are really beautiful, too." At the time of our chat his third wife had just left him for a Frenchman and he was discouraged. She had lost interest in him.

Women sometimes report that their taste in men changes around ovulation, as does the way they see men. They say they're more drawn to Don Juans, and less likely to relate to a man as a person. In short, they're more likely to see him as a tempting hunka burnin' genes.

The biological self is petty and quite cruel, and strangely enough very easily finds imperfections while at the same time caving in to really low standards. Some of the petty crap in my head about my boyfriend says: he's so WHITE, I need a dark, exotic, and mysterious man! His hair is thin; I don't want my children to have thin hair. The voice inside assesses and rejects one's current mate based on self-serving, shallow ideas that have to do with physical characteristics or status.
—Lisa

Strictly speaking, humans may not experience the immediacy of the Coolidge effect (unless they're at an orgy). For us, habituation more often takes the form of *decreased sexual responsiveness with long-term mates.* We may be more like monkeys. When male monkeys were paired repeatedly with the same females (who were *always* in the mood, thanks to daily hormone injections), the males copulated less and less frequently, and with declining enthusiasm, over a three-and-a-half-year period. Yet these slackers hurriedly changed their ways when novel females showed up.[8]

Could our mammalian brains be meddling with our capacity for sustaining intimate relationships? (The mammalian brain lies beneath the rational brain. It governs sex and love and is surprisingly similar in *all* mammals.) Most mammals do not form pair-bonds as stable as ours. Yet even among our few monogamous mammalian cousins, no species is *sexually exclusive*. They burrow together and co-parent, but they are frequently impelled to gather genes from strangers on the side. Those enterprising genes like to keep gene pools nice and fresh. Habituation to one's partner apparently serves evolution's goals by making novel partners look *tempting*. Think of it this way: If sexual fidelity guaranteed more and fitter offspring, no mammals would fool around.

Mammals generally have rigid periods of being in heat, dictated by hormones, while humans can have sex whenever the urge arises. However, our hormones, too, regulate us. Unfortunately our version seems to be like starting and stopping in heavy traffic. Between passion bouts, we're likely to find a mate increasingly exhausting, jealous, or impossible to please. And our mate is likely to find us self-absorbed, unhelpful, or unaffectionate— except when pursuing sex.

At the start of our marriage, we slept together nude. Soon she started wearing underclothes. She gradually stopped enjoying having me put my arm around her or cuddle up to her. Sometimes, with little or no provocation, she would sleep in another room, which seemed rather callous, and left me feeling lonely and frustrated. Sex grew less and less frequent, and finally she moved into another room, permanently. I was going on the assumption that if she could just enjoy sex more, i.e., have more orgasms, we would have sex more often and my needs would be better satisfied. So, I was always trying to give her a good pounding. Oh well. . . .—Brent

Research confirms that as the duration of partnership increases, sexual desire declines in women—while desire for tenderness declines in men.[9] This miserable program can keep us partner-hopping, adding mating opportunities on the side—or just plain frustrated, baffled, and bad tempered. And we never suspect that the drive to *exhaust* sexual desire is playing a role in this familiar pattern. Instead, we believe that sexual satiety is a good bonding strategy for mates. As we'll see, there is reason to suspect that it actually speeds the process of habituation, subtly shifting lovers' perceptions of each other for the worse.

Remarkably, past sages of various traditions observed that sexual satiety indeed drives partners apart, causing feelings of depletion and disharmony. They also discovered a way around the problem. They recognized that there are *two* fundamentally different approaches to lovemaking, depending upon its purpose.

Fertilization-driven sex is for procreation. Climax launches sperm to meet egg. In contrast, bonding-based sex has harmony and well-being as its primary objectives. *Both methods entail intercourse* to ease sexual tension effectively. Fertilization-driven sex achieves this goal with a neuro-chemical crash followed by a surprisingly slow return to homeostasis (that is, pre-orgasm balance). Bonding-based sex eases sexual tension via gentle intercourse mingled with deep relaxation and lots of soothing affection, leading to refreshing feelings of satisfaction and lingering equilibrium.

Making love is like inflating a balloon. Having an orgasm is like popping the balloon, but if you finish without an orgasm you are like a balloon that takes several days to gradually deflate, leaving you much longer to enjoy the inflated feeling.—Rob

---

HOW DID THAT WORK OUT?

Theory is great, but after years of fitful explorations I was lucky enough to meet a partner willing to experiment open-mindedly with this unfamiliar approach to intercourse. When we got together ten years ago, my husband, Will, and I began our relationship with bonding-centered lovemaking. We emphasized generous affection, and did not pursue orgasm (although orgasm still occurred on rare occasions). This type of lovemaking is an ancient practice that is hinted at in various traditions. I now think of it as *karezza* (from the Italian for "caress," pronounced ka-RET-za), a term coined almost a century ago by a Quaker doctor.

The technique is not based on control. [During intercourse] you are not seeking to avoid orgasm or to manipulate your bodily energies; you are merely closing your eyes, feeling those energies stream into your heart, head and genitals and those of your lover, and allowing them to circulate. . . . You are always relaxing, relaxing, falling back into the heart. Effortless awareness is the key. All your energies will be drawn upward, diffused throughout the body. . . . As this takes place, lustful tendencies will be transmuted into feelings of love and the need for conventional orgasm will lessen.[10]

When we looked back a year after beginning this practice, we had to admit that we were amazed. Life wasn't perfect, but there were definite, positive changes. No more yeast infections or urinary tract infections for me, no more alcohol abuse or chronic depression (or prescription antidepressants) for Will. Lovemaking was less intense, but left us more contented. Even now, we never seem to tire of each other's touch, and actually enjoy helping each other. Best of all, there is a very welcome, lighthearted playfulness in our relationship, which allows us to laugh about, and resolve, most sources of friction effortlessly.

As a human sciences teacher who cheerfully pores over medical abstracts for hours at a time, Will was curious to see if science could shed any light on these improvements. He delved into research about oxytocin, the so-called "cuddle hormone." This material went far toward explaining why selfless, non-goal-oriented lovemaking might have enhanced our health and countered depression[11] and addiction.[12] For example, HIV-positive patients survive longer when in relationship.[13] Wounds heal twice as fast with companionship, as compared with isolation.[14] In primates, the caregiving parent, male or female, lives longer.[15] Oxytocin is probably the chief hormonal player behind all of these gains.

My husband also realized that, by taking it easy and avoiding climax during our karezza lovemaking, we were apparently benefiting from less dramatic fluctuations in our brain chemistry. This is because orgasm is experienced in the brain. It's a complex sequence of neurochemical-hormonal events even more than a genital event. For example, you can stick an electrode in someone's brain, or spinal cord, and produce the sensation of orgasm without touching *any* genitals.

Instead of an electrode, the body uses a spike of neurochemicals to trigger the sensation of orgasm. What goes up at the moment of orgasm must come down. Although scientists aren't generally acknowledging that there is a post-orgasmic letdown, evidence of it has already turned up in the research of those seeking to develop sexual enhancement drugs. This subconscious cascade of neurochemical events, which appears to take a full two weeks to return to homeostasis, is behind the ability of Cupid's poison to sour our relationships.

Forget breast implants. It's never about big or little, or short or tall, or blonde or brunette. It's only about "old" and "new." Hugh Grant had Elizabeth Hurley at home, and he wanted Marvin Hagler in a wig.
—Bill Maher, comedian

During this recovery phase lovers may feel needy, irritable, anxious, depleted, or desperate for another orgasm (to ease related symptoms). They don't realize that they are temporarily off balance. This is a recurring trigger for disharmony and compulsive behavior, and it's built right into our romantic relationships. Yet this recovery phase is nearly invisible to sexually active adults, because at first we typically try to resolve any uneasiness with *another* orgasm. This instinctive response pushes us toward further sexual satiety—and subsequent emotional distance. You have to hand it to those genes of ours. It's a clever way of making sure we engage in as much fertilization-driven sex as possible—before losing our desire to remain sexually exclusive with a mate.

Thanks to this innate program, we seldom discover the sense of well-being and contentment that accompanies the move toward equilibrium using karezza, that is, bonding-centered lovemaking. Instead we tend to focus on blaming each other for our changed feelings. "If only he would be more affectionate or supportive." "If only she would stop processing her feelings and just have sex."

As we will see, this post-orgasmic recovery period is likely to underlie such diverse phenomena as the one-night stand, the sexless marriage, infidelity, and porn addiction. It contributes to the common experience that the honeymoon seldom lasts longer than a year. It is why close friendships that bloom into love affairs often turn sour.

The bottom line is that the subconscious mating program behind our spontaneous sexual appetite works perfectly for maximum gene proliferation. It just doesn't happen to have our individual well-being at heart. Dutch scientist Gert Holstege, who reported that his brain scans of men ejaculating look like brain scans of people shooting heroin,[16] once remarked that we are all addicted to sex.[17] He was acknowledging that sexual impulsiveness *naturally* leads in the direction of satiety—and, given opportunity, even compulsion.

MATING AND BONDING, THE TWO PEDALS

If we do what we've always done, we'll get what we've always gotten. We're wired that way. Yet we don't just possess a mating program. We also possess a bonding program. It originated as a mechanism for bonding infant mammals to their caregivers, but it has also evolved to encourage us to fall in love—for a while (pair-bond). It works on a mutual exchange of subconscious cues, behaviors that we're encoded to find pleasurable at any age. As we will see, we can refine our innate inclinations by using these bonding behaviors to strengthen our enthusiasm for lasting intimacy indefinitely—especially if we're willing to transform intercourse itself into a bonding behavior when procreation is not desired.

Lack of cuddling eventually leads to lack of desire for it, whether through laziness, habit, resentment, or indifference. Cuddling (all affection included) causes the desire for more. It is a beneficent biofeedback machine, just as the absence of affection seems to be the opposite. Everyone will be familiar with young lovers seeming unable to get near enough to each other. Well, although we've been married for ages, we've experienced the same, repeatedly, as a result of initially scheduling cuddling—even a minute a day—and watching it snowball.—Keith

Humans experiencing companionate love feel calm and secure and experience social comfort and emotional union.[18] Given the powerful psychological and health benefits of happy union, karezza lovemaking may prove surprisingly beneficial for socially monogamous mammals like us.

I now think of our mating and bonding programs like two pedals that drive our intimate relationships. The mating program (the urge to exhaust ourselves sexually as thoroughly as possible) is the "habituation pedal," because it so often causes partners to get fed up with (habituate to) each other. The bonding program, on the other hand, is the "harmony pedal," because it makes togetherness more deeply satisfying. With this simple knowledge, we can steer for the results we want.

While Will was learning about the hidden endocrine cycle of sexual satiety, I continued to root around in the esoteric attics of some of the planet's most influential religions. There's a surprising amount of lore about how intimate relationships can serve as a path to deeper union and clearer spiritual perception. We don't hear much about this material because the better-known religious directives focus almost exclusively on social conventions and generating more believers.

In the familiar doctrines, the concept of continence equates with the sexual abstinence of monks and nuns. Yet it appears that some of our most inspiring spiritual teachers have alluded to the transcendental power of sexual continence during intercourse, within intimate relationships. I'll share some of what I found in the Wisdom segments between chapters.

WHY NOW?

Obviously, humanity's subconscious mating agenda is not a new challenge, but there are two developments that make it more urgent to cultivate authentic harmony between couples. First, our culture has changed. Until recently, across much of the globe, church and state kept a rein on sexual expression. Marriages were often arranged. Divorce was first impossible, and then heavily censored. Birth control was unavailable or prohibited. And unsanctioned relationships were strictly punished. All these features of life ensured that any emotional separation between partners was partly masked by the fact that they had to continue to live together and raise their inevitable children. These circumstances also meant that there was just plain less fooling around after the honeymoon period (in most couples' lives). That left relationships stagnant but less volatile.

Today social and civil sanctions in the West cannot hold mates in artificial bondage. This means that our underlying mammalian mating programming is ripping couples, and families, apart with increasing efficiency. As we no longer live in tribes based on mutual support, this outcome is agonizing for all concerned.

Moreover, with each new generation there may be fewer "swans" (couples who escape habituation). When researchers looked at marital happiness across generational groups, they discovered that the oldest couples were more likely to be somewhat happier. Analysts put this down to the fact that older couples married when people held more pragmatic views about marriage, support for marriage was stronger, and couples were more committed to the norm of lifelong marriage.[19]

However, there may be a second very potent, but unacknowledged, factor at work. We are guinea pigs in a massive international experiment. Today's titillating media routinely evokes supranormal (that is, above-normal) sexual stimulation in our brains. Consider these titles from mainstream men's and women's magazines: "Sex with Someone New—Every Night" (via acting out sexual fantasy) and "How to Find *His* G-Spot." Or Chile's precocious under-eighteen youth, whose enthusiasm for casual sex is boggling minds like nothing the country has witnessed before.[20]

This focus on sexual gratification speeds up the involuntary workings of our mating program by urging ever-more-rapid sexual surfeit (and subsequent disinterest) between lovers. The result is often shorter intimate connections, and increasing distrust between the sexes—frequently leading to despair about relationships and unhealthy isolation. In essence, our innate program for genetic success is working so efficiently that it's finally on the verge of backfiring. The wedge of mistrust and disillusionment between the genders is widening.

Q: What's the difference between a new spouse and a new dog?

A: After a year, the dog is still excited to see you.

Yet the more my husband and I learn, the more we realize that everyone is fundamentally innocent. We, our exes, you, your exes, and all our parents have only been doing what our genes programmed us to do, that is, get bored, tired, or irritated, be disappointed with each other, (often) fool around, break up—and start it all again. We had no idea that orgasm is not mere pleasure or release, but that satiation tends to cause us to devalue or alienate our mates. Avoiding sex doesn't solve the problem because sexual frustration continues to build without resolution.

On the other hand, pursuing orgasm nonstop to relieve tension poses its own hidden risks of habituation and compulsive behavior. Some sexual tension is natural. It's there to encourage us to connect with mates. Yet, as we will see, especially intense sexual frustration can be the result of an urgent desire for relief from feelings of restlessness, irritability, and apathy—feelings that sexual satiety *itself* can bring on. Resolving the latter with *more* sexual stimulation can send us into a downward spiral. We can escape by moving toward enlivening equilibrium using the bonding behaviors and approach to lovemaking mentioned earlier.

Meanwhile, one can sympathize with the outrage of religious fundamentalists and aggrieved feminists at the current chaos. Too many people are indeed seeking relief for inflamed libido using casual sex and porn. However, our righteous critics may find that mastering bonding-based lovemaking also eases their harsh judgments of others. In any case, shaming those caught in the passion cycle, male or female, has the unintended effect of making the search for sexual gratification more compelling. If we want to explore the power of karezza to increase the stability and harmony in our intimate relationships, we have to address our current habits compassionately and creatively—without blame. Those habits are the outcome of a logical experiment: determined pursuit of orgasm in the belief that it would increase our psychological health and well-being. Our task now is to appraise the results as honestly as we can, and then choose our direction consciously.

The good news is that moving beyond impulse, to conscious equilibrium in our sex lives, tends to furnish a sense of inner wholeness. For example, my husband and I now feel less susceptible to manipulation of any kind, whether by advertisers, politicians, or others. You, too, may find that without the feelings of lack, uneasiness, and neediness that mysteriously show up after exhausting sexual desire, you simply aren't as vulnerable to temptations like junk food, reckless spending, or fear-based manipulation.

WHY ME?

To explore karezza I had to set aside the popular wisdom of the last six decades. It holds that orgasms are purely a source of pleasure and beneficial release, which, if not forthcoming spontaneously, should be pursued by such means as are available, both natural and artificial. My explorations contradicted that thinking and slowly led to a personal paradigm shift. I no longer think of orgasm as a genital event that ends shortly after climax. Instead, I'm intrigued by orgasm's lingering neurochemical realities and what they mean in terms of our perceptions of each other, the quality of our relationships, and our evolution (both physical and spiritual).

As it turns out, various disciplines have uncovered vital pieces of this other paradigm. Evolutionary biologists observed that our genes' primary goal is not necessarily harmony between mates, but rather greater success for themselves. Neuroscientists uncovered the fact that potent sexual stimulation affects the brain somewhat like an addictive drug. Psychiatrists and psychologists observed that shifts in our subconscious *feelings* toward individuals radically change our *perceptions* of them. And little-known texts from various spiritual traditions revealed an intimate union between men and women, which brings them back into harmony with each other and their neighbors.

Alas, the inhibited flow of information between disciplines sometimes hampers insights that integrate diverse perspectives. Biologists tend not to refine their conclusions based upon intriguing parallels in ancient texts; neuroscientists have not studied the effect of neurochemical fluctuations on how lovers perceive their intimate partners in the course of their return to homeostasis after orgasm; and psychologists and psychiatrists are discouraged from contemplating the merits of sex without orgasm because Freud, Kinsey, and others caused it to be viewed as a paraphilia (sexual disorder). As a result they conflate the terms "sex-positive" and "orgasm-positive." Finally, theologians familiar with the texts I studied are often inclined to ignore the wholesome possibilities of sex outside of propagation, on the assumption that their Creator cares only for mankind's unfettered multiplication.

Unconstrained by any of these disciplines, I collected clues from all of them. I discovered that there was a remarkably strong case to be made for why humans might want to master *another* approach to intercourse for when conception is not the goal.

You may be wondering what motivated me to explore making love without orgasm in the first place. After all, our mating program is subconscious and has been with us since before we were human. We're not *supposed* to notice it. In fact, none of us can really see the challenge we're up against until we unhook from our mating program by experimenting with another way of easing sexual tension for an extended period of time, and *then* return to fertilization-driven sex to experience the difference.

14

For better or worse, I had ample opportunity to make that experiment. I was very drawn to the idea of Taoist lovemaking when I read my first book about it, but very confused about the instructions for *doing* it. I was sure that passion fitted into the equation *somewhere*. As a result, my love life resembled the movie *Groundhog Day*, where the main character seems doomed to relive the same events over and over forever.

In truth I was slowly learning some of the basics about our subconscious mating program. They didn't perfectly fit my understanding of the Taoist model I was trying to follow. Yet, remarkably, they did line up with the science my husband unearthed years after we met and began trying karezza.

In sharing what I've learned, I'll begin with my earliest teacher: my own experience. It zigzagged quite a bit as I set out to explore some ancient ideas that promised greater relationship depth and harmony. Gradually I realized that I was not the only one plagued by fragile relationships; separation was actually creeping into *most* intimate relationships of any duration. Other unexpected insights followed, and the next two chapters relate some of the "ah-ha's," as well as the bruises I sustained, during my early efforts. I think of this period as the "yin," or receptive, phase of my adventure, because I did my best to stay open to the insights entering my life, even though they were not scientific, and did not fit my worldview at the time.

After Will arrived, the objective information he turned up complemented my earlier, subjective observations in quite unexpected ways. I think of this phase as the "yang" phase, because Will's input (based on the current understanding of many insightful researchers) provided a much fuller, more grounded, understanding of what I had experienced and observed. His material, which shapes Chapters Four (At the Heart of the Separation Virus), Five (The Passion Cycle), Six (The Road to Excess), and Eight (Science That Binds), reveals the workings of our subconscious mating and bonding programs in scientific terms.

Even if you don't think you like science, you may find this material surprisingly absorbing. We'll consider how our domineering genes manipulate us to fulfill their agenda at the expense of our unions. We'll look more closely at the orgasm cycle, and consider what current findings can tell us about how it sometimes becomes a slippery slope to compulsive behavior. We'll also examine possible reasons behind karezza's ability to contribute to healing, balance, and stronger emotional bonds.

In Chapter Seven (Learning to Steer) we'll address how we can shift the balance between our mating and bonding programs. Chapter Nine (Bridging the Gap) explains how we came to use orgasm as "mood medicine" and why that strategy can fail pair-bonding mammals like us. It also suggests strategies for introducing others to the concept of karezza. Chapter Ten (The Path of Harmony) recaps the practice of karezza itself.

Be aware that the chapters with practical suggestions are perhaps the *least* important parts of this book. Once you understand the origins and mechanics of the challenge mankind faces, you, too, may find your own way toward the option of generous, affectionate karezza. Until you have fully integrated that information, all practical suggestions for eluding your subconscious mating program are likely to prove pleasant, but somewhat empty, exercises. In fact, you could end up in a *Groundhog Day* loop of your own.

TAOISM

In these Wisdom segments between chapters, we'll look at various texts and traditions that record insights about lovemaking directed toward deeper union between partners rather than fertilization. The excerpts are interesting primarily because they exist at all—not because they reflect mainstream doctrine. Who would have thought there was so much lore about the potential hidden in intimate relationships?

One of my favorite accounts of bonding-based lovemaking is contained in the *Hua Hu Ching,* a little-known collection of teachings attributed (as is much Taoist wisdom) to master Lao Tzu. In the Walker translation,[21] which includes material passed down orally, Lao Tzu warns:

> Although most people spend their entire lives following the biological impulse, it is only a tiny portion of our beings. If we remain obsessed with seeds and eggs, we are married to the fertile reproductive valley of the Mysterious Mother but not to her immeasurable heart and all-knowing mind.[22]

And:

> If you wish to unite with her heart and mind, you must integrate yin and yang within and refine their fire upward. Then you have the power to merge with the whole being of the Mysterious Mother. This is what is known as true evolution.[23]

He explains further:

> The first integration of yin and yang is the union of seed and egg within the womb. The second integration of yin and yang is the sexual union of the mature male and female. Both of these are concerned with flesh and blood, and all that is conceived in this realm must one day disintegrate and pass away.[24]

17

So far we are on familiar ground, but then Lao Tzu suggests that there is an entirely different experience open to us through union.

> It is only the third integration which gives birth to something immortal.... The new life created by the final integration is self-aware yet without ego, capable of inhabiting a body yet not attached to it, and guided by wisdom rather than emotion. Whole and virtuous, it can never die.[25]

Lao Tzu advises that this mystical union of yin and yang can be achieved through sexual intercourse.

> Because higher and higher unions of yin and yang are necessary for the conception of higher life, some students may be instructed in the art of dual cultivation, in which yin and yang are directly integrated in the tai chi [disciplined practice] of sexual intercourse.... If genuine virtue and true mastery come together ... the practice can bring about a profound balancing of the student's gross and subtle energies [otherwise it can have a destructive effect].[26]

Indeed:

> The result of this is improved health, harmonized emotions, the cessation of cravings and impulses, and, at the highest level, the transcendent integration of the entire energy body.[27]

My husband and I have already experienced some of the benefits mentioned as a result of making love frequently and affectionately, without pursuing the overstimulation of sexual satiety. We have noticed definite improvements in our health, greater emotional balance and harmony, and decreased cravings.

Here are two other sections from the *Hua Hu Ching*, offering additional pointers.

Section 69

A person's approach to sexuality is a sign of his level of evolution. Unevolved persons practice ordinary sexual intercourse. Placing all emphasis upon the sexual organs, they neglect the body's other organs and systems. Whatever physical energy is accumulated is summarily discharged, and the subtle energies are similarly dissipated and disordered. It is a great backward leap.*

For those who aspire to the higher realms of living, there is angelic dual cultivation. Because every portion of the body, mind, and spirit yearns for the integration of yin and yang, angelic intercourse is led by the spirit rather than the sexual organs.

Where ordinary intercourse is effortful, angelic cultivation is calm, relaxed, quiet, and natural. Where ordinary intercourse unites sex organs with sex organs, angelic cultivation unites spirit with spirit, mind with mind, and every cell of one body with every cell of the other body. Culminating not in dissolution but in integration ["not in separation but in merging"?], it is an opportunity for a man and woman to mutually transform and uplift each other into the realm of bliss and wholeness.

Section 70

The cords of passion and desire weave a binding net around you.... The trap of duality is tenacious. Bound, rigid, and trapped, you cannot experience liberation.

Through dual cultivation it is possible to unravel the net, soften the rigidity, dismantle the trap. Dissolving your yin energy into the source of universal life, attracting the yang energy from that same source, you leave behind individuality and your life becomes pure nature. Free of ego, living naturally, working virtuously, you become filled with inexhaustible vitality and are liberated forever from the cycle of death and rebirth.

Understand this if nothing else: spiritual freedom and oneness with the Tao are not randomly bestowed gifts, but the rewards of conscious self-transformation and self-evolution.

Other ancient Taoist sex manuals, such as *Secrets of the Jade Chamber* and *The Dangers and Benefits of Intercourse with Women,* also refer to the phenomenon of man and woman achieving immortality together through conservation of sexual energy. *Dangers and Benefits* says it is achieved

---

*Lao Tzu presumably knew nothing about neuroscience, but, as we'll see, "dissipated and disordered subtle energies" is a surprisingly good description of events in the brain after orgasm.

through a combination of deep penetration, low arousal, and visualizations of energy moving through the body.[28] *True Transmission of the Golden Elixir* describes a spiritual parthenogenesis, "forming the holy fetus," dependent upon conserving one's life force energy. *Exposition of Cultivating the True Essence* explains that sexual alchemy is only possible when the unstable male sexual energy (1) is aroused without "bursting out," (2) welcomes the more stable yin energy, and (3) fuses with it.[29]

> The Chinese legends speak of a golden age when all men lived in harmony with nature and transmuted their seed up as naturally as you or I breathe.
> —Mantak Chia,
> Taoist teacher

This lofty objective of spiritual union between equal partners eroded in later Taoist writings—first into plots for "stealing" the sexual energy of the opposite sex, and more recently into techniques for men and women to produce multiple-orgasms in themselves and each other. In short, even the Taoists haven't always been able to resist the tug of humanity's subconscious mating program—perhaps because they lost sight of the gifts of deep emotional bonds between mates. Still, I am very grateful to the Chinese for preserving some of the oldest accounts of controlled intercourse. They confirmed my own experience in surprising ways.

Scholar Douglas Wile, who translated and analyzed numerous early Chinese texts on sex, observed that, "For the Christian, sex is for procreation; for the Chinese orgasm is for procreation, but sex is for pleasure, therapy and salvation."[30] As we will see in the next Wisdom segment, early Christians may also have taught that sex was for salvation.

CHAPTER TWO

ELEPHANTS IN THE LIVING ROOM

By avoiding sexual satiety we can use intimate relationships to evoke feelings of optimism and abundance more
consistently.

Orgasm can set off mood swings and perception shifts that
linger for approximately two weeks.

These changes affect both sexes, and masturbation produces
them, too.

Have you ever fallen in love with someone who loved you back? What an experience! Suddenly the world begins to make sense. With higher voltage you flow with inspired ideas. Life takes on a rosy glow, and the wings and halo of your loved one are clearly visible. Yet, if things take their normal course, you will soon look back on this brief interval of heightened awareness as the honeymoon period, and regard it as a once-in-a-romance sprinkling of fairy dust.

In fact, something quite real is going on, biologically and, perhaps, energetically. It is actually enlivening you, expanding your perception, and profoundly changing your body chemistry. According to various spiritual traditions across the globe, the connection between lovers is potentially nothing less than a path to enlightenment.

However, most of us never make it anywhere near the penthouse of spiritual insight. Instead, we get off somewhere around the third floor and swiftly begin that familiar downward spiral into the mundane, too often followed by a nosedive into the basement. This happens because the physical part of us is operating on biological autopilot and we have assumed its will is our own.

My education about the hidden potential in relationships began with just such a crash. Some years back my sister, weary of watching the turnover in my love life, gave me a book with a title like *Marrying the Man of Your Choice*. I had tried all of the mainstream advice for sustaining relationships with little success, so I figured, why not? The book insisted that I needed to write a detailed description of my ideal mate. So I did.

Sure enough he showed up within a year. Not only that, a couple of months before Paul and I met, he attended a party whose host had hired a psychic as a party gag. The psychic told Paul that he would meet me by a certain date, giving him my age, my profession, the element of my astrological sign, and several other surprisingly accurate things. We met at a business conference in New York City two days before the date the psychic named. It certainly *felt* like a heavenly match. Shortly after conventional sex entered the picture, however, the relationship blew apart. And every time we got back together again, it blew apart again.

At the time I made no connection between the pursuit of orgasm and the recurring friction between us. I felt like a random bolt of lightening had just reduced another of my precious unions to ashes. It was excruciating to watch a relationship with someone with whom I had experienced such a profound, seemingly fated, connection crumble despite all efforts to save it.

"BE CAREFUL WHAT YOU ASK FOR … YOU MAY GET IT"

Although I was a business professional, I had recently begun experimenting with the concept that inspired insight is available for the asking. I figured that a sound way to prove that the idea was bunk was to try it for a while. Besides, the results I was getting in my love life using rational strategies were disheartening. So I focused on the question "Why are my relationships crumbling?" An answer arrived almost immediately—although it proved to be only one strand of a larger tapestry, which ultimately grew into this book.

That same week I ran into my first Taoist lovemaking manual.[31] It recommended another method of making love. Instead of rushing for climax, lovers opt for a wave-like approach, with an emphasis on deep relaxation between periods of gentle intercourse. The instant I read the descriptions, I knew what I had always been seeking in intimate relationships:

> It is a very powerful experience which I feel in every cell, every particle of my being as an exquisite, ecstatic melting. The feeling of connection with my partner is profound. My whole being is shared with his, and his with mine, as one flow that knows no boundaries.... I am always in awe of the tremendous power residing in male and female.... There is a sense of all the time in the world, of being in eternity, and of having more and more energy available.[32]

There was a *slight* hitch. To move toward this experience one had to pass up conventional orgasm. Sadly, Paul's wild-and-crazy side didn't extend much beyond the odd party-psychic reading, and he certainly had no interest in exploring unconventional sex. Shortly thereafter I was transferred to Europe. Foiled again.

The Taoist book went back on the shelf, but within two years my life took a radical new direction. I turned down a promotion to my company's headquarters in order to pursue my spiritual studies. This surprised those who knew me well, as I was hardly a candidate for an ascetic lifestyle. Also I had been an arch-atheist from the age of twelve—when I learned of slave ships and concentration camps, and decided that no God would allow such things to happen.

However, a few years earlier, through an unexpected constellation of events, I had attended a seminar called "The Silva Mind Control Course." It was my first exposure to the idea that our thoughts, beliefs, and expectations shape our experience, a concept I was quick to denounce as hogwash. To prove my point, I tried one of the relaxation-affirmation techniques in a halfhearted fashion, and was thoroughly annoyed when it worked. The stress headaches that had plagued me for years stopped. Resentfully, I purchased a book on creative visualization—and gradually shifted from cynicism to optimism as I became more productive and happier. My relationships grew more loving, but remained just as fragile. It seemed that I had more inner work to do.

Meanwhile, I found myself thinking in larger terms, which ultimately expanded widely enough to encompass both evolution *and* a conception of the Divine (making me Richard Dawkin's worst nightmare). I began to think of creation as a sort of exploding mushroom cloud of unending creativity with an infinite number of planes of existence with unique characteristics. What if, within this grand benevolent, yet impersonal, kaleidoscope, we sparks of the Divine had the freedom to conduct whatever collective experiments we chose?

In my next incarnation I want to live my life backwards. You start out dead and get that out of the way. Then you wake up in an old people's home feeling better every day. You get kicked out for being too healthy, go collect your pension, and then when you start work, you get a gold watch and a party on your first day. You work for forty years until you're young enough to enjoy your retirement. You party, drink alcohol, and are generally promiscuous, then you are ready for high school. You then go to primary school, you become a kid, you play. You have no responsibilities, you become a baby until you are born. And then you spend your last nine months floating in luxurious spa-like conditions with central heating and room service on tap, larger quarters every day and then Voila! You finish off as an orgasm! I rest my case.
—Woody Allen

I was especially intrigued by the theory that we humans unconsciously mold aspects of our collective experience with our beliefs. Looking around at the planet's inequities, nonrenewable energy habits, and constant bickering, I could see that if our thoughts were shaping our existence, we were thinking some very self-sabotaging thoughts. Could our thoughts be giving rise to scarcity, defensiveness, greed, shortsighted thinking, and uneasiness between the sexes? If so, who was thinking all these counterproductive thoughts?

At the same time, I was determined to see if the claims in my sacred sex texts had any merit. Could mates—by avoiding sexual satiety—use intimate relationships to create feelings of abundance, wholeness, optimism, stable affection, and expanded awareness? Might humankind shape a very different experience if these claims were true?

It hadn't yet dawned on me that by using each other for sexual satiety and procreation, we might inadvertently be churning out the defensiveness, anxiety, and scarcity that puzzled me.

[According to the ancient Chinese] orgasm should not be compared with our normal state but rather with our postcoital condition.... Coitus reservatus is then experienced not as an unbearable itch or pressure, but fullness and vigor.[33] *—Douglas Wile, sinologist*

DOÑA QUIXOTE SETS OUT

A fascinating journey had begun. It was not without bumps, however. Swiftly I discovered that, even with good intentions, it is not so easy to leave current sexual habits behind. My first attempt to crack the code was with Alex, whom I met in a workshop at a spiritual community in Scotland. A deeply spiritual man, he was taking a break from his psychology practice to travel from Canada around the world and visit various inspirational sites. After the seminar we returned to my home on the European continent.

I dusted off my Taoist lovemaking book, and we decided to try making love without ejaculation. Its male author believed that loss of semen, not orgasm, was the chief drawback of conventional sex. I took his word that this was a *male* issue, and that women's orgasms were risk-free. I certainly knew no better—yet.

> Never be afraid to try something new. Remember, amateurs built the ark. Professionals built the Titanic.

The book contained lots of tips on how men could gain mastery over the urge to ejaculate. It recommended tightening the muscles around the prostate gland, clenching the teeth, counting breaths, and various other forceful techniques—all of which I later learned are not nearly as effective, or healthful, as a very gradual, more relaxed approach to intercourse itself.

In any event, Alex insisted that he did not need any instructions. When we made love, however, it was business as usual. That is, he ejaculated. And for the next several days exactly the same thing happened, despite his genuine intention to avoid orgasm. I kept suggesting he study the manual but he was growing increasingly irascible. When I pointed out that, according to the book, his short temper might be due to the effects of orgasm itself, he blew.

"You are crazy to suggest ejaculation has a negative effect on men," he bristled. "I'm a psychologist. If that were the case, I would know about it. If you keep talking like this, you're going to be in a mental institution explaining this to your shrink!"

I could see that further argument would just make things worse, and it occurred to me how nice it would be if he just got on the next train! I managed a stony silence. Finally he exploded, "I can see you are not going to listen to a word I say until I read that book!"

"That's right, Alex," I admitted.

"Okay, what do I have to read?"

I showed him the four or five pages that explained the techniques mentioned above for men to avoid orgasm.

He flipped through the directions and announced, "Let's go try it."

At that point I was ready to give up the whole idea. This rather unchivalrous invitation did not resemble any of my mental images of inspired union. Still, I longed to know if the ideas had any merit.

We made love according to the instructions. He clenched and counted and completed the encounter without ejaculating. Then he amazed me by saying, "I do not believe it. I don't feel unsatisfied. I don't have ... uh ... blue balls. *Thank you for teaching me this!*" As astonishing as his newfound enthusiasm was, an even greater surprise followed. Over the next twenty-four hours he was a different man. His anger evaporated and his heart opened. Whereas before he had assured me that he did not need a partner because he was on a spiritual path, now he opened up and talked about how much he had always wanted a mate and was confused by his inability to stay in relationship.

The biggest shift of all was that he saw me in a completely different light. Forgetting all about institutionalization, he said, "You are so spiritual and generous. God must be really proud of you for sticking to this despite so much resistance." I felt transformed also. My heart cracked open with gratitude and I could clearly see his angelic qualities. I remember thinking, "Thank you for showing me this man's true beauty."

I vowed that I had just had my last pointless meltdown with a lover. I could taste the potential for mutual adoration and satisfying intimacy in the new concept and was more determined than ever to master this unconventional approach to sex.

As it turned out, I had more senseless meltdowns ahead because some of the vital clues about how one eludes our genes' mating objectives were missing from the sacred sex manuals I devoured. Despite thrilling breakthroughs, my results were erratic. Alex had shown me the *potential* in the concept, but we hadn't mastered how to stabilize the benefits. Fluctuating feelings (feeling deeply in love one day and guarded the next) were even more frightening than consistent emotional distance. They made love seem unreliable. This seemingly inexplicable fluctuation needs to be avoided if couples want to stay closer over the long run. Eventually I would learn that a gradual approach and consistency over time were critical factors.

Meanwhile, good intentions and lofty aspirations were clearly not enough. Whenever I inadvertently slipped into earlier habits of foreplay and ejaculatory sex, relationship disharmony erupted.

As we were falling asleep after making love, I noticed that my lover still had a strong erection. We had just started experimenting with avoiding orgasm during sex, so I asked him, "Isn't that making you uncomfortable?" I could hear a big smile in his voice as he replied, "No, I love it!" And when we woke up during the night, I found out why.—Kaiya

---

A SUBTLE SENSE OF LACK

Hard as it was to accept, orgasm indeed seemed to be the deciding factor. However blissful the encounter itself, a strange separation or uncomfortable alienation showed up over the days following my partner's climax(es)— and it lingered for about two weeks. Remember the movie *When Harry Met Sally*? Billy Crystal said that thirty seconds after making love he wants to get out of bed and leave. When I asked a man about it, he replied, "Yeah, I guess that is how most men feel. 'Boom, I'm done! Elvis has left the building. The fat lady has sung. Thank you—and goodbye.'"

Clues began to turn up that confirmed what I was experiencing in my personal life. At first I only saw the post-orgasmic shift in *men* and in their writings. For example, here is another example of a man's urge to leave after making love, which also shows our modern tendency to consider *anything* but sexual satiety as the culprit for our post-orgasmic uneasiness:

No matter who the woman was, I was as good as gone the moment we made love. It was at that moment that I always touched something taboo—perhaps my mother, perhaps my pain—and I would have to fly away.... I worried and waited for the most appropriate moment to take flight. If I didn't fly away I ran them off. Either way I knew I couldn't be with them.[34]

27

It was obvious to me that a subconscious urge to get away after sex makes a woman look less appealing, even if a man sticks around. I began to think of the shift as "the poison on Cupid's arrow," a sort of hangover, or temporary phase, of subtle uneasiness, which follows that "I'm done!" feeling, and colors perception for the worse for weeks.

Were post-orgasmic shifts like these contributing to humanity's nonsensical notions about sex? If a man can feel anxious enough to bolt after sex, couldn't he also feel uncomfortable enough to conclude that the other gender is treacherous or repugnant, that circumcision is appropriate to reduce sexual desire, or that an angry deity is punishing humans for engaging in sex? Years later I learned that a nineteenth-century theology graduate had reached the same conclusion I had:

> Exhaustion and self-reproach make the eye evil not only toward the instruments of excess, but toward the person who tempts to it.... This undoubtedly is the philosophy of the origin of shame after the fall. On the same principle we may account for the process of "cooling off," which takes place between lovers after marriage and often ends in indifference and disgust.
>
> In contrast with all this, lovers who use their sexual organs simply as the servants of their spiritual natures, abstaining from [climax] except when procreation is intended, may enjoy the highest bliss of sexual fellowship for any length of time, without satiety or exhaustion; and thus marriage life may become permanently sweeter than courtship or even the honeymoon.[35]

Even if someone doesn't feel guilty after sex, might not his perception of himself and others shift for the worse? Here's what actor Hugh Grant said *about himself* not long after he was caught with Divine Brown in 1995:

> I don't give a f**k about the morality of it.... I didn't care. Everyone's a dirty beast.

If we're all just "dirty beasts" then it's easy to overlook any loftier aspects of our characters and rush for the lowest common denominator of sexual behavior. Perhaps post-orgasmic perception shifts are contributing to a general cynicism and casualness toward sex. Many blame the Christian religion and its proscriptions about sex for today's unhealthy sexual attitudes (a point of view with some justification). Yet, as I continued to dig for clues, I learned that Cupid's poisoned arrow predated Christian influence.

For example, two thousand years ago Roman poet Ovid cynically advised using the pursuit of orgasm to the point of disinterest as a "cure for love":

Sate Yourself With Her

… Are you a prisoner of Love, unable to get away because of your tender feelings? … Go! Enjoy your girl with complete abandon, night and day. Let loathing end your malady. Even when you feel like you've had enough, stay on until you're overwhelmed and surfeit destroys love, leaving you no pleasure in her company.[36]

And what about these lines from the ancient *Greek Anthology*?

Once plighted, no men would go whoring;
They'd stay with the ones they adore,
If women were half as alluring
After the act as before.[37]

At last I accepted that the shift in a partner's perception of me, which I had often sensed after bedroom fireworks, was not strictly a product of my issues or even his. It was real. It was also both involuntary and preventable. That is, partners could not seem to stop the shift from occurring without addressing the underlying cause: sexual satiety. What a horrible thought!

I consulted my sacred sex texts again. There it was in black and white: Intercourse is beneficial, but orgasm brings with it a host of problems. Symptoms could include feeling drained, irritability, energy imbalance, health problems, and, most significantly, a growing aversion to one's sexual partner.

Eventually a man can develop feelings of indifference or hate for his sexual partner because he subconsciously realizes that when he touches her, he loses those higher energies that could make him a truly happy man.[38]

This is a worldwide phenomenon, too. For example, the Hulis, aborigines of New Guinea, also known as "Wig Men," have a traditional distrust of women, believing that females take their powers from them. As a result, they live apart from their bare-breasted wives and cook their own food. Sex is reduced to a brief encounter—not unlike many encounters of today's Western warriors. Not all Wig Men are sporting wigs.

Of course, lovers do not always project their post-orgasmic uneasiness (conscious or unconscious) onto their mates. Consider the words of psychologist Herb Goldberg in *What Men Really Want:*

> The defensive nature of masculinity creates in men a deeply wary and negative experience of the world, which they see as a place where there is never enough power, control, security or independence.[39]

There it was, the "sensation of lack" leading to defensiveness and a "them versus me" mentality, which had puzzled me. However private the act of intercourse, its repercussions were quite possibly shaping our *collective* experience. Certainly, at any given moment a lot of us are hotly pursuing sexual satiety for all we're worth. And many of the rest of us are pining for a sweetheart—another sense of "lack." I was staggered by the implications.

The world is full of obvious things, which nobody by any chance ever notices.
—Sir Arthur Conan Doyle

As the light went on, I felt like I had just discovered an elephant in my living room that had been there all along, mindlessly trampling my relationships and clouding my lovers' perceptions of me. Was it, along with everyone else's elephants, also creating feelings of lack and defensiveness across the globe?

"OBJECTS IN MIRROR MAY BE CLOSER THAN THEY APPEAR"

My friend Anya had a new lover, Rafi. He had grown up in a culture where artificial birth control virtually did not exist, so in order to decrease the chances of impregnating his girlfriend as a teen he had learned to pass up ejaculation. He regarded it as perfectly natural to explore a non-ejaculatory approach to sex with her. She was thrilled. Their lovemaking was sensational, cosmic, lengthy (the phone was once off the hook for four days while I dialed in vain), and her capacity for multiple orgasm as boundless as ever.

But cracks were appearing. A few weeks into her romance she finally called and asked hesitantly, "Do you think there's any chance orgasm is a problem for women, too?" I was listening very carefully. During the preceding months I, too, had finally found a lover who controlled himself easily, but who obviously enjoyed that I climaxed so effortlessly. However, we were certainly not tapping the mystical bliss and union I had read about in the sacred sex books. Instead I was noticing an ugly emotional friction flickering between us.

The issue of the effect of orgasm on women is obscured by the fact that most sexual advice—even esoteric—assumes that orgasm is no problem for women because we do not ejaculate semen. For years I fell for this cheery assumption. Now, however, events were conspiring to bring certain unwelcome truths to my attention.

From the time of her phone call, Anya and I compared notes like scientists in a laboratory. Regardless of other variables affecting our love lives, within a week or two after orgasmic encounters (even if only the woman climaxed), trouble would erupt. Anya tended to become weepy, oversensitive, ineffective, and discouraged. I tended toward a razor tongue, impatience, pessimism, and analyzing the obviously irreconcilable differences between my lover and myself. Mood swings, which Anya and I had once knowingly blamed on the fallout from our partners' post-ejaculation blues, haunted us both. Why was this happening?

Women's Bumper Stickers:

Next mood swing:
6 minutes

All stressed out
and no one to choke

You have the right to
remain silent, so shut up!

Caution: zero to "bitch"
in 8 seconds

Do not start with me—
you will not win

My last relationship was short. She practically begged me to make love—and she had an orgasm and everything—but immediately she wanted to run away. A few weeks later, after she slowly warmed back up, we did it again, and she seemed to have a ... fine time again. Then, only a few days later, she informed me "orgasm was a petty experience" compared with her spiritual practice. In fact, she told me she was afraid she could get really hooked on sex. (I remember thinking to myself how horrible that would be.)

And that was pretty much the end of our relationship. She announced that I was less spiritually evolved than she was and broke up. Since I had read the material on your Web site, I tried to tell her that she was having a separation hangover. But she was buying none of that—although she did sort of see it after a few months had passed. I think orgasm's doing the opposite of what women want it to.—Ken

Most women are certain that today's focus on women's orgasm is an idea whose time has come. After all, for millennia the heavy boots of patriarchy have stomped on women's sexuality. Women were relegated to the role of brood mare, forced to let men have their way with them with no attention to *their* way, and so forth.

As one liberated male explained, "Women have thousands of years of missed orgasms to make up for"—a noble task at which he was diligently beavering away. It is certainly true that many women regard learning to climax as a breakthrough because they previously felt they were missing out on something.

Now, though, Anya and I squirmed as we asked ourselves the same hard questions we had asked about the effects of sexual satiety on men. What if some sort of perception shift resulting from orgasm also left *us* with feelings of lack? How might sexual hangovers manifest in women's experience? How about all-around bitchiness? Making him wrong about everything? Reaching for antidepressants? Avoiding sex? Overeating? Excessive fondness for one's vibrator? Feeling unable to cope? Insane jealousy? Fortune hunting? Romance novel addictions? Compulsive shopping, or even kleptomania? Tears and emotional blackmail? Neurotic, needy, controlling mothers—and wounded kids?

Why, it looked like a list of complaints from the minutes of a men's support group meeting. And maybe we women could not do much to prevent our flashes of bottomless-pit neediness and destructive overreactions unless we, too, addressed this unsuspected cause of our natural, but avoidable, sense of deprivation. One weary veteran was right on the money:

Are women crazy, or do I, without knowing exactly how, somehow make them as irrational and volatile as they seem to become after we get involved? They're rarely like that until after we get "serious."[40]

When at last I put on my elephant-hunting spectacles and observed my own behavior objectively, I had to admit that I could stay really loving after orgasm—for about five days at the most. Then my whole world started to look *different,* and the only thing I was sure of was that my distress was due to my partner. The effects came and went for about two weeks, and I was sometimes at my very worst just before the end of that time.

Tragically, today's media insists that women's happiness is utterly dependent upon pursuing orgasm to the point of surfeit (rather than bonding behaviors and trusted companionship). If we aren't happy after we learn to orgasm, it's because we haven't mastered multiple orgasms. And if we aren't blissful then, we must be missing out on the even more intense experience of ejaculatory orgasms (yes, for women). Genitals not exploding at will in the bedroom? No problem, sexual enhancement pharmaceuticals with high price tags and unknown side effects are on the way.

I've learned to control my ejaculation because I don't like feeling fatigued during the following days. But I often don't want to bring my girlfriend to orgasm either, because (I'm not joking here) she just finishes like that—and rolls over and goes to sleep. I'm left totally energized, unable to sleep. I must add that it was very good to experience the other side of the coin.—David

This media blitz to inflame yearning doesn't just sell magazines and the items advertised in them. It is also misleading us about where happiness, well-being, and harmonious relationships lie.

It dawned on me that women who do not orgasm easily might actually be ahead of the rest of us—provided they realize there is no reason to amp up unnecessary frustration in pursuit of the "Holy Grail" of orgasm. At some level women who don't settle for orgasm as the measure of their sexual satisfaction may be holding out for the bonding behaviors that would deepen their relationships and offer both partners more satisfaction. It may even be that gentle, generous lovemaking, with no performance objectives, is the best possible way for women to unblock their sexual energy, and that forced orgasms only make it more difficult for them to fall into relaxed, openhearted, union.

Not long after Anya and I faced the facts, I came upon a clue in black and white that confirmed what we had learned the hard way. A tantra teacher in India wrote:

[If a woman does not relax into a transcendental state during sex] she will have the nervous orgasm, which is short-lived and followed by dissatisfaction and exhaustion. This is often the cause of a woman's hysteria and depression.[41]

Depression is highest in the USA. It's clearly dysregulated for some reason.
—Randolph Nesse, co-author of *Why We Get Sick*

Not to mention that of her mate.

Our experience suggested that women may not want to make the same innocent error men have of believing sexual satiety is the point of sex. In fact, as I listened to people's stories, I saw that a lot of misery could probably be avoided by mastering another way of making love. Scenarios like this one brought up both compassion *and* a desire to share what I was learning:

> This relationship was supposed to be different. We were bonded in spirit. But within six months we had fallen into the abyss of all that was unholy between man and woman. My physical and emotional health was severely depleted. Depression was a constant companion. Our relationship was fragmented and wounded. How could I have experienced Divine Oneness and now feel such separation from my husband? How could I endure the pain of not knowing how to close the enormous gap between us? What had happened during my marriage that warranted the comment from a new friend that I was the saddest looking woman she had ever seen? Before my marriage I was a professional educator, vibrantly alive. A year into it I felt drained of all but enough life force to survive.[42]

"BUT I FEEL GREAT AFTER ORGASM!"

Skepticism is healthy. Make your own investigations. First, check your timing. Is your relationship in the "honeymoon high" phase? In the early stages of romance, few people can spot the perception shift after orgasm, thanks to the drug-like buzz of new-romance neurochemicals. Unfortunately, the effects of this booster shot will wear off within two years (if not far sooner), and pursuing sexual satiety may actually speed this process, as we'll see.

Second, get out a calendar and track events for yourself—both orgasms and mood swings over the following two weeks or so. Women (especially) can sometimes feel elated for several days after orgasm, and *then* see things turn sour quite unexpectedly. In fact, some of us suffer our most pronounced changes in mood and perception near the *end* of the two-week cycle.

What I have experienced first-hand is that orgasm with a partner, or on my own, definitely triggers addictive tendencies, as well as old neurotic emotional patterns. I still have emotional issues to work through, and I still create obstacles for myself, but avoiding orgasm gives me a more sound foundation to work from. My intuition is heightened, my intellect is more powerful, and I just feel better about myself overall. I also get along with people better, and I can handle stress much more competently. I've achieved a level of emotional stability that I never had my entire life. I react much more appropriately to life's ups and downs, while I used to just fall apart.—Bette

---

This hangover is subconscious for both men and women, although men usually acknowledge it more readily because so many of them have experienced the urge to bolt after sex. In contrast, we women sometimes feel unusually clingy, jealous, or determined to remodel our mates—emotions that certainly don't feel like an urge to separate. Without realizing it, however, we are engaged in *separating behavior* that can drive a partner away. Either way, our powerful genes win the mating sweepstakes—if someone fools around.

Post-orgasmic feelings can make a mate's endearing habits look like annoying flaws. They can also affect women's judgment adversely in other ways. A friend shared her experience:

I've always been a very sensual woman. I could have five and as many as nine orgasms in a single encounter. After such events I often felt a sense of having conquered my partner rather than having been with him in a romantic, mutually loving exchange. I usually felt distant from him emotionally; I would play silly power games, word games, put-downs if I thought I was superior, or else just go off shopping if I thought it was going well. That was my biggest weakness. I'd spend a fortune on expensive clothes and jewelry, fantasizing about our wonderful social life together where I'd be a star or center of attention in all my finery with this great guy and me together.

Within days I'd become weepy and reminisce about very sad periods in my life and fall into a mild depression. If I did this with the guy present, I wanted him somehow to say the right thing and ease the pain, be the protective man. However, men never seemed to say the right thing or not often enough for the depth of my despair. Sometimes I'd grow possessive and phone or try to be clever in how I'd contact him because I was needy and wanted his attention and wanted it there and then—no matter what else was pressing in his life or mine.

Then when a guy didn't come up to snuff—too weak and tired and unreliable, or had fled off to the next conquest to escape the drain of a now-possessive or demanding woman—I'd be left with my expensive purchases and not able to pay my phone bill.

As you observe yourself (or your female partner), you, too, may see the connection between cause and effect. Watch for unspecified malaise, greater discomfort before or during menstruation, flaring temper, weepiness, harsh judgments, irrational spending, and a dismal sense that you have chosen a partner who is just not right for you. Above all, watch for friction between you and your sweetheart during the two weeks after one of you has an orgasm—whoever, or whatever issue, seems to cause it.

If you are living with a partner, chances are your distress will be projected onto your mate (especially after the neurochemical honeymoon wears off). Ask for honest feedback. Do the good feelings of orgasm outweigh its costs when you take into account the complete cycle of sexual satiety? As we'll see shortly, our genes' mating agenda is temporary, fertile bonds followed by restlessness. You are merely their puppet while you follow their script. When you learn to outsmart them, you may find that the issues you believed were causing the discord between you and your partner grow more manageable.

This new way is having profound results in our marriage and in other areas of our lives. We are happier. We don't fight nearly as much. Our kids seem more relaxed and secure. I now have a different, lower-paying job, but the stress has been minimal, and my wife and I have even started a small business together. All in all, I think we are on the road to a much more fulfilling marriage and life.—Lawrence

ROWING IN THE SAME LEAKY BOAT

My quest was obviously taking some unexpected directions. One thing was clear, however: Men and women were in this together. Evolution had shaped men to fertilize with gusto, but it had also shaped women to draw those sperm to their targets with powerful magnetism. Yet both men and women benefited from dodging Cupid's poisoned arrow by learning to make love without reaching the point of "enough, thanks." This meant that if men wished to become "safe pilots," to use Taoist terminology, they needed to learn sexual self-discipline. But women needed to check their inner temptresses at the bedroom door and find other satisfying ways of nurturing their mates. Both sexes would have to move beyond their automatic responses if they wanted to experiment with the mystery of bonding-based sex.

Loving means much more than sex—it means being comfortable with the whole wide gamut of both pleasant, unpleasant, sexy and not-so-sexy aspects of sharing life with a real human, man or woman. Once you have reached this point where you are not going to objectify each other, then it's almost impossible to step into conventional, default roles of relating without immediately feeling sick.—Niki

I was flooded with compassion for everyone. What bad luck that an effective tool for harmony and more balanced perception should be veiled by our most compelling urge: the urge to quench our sexual thirst. How sad that our very efforts to love each other could evoke lingering feelings of depletion, neediness, and resentment—giving rise to thoughts of scarcity and the belief in a need for defensiveness.

On the other hand, think of the potential! If we were collectively doing all this to ourselves, then *we could change it.* By understanding that orgasm is merely the peak of a longer, self-defeating cycle, we could alter our love-making to produce lingering feelings of satisfaction and excess energy instead. Intimacy would be perceived subconsciously as a source of lasting well-being, rather than a depleting sacrifice leading to resentment and aversion.

TELLTALE SIGNS?

In his book *Sex, Time and Power,* Leonard Shlain points out that compared with other species humans display some surprising characteristics. Men masturbate to ejaculation far more often, and more intensely, than other species.[43] Women are far more drained by their menses than other species are. Humans also engage in exclusive same-sex pairing more than other species.

Could these behaviors be linked to the fact that we are able to have sex anytime, unlike species with rigid mating periods? As we'll see, it seems that our genes have chosen *another* way of making sure human emotional bonds don't jeopardize the potential for even greater genetic success: recurring draining feelings of uneasiness and resentment. These, in turn, leave us vulnerable to groundless irritation, hypersensitivity to sexual cues, discouragement, and weakening emotional bonds. Could our post-orgasmic feelings also be reflected in our lives as draining conditions, such as heavy menstruation and compulsive masturbation?

Chinese Taoist sages taught that both sexes had the power to revitalize themselves by cultivating their sexual energy to avoid loss of vitality. To make their point dramatically, they equated the loss of one drop of semen with the loss of 100 drops of blood.[44] Men were taught "sexual kung fu" to refine the sexual energy residing in sperm instead of ejaculating. Women were advised to mitigate their periods in a similar practice known as "slaying the red dragon." Today, many of us are engaged in sexual behavior that is the very opposite of such careful cultivation.

The ancient Taoists who claimed that loss of semen or blood caused the depletion they experienced were probably incorrect. As it turns out, neurochemically induced *feelings of depletion* appear to be the prime culprit in both sexes, as we'll see in Chapter Five. However, the Taoist method of avoiding those self-sabotaging feelings was very insightful indeed.

THE PITFALLS OF SELF-SUFFICIENCY

Meanwhile, there was a more immediate question on my mind. What happens when one is without a mate? Clearly sexual energy is too dynamic to sit on indefinitely, and I had no wish to become a passionless husk. I sensed that my mission was to learn how to become more alive, not less.

The texts I was studying suggested that sexual energy could be carefully refined and directed toward heightened spiritual awareness, even without a partner. Sages insisted that orgasm somehow drained sexual energy before it could be used for that higher purpose.

In my experience, there are actually two ways to be celibate while waiting for the right partner, and I've been both. One is about repression of sexual energy. Fighting your sexual desire out of fear can cause physical and emotional complications, sexual fantasies, and even perversion (as seen in the media coverage of Catholic priests and child abuse). The other kind, though, is about transformation of sexual energy. This is the kind that benefits me. It is difficult to distinguish at first, and I think most people who attempt to give up masturbation almost certainly will experience discomfort in the beginning.

Transforming sexual energy basically means using it for a higher purpose, such as personal growth, spiritual practice, service to others, and so forth. In my case I went back to school and amazed myself with my academic performance. I can honestly say that my physical and emotional health are much better than when I was masturbating frequently, and I still have a healthy sex drive, as far as I can tell! But I learned that I could not just stop masturbating, yet continue doing everything else the way I did before I stopped, such as isolating myself, or zoning out with TV. I had to use the energy toward a larger goal. It seems that finding a partner kind of happens on its own. I'm just starting to date again after two years. Phew!—Caitlin

Of course I didn't take the sages' advice at face value. I conducted my own experiments. They revealed that masturbation consistently set off mood swings during the following two weeks. I concluded that seconds of intense pleasure were a high price to pay for two weeks peppered with erratic shifts in outlook. I also noticed that my sense of connectedness and clarity during my spiritual practice flickered or faded during that time. I began to understand why Tibetan Buddhists referred to orgasm as "the killing of the inner Buddha."[45] As I grew to relish the comforting sense that I was "in the flow," I gradually drifted away from masturbation without any inner conflict.

> *In these months of long-distance relationship I have clearly noticed how, when I do not masturbate, my affection and love for my girl-friend increases. I can see that in the way I write to her as well as a very nice overflowing feeling of love tangibly felt in the area of the heart. But after masturbating there is a change in that. The feeling of love (albeit still there) gets less, and the way I write to her changes, too. I sort of become more aloof, and that is reflected in my words. After about two weeks of not masturbating things change back again.—Jeremy*

But what to do with my sexual energy? Some esoteric sex manuals advised solo energy practices to draw the sexual energy upward and circulate it throughout the body. These techniques provided some relief, as did meditation, but it became evident that a partner was vital for stabilizing my sexual energy over the long term, now that orgasm was off the menu. I liked the sound of a joint effort, but it was also unnerving to contemplate relinquishing the illusion of self-sufficiency.

While I was discovering the surprising benefits of containing and redirecting my sexual energy, most of Western womanhood was galloping off in the opposite direction. Masturbation was hot! Women's magazines were blaring the message from every checkout counter: *The Clitoral Truth: The Secret World at Your Fingertips, Sex for One: The Joy of Self-loving,* and so on. Good ole do-it-yourself sex appeared to be the obvious solution in lots of situations—and good, clean fun, too.

Energy Circulation

Want to try a quick energy circulation exercise? Close your eyes, tighten the muscles of your pelvic floor, and draw the energy up your spine to the top of your head. Then imagine drawing it down the front of your body and storing it in your navel.

Masturbation is natural, of course. It's good to be at ease with your genitals and what they can do. In eager young men masturbation also serves our genes by ensuring that highly motile—that is, fresh and fertile—sperm are always at the ready. What is *unnatural* (in the sense that our ancestors would have faced nothing like it) is the quantity and intensity of today's sexual stimulation.

As we'll see in Chapter Six, intense stimulation to the point of (temporary) sexual exhaustion by any and all means has powerful, unsuspected effects on the brain. Briefly, the post-satiety period can be uncomfortable—and another orgasm instantly makes you feel great, or at least puts you to sleep. Yet in the wake of that relief follows another period of uneasiness. Without realizing it you can end up masturbating to self-medicate your recurring discomfort, with a net loss in overall well-being. Worse yet, if you mistake your cravings for true libido, self-restraint can seem unattainable.

I've kinda stopped the do-it-yourself sex. Feels better. Imagine that: masturbation makes the frustration worse.—Kevin

We humans evolved in tribes. Our sense of genuine well-being is dependent upon physical contact and mutual support. Given that we're not well suited to our isolated modern lifestyles, it's no wonder that many of us are self-medicating any way we can, and trying to content ourselves with two-dimensional mates or fictional heartthrobs. Fortunately, there are billions of three-dimensional solutions to our fundamental problem living side-by-side with us.

Woke up very clear, as though I've been in a dream. Porn has become a temptation, rather than the overriding compulsion it was. Yesterday I met an adorable woman. If I could look into her clear and gentle eyes each day I would never need to look at porn again ... because the beauty of actual magnetism that is felt with another goes so far beyond anything an orgasm in front of a PC can give. I feel like I'm reclaiming my life.—Kurt

It is sad that today's hypersexuality trends so swiftly push us away from each other. I was beginning to figure this out, but was still somewhat aghast by what I was learning.

CHRISTIANITY

Imagine for a moment that Jesus actually taught a sacramental inter- course that heals the separation impulse between intimate partners with a view to attaining spiritual awakening, rather than producing children. Would there be *any* evidence to support this possibility? Surprisingly, yes, although you will not hear a whisper of it in mainstream Christianity.

First, let's consider a bit of context for this radical idea. Beginning in 312 CE, Constantine and his successors gradually placed the might of the Roman Empire behind a single Christian sect. According to scholar Elaine Pagels, it comprised only half of the world's Christians.[46] From that time onward, the "winners" determined Christian doctrine, reviling and suppressing other, and even *earlier,* accounts of Jesus's teachings. Until sixty years ago, the world knew very little of the "losers," the more mystical, less formal sects of early Christianity.

Then some very old texts turned up in a cave in Upper Egypt. They are known as the Nag Hammadi codices. These texts offer an intriguingly different picture of early Christian beliefs. They state that the defects of this world are due to the fact that it is the handiwork of a flawed angel, or demiurge.

> In the beginning the universe was created. This has made a lot of people angry and been widely regarded as a bad move.
> —Douglas Adams, author

They also emphasize the androgynous nature of the Divine and record that Adam was immortal and whole—until he separated from Eve by "begetting beasts" (physical children) instead of engaging in sacred union. They say that Jesus returned in order to heal the separation between the sexes in a mystery called the sacrament of the bridal chamber. Here is a sprinkling of intriguing passages from the Gospel of Philip:

> The embrace that incarnates the hidden union [is] not only a reality of the flesh, for there is silence in this embrace. It does not arise

from impulse or desire; it is an act of will.[47] ... Seek the experience of the pure embrace; it has great power.[48]

The union is in this world man and woman, the place of the power and the weakness.[49] ... There are two trees growing in Paradise. The one bears animals, the other bears men. Adam ate from the tree which bore animals. He became an animal and he brought forth animals.[50]

All will be clothed in light when they enter into the mystery of the sacred embrace. If the woman had not been separated from the man [through incorrect union], she would not die with the man. Her separation was the origin of death. Christ comes again to heal this wound, to rediscover the lost unity, to enliven those who kill themselves in separation, reviving them in union.[51]

The holy of holies is the bridal chamber, or communion.[52] ... Man and woman unite in the bridal chamber, and those who have known this sacred embrace will never be separated. Eve separated from Adam because she did not unite with him in the bridal chamber.[53]

[We] are reborn by the Christ two by two. In his Breath, we experience a new embrace; we are no longer in duality, but in unity.[54] What is the bridal chamber, if not the place of trust and consciousness in the embrace? It is an icon of Union, beyond all forms of possession; here is where the veil is torn from top to bottom; here is where some arise and awaken.[55]

They have risen above attraction and repulsion.[56]

Another Nag Hammadi text, the Exegesis on the Soul, is an allegory about the soul's return to the Father, but might it not *also* contain clues about the mystery of lust-free union? Consider this description of the sacrament of the bridal chamber:

Since that marriage is not like the carnal marriage, those who are to have intercourse with one another will be satisfied with that intercourse. And as if it were a burden, they leave behind them the annoyance of physical desire and they [turn their faces from] each other. But [once] they unite, they become a single life.... Wherefore the prophet said (Genesis 2:24) concerning the first man and the first woman, "They will become a single flesh." For they were originally joined to one another when they were with the Father. . . . This marriage has brought them back together again.[57]

The ultimate goal, as various Nag Hammadi texts make clear, is an experience of wholeness that recreates a gnosis (knowledge) of our divine androgyne origins. The Gospel of Philip suggests that this is the way the Christ is reborn in mankind. As we saw, the ancient Taoists also recorded that the practice of controlled intercourse could give birth to a nonphysical "holy fetus."[58] I suspect that this concept of giving birth to the Christ two-by-two is behind such gnostic references as imperishable seed, divine conception, rebirth, incorruptible body, and so on. Might it also have been the original meaning of immaculate conception?

Although most fundamentalist and Catholic Christians seldom acknowledge it, Jesus didn't recommend procreation. His objective was helping mankind to achieve spiritual transcendence. His lack of attention to reproduction is apparent even in the canonical gospels in the New Testament. In the Nag Hammadi Gospel of Thomas, Jesus is far more explicit:

[Jesus] said to [her], "Lucky are those who have heard the word of the Father and have truly kept it. For there will be days when you will say, "Lucky are the womb that has not conceived and the breasts that have not given milk."[59]

Procreation was definitely *not* on the minds of the early Christians, who were willing to leave families behind entirely to spread the good news.

Mainstream Christianity assumes that Jesus was celibate. However, the sacrament of the bridal chamber is clearly not a solo mystery. The Gospel of Philip records that Jesus had a consort in Mary Magdalene, whom he used to kiss often on the [mouth].[60]

Scholars are slow to accept that these unfamiliar concepts may once have been at the heart of Christianity. However, religious scholar Dennis R. MacDonald acknowledges that soon after the time of Jesus, and certainly by the time Saint Paul wrote the material in Galatians, there was already a widespread oral tradition—evidence of which has come to light via Egypt, Syria, and Greece—to the effect that Jesus had taught, "You enter the

Kingdom of Heaven when male and female become one."[61] Incidentally, Helmut Koester of Harvard University has suggested that some traditions in the Gospel of Thomas may *predate* the gospels of the New Testament.[62] Princeton's Elaine Pagels believes that the Bible's Gospel of John was written to counter the widespread influence of Thomas, which encourages believers to know God directly rather than simply believe in Jesus.[63]

According to scholar Michael A. Williams, the early believers who lived by these principles were apparently devoted Christians, widely admired for their integrity. In his view, as the Church sought dominance, its fathers produced rather standard, scandal-filled polemics about them. As a consequence, religious scholars later segregated and marginalized these early believers with the label "gnostics." Williams also notes that as late as the second century CE, there was a Christian movement in the Rhône Valley that practiced a rite called the "bridal chamber," which he believes was most likely some version of the "undefiled marriage" described in the Gospel of Philip, in which desire was renounced and transformation of the couple was the goal.[64]

In *Just Love: A Framework for Christian Sexual Ethics,*[65] religious scholar Margaret Farley reminds us that the early Christians were not necessarily sex negative even though they were concerned about the power of unbridled sexual desire to interfere with their spiritual clarity and corrupt spiritual love between men and women. Scholar Peter Brown records that celibacy was not the only solution proposed. Spiritual marriage *(syneisaktism)* was another.[66]

In a relationship practice that was apparently widespread during the first several hundred years of Christianity, a devout couple would cohabit under the condition of strict continence. According to scholar Elizabeth A. Clark, the origin of the practice is unknown, but might it not have been a watered-down version of the mystery of the sacrament of the bridal chamber described in the Nag Hammadi texts?

Almost 400 years after the time of Jesus, Archbishop Chrysostom said this in condemning this popular practice of taking a spiritual bride:

> The notion that this pleasure and love can be keener than that afforded by living together in a legal marriage probably astounds you, [but in the case of a spiritual bride] there is no intercourse

which can restrain and relax the frenzy of nature, nor do labor pains and childrearing dry up her flesh; to the contrary, these virgins stay in their prime for a long time, since they remain untouched.... These women retain their beauty until they are forty.... Thus the men who live with them are stirred by a double desire; they are not permitted to satisfy their passion through sexual intercourse, yet the basis for their desire remains intensely potent for a long time.[67]

As theologian Charles Williams observed, the harsh suppression of this phenomenon by the Church means that we unfortunately know nothing of the cases in which a chaste union's power to overcome the drawbacks of passion succeeded. The Synod of Elvira (305) and the Council of Nicaea (325) forbade it altogether, for fear of scandal.

The great experiment had to be abandoned.... It was one of the earliest triumphs of "the weaker brethren," those innocent sheep who by mere volume of imbecility have trampled over many delicate and attractive flowers in Christendom.... The Church abandoned that method in favor of the marriage method, which [Paul] had deprecated, and eventually lost any really active tradition of marriage itself as a way of the soul. This we have still to recover.[68]

Today we view these early Christians, with their lofty ideals for intimate unions and their sacred texts hinting at an unfamiliar form of continence, through two thousand years of dark glass furnished by the Church fathers and their successors. These well-intentioned latecomers reshaped the rules of the family away from ambitious spiritual goals in favor of procreation and social stability based on the imperial Roman model of *paterfamilias*.[69]

Could the "winners" have misinterpreted some of the original message when they advocated "celibacy as a spiritual path, and, for lesser souls, a sacrament of marriage strictly for procreation"? This doctrine leaves biology triumphant, and discounts the power of love between lovers to lead to an experience of the Comforter (Paraclete). Considering the mind-altering properties of sexual satiety, it may be that the sacramental intercourse hinted at in the Nag Hammadi codices, and even the "spiritual marriage" as practiced by other Christians, could both promote harmony between the sexes and greater inner peace, quite apart from any deeper mystery.

CHAPTER THREE

A Whale's Tail

The most effective way to see the benefit of karezza is to try it for a minimum of three weeks and then return to conventional sex.

With conventional sex, decline in marital satisfaction during the first year or two of marriage is standard.

Excess libido can be the *result of* sexual satiety.

After several years of experimentation, I had the sense that there was a bigger picture forming than I could yet see. I had learned a lot, but I also had more questions than ever. It was apparent that the fallout after orgasm led to clouded perception for both men *and* women. It was also clear that it often gave rise to uneasiness and anxiety—particularly between mates. The good news was that making love without sexual satiety yielded a refreshing lightheartedness that increased with consistency. Those few people I knew who were willing to experiment felt better and more in control of their lives when they cut back on orgasm, even while on their own.

Yet it was decidedly *awkward* to try to explain any of this to someone who hadn't already experienced the benefits—let alone to a new lover. As a friend wrote:

> I've just begun a new relationship, but I don't think I'm ready to share this idea with her. I really like not having the ups and downs of orgasm. But I don't know that I am sure and confident enough in myself or my convictions about this approach to advocate it to

another. So I think I am going to end up starting with conventional sex. And to be honest, I think it would end up that way anyway! Of course, I will not make orgasm my goal. Eventually I think that will lead to not climaxing, and then to talking about it. I don't know that I can start it the other way—not yet.

Six months later he took a job in another state, after breaking up with her five times. Yet I totally understood his point of view. Even for someone with an open mind and ample courage there's a big difference between grasping a concept and living it with a second person. Suppose you aren't sure about the connection between orgasm and disharmony but you try the ideas with a lover and see the benefits. Wouldn't you always still wonder if your relationship might have been just as harmonious—or even better—with great orgasms in the mix? We naturally question anything that leads away from fertilization-driven sex.

My own irregular learning curve suggested that a person has to try karezza for several weeks and then go for orgasm—with the same partner —in order to make a meaningful comparison. In theory one could also start with conventional sex and then backtrack to try karezza. Yet I never made much progress in a new relationship unless I *began* a relationship with karezza.

New relationships are very thrilling. Biology drives us together with fireworks. It never seems like a good idea to try a tamer approach to ease sexual tension at the beginning of a relationship. "What? And miss all the thrills of that exciting honeymoon neurochemistry? Are you *crazy?*"

Yet whenever I started a relationship by yielding to my mating program I ran into problems. One was that orgasm seemed to have an addictive quality to it. Once passion was ignited, it tended to rage until it burned itself out naturally. As the flames diminished, both of us instinctively used passion to try to restore the intensity of our connection. That actually sped up the natural flattening of sexual desire between us.

As the brain's pleasure centers light up, they bring not only joy to the moment of sex but also the appetite for more and more sex.... The more we have it the more we want it. It is the ultimate addiction.
—*Joann Ellison Rodgers,* SEX: A Natural History

By the time my lover and I reached the familiar impasse just over the crest of this "ultimate addiction," my perception of him and his of me were suffering. The fallout period turned out *not* to be a good starting point for an approach that called for sidestepping hot foreplay and orgasm. Especially during the first two weeks after conventional sex, lovemaking without orgasm seemed like a really *bad* idea. Paradoxically, cravings for orgasm were often more demanding than during our pre-orgasm courtship. (We'll see why later.) Even when I persuaded a partner to experiment with the alternative during the recovery period, our efforts were mechanical and interspersed with periods of emotional friction. The benefits seemed as ephemeral as bubbles, and we tended to give up, return to our genes' script, and eventually separate.

All the same, I was becoming joyfully optimistic about intimate relationships due to my brief glimpses of harmony. What a relief to know what had been eroding my relationships and, theoretically at least, how to get around it!

"BUT WHAT ABOUT HAPPY MARRIAGES?"

Of course, I couldn't help wondering about the long-term, contented marriages of some of my friends. How were *they* eluding Cupid's poisoned arrow? I began by asking some women I knew well if they had ever sensed an uneasy emotional distance from their mates after lovemaking.

"I've had to quit making love with my husband entirely," confessed an English friend in a small study group I attended while living in Belgium. "It always set off days of inexplicable depression." Moved by her admission, a German friend chimed in: "After sex I used to get up and go into the bathroom and sit on the tub and cry. I could not imagine what was wrong with me. I had a nice husband, two wonderful kids, and all the money we needed." A third (Danish) was also virtually sexually estranged from her husband and *somewhat* comforted to know the others were sleeping in separate bedrooms from their spouses, too. All were attractive, otherwise compatibly married, and quite comfortable with massage, intimacy, and looking at their issues.

Yet all of them opted to let sleeping husbands lie rather than suggest a new approach to lovemaking. Hilde made a brief experiment first. She asked her husband if he would make love, but skip orgasm. After months of weighing involuntary celibacy against "insane ideas," he agreed. They tried it once, without the gradual exchange of energy over the preceding weeks, which I was learning was necessary for best results. "The next day," she told me, "we were like teens in love. We took a walk in the woods. He even lifted me over a fence that unexpectedly barred our way. We giggled the whole way back to the hotel."

The results, though encouraging, were short-lived. The next time they made love, he begged to ejaculate because it was his birthday. She acquiesced. "Within days he seemed to age ten years. I just can't stand the thought of touching him," she confided. Years later, their unresolved emotional and sexual distance was still a bitter drain on both.

Later I discovered that lack of sexual desire is the most common problem clients bring to sex therapists. I also spoke with a couple so harmonious that they were the envy of their friends for years. Then they shocked everyone by divorcing—on the theory that something must be terribly wrong because they were not ever having sex, though they still loved cuddling. Their experience was certainly not unique. Oprah's protégé, Dr. Phil, once remarked that sexless marriages are "an undeniable epidemic."[70]

Traditional sexual advice never made sense to me. As a single person I'm supposed to let go of my sexual frustration. But then once I have a partner, I have mostly to worry about how to keep my sexual desire going. How can anyone be expected to split her life into such completely different behaviors and attitudes based on relationship status?—Anne

---

The phenomenon of disappearing sex drive wasn't exclusive to women. "I lived with my boyfriend for quite a while before we got married during college," confessed a girlfriend.

We were nuts about each other and very sexually active. But shortly after we married he began to pull away from me sexually. He couldn't explain why, and I couldn't bear the pain of knowing that something was wrong between me and my closest companion with no way to understand it or resolve it. I had an affair with a fellow student. That soothed my wounded ego, but it also made me feel horrible. I'd always prided myself on being honest and genuine, and yet my actions were totally the opposite. But it seemed like losing that sense of closeness with my husband made me feel so desperate that I had very little choice.

In short, the more closely I examined successful marriages, the more I found

Since sexual intercourse is not hindered in a relationship with a wife, it serves to still passion and often leads the man to satiation, greatly reducing his desire.
—John Chrysostom,
fourth century CE saint

gaps in them. True, in the happiest marriages, the partners were somewhat content with the compromises they had constructed. Upon careful inspection, though, the separation between mates was still evident. Instead of exhibiting immunity to the poison on Cupid's arrow, most marriages established that it was more potent than I had first imagined.

THE BERMUDA TRIANGLE OF RELATIONSHIPS

Eventually I realized that studying the different reasons couples separate or trying to figure out who was at fault shed no light on the bigger issue. While conventional sex was in the mix, if couples resolved one source of friction, another arose to take its place. The challenge was best viewed simply as a separation mechanism that shows up in different ways.

Once I realized separation was almost *always* present, I found myself devising a simple tool for pinpointing where the separation lay in a union (including those of my past). I nicknamed it the Bermuda Triangle of Relationships because separation tends to creep into committed relationships in one of three ways: (1) the sexual attraction between the partners fades, (2) they become less available to each other sexually even though there is still an attraction between them, or (3) the couple's monogamous commitment breaks. With any of these three cornerstones removed, the relationship is usually badly crippled, even if it survives. As I looked around, I saw that even the best matches all too often found their way into this puzzling Bermuda Triangle despite all efforts to stay on course.

The subtlest way partners separated was by becoming largely unavailable to each other sexually, despite the obvious spark between them. The reasons for separation often appeared to be beyond their control: incompatible sleeping habits, professional needs to live in different locations, snoring, children's demands, illnesses, inexplicable fatigue, sexual dysfunction, and so on.

Many couples blamed their lack of libido on fatigue, but if they divorced I noticed that they found plenty of time for passionate romance, so I began to suspect that exhaustion might actually be one more way of unconsciously avoiding the fallout from sexual satiety. In *For Women Only,* authors Jennifer Berman and Laura Berman list various techniques that their patients use to avoid sex, from the age-old strategy of feigning sleep to the quite modern practice of taking on household night-owl projects.[71] And women are not alone. Unfortunately, this tactic often denies both mates much needed nonsexual affection, too.

The other night I decided to surprise my husband. I sent the kids to stay at my mother's for the night. I donned a leather bodice, stiletto heels, and put on a mask. My husband came in from work, grabbed the TV remote and a beer, and said, "Hey Batman, what's for dinner?"

I saw that substance abuse was another common way that couples kept a distance sexually. With a few too many glasses of wine or habitual marijuana use, many were able to "medicate" their post-orgasmic discomfort and drift in a haze of pseudo-intimacy for years. From the outside their unions often looked all right.

The most overt way that couples separated was by breaking their commitment. The relationship fell apart, or the partners opted for an open marriage. "One in five adults in love with someone other than partner," proclaimed the UK *Telegraph* recently based on a study.

A sense that you have somehow married the wrong person makes ongoing commitment problematic. Often one spouse opts for the noble-sounding ideal of needing more personal space, or both decide they are growing in different directions, and they divorce. Is this problem widespread? In 2002, the U.S. Census Bureau predicted that half of all recent marriages would end in divorce.[72] Since then the divorce rate has dropped slightly, but more couples than ever *never marry.* Their breakups aren't counted in divorce statistics.

As I measured everyone's favorite fairytale couples against my Bermuda Triangle model, I realized that I had a whale by the tail. Separation was affecting the majority of couples to some degree. Years later I am still struck by how few exceptions there seem to be. When my husband and I give talks about Cupid's poisoned arrow we are inevitably stunned when some of the most loving couples in the audience—couples who seem like they should be telling the rest of us the key to happy marriage—come up afterward and say: "We know exactly what you're talking about and we want to learn more. We want to stay in love."

"YOU JUST HAVE TO FIND THE RIGHT PERSON"

Longtime marriage counselor and author Willard F. Harley, Jr., practically acknowledged the source of the problem in his book *Love Busters:*

> I want to emphasize that [the utter selfishness that so often splits couples up] is normal in marriage. You might think you're married to a crazy person or you may think you're crazy....
>
> I'm thoroughly convinced that it's marriage itself, or more specifically a romantic relationship, that makes communication so difficult. It's not the differences between men and women.... [Those I counsel] have very little trouble resolving conflicts when not in romantic relationship.[73]

What I was learning suggested that the relentless tug of the Bermuda Triangle can't be overcome with good communication, superior compatibility, avoiding sex before marriage, and so forth. Why? Because it was somehow linked to sexual intimacy, which is obviously an integral part of any healthy marriage. I sometimes think of this creeping separation as a "virus," because it subverts a healthy element of union—intimacy—and transforms it into a means of damaging the host relationship. Falling in love was great; watching attraction die was awful.

I wasn't about to accept that fertilization-driven sex was the only factor in people's deteriorating love lives, and yet there was a discouraging similarity to most couples' results. I began to wonder if the challenge in intimate relationships was not *whom* we marry but rather *how* we make love. My suspicions grew stronger when I happened upon "the honeymoon study." Doctor Kiecolt-Glaser set out to discover whether stress hormones rose during marital conflict. To isolate short-term stress she chose ninety newlywed couples out of the whopping 2,200 newlywed couples she and her colleagues interviewed. Only the most blissful, healthiest, wealthiest, most stable couples were selected.

Kiecolt-Glaser discovered that conflict indeed raised stress hormones (with possible implications for lowered immunity to disease). However, in following up with the couples, she *also* discovered that across the board, they reported decreased satisfaction in their marriages by the second year. As Kiecolt-Glaser put it, "Declines in marital satisfaction appear to be a stable response to the first year or two of marriage." That's scientist-speak for "the poison on Cupid's arrow had taken effect." By release of the study, a fifth of her blissful, ideally suited couples had already divorced.[74]

Relationships are failing despite marital therapy and efforts to support them.
—Savulescu and Sandberg, ethicists

No wonder marriage counseling so seldom keeps couples together. Something larger and quite impersonal is at work, and I was to learn more about its biological basis just a few years later.

MORE AWKWARD QUESTIONS

Hearing about the unsuspected gaps in friends' love lives wasn't the only awkward aspect of my quest to understand more. Every book I could find about Taoist lovemaking, or even tantra (the Hindu tradition that encompasses sacred sexuality), insisted that there was a powerful synergy unique to the carefully cultivated union of yin (female energy) and yang (male energy). What did that mean for my gay friends? My friends with physical ailments that hampered their lovemaking? Or those who weren't yet ready for intercourse?

I dug through various ancient texts looking for answers. The Taoists certainly weren't squeamish or moralistic about same-sex behavior. Sex between women was considered a neutral practice called "polishing the mirror" (although orgasm was viewed as draining for women as well as men).[75] However, the Taoists warned that casual sex between men, "dragon yang syndrome," was too draining due to overstimulation (and sexual exhaustion), and therefore a potential source of health problems.

Anyone without a partner of the opposite sex was advised to refine his or her sexual energy, or supplement same-sex activity, using the solo exercises that I had learned, and to seek other sources of yin or yang energy.

> The male energy can be found in such sources as the sun and the mountains, and the female in such sources as the earth, the moon, and the lakes.[76]

The Taoists advised against frequent masturbation and orgasm, independent of sexual orientation. They observed that climax actually ratcheted up sexual desire, while also being depleting.[77] This seemed paradoxical until I thought about it for a while. I realized that for me, too, sexual satiety could subsequently increase the hankering for hot sex—perhaps to expel the gloom of the emotional friction or distance during the "hangover" period. Pursuing orgasm after satiation seemed to be the equivalent of eating when feeling anxious, even if one is not hungry. We will return to this point in Chapter Six when we look at how orgasm can become compulsive.

The Taoists regarded hypersexuality, or "expenditure without restraint," as the predictable outcome of pursuing sexual surfeit without first restoring inner equilibrium—not as evidence of true libido. In fact, in their view, premature ejaculation, discomfort after orgasm, wet dreams, and "lustful thoughts" were often indications of depletion, not surplus, of sexual energy. Their solution? Avoid depletion in the first place.

I'm taking notice of my feelings after orgasm. Immediately the urge completely disappears. I think "But why was I so desperate?! Who was pulling my strings? How was that sooo necessary?!" It feels like something really takes control of me, and it's very difficult to describe. Second, after orgasm I feel ... neutered. Like all my manly essence has been taken away, like a sissy boy: weak, shy, and introverted. It's really unsettling. Before I felt more like a man.—Dennis

---

Were many of us caught in hamster wheels of hyperactive sexual pursuits that were only increasing our discomfort? While I was pondering my sexual energy with new respect, a drama unfolded in my life, which increased my motivation to share what I was learning.

WAKEUP CALL

A friend brought an appealing young man to a party at my home. Lars was a gifted graphic designer, sensitive, sincere, courteous, and somewhat shy. He was accompanied by a polite, and much older, woman. I didn't realize they were lovers.

A few weeks later the friend who had brought them both to my house showed up again. He was shattered; Lars was dead.

Apparently Lars had only been with the woman a few months. And during that time he'd experienced periods of utterly uncharacteristic, violent behavior. For example, he got into fights in bars and had even been threatened with arrest. My friend, who had known Lars's whole family for years, also talked with his lover after Lars's death. She told him Lars had become sexually aggressive. The night of his death the woman had refused to participate. She went into another room to lie down. He came in later, sat on top of her, and demanded that she make love. She said no. He pulled a gun from behind his back and shot himself in the head.

Now, it's possible that there was no link whatsoever between his emotional-behavioral deterioration and his sex life. It was clear to me, though, that some sort of severe imbalance certainly corresponded with the period of their intimacy. Deeply affected by this tragedy, I made a solemn promise never to use my seductiveness to put a lover at risk. I was also committed to discussing the careful management of sexual energy with anyone who showed the least curiosity.

THE GLAMOUR HOOK

While living briefly in Manhattan I worked for a friend who owned a gay nightclub. As cabaret room manager, I designed posters for drag queens, made many more gay friends, and had lively discussions about gaps between the genders. Initially, I was amazed at the open-mindedness of my homosexual friends. Then it dawned on me that people drawn to same-sex relationships have probably spent more time pondering the reasons for alienation between the sexes than anyone but me. Far from being threatened by my ideas, many related easily.

Some had also experienced the post-orgasmic hangover. One friend told me this story:

> After six months of celibacy during a training program, one of my first stops was a gay beach where I had sex. I was amazed at the depth of the depression that followed within days. It made me think back to the times when I visited such beaches regularly in Holland. I was always sick. Maybe some people aren't affected by it, but sex the way I've been using it does create a hangover for me.

My closest buddy in New York was a man I had known for years while we both lived in Brussels. I loved him like a younger brother, but our friendship was challenging for me. Mark shared that he masturbated relatively infrequently, as compared with another gay friend who had transformed his second bedroom into an altar to pornography (pre-Internet). But whenever he did, it was soon followed by a devastating loss of self-confidence. Some event would unnerve him completely, such as a discussion with family members, who were not thrilled about his bumming around without a career. That is when he would go off to the bushes, feeling worthless, in search of a thrilling dose of temporary oblivion.

It took him some time to spot the pattern, but he finally quit masturbating. Not only did he forsake the park shrubbery, but within a few months he got together with one of his early lovers, with whom he had lost contact ten years earlier. It was Mark's first real relationship. Despite my evangelism about orgasm, both occasionally ejaculated, and their relationship was volatile. Finally, when Eric was out of town for a few weeks, Mark decided to stop mooching, get a job, and separate from him.

He went to work for a brand new Barnes & Noble bookstore, which had a clever strategy for appointing managers. It threw all 450 employees into a four-story building together as equals. Boxes had to be unloaded, moved around, and unpacked, so teams spontaneously formed and leaders appeared. I often stopped by to visit, and I was dazzled as Mark bloomed into a brilliant natural leader: charismatic, hardworking, funny, reliable, and a genius at kidding slackers into full participation (after all, who knew more than he did about evading work?).

He also crackled with a magnetic, thoroughly masculine electricity I had barely glimpsed, but which he now wore as naturally as any team captain. He flirted with everyone in a lighthearted way, and everyone, of both sexes, wanted to work with him. It came as little surprise that he was promoted twice in the first two weeks.

The last day before Eric's return, Mark told me that he was feeling torn. He was acutely aware that before him was an open gate to a totally different lifestyle, and he, too, was enjoying his transformation. But it was also scary.

That evening panic set in. He visited a Times Square porn theater and jerked off. His earlier persona swiftly reappeared. He decided to stay with Mr. Wonderful (his nickname for Eric) "because his apartment was so nice." He began to offend people at work with his manipulative gossiping, and it was not long before he quit his job at the bookstore. As he explained, "Eric needs me to help him select *fabric* samples and I just *love* fabrics!"

Evidence was piling up that orgasm had the power to shift perception and self-image. Was this harmless little habit shaping our choices without our awareness?

The Bible contains six admonishments to homosexuals and 362 admonishments to heterosexuals. That doesn't mean that God doesn't love heterosexuals. It's just that they need more supervision.
—Lynn Lavner

BEYOND RESENTMENT

A couple of years later, a friend (whom I had not known was bisexual) introduced me to Kate, who was passing through town. My friend, who enjoyed drama, had "forgotten" to tell me Kate was homosexual and insisted that she would find what I was learning of great interest. Right. "On a 1–10 scale of lesbianism, I'm about a 15," Kate later told me. "I've never slept with a man. I can't even stand the thought of it. I love women, though."

However, that first evening I missed the signals: the discreet rainbow earring, the black leather jacket, and the defiant glint. I only saw a brilliant engineer with a remarkable ability to concentrate, a broad-ranging background in spiritual matters, and a powerful will, who asked some of the best questions I had heard. Thus began a lively cross-country exchange between two very determined women—which continues to this day.

We were both avidly studying some of the same spiritual texts, and enthusiastically recommended books to each other. When the topic of forgiveness came up, I remarked that she seemed to forgive women *anything*, but became completely exasperated whenever a man did something she didn't like.

Kate got very quiet. "I'll work on it," she said, with the grim determination of a true spiritual warrior. A week later, I got an e-mail from one shocked lesbian! Following deep spiritual work on releasing resentments she was harboring toward men, Kate was asked out by a male colleague— a first. The day of their date she suffered a horrible migraine, but the evening was quite a surprise. She ended up telling him all about herself. Nonplussed, he only wanted to know if they might have a future together. Probably not, since she was about to take a job in another state.

A few months later something had definitely shifted. Men, whom she had previously viewed as thick-witted obstructionists, now fell over themselves opening doors, grinning, offering help, furniture, and information. "And when I wear a skirt they say 'Good morning' to my legs," she laughed. "Of course, I like women's legs, too."

When I next saw her, she was glowing. Gone were all traces of defensive impassivity. She still had powerful desires to hang out at lesbian bars and Web sites, but, to my surprise, she did not announce her sexual orientation at her new job, opting for neutral. With virtually no female colleagues or leisure time, she became attracted to some of her male colleagues and began dating them. She has been living with one of them for over a decade now.

Today she is a supportive manager and senior engineer in an otherwise all-male, extremely high-pressure engineering firm, with numerous men reporting to her. They think she is wonderful, and drop everything to help her when she needs quick support on a project. "People are saying such enormously good things about me that it's embarrassing," she told me recently.

I was learning that forgiveness, like orgasm, has the power to shift perception. Or, to state it differently, resentment is a surprisingly effective obstruction between the sexes—but it's a choice.

MATING VERSUS BONDING

As a straight person, I initially found this fluidity among my homosexual friends confusing. I was under the mistaken impression that *homosexual* was just like *heterosexual,* except with the magnets reversed. These days however, everyone seems to be on one spectrum, and it's a surprisingly fluid one. At the institute where I met my husband, all of the women in a recent incoming class announced they were "bisexual" or "pansexual" in response to a public question posed by a young man who seemed to be trying to find a sweetheart without making any offending assumptions. I don't know if he concluded that the glass was half-full or half-empty.

Just recently I found that psychologist Lisa Diamond, author of *Sexual Fluidity,*[78] has confirmed that fluidity (especially, although not exclusively, among women) is the *norm.* When she tracked eighty non-heterosexual women for ten years, she discovered something quite unexpected. Some reported falling in love with, and developing sexual desire for, individual men in their lives. At first Diamond thought that they were either mistaken about what they were feeling, or confused about their own sexual orientation. However, she continued to listen and study.

Every two years about a third of the women changed their category among such labels as "lesbian," "bisexual," "heterosexual," or "undefined." Sexual fluidity was obviously quite typical. Although Diamond acknowledges that women experience sexual fluidity more frequently than men, she points out that "any individual should be capable of experiencing desires that run counter to his or her overall sexual orientation."*[79]

Eventually she evolved a model to fit the facts she observed: While the goal of sexual desire is sexual union for the purpose of reproduction, romantic love is governed by the attachment or pair-bonding system, with its goal of maintaining an enduring bond between two individuals.[80]

Affectionate love (bonding) is thus more aligned with caregiving and emotional attachment than desire to mate. Bonding calls on the same functions of the brain that attach caregivers and infants. Obviously, caregivers

---

*Diamond cautions that no one should confuse plasticity (the capacity for sexual orientation to change) with choice (the ability to change it at will). In any case, the fact that sexual identity may turn out to be more like religion than race, and somewhat fluid rather than fixed, is irrelevant to the discussion of equal rights for sexual minorities.

love both boys and girls, so this bond is neither gender-specific nor always tied to sexual desire.

In contrast to affectionate love, erotic (mating) feelings have much in common with addiction to alcohol or drugs. Intense neurochemical messages ensure that we become "hooked" on a mate, at least for a while. (More on the mechanics of this process in the next three chapters.)

TEAMING UP

By this point in my quest, additional gains from making love without orgasm were obvious to me. Up until I began experimenting with it, I had to take antibiotics almost every time I made love just to avoid urinary tract infection. I never needed them again. Yeast infections stopped, too. (Incidentally, a friend of mine with genital herpes, who also experimented with karezza, noticed that outbreaks did not occur except when he wandered back into a search for passion.)

Meanwhile, my travels had carried me to California, where I was working at an institute that taught traditional Chinese medicine and massage. I asked Will, the anatomy and physiology instructor, to read the material I planned to post on my Web site. I figured he would prove a good critic.

As it turns out, he had a lot more to offer. We have been married for almost a decade and together for two years more than that. He is a wonderful co-explorer, remarkably willing to think outside the box. We began our relationship with karezza (although I didn't yet know of that term), avoiding orgasm as much as possible.

I had figured out—the hard way—that it was virtually impossible to switch from conventional intercourse to karezza lovemaking overnight. Trying to make love as usual but without orgasm "cuts the balls off of sex," as a male friend observed. To explore karezza, couples need a clear target and a transition period with lots of affectionate contact.

To ease this process, I had collected a three-week series of playful activities called the Ecstatic Exchanges (available at the end of this book). The goal of the Exchanges is to offer couples lots of ways of being affectionate without unconsciously drifting into familiar foreplay routines and overheating each other. The Exchanges call for abstaining from intercourse during the first two weeks, so that experimenters can move beyond the hangovers from their most recent orgasms. They keep some sleeping garb on. The third week includes slow, relaxed intercourse on every third night.

Here is Will's account of his early experience, written after about ten months:

> When I agreed to try the Exchanges, I had my reservations. Number one, I'd never been able to sleep comfortably through the night, even with my ex. Number two, I wasn't thrilled about making love according to some recipe that sounded like *it* would tell *me* when I could have intercourse. Three, I didn't know Marnia *that way,* and it felt weird to start on a program that envisioned making love some weeks down the road. Four, I liked masturbating as much as anyone (about three or four times a week), and I knew I'd have to give up ejaculation while trying the Exchanges.
>
> I had read her material, though, and it perfectly described the roller coaster of my previous relationships. Finally, I understood why I'd always pulled away to find my own space, or gotten into pointless arguments with my lovers. I wasn't convinced that the effects of orgasm lasted as long as Marnia said, but I had never avoided orgasm long enough to find out. In any case, I sensed that this approach to sex might be an improvement. A few months earlier I had broken up again with the mother of my son, with whom I'd had a painful, on-and-off-again relationship. I'd started drinking immediately after we got together the first time, fifteen years earlier.
>
> By the time I started the Exchanges, I was in financial ruin and my drinking had increased to the point where I knew I was an alcoholic—although I was keeping my addiction in the closet by leaving campus to binge whenever I could. I was spiraling downward and I didn't know how to get myself back up. I decided it was worth a try.
>
> Some effects of the Exchanges were surprisingly rapid. After only three days I felt more comfortable and relaxed in my body. Kissing started to feel like a whole different experience—like my first kisses many years earlier. Outcome-based sex fell away. And my focus on my genitals started to shift to more of a focus on sharing.

Other changes followed. My pattern of being unable to sleep with someone else disappeared, though the first few nights were challenging. Now I love touching her if I awaken in the night before we fall back asleep.

The addiction took longer to address—in part because I tried to hide it while I struggled to stop on my own, repeatedly, and with no success. When it came out in the open I was sure she would leave, but she didn't. Instead we became closer partners through addressing it. It has been more than six months since I've had any alcohol, and I haven't had cravings or withdrawal symptoms. Occasionally I've had some thoughts about drinking, always following overheating her or myself. Previously, I used alcohol to escape from the pain of relationship. But with this approach the relationship has been a source of inspiration and strength.

I haven't ejaculated at all since the relationship began ten months ago, and the desire to have orgasm isn't really present—though I'm sure I could if I wanted to. There have been no ill effects from not ejaculating. I've had only one experience of genital discomfort, which occurred when she overheated me with classic foreplay.

The biggest difference between this relationship and my others is that we feel like teenagers, even though we're in our forties. We spend time kissing most days and make love frequently. The energy's been like that between us from the beginning—except for a few detours into "relationship hell," brought on by too much passion, which led to her climaxing. The detours have convinced me that if we were engaging in conventional sex, my relationship with her would be as dismal as any of my past relationships.

I've seen big changes in other aspects of my life, too. My finances are sorting themselves out, and my professional life is expanding in directions I'd always wanted it to—but was unable to take it before. The opportunities continue to flow to me effortlessly and work out great. I have a lot more confidence in myself. I'm calm and focused. And I'm now comfortable with being in a partnership instead of seeing myself as a separate entity who happens to be involved with someone at the same time. I'm much more optimistic about relationships.

A TOUGH LESSON

Unfortunately, merely avoiding orgasm doesn't guarantee lasting harmony. Will and I learned this the hard way. Lulled into complacency by the easy harmony between us, we began making love whenever we felt like it. Up to that point we had been making sure that we did a lot of non-goal-oriented snuggling at least every other night.

Cracks appeared, but we did our best to ignore them. Without even noticing, we drifted away from the thoughtful exchanges of touch and more toward standard "let me feel you up" foreplay. Then our sleeping went out of sync. Will awakened earlier and earlier. If he got up and left for his office, it created an emotional rift between us, and if he stayed he was so restless that I felt obliged to try to comfort him. Both of us were exhausted by early evening.

My libido fell off to an alarming degree, but I did my best to remain sexually receptive, hoping that things would come back into balance when Will felt more nourished. Instead, he grew hungrier. We sometimes made love when I was not really ready, in a misguided attempt to regain the closeness that was fading. To me it felt like I was nursing an increasingly demanding infant, and I was astonished at how draining it was—and how resentful I felt. He felt confused and frustrated. As he said, quite logically, "I am only touching you as I always have, and if you now don't like it, you must not love me after all."

When I suggested that we back up and try the Exchanges again, it became obvious just how far off course we had blown. "If I tried to do what you are suggesting, I'd feel neutered," he cried. "You're trying to take away all my sexual pleasure!" Ugh. This did not sound like Will. After all, while doing the Exchanges and for months afterward, he had been amazed at how satisfied he felt, whether it was a lovemaking night or just a snuggle night. Why did his happiness and manhood now hinge on yielding to the very impulses we had formerly avoided with such good results?

WHERE HAD WE ERRED?

As it turned out, we had made two mistakes—although we didn't fully realize the second one at the time. First, when we stopped making love on a schedule, we unintentionally turned our controls back over to biology. Will, a typical, red-blooded male, is programmed to pursue all potential sexual opportunities. Without regular non-intercourse nights, it was his biological duty to rev up constantly—just in case. He was like a car engine that was semi-overheated all the time. This problem was prevented during the Exchanges because we always knew when we would—and would not—be having intercourse. Structure was actually soothing.

Second, we had drifted away from engaging in lots of non-goal-oriented affection. Therefore, our nervous systems never got a chance to relax into the healing comfort of our initial time together. As we realized much later, this also meant we weren't consistently exchanging the signals that the mammalian brain associates with bonding.

For such innocent mistakes it took surprisingly long to undo the damage. Not only had our future together come into doubt, but also our mutual magnetism, which had once been utterly reliable, was not there to pull us back together. Ouch.

First, we attempted to return to having intercourse on a schedule. That failed. No electricity was flowing, our hearts felt guarded, Will's touch was still hungry, and I had a dream orgasm, which meant another two weeks of unbalanced energy. Crises at work drained our energy. Our lives seemed caught in a bizarre downward spiral on every front.

We realized that if what we had learned was correct, we would have to reorient our nervous systems completely, again, toward giving and away from craving, even though it meant another uncomfortable withdrawal period. We were badly frightened. As Will said: "I just don't think I can do it. I don't know how to touch you."

With heavy hearts we put some sleeping garb back on anyway and began the Exchanges. Could they work twice, especially given our state of mind? *Had they worked at all?* Every gain of the past year came into question. Maybe we had just been kidding ourselves. Maybe our harmony was merely a product of temporary honeymoon neurochemistry. Maybe Will's addiction and depression had disappeared for other, unrelated reasons. Maybe there was no way to best biology. I felt doomed to become a "scaggy hag." Certainly the dark circles that had appeared under my eyes during the preceding weeks suggested there was no escape. Even my complexion had taken on a new pallor.

At first time stood still. Though we were both as caring and affection-ate as possible, the Exchanges now felt dry as dust. Will made a concerted effort to avoid flipping on his sexual hunger switch. As he described it, he touched my whole body as if one part were no more important than the other, rather than focusing on his favorite bits. He decided to try to tune into my response to his touch instead of concentrating on his own sen-sations.

I made every effort to be affectionate and return his affection even when tired. Within a couple of days things lightened up between us, but initially it felt like the camaraderie between condemned prisoners sharing a final meal. However, we were definitely sleeping better and better, and on the same schedule again.

After about six or seven days we passed a turning point. Will com-mented that he felt noticeably calmer and less agitated. Our "I love you's" took on a new enthusiasm, and we laughed a lot. Both "intercourse" nights and "just snuggle" nights regained their former tenderness and content-ment. We felt optimistic again. Our careers took forward jumps and we *looked* better. The last thing to recover was my libido. Clearly my subcon-scious had registered "feeling devoured" as an uncomfortable experience, even though Will had never been aggressive or even openly demanding.

For several years after this experience we returned to the Exchanges whenever we found ourselves drifting toward a goal-oriented focus. Soon a night or two of conscious, generous affection was enough to pull us back on track.

At last convinced that we were onto something worthwhile and repeat-able, Will surprised me one day by saying, "I think I'll see if there's some relevant scientific research." He was certain that there had to be physio-logical realities behind the benefits we were experiencing. The material he uncovered is so fascinating that, with his help, I will weave it into the remainder of this book.

HINDUISM

A collection of lore about the concept of lovemaking without sexual satiety would not be complete without mentioning tantra. Yet few subjects are more bewildering than the concept of beneficial synergy between mates in the Hindu religion. On the one hand, there is the belief that creation itself arose from the divine sexual union of male and female.[81] There is also the legend of Parvati, a primary personification of the Divine Feminine. She willingly chose grueling spiritual asceticism and privation in order to win her divine consort Shiva, unite with him, and thus bring love back into a forlorn world. (Shiva had abandoned the world in favor of ascetic solo practice after her death in a prior incarnation.)

On the other hand, the term *tantra* can create more confusion than clarity. Tantra comprises both a celibate tradition known as the "right-hand path" and a sexual tradition known as the "left-hand path." Moreover, there exist both a Tibetan Buddhist tantra (to be discussed later) and the classic Hindu tantra. Finally, even within classic tantra, streams diverge—and have shifted with time.

Although there are now as many different sexual-tantra recipes as there are cat breeds, classic Hindu sexual tantra was not about mutual enlightenment or deeper union. Despite the showy display of worshiping the divine god or goddess in a shared ritual for raising the kundalini energy (refined life force energy), the *maithuna* (or "twinning") ritual apparently developed for solo spiritual pursuits, not as a mutual, or ongoing, cultivation of sexual energy for spiritual purposes.

Author James Powell traces the roots of tantra back to a sexually permissive, *matriarchal* society in India. A favorite divinity of these early worshipers was the lusty Krishna—a dark blue fellow who was a sort of sexual Pied Piper, luring otherwise well-behaved married women from their beds to orgies in the wild.

Some worshipers of Krishna formed couples. They would stimulate intense, even violent, erotic emotions in themselves by reading and chanting the amorous adventures of their God. They would then perform sexual yoga, in which the male would play the part of Krishna and his partner the role of one of the cowherd girls [of the Krishna myth]. Love rituals were performed in large circles. It was felt that more intense erotic emotion could be produced if the women in such rituals were the wives of other men.[82]

Later, tantra moved in a decidedly patriarchal direction under the Brahmans. Retained semen was equated with light and spirituality. Women were increasingly viewed with suspicion because they tempt men to lose semen. As a consequence, men believed that their health and spiritual power depended more upon keeping their seed than upon synergistic union.

A strong emphasis on celibate spiritual practice arose. Even among spiritually minded householders (men with families), the goal seems to have been to avoid ejaculation by limiting intercourse strictly to sex for procreation. For example, in *Autobiography of a Yogi*,[83] the late Paramhansa Yogananda reported that his parents had sex once a year for purposes of procreation. Similarly, a devotee of the late Baba Muktananda told me that householders could consider themselves celibate if they had sex only once a month.

Some yogis sought to use ritualized sex for spiritual purposes (the left-hand path). Far from seeking mutual enlightenment with a partner, the yogi sought to awaken his own Feminine Principle within—residing in the form of the kundalini energy coiled at the base of the spine. Its release ideally manifests as psychological androgyny. The most powerful method of arousing the kundalini was said to be the sexual embrace—preferably with a young virgin. Virgins were believed to be full of spiritual power and capable of initiating one into the flow of subtle energies. (Similar beliefs were popular in China around the same period, and the Chinese ultimately trafficked in pre-pubescent girls in order to harvest their yin energy just before their first periods, when it was allegedly at its peak.) For yogis, this ritual lovemaking had nothing to do with romantic love. The woman was revered not as a woman but as "the Goddess"—and it didn't much matter if she were a total stranger.

Not surprisingly, the left-hand path of sexual tantra fell into disrepute in its native land and went underground. In the view of yoga scholar Georg Feuerstein, much sexual tantra came to resemble black magic (or sex magick). It calls for exerting power over others and disregarding their well-being in search of personal gratification. According to Feuerstein, the self-centered focus of many tantric practices is revealed by their preoccupation with pursuit of orgasm, perhaps after partners have aroused each other for the purpose of achieving an altered state of awareness.[84]

Feuerstein counsels that genuine tantra of either path (right or left) is a mystery that seeks to transcend the illusory self (ego) by awakening the body's erotic potential while one's energy is contained. The goal is bliss, a beyond-the-body state of communion with the Divine, not a heightened state of sensory pleasure. Classic tantra recommends techniques for transforming, or moving beyond, passion. In contrast, Western teachers frequently adapt its methods to increase passionate intensity—and gratify the ego's desires.

As Feuerstein explains, at orgasm the creative tension that could serve as a bridge to ecstasy is lost. The whole point of avoiding orgasm is to accumulate the subtle force or nervous energy called *ojas,* which is wasted the moment the nervous system fires during sexual stimulation.

[It's not semen loss that's the problem.] It's actually the firing of the nervous system during sexual stimulation. That applies to both men and women.—Georg Feuerstein

In *Sacred Sexuality,* Feuerstein records that openhearted lovers, tantric or otherwise, have spontaneously stumbled upon the experience of communion:

[After a night of lovemaking] I felt as though I was conscious or constantly awake on some higher plane. The entire day I remember feeling totally and perfectly relaxed. In this perfect relaxation I stood outside of time. To say there was no beginning or ending of time would seem irrelevant. There was simply no time.... [I was aware that everything material] was all spontaneously and playfully arising from one great source.... Somehow I had become infinity with eyes. I felt as if I had just been born in that moment, or that I had been asleep all my life and had just awakened. I also remember thinking that this was the true condition of everyone and that everyone could know this.... I remained in this state of edgelessness for about three weeks, and life was intensely magnified.... I ate almost nothing during this period.... I remember telling my lover that it felt as if my spine were plugged into the "universal socket" and that it was a source of infinite energy.... During this time I was more creative than I had ever been (or have been since) both at work and outside of work.... I also became prescient, seeing into the future and then later experiencing the scenes I had foreseen down to the last detail.... I loved everyone, including my lover, the same, infinitely. There was really no one separate to love.[85]

CHAPTER FOUR

AT THE HEART
OF THE SEPARATION VIRUS

No species of mammal is sexually monogamous, including humans. Multiple mates improve our genes' chances of making it into the future.

Urges, drives, emotions, and moods equate with neurochemical changes occurring in the part of the brain common to all mammals.

Dopamine, the "craving" neurochemical, stimulates the brain's primitive reward circuitry. It drives us toward new mates and sexual satiety.

Crime investigators follow the money, but anyone trying to understand the widespread disharmony in human intimacy would do well to follow the genes. The impersonal selection process of evolution tends to conserve behaviors that work—that is, behaviors that lead to the most genes flowing into the future in the form of progeny. Impulsive desire ("I'm hot for you, Baby!") and romance obviously serve this end, so intoxicating honeymoon neurochemistry makes perfect sense. Yet so does a less obvious behavior: producing offspring with different mates.

Could it be that we are molded to sour on (habituate to) our mates after a time, and even to find them annoying, unattractive, or utterly unreasonable? Could our blueprint also be behind the tendency to speed a mate's departure by *becoming* irritating and unreasonable? These are unnerving thoughts, but if these behaviors favor our genes' chances of proliferation, then it's likely that we *are* programmed for them. Indeed, restlessness and disharmony could be as much a part of our mating program as initial infatuation and pairing up.

If this programmed disharmony seems implausible, consider the fact that a matriarch elephant and a herd stallion drive off adolescent males—even their own sons—when the moment comes. They don't realize they are serving their genes by preventing inbreeding and planting descendants in other herds. They just know they want those guys out of the herd, even though banishment is harsh and many adolescent males don't survive.

Your genes aren't concerned with your lasting happiness. They view you as just another bus in a long, complex journey to their chosen destination: more descendants. They have programmed you accordingly.[86] They don't care whether you paint the ceiling of the Sistine Chapel, have a lot of friends on Facebook, discover the meaning of life, or fail to pay your taxes. They're concerned with making more copies of themselves in the form of babies—who will make their own babies. Did Michelangelo have kids? If not, his genius is irrelevant from biology's perspective. Cockroaches, on the other hand, are real champs.

Genes never sleep. Instead of a blissful "they got married and lived happily ever after," gene fairy tales end with offspring and more offspring—any way the genes can get them. As surely as they drive couples down the wedding aisle in the first place, our genes will push us toward betrayal whenever infidelity is in their interest.—Burnham and Phelan, authors of *Mean Genes: From Sex to Money to Food: Taming Our Primal Instincts*

Lasting contentment is bad for genes. If you have your children with different mates due to your inability to remain faithful, their immune systems and other traits will be less similar. So, for example, if a deadly new organism appears, chances are better that one of your children will be able to fight it off. This is one reason genes drive us to have affairs, divorce and remarry, and avoid incest.

Our genes' tactics once sustained scanty populations. Now they foster unwanted pregnancies, the spread of sexually transmitted disease, heartache, and overpopulation. They may have molded our rational brains, but planetary welfare is not among their preprogrammed priorities. If our rational brains ruled us, our population would not be growing exponentially. When it comes to mating, our rational brains are not in charge.

Our attraction to voluptuous curves or alpha male traits is instinctive—and powerful. One result is that romances are initially more intoxicating—and ultimately more fragile—than friendships and family ties.

This city is full of such beautiful women, and I often find myself thinking I'd totally settle for having my girlfriend as just a friend if it meant I could have assorted meaningless trysts with others. I know I'd be emotionally unfulfilled, and I could never really treat another person as an object. Still, it's clear that my brain wants me to choose my girlfriend to mother my children—and then have some lanky Indian girl as a mistress or whatever. Damn evolution to hell.—Jordan

---

PLANNED OBSOLESCENCE

From your genes' perspective, monogamy is as risky as putting all your eggs in one basket. This is easy to see, because only a few dozen mammals, of the nearly 4,000 species, mate for life—and DNA testing reveals that while some hang out together, they still occasionally fool around on the side. (Same goes for those lovebirds. They are technically only lifelong companions, or socially monogamous, as opposed to totally faithful.) As Will says, "In the poker game of life, holding onto the 'monogamy card' meant a losing hand." The instinctual urge to collect improved and assorted genes is wired into the mammalian brain—and you are a mammal. This urge is at the heart of the separation virus. It's what makes Cupid's romance-producing arrow turn toxic.

In most species this inclination to add mates is drama-free. Once a bull fertilizes a cow, pheromone signals (airborne chemicals that turn switches on and off in the brain) ensure that he does not return to her that mating season—although a second enterprising sperm donor may still find her cute enough for a romp in the hay when the competition isn't looking. This arrangement seems to suit all concerned.

Not all species are so lucky. Species like ours—for whom reproductive success is best served by shared parental support—are destined for inner turmoil. We are programmed to love falling in love. Yet we are still stuck with that ancient mammalian program to find *novel* mates enticing—when opportunity knocks. This creates an uneasy tension that can be seen even as far down the food chain as the prairie vole (a small mouse-like critter). "Monogamous" female prairie voles have been observed to entertain stray males at home—and then viciously chase them off after their visitors' dissimilar genes are safely stowed.

Not every human being is equally predisposed toward monogamy. We have assorted mating strategies—such as the good lover, the good provider, the good companion, or the good-looking specimen—which are no doubt reflected in a diverse range of characteristics, genes, and gene expression (the process by which genes are turned on and off). For example, some women may be more likely to trade off evidence of a man's genetic fitness in the form of symmetry, strong jaw line, and muscle size, for evidence of his willingness to invest in, and care for, offspring. Yet, we're all apparently programmed for some degree of friction between the rewards of emotional bonding with a mate and the rewards of sex with a novel partner.

The only species I know of in which there seems to be 100 percent monogamy is a flatworm that lives in gills of freshwater fish. Males and females meet each other as adolescents, and their bodies literally fuse together, whereupon they remain faithful until death.

—David P. Barash, co-author of *The Myth of Monogamy*

To varying degrees, we are fashioned for genetic success—and relationship fatigue.

As we will see, this doesn't mean that every intimate relationship is doomed to fall apart, or that every mate will be unfaithful. It means that *as a species* we are programmed to tire of our mates—or be sexually attracted to other mates. Assuming you want different results, you can either take your chances that your union will be one of the few exceptions to the rule, rely solely on your sterling character (and that of your mate), or learn how to elude your genetic autopilot. The latter is a lot easier to do once you understand where your autopilot's subconscious mating and bonding commands emanate from, how your autopilot signals you, and what behaviors allow you to change the volume of those signals.

MEET YOUR MAMMALIAN BRAIN

Where do we fall in *and* out of love? To answer that question, imagine conducting an archeological dig—inside your skull. If you start at the front

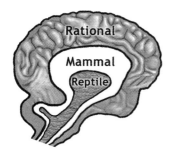

and top of the brain and burrow down, you eventually arrive at parts of the brain that evolved millions of years ago. An effective, if simplistic, way to understand this is by envisioning your brain in three layers. This model, proposed by neurologist Paul MacLean, separates the brain into several regions, once thought to correspond to mankind's evolutionary history. The region at the core governs our mechanical behavior (reptilian brain), and the more recently evolved regions govern our emotional behavior (mammalian brain) and rational behavior (rational brain). All three regions are connected by an extensive set of nerves. They continuously interact, and evolve together.

Our so-called reptilian brain governs self-preservation, aggression, and the most basic life-sustaining processes, such as respiration, circulation, sleep, and muscle coordination. It is instinctive, and repeats the same behaviors over and over. The next region can be thought of as our mammalian brain. It's often called the limbic system, or emotional brain. Like the reptilian brain, it has been around for at least 150 million years. Emotional bonds between parent and offspring grew stronger as the mammalian brain evolved. ("Warm and fuzzy" does not describe the relationship between an iguana and her hatchlings.) The mechanisms in this part of the brain are pretty much the same in us as they are in all mammals, such as dogs, rabbits, or rats.

The mammalian brain's neurochemical releases color how we see the world on a given day—and whether we approach, or avoid, something or someone. It is the place where thoughts affect bodily function. It governs emotions, such as fear, joy, and anger. It is the seat of most of our drives and desires, including hunger, mate selection, and sexual urges.

Indeed, in all mammals this part of the brain is integrally involved with getting the right sperm together with the right egg—at the right moment. It's where we experience orgasm. It's also concerned with moving mammals on to their next mates or,

When a man marries his mistress, she leaves a vacancy.
—Sacha Guitry

in those few species that team up to parent, motivating both bonding *and* "extra-pair couplings" (fooling around). Here is where we fall in *and out* of love.

Our rational brain has surprisingly little say about these phenomena. For example, women tend to find mates attractive based in part on body odor. The scents that appeal to them correlate with genetic advantages for potential offspring rather than long-term emotional or intellectual compatibility. Specifically, a woman is drawn to a partner whose aroma indicates immunity that is diverse from her own—and would result in babies who can fight off a greater variety of infectious microbes.[87] The mammalian brain has even gained the nickname "the smell brain."

Male: Hey, Baby, how do you like your eggs in the morning?

Female: Unfertilized.

It is set up to learn how to repeat what's pleasurable and avoid what's disagreeable. (Chocolate, *good*. Hot stove, *bad*.) It's the primary hub of emotionally charged memories, both positive and negative. On this basis, your mammalian brain decides whether your rational brain has a good idea or not—that is, whether it feels *true* and *right*. It is therefore a big component of your inner compass, and is especially strident when you are stressed, or have been skewered by Cupid.

The rational brain, or neocortex (cerebrum), evolved even more recently. It is actually present in all mammals, but much expanded in dolphins and humans (and other primates). It allows us to invent things and think abstractly.[88] However, we humans may turn out to be a flash in the pan, while animals of other evolutionary lineages will prove far better suited to the challenging conditions we are using *our* brains to bring about.

In humans the neocortex makes up two-thirds of total brain mass. Yet impressive as it is, it relies heavily upon the mammalian brain when weighing choices. In fact, the rational brain spends most of its time planning and executing the desires of the mammalian brain. It may rest atop the mammalian brain, but it certainly doesn't dominate it. Indeed, the mammalian brain can normally hijack the rational brain whenever it perceives a need.

Evolution tends to conserve structures and strategies that work. ("If it ain't broke, don't fix it.") The mammalian brain drives the behaviors that pass on genes with such efficiency that it apparently hasn't evolved much in the last hundred million years—as you can see in this next illustration (also drawn from MacLean's work).

It has similar parts, wiring, and functions in all mammals, and the same neurochemicals turn its functions on and off, whether the behavior is mothering, mating—or moving on.

Scientists aren't studying rat brains to figure out how to help rats with their addictions or erections. They study them because our brains have so much in common. Rats can become addicted to the same drugs we can, and sexual enhancement drugs that alter *their* mating behavior are likely to alter *our* mating behavior. Rodents and primates evolved from common ancestors.

In the next chapter we'll see what neuroscientists are learning in the quest to manipulate our mating behavior for commercial gain. But first let's look at some of the tricks our mammalian brain gets up to in our love lives—so we can learn to maneuver it.

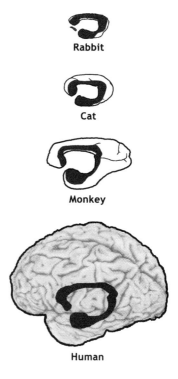

The mammalian (limbic) brain drawn to scale in four different mammals

RUTHLESS EUGENICS—OUR MATING PROGRAM

Your genes can't politely request that you make more babies. Instead, they have shaped you to want to engage in the behaviors that, on average, lead to more babies. Some of these behaviors are quite splendid, and may even be related to the rapid development of the rational brain. Geoffrey Miller has suggested that intelligence, musical talent, a sense of humor, empathy, and creativity all evolved because these qualities put potential mates in the mood for love.[89]

Certainly, making a baby may be the farthest thing from your rational mind during sex. Yet your crafty genes frequently achieve their goal, because neither your drive to seek sexual gratification nor your wandering eye changes just because of your shaky financial situation, your awareness that the world's population is swelling ominously, or the wisdom of preventing unwanted pregnancy.

What does our basic mating program look like? It's very similar to that of other socially monogamous mammals. A glimpse at the world's few remaining hunter-gatherer tribes is instructive. These people are thought to exhibit the behavior of our common ancestors during the many thousands of years that our brains operated without modern customs. So what did anthropologists find when they studied the !Kung of the Kalahari and the Mehinaku of South America? Lots of impulsive sexual behavior and romance, constant churning in intimate relationships, and much attendant heartache. (As we'll see later, earlier anthropologists also recorded numerous taboos calling for sexual abstinence under various circumstances, often to increase abundance and vigor.)

There were a few surprises. Experts had assumed that men and women have very different mating strategies. After all, women invest a lot of time and resources in each child. In theory, they should be choosier about mates. Men, on the other hand, can pass on the most genes by pollinating as many flowers as possible. Yet it turned out that hunter-gatherer women are just as promiscuous as men. It's certainly to a male's genetic advantage to sow his seed far and wide. But a woman's genetic advantage lies in seeking a mate who looks like he has good genes—and is a good provider with lots to invest in offspring. Who says they have to be combined in one guy?

Nevertheless, unlike the primates that are our closest genetic mirrors, humans thrive with high male investment in their offspring. Human babies, with their large skulls, must make it through the birth canal long before they're as fully developed as other mammal infants. They're helpless (and clueless) for longer, too, which is one reason it is so tough to be a single mom. Hunter-gatherer mothers typically obtain the support they need by sleeping around (and collaborating with other women). In this way, they persuade various men that a child could be his. (They may also be creating doubt about paternity to protect their children. Even today, stepchildren experience physical abuse and homicide at disproportionate rates.[90]) This tactic assures Mom more resources, increased protection, and help in preparing the child for adulthood. A !Kung San hunter-gatherer told an anthropologist the following:

One man can give you very little. One man gives you only one kind of food to eat. But when you have lovers, one brings you something and another brings you something else. One comes at night with meat, another with money, another with beads. Your husband also does things and gives them to you.[91]

⁓

Remember, our ancestors lived in tribes. Children weren't totally dependent upon insular couples; they were literally raised, as Hillary Clinton says, by a village. Monogamy was not as important a factor as it is in our isolated modern lives. In fact, it is likely that the part of our mating program that bonds us emotionally to our lovers for a time is—evolutionarily speaking—an afterthought, an adaptation of the fundamental mammalian parent-child bond.

> My mom said the only reason men are alive is for lawn care and vehicle maintenance.
> —Tim Allen

Even so, this capacity to form romantic pair-bonds offers a way to steer for harmony. As we'll see later, we can use our rational brain to activate, and sustain, our bonding program above our mating program.

In today's insular families, monogamous men may seem like good insurance for seeing a woman's genes safely into the future. However, the mammalian brain hasn't caught up with this change. For example, a woman who feels like her "needs aren't being met" by her spouse may unconsciously be gearing up to do some gene shopping at her next ovulation. Did you know that women are more prone to be unfaithful during the fertile days of their menstrual cycles?[92]

Being a woman who is extremely sensitive to my ovulation cycle, I can ATTEST that I am personally vulnerable to "good DNA subjects" (i.e., good-looking men) when I'm fertile. This tendency is totally gone at every other time of the month. When my biological process is at bay, I relate with people on a more intellectual, or culturally relevant, level. It's quite bizarre.—Jasmine

Throughout the animal kingdom there's a female drive to shop for good genes and a corresponding male impulse to display outstanding traits. When selecting mates on genetic autopilot, women, like many other females, are more likely to go for qualities that make their male offspring effective gene transmitters. Peahens choose the peacock with the biggest tail display, even though his fancy tail makes getaways more uncertain. Cow seals pick the bull with the most blubber, even though he can hardly budge on land. And a woman may find a fling with a square-jawed, symmetrically featured Don Juan appealing *because* he can easily seduce her (and everyone else)—even if she certainly wouldn't want her daughter engaged to such a guy.

All these discriminating females unwittingly gamble that their male offspring will inherit the same tail, blubber, or magnetism—and be more attractive to the females of the next generation. In this way, our heroines' genes live on, even though their love lives may be brief, or emotionally excruciating.[93]

MORE ON THE MONOGAMY CHALLENGE

Need more proof that women are wired to seek action on the side? Consider the fact that men's mammalian brains are programmed to assume infidelity in their mates and adjust sperm output accordingly. The more time couples spend together between ejaculations, the fewer sperm the man delivers during intercourse. That is, males apparently assume sperm competition in mates who have been out of sight. Regardless of a male's sexual activity in his mate's absence, he will ejaculate as many as four times more sperm when she returns. This improves his chances of fathering offspring, whatever she has been up to. No one knows how this mechanism works, but biology can clearly manipulate our behavior without our conscious participation.[94] This characteristic evolved *because* women tended to fool around during absences.

Men also apparently unconsciously sense when women are ovulating—not unlike other male mammals, which instinctively pursue females when in estrus. In a recent study, strippers who were ovulating averaged $70 in tips per hour, while those who were menstruating made $35, and those who were neither ovulating nor menstruating made $50.[95] Women also report that when they're ovulating, their partners are more loving and attentive and, significantly, more jealous of other men. "The men are picking up on something in their partner's behavior that tells them to do more mate-guarding," said researcher Martie Haselton.[96]

Men, too, are programmed to shop for genetic opportunities. As Leo Tolstoy, an (apparently) faithful husband and father of thirteen children, put it:

> In life this preference for one [lover] to the exclusion of all others lasts in rare cases several years, oftener several months, or even weeks, days, hours.... Every man feels what you call love toward each pretty woman he sees, and very little toward his wife.... [And] even if it should be admitted that Menelaus had preferred Helen all his life, Helen would have preferred Paris.[97]

A new potential sex partner feels like one of the most effective "cures" for the post-passion blues. It stimulates instant focus and motivation. Yet this state of mind is actually a slightly altered state. It affects judgment adversely in both sexes.[98]

The subconscious, neurochemically enhanced lure of a novel mate has power. It is rumored that Gandhi turned it to his strategic advantage. While he was fasting to protest British colonialism, he reanimated himself by sleeping between a pair of virgins (enticing, if unexploited, fertilization opportunities). His subconscious response to their presence apparently did rouse much-needed motivation, which he carefully transmuted to cope with the stress of fasting. He had long since given up sex with his wife, of course, in favor of celibate spiritual practice. History has not recorded whether Mrs. Gandhi conducted a similar experiment to raise her spirits in the absence of her husband's attentions.

A man may love his mate and his kids. Yet, not unlike a woman, if he yields to his *default* mammalian programming, he is likely to nip out and have sex now and then, even if he remains attached to his family. As psychologist Lisa Diamond has pointed out, our program for sexual impulse is not the same as our program for bonding. I'll have a lot to say about that later on.

Meanwhile, we may reluctantly accept that we are "in lust" with that manly political presence or gorgeous young starlet with many child-bearing years ahead of her because our mammalian brain sees, stamped right on the hot one's forehead, "MARVELOUS GENETIC OPPORTUNITY." Yet most of us have a lot of resistance to the idea that we're *divorcing* because of a subconscious mating program. This is because we rationalize our mating decisions. It gives that large, new part of our brains something to do.

FAITHFUL BUT IRRITABLE

Conservative authorities have long tried to convince us that the key to happiness is getting married, staying married, and reproducing. Yet this advice often ignores the unrelenting pressure on us to be the best gene machines possible. Many of us manage to remain married and even faithful to each other, but few of us are able to shut out the mating urges emanating from our mammalian brains. Those signals, which would have successfully moved our hunter-gatherer forebears on to additional partners, can make us feel dissatisfied and resentful. We may find ourselves wondering what it would be like to be with so-and-so, feeling bored with our love lives, not liking a partner's way of touching us, turning to porn, and so forth.

Not surprisingly, this disharmony tends to show up right where our single-minded genes want us to take action—in our sex lives. Dr. Domeena Renshow, head of the Sexual Dysfunction Clinic of Loyola University, suggests that eighty percent of Western divorces are due to tension in couples' sex lives, and that fifty percent of couples who stay married also have problems in this area.[99] Italian researchers found that some of this tension may be the result of diverging testosterone levels—controlled by the mammalian brain. Testosterone is a factor in sexual desire for *both* sexes. In new lovers, women's testosterone levels are higher than normal and men's are lower than normal, which helps synchronize sex drives. Thereafter, the levels diverge. Two years later, they have returned to pre-romance levels,[100] and the urge to "make a baby" with someone else can easily arise.

Eighty percent of married men cheat in America. The rest cheat in Europe.
—Jackie Mason

Another change that mates have to contend with is that their "altered-state" honeymoon neurochemistry wears off. Italian researchers noticed that new lovers and patients with obsessive-compulsive disorder have something in common: low levels of the brain chemical serotonin.[101] With time, serotonin levels bounce back, which can be a relief. Yet it also means that lovers are no longer as obsessed with each other ... and more likely to notice other potential partners. Intense romantic love also correlates with high levels of another brain chemical, nerve growth factor, which may elevate mood. Within twelve to twenty-four months, the levels of NGF are no different from those of controls who are single, or already yawning in long-term relationships.[102] Romantic love generally fizzles, due to its unstable nature.

Research reveals that open conflict is greatest among couples in their twenties and thirties (when sexual activity is most frequent). However, even if mates demonstrate greater resignation as habituation sets in, they continue to find one another more irritating and demanding the longer they are together.[103] As we'll see, this may be because they lose the benefits of close touch and companionship (bonding behaviors). Significantly, study participants did not perceive that relationships with children or friends were more annoying and demanding with time.

[Passionate new] partners have a kind of tense, jittery restlessness, but actually they are exhausted. . . . The hangover after sex excess is often more damaging than one after alcohol. [Physiological changes] cause loss of energy, vigor, happiness and, eventually, love.
—Rudolf von Urban, MD, author of *Sex Perfection and Marital Happiness*

All of this research suggests that mates are not only wired for lust, attraction, and attachment—but also for disenchantment. Even if you manage to stay married to your one true love, this built-in separation program can kindle frustration, reactivity, a sense of resentful stagnation, and cravings. In some ways, commitment can make spouses even crankier than couples without formal commitments, because it is stressful to experience a buildup of unpleasant feelings with no easy way out. As someone quipped, paraphrasing Dr. Samuel Johnson, a golden wedding anniversary is like a dog walking on two legs. The marvel is that it occurs at all, even if done poorly. In short, disenchantment is natural, so don't feel like a victim if it happens to you. On the other hand, it's not inevitable; you can elude the poison on Cupid's arrow.

QUESTIONING COMMITMENT

Meanwhile, it's no wonder that so many people are questioning the value of commitment in relationships.

> In the first decade of the 21st century, the proportion of Americans in every racial and ethnic group who were never married has continued to grow by double digits. . . . Soaring divorce rates have leveled off, most experts agree, but one reason may be that the dissolution of live-in relationships are not taken into account.[104]

Certainly it's logical to wonder—especially when in a committed relationship—if you would be best off if you simply yielded to biology and quenched your sexual desire with multiple partners, as did your forebears. If "natural" improves your diet, maybe it will work for sex.

Professor: Why do we fall in love with such intensity?

Student: To get us out of one relationship and into another one?

Yet from a genes' eye view, there is an important distinction between eating and sex. Sure, you're designed to eat, if only to keep you in the procreation game. When it comes to sex, your welfare is pretty much immaterial. For example, look how humans throw caution to the winds to pursue a genetic opportunity even if it threatens their individual survival. Think of a woman who insists on getting pregnant despite medical warnings that her life is at risk. Think of young Saudis who chance severe punishment and death to spend time together before marriage. Think of Romeo and Juliet.

Natural, in the sense of "instinctive," is not always a reliable compass for well-being or fulfillment in our lives. In fact, sexual impulsiveness can *naturally* push us away from one of the best forms of health insurance available on the planet: close, trusted companionship. Why, then, do we leap at these high-risk, high-cost opportunities with such fervor?

THE LINK BETWEEN BODY AND MIND

Perhaps you have had this experience: You are cheerfully sauntering along when suddenly . . . smack! Hit by an arrow—or was it a tank? Oh my God! Has anyone ever felt like you are now feeling? Surely, with passionate intensity like this, you and your new heartthrob can defy the odds and live happily ever after, right? Not necessarily. This intensity is not glue; it's motivation.

How does our friend Cupid do it? Well, he dips that arrow in a lot of neurochemicals that evoke powerful "I gotta have it!" signals in our mammalian brain. Let's examine this motivational system in simplified terms, so we will be able to understand later why sexual satiety can dampen it so effectively.

Did you know that there are tiny signaling substances flowing through your body and brain, controlling everything you do and think—from blinking your eye and breathing to fighting an infection and, possibly, remembering last New Year's Eve? The two most common terms for these chemical messengers are *hormones* and *neurotransmitters*. By definition, hormones are chemical messengers released from glands, such as testosterone and estrogen, which circulate in the blood. Neurotransmitters, as the name suggests, transmit information from nerve cell to other nerve cells or organs. Examples would be serotonin and dopamine. Scientists used to differentiate between hormones and neurotransmitters, but as they've learned more, they've found that many hormones affect nerve cells in the brain, and many neurotransmitters are at work throughout the body. We'll just use the term "neurochemical" for both.

There are probably hundreds of different neurochemicals, each with its own message. Every mood, desire, urge, and feeling of love or fear corresponds with a swing in neurochemicals. When you know a bit more about how they work, you'll understand why particular behaviors can accelerate or combat relationship erosion. We'll focus on the most important neurochemicals for our narrative.

The mammalian brain is the control center for all the neurochemicals that bond us to mates—or lead to heartache and separation. The same neurochemical can affect body and mind *differently*. For example, an important neurochemical, which has effects on both body and mind, is oxytocin. At birth, the mammalian brain releases oxytocin out into the mother's blood to cause the labor contractions that push out her infant. When the mother sees her little darling, the mammalian brain also releases oxytocin backward into the brain, so the mother falls head over heels in love. Ideally, she bonds with, and protects, her child indefinitely.

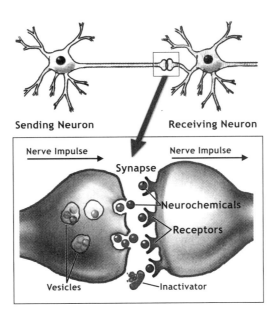

Two nerve cells (called neurons) using neurochemicals to communicate

In fact, oxytocin is what enables *all* of us to fall in love.

What is happening to her mammalian brain? To understand Mom, and more important, Cupid, we need to know a bit more about how nerve cells communicate. The illustration shows two of the 100 billion nerve cells that make up the human brain. If a nerve cell becomes excited with a thought or memory, that excitement is electrical. Like a lighted fuse, a wave of electricity starts at one end of the cell and zips along to the opposite end. The electrical current reaching the end of the cell causes a release of neurochemicals into the synapse (the small gap between cells). The neurochemicals act as little keys that unlock padlocks on neighboring cells. These padlocks are *receptors,* and when they are "unlocked," the neighboring cells, too, become electrically excited. All your experiences, moods, behaviors, and memories correspond with specific combinations of activated nerve cells.

Mom sees, touches, and smells her baby. With each experience, more sets of nerve cells are recruited as oxytocin floods certain synapses. Networks of connected nerve cells fire like dominoes falling. With specific pathways in her brain flipped on, Mom activates a crucial genetic program.

Electrical impulses now flow freely along the connected nerve cells like swiftly burning fuses, telling her that this experience is *very* rewarding. Neurochemicals are the matches that light those fuses. Indeed, each pathway has neurochemicals that will turn it on or off, and up or down (in intensity).

To produce thoughts, feelings, and memories, several neurons actually fire in sequence. These groups of interconnected nerve cells are called pathways or circuits. Also, the neurochemicals released at the synapse between cells determine which neurons fire and which stay quiet. For some the message is "fire"; for others it's "stop." This is how your brain regulates itself and prevents chaos. It turns on some pathways while simultaneously turning off others. Mom's love and bonding pathways are cranked up, while her fear and pain pathways are turned down. A similar combination of events allows us to fall in love.

You have countless pathways or circuits in your brain. Some are innate, like those that activate breathing, swallowing, or yawning. They are just waiting for the right stimulus to light them up. You create other pathways throughout your life as you form memories, perfect your kissing, or learn to stay on that snowboard.

The mother-child bond is innate. It lies there like a new highway yet to be driven upon. It just needs to be flipped on, although events can interfere with it. For example, mothers with drug addiction or severe depression may be unable to connect with, and nurture, their children due to neurochemical imbalances that prevent strong connections from forming between the key nerve cells.

Scientists believe that bonding with your children and falling in love with a mate are existing pathways, waiting to be turned on—and off. The "switch" is the right neurochemicals in the right synapses. As we'll see, specific behaviors can encourage that switch to flip on or off.

URGES ARE SIGNALS

The rewiring of Mom's brain is dependent upon two equally important events: her production of more oxytocin, and her mammalian brain becoming more sensitive to the oxytocin she makes. Nerve cells can become more or less sensitive to neurochemicals, as needed.

A nerve cell with fewer receptors—becoming less sensitive. Causes dramatic decline in number of electrical impulses on receiving neuron.

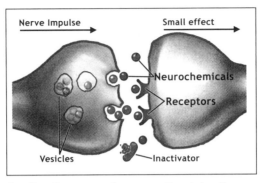

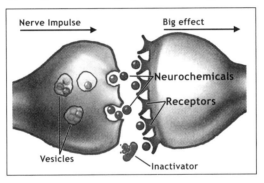

A nerve cell sprouting more receptors—becoming more sensitive. Results in more electrical impulses on receiving neuron.

As we'll see in a moment, *both of these events are involved in the highs and lows of sexual relationships.* Cells adjust by sprouting more receptors (to become more sensitive), or decreasing them (to become less sensitive). Think of little hands reaching out to grab hold of the neurochemicals. The more hands you have, the more you can grab; the fewer hands, the less you can grab.

Addiction has been carefully studied and it is tied to a change in receptor quantity. Let's use cocaine addiction as an example. Cocaine causes a massive spike of dopamine and blocks its removal from the synapse. (Dopamine is a neurochemical related to reward and addiction—as well as sexual desire.) The synapse is flooded, which produces a prolonged excited state. This is too much of a good thing. The receiving nerve cells say, "Enough is enough!" If someone screams at you, you cover your ears. Nerve cells accomplish this by getting rid of dopamine receptors, which paradoxically can make you seek even more stimulation. As we'll see in the next chapter, other key receptors also decrease after orgasm.

With repeated use of cocaine, dopamine receptors decrease and cells become less sensitive to dopamine. For the cocaine user this means that no matter how much dopamine his brain makes, it will not be enough to fully activate the circuitry that makes him feel good. Simply put, too little electricity is flowing through the circuit. (Think of a flashlight with fading batteries.) This is one of the main reasons that addicts have such cravings. They want to feel normal again. In essence, they want their dopamine receptor numbers to return to normal, so enough electricity flows through their "feel good" batteries. However, until their brains have been all the way through withdrawal and their dopamine receptivity is regulated again, they won't experience normal levels of pleasure from everyday things, such as chocolate ice cream, foreplay, or watching a favorite TV show.

These changes occur in the centerpiece of the mammalian brain, in an ancient pathway known as the *reward circuitry*. It evolved to push our ancestors to repeat behaviors that encouraged their survival—and the passing on of their genes. Our reward circuitry is small, but mighty. It drives us to connect with others, eat, drink, take risks, pursue romance, and especially to make

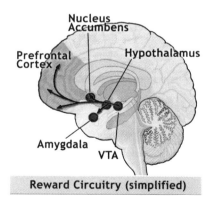

Reward Circuitry (simplified)

babies. Without this mechanism, we would feel no pleasure, and could not fall in love. The pathway starts above the brainstem, passes through key centers of our mammalian brain, and ends at the front of our rational brain.

YOUR INNER COMPASS

Try as you might, you never make a decision without consulting your reward circuit. And it's a good thing you do—much of the time.[105] It helps you know instinctively which course of action is likely to be most rewarding. It also helps you assess other people, so you know whom to trust and love. Mr. Spock notwithstanding, people with damage to this part of the brain, who must rely solely on the logical skills of the rational brain to make decisions, cannot make sound decisions.

Your reward circuitry, although blindingly efficient, has a couple of major weaknesses. First, evolution shaped it over many millions of years. This means it is not well suited to aspects of modern life that have recently changed a lot. For example, sugar was scarce in our ancestors' environments, but it is everywhere in today's Western diet. Alas, you are programmed to grab high-calorie foods without thinking.

I can resist anything but temptation.
—Oscar Wilde

Second, your reward circuitry serves your genes before it serves you. You may want a long, healthy life with a harmonious intimate relationship. Your reward circuitry, however, is programmed to urge you to behave impulsively at times, so that you engage in behaviors that favor passing on your genes via different mates. The result? You are likely to experience especially loud, gut-level impulses from this trusted, but somewhat treacherous, part of your brain. It can twist your values without your conscious awareness.

DOPAMINE—THE SHARPEST ARROW IN CUPID'S QUIVER

Dopamine is the prime gadfly that activates your reward circuitry, where it equates with eager anticipation. A little bit of dopamine activating the right nerve cells makes life seem worth getting up for in the morning. Too much, and you may bounce around like popcorn; too little, and you may sink into apathy instead.

Dopamine itself is what motivates you. You're not craving ice cream or sex with that film star. You don't even want to win the lotto or bungee jump. You're actually seeking more stimulation of your reward circuitry. The bigger the surge of dopamine in response to some activity (or person), the greater your perception that it is rewarding. Chocolate cake triggers more dopamine than boiled Brussels sprouts.

Our entire economy plays upon our evolutionary drives. When you enter a movie theater and smell the popcorn, your dopamine rises and stimulates your reward circuitry. You crave that tub of buttery corn. Similarly, the supermodel next to the new BMW signals your mammalian brain that sex, money, and status are right there, in exchange for your credit card. Such a deal.

When we chase things in our lives, we're not after the *things* as much as the *feelings* associated with high dopamine. Hedge-fund moguls didn't need any more money, but their dopamine rose at the chance to outsmart others via those treacherous credit default swaps. No wonder deregulation *felt* like a great idea. The same highly motivating dopamine feeling is behind the drive to be Number One. Both the alpha chimp in a troop and a tycoon like Bill Gates raise their dopamine by dominating others. The washed-up boxing champ who keeps coming back is missing the dopamine of going for another big win.

Addictions, too, are governed by the reward circuitry. So, for example, junk food, gambling (in casino or stock market), porn-masturbation, alcohol, and shopping can all increase dopamine if they appeal to you. It's why they can become addictive, as we will see.

ENTER CUPID

Our reward circuitry is also where we fall in and out of love. Either we perceive someone as rewarding—that is, our dopamine surges at the thought of being with him or her—or we don't (no surge). Think back to the Coolidge effect. When the bull approaches a cow he has already serviced this season, no dopamine surge. Unserviced cow? Big surge.

> Instead of getting married again, I'm going to find a woman I don't like and give her a house.
> —Lewis Grizzard

This mechanism is subconscious; the rational brain isn't calling the shots. *You cannot force yourself to fall in love or stay in love,* any more than you can will yourself to digest a meal or fall asleep. Unless you do something to steer around your underlying mating program, you are likely to fall in and out

93

of love only on Cupid's commands—despite your best intentions and most sincere vows.

Not only does dopamine rise as we become aroused, it also surges for novelty and taking risks. Suppose your reward circuitry stops responding positively to your mate. The chance to have condomless sex with your co-worker in a dicey tryst may seem like a great idea—regardless of the reality.

"When sex evaporated from my marriage bed," recounted a friend, "I thought that what had been missing was passion." Continuing:

> In fact, I prayed for the return of what I called "passion" in my life. It surfaced in the form of a red-haired Scorpio who looked excellent in hot pants. At some point during the stormy ride that followed, I stumbled upon a dictionary definition of passion. *"Any intense emotion,"* it said, *"such as the sufferings of Jesus upon the cross."* Sure enough, I had found passion, all right. Brief as it was, our relationship made crucifixion look kind of appealing. It also resulted in twins.

Dopamine is released in response to *expectations*—rather than actual levels of pleasure. Something that is better than expected results in a bigger surge of dopamine. Think of hitting the jackpot while gambling. In fact, your reward circuitry readily learns to ignore familiar sources of pleasure in favor of things that initially registered as "unexpectedly compelling," whether or not they still provide pleasure, or have even grown unpleasant. This is why clicking onto porn Web sites can leave a big impression. It's also why sex with the same partner can become routine—unless you are managing your dopamine levels with karezza and bonding behaviors.

Buddha's Second Noble Truth: Suffering is caused by craving and aversion.

A dopamine surge is like the rake of a cowboy's spur. It urges you to exert yourself endlessly, to want the best of whatever is on your horizon, and even to seek out new horizons. This is good when directed toward completing a workout or getting a degree. Yet if you aren't using your rational brain to help steer, this primitive mechanism can set you on one meaningless quest after the other in search of a brief sense of eager anticipation—and no lasting fulfillment. This is why chasing the dopamine surges related to junk food or affectionless sexual stimulation is more likely to lead to recurring dissatisfaction than happiness.

Consider what happens when sadistic scientists put a starving rat on one side of a grid with electric current running through it and food on the other side. The rat will not cross the pain-producing grid. Yet put a rat with an electrode planted in her reward circuitry on one side of the grid and a lever she knows will stimulate her reward circuitry on the other, and she'll dash across the grid to tap that lever nonstop.

Stimulation of her reward circuitry becomes her top priority, because it's telling her inner compass that a big reward is just around the corner. She will ignore food, even if starving, or abandon her unweaned pups just to tap that lever until she drops. If the rat is male, he'll ignore a receptive female to tap it until *he* drops.[106] Humans implanted with similar electrodes (decades ago) experienced a constant urge to tap their levers, as well as intense sexual arousal—but not pleasure or orgasm itself. They also reported an undercurrent of anxiety.[107]

Intense stimulation of the reward circuitry (which some call the pleasure-reward pathway) is so overpoweringly compelling that the anticipated reward eclipses the fear of pain. As we've seen, instead of an electrode your body uses surges of dopamine to activate your reward circuitry.

If you've ever had an orgasm it won't surprise you to learn that dopamine shoots up as you become aroused, and peaks at climax.[108] It also rises as you pursue a novel

> The passion you fulfill is the passion you kill. The most wonderful, soaring feeling known to all mankind ... amounts to no more than a narcotic high, a temporal state of mania.
> —Neely Tucker, journalist

mate—and more so when she or he plays hard to get. These are the most powerful dopamine surges available to you (short of taking drugs). They can, in fact, lead to altered states if sufficiently intense. You can get as high as a kite—and not necessarily in a good way—on your own chemical messengers. (We'll talk about ways to achieve a more balanced, yet also pleasurable, neurochemical state later.)

Orgasms and potential new mates are compelling largely because of the dopamine released in our reward circuitry. Indeed, anthropologist Helen Fisher found that MRIs of those who are infatuated reveal that their reward circuitry is activated.[109] That is, romantic love is not an emotion, but rather a *drive*, activated by your response to that special someone. Whether her subjects were feeling euphoric or anxious about their romances, they were equally motivated by dopamine to *be with their beloveds.* On the other hand, when deprived of their beloveds, they suffered intensely.

Think about it. If you're designing a species and you want to make sure it does things that are crucial for survival—like eating and reproducing—you create a system that's all about pleasure so it wants to repeat those things. Then you have dopamine make those behaviors become automatic. It's brilliant, really.

—Nora Volkow, Director of the National Institute on Drug Abuse

When falling in love, the parts of the brain that aid with judging character and looking ahead, and the parts that protect us from harm, are switched off. When in this altered state, we're blind to faults and flooded with the neurochemicals of reward. This is why every mother knows that her newborn is the most beautiful baby on the planet. Infatuation lights up the same areas of the brain as drug addiction; and a romantic breakup can feel like withdrawal from drug use.[110]

Perhaps you begin to see why lovers committed adultery even when the punishment was to burn at the stake. By means of this effective, well-hidden mechanism deep in the mammalian brain, our ambitious genes often persuade us that any sacrifice is worth the pursuit of passion (and risk of pregnancy).

CORTEZIA

According to the late Swiss scholar Denis de Rougemont,[111] when the heady combination of reckless passion and adultery that was woven into the *early* Hindu tantra arrived in Western Europe during the Middle Ages, it merged with another ancient stream of thought—and the result was incendiary.

Tantric concepts migrated to the West, apparently through the impassioned poetry of the Muslim world under the umbrella of divine passion, or *fana* (the "passing away of the self"). Fana was the theme of mystical Sufi love poetry and song. (Some Muslims consider the Sufis heretics, just as mainstream Christians have often condemned mystically minded Christians as heretics.)

In due course, fana inspired the Spanish Moors. For example, here is a passage from *Bezels (Seals) of Wisdom* by Sufi mystic and philosopher Ibn al-ʿArabi, who was born in Spain in 1165:

> Contemplation of the Reality without formal support is not possible.... Since, therefore, some form of support is necessary, the best and most perfect kind is the contemplation of God in woman. The greatest union is that between man and woman.

Fana then tootled across the Pyrenees in the refrains of wandering minstrels into what is now southern France. There it encountered a version of Christianity, which may have migrated westward from Bulgaria, and beyond, or arrived with Mary Magdalene very early in the Current Era.[112] (In Bulgaria, Christians with similar beliefs were known as the Bogomils. "Bogomil" means "beloved of God.") Either way, Fana collided with the devout beliefs of a group who came to be known as the Cathars.

The Cathars were a rather chaste group of Christians who retained a lot of the so-called gnostic ideas of primitive (pre-papal) Christianity.[113] They preferred to avoid procreation, placing their attention instead upon preparation for reunion with the Divine. They believed the "Good God"

was not the creator of the corrupt world, and they passionately worshipped the Lady, the feminine aspect of the true God. The Cathars also believed that the love of man and woman should be as pure as their spiritual love for the feminine aspect of God, although little else is known about their actual practices.

The word *cathar* means "pure" in Greek, and that is how the Cathars are remembered. The influence of Cathar purity ultimately drove the Church to tighten up on many lax practices, such as priests' openly keeping mistresses—a practice so common that that there were laws enabling priests to pass property on to their heirs. The impassioned purity of the Cathars also indirectly inspired the Protestant Reformation and the Quaker movement.

Widespread admiration for the Cathars—amid the rampant corruption of the Church—swelled Cathar ranks. The Church branded Cathars as heretics. (A "heretic" was anyone who believed he could have a relationship with God *without* the authority of the Catholic Church.) The result was a hideous crusade throughout the Languedoc region of France (which in those days still spoke a language closer to Latin than French itself was).

The Church burned alive or otherwise murdered as many as one million fellow Christians—suspected Cathars—including whole towns, right down to the infants. Guillaume Belibaste, the last Cathar recorded to have burned at the stake in 1321, is said to have prophesied that "at the end of seven hundred years the laurel would again turn green,"[114] implying that the principles of "the true Christianity" would return to the world's attention.

Persecution sent the movement underground and into decline. However, the troubadours of Provence spread elements of chaste romance and the idealization of women throughout Europe under the guise of *cortezia,* the courtly love tradition. In this way it transformed from an underground religious movement into a code of manners for the upper classes also known as chivalry. Once a radical change in mores, the code of chivalry still lingers in such mundane routines as men holding doors for women or rising when a woman enters the room.

De Rougemont also traces the unrealistic Western desire for an all-consuming, undying passionate union to chivalry. De Rougemont has a point; the passionate burn of honeymoon neurochemistry is not sustainable. Sustainable romance emphasizes bonding neurochemistry, as we will see in later chapters. However, as Frenchman Jean Markale has explained, courtly love was never intended for marriage and family. It was an attempt to regain the paradisiacal condition at the dawn of time by overcoming the separating force of fertilization-based sex. (The word *sex* derives from the Latin word *secare*, "to sever.") Courtly love was a sexual initiation based upon purity of motive (putting love before lust) and a bond between lovers that was so complete and selfless that a third, spiritual entity was created.[115]

Courtly love definitely had elements of sexual self-discipline for a higher purpose. Some suggest practices calling for self-restraint originally evolved as preparation for the profound purity of becoming a Cathar *parfait* (holy man or woman) later in life.[116] "Embracing, kissing, often completed by caressing, are the carnal maneuvers courtly love permitted to the lover. *Le jazer*, going to bed could be probative and chaste."[117]

Cortezia knights pledged themselves to unavailable lovers—married ladies with whom they would (in theory at least) never have procreative sex. By sublimating their unrequited passions, these suitors harnessed their energy for spiritual and physical quests. They were rewarded with favors from their ladies, which seem to have ranged from smiles, tokens, and kisses to sleeping together in the nude and even intercourse ("becoming total") without ejaculation.[118] The ideal was a shared and faithful love, a morally uplifting love, a desire for greater spiritual light.

The most powerful practice of the tradition was the *penetrating gaze*:

> When two pure and sincere lovers look each other in the eyes as two equals, they are feeling … such joy in their hearts that the gentle feeling that is born there reanimates them and nurtures their entire heart. And the eyes through which this tenderness passes back and forth are so loyal that neither of the two lovers can hold anything back for solely their own benefit.[119]

Altruism was a key concept of courtly love: "Flee avarice as if it were a dangerous plague and, in contrast, be generous." Another was the avoidance of excessive lust: "He whose lust is too great does not truly love."[120] A principal tenet of chivalry was *E d'amor mou castitaz* (From love comes chastity).

Incidentally, it is believed that some of the troubadours of the courtly love tradition who sang ballads to their ladies were actually singing about the Cathar version of Christianity, with its fervent reverence for the Lady (the feminine aspect of God). Perhaps due to widespread pro-Lady fever, many cities constructed great cathedrals in honor of Jesus's mother, Mary, during this period, including Notre Dame de Paris.

It was also around this same time (the thirteenth century) that the mystical Jewish Kabbalah texts, known collectively as *The Zohar*, appeared in Spain.

However, according to scholar Moshe Idel, the kabbalists put mystical union in the service of procreation, in contrast with traditions that put nonprocreative intercourse into the service of mystical consciousness.[121]

> For the Kabbalist the ultimate sacrament is the sexual act, carefully organized and sustained as the most perfect mystical trance.
> —Kenneth Rexroth,
> author of *The Hasidism of Martin Buber*

Elsewhere in Europe, underground traditions advocating sex magick rituals—which often bore little resemblance to the chivalrous self-restraint of cortezia—also appeared. Subsequent centuries gave rise to colorful blends of kabbalist, tantric, and Asian practices, which influenced the Rosicrucians and Freemasons, as well as the writings of Emanuel Swedenborg and William Blake.[122]

Perhaps in rebellion against Church suppression, some of the sex magick schools ritualized (and still ritualize) orgasm and sex in some rather extreme and risky ways. Such rites produce intense stimulation, which can throw practitioners onto a neurochemical roller coaster that we'll examine more closely in the next two chapters.

CHAPTER FIVE

THE PASSION CYCLE

Orgasm sets in motion a cascade of programmed neuro-chemical events, which may continue for approximately two weeks. They change how we feel and how we perceive the world around us, especially a mate. They can speed habituation.

Changed feelings may be subtle and take many forms, such as irritability, cravings for orgasm, fuzzy thinking, emotional neediness, overreactions, and fatigue.

As the mammalian brain triggers habituation, the rational brain generates rationalizations for incompatibility.

The passion cycle can activate the amygdala's stress response, causing us to misperceive a partner as a threat.

A visitor to my Web site wrote:

I think the force of habituation is the real killer of relationships. I recently watched an old video of my wife and me visiting my parents with our kids. I was utterly transfixed by my wife—who looked gorgeously, awe inspiringly, achingly desirable!

The real gut-wrencher was the impression I had that I (in the video) had got so used to being around this delightful creature that I was taking her utterly for granted. I was probably even spending a lot of time complaining to myself about various things she did or didn't do that weren't quite up to expectations. I mean, why wasn't I just loving her???!!! The realization that I am running the risk, right now, of failing to fully appreciate my wife hit me like a ton weight. I envisaged myself, aged eighty, looking back at videos of us today, showing me equally incapable of being intoxicated by my wife, but drooling at images of how she is now.

How does this habituation (feeling of boredom, or "same old, same old") creep into relationships? Let's look at a factor that few of us ever consider—or want to consider.

THE ANTI-LOVE POTION

While you're declaring your undying love as orgasm approaches, your body is preparing to play a nasty trick on you. The very intensity of your glorious crescendo will trigger a cascade of neurochemical events, which have the power to shift your perception without your awareness. These neurochemical shifts can affect your judgment and how you experience the world. Above all, they can easily tarnish the way you see your lover, and create emotional distance between you. Male or female, it may be *two weeks* before you are completely free of their effects.

This is the two-week passion cycle, or orgasm cycle. It is perhaps the highest cost of fertilization-driven sex—and a prime reason to master a second way of making love for when conception is not desired. (Kids are expensive. Keeping two households going when unions deteriorate is even more expensive.)

Everyone's experience of the passion cycle is somewhat different. In most people the cycle's effects remain subconscious. For example, neither my husband nor I made the connection between orgasm and subsequent malaise earlier in our respective sex lives—although we experienced a lot of both. It was only when we explored karezza (making love without orgasm) that we became aware of a steady increase in lightheartedness and harmony.

Not only have we noticed improvements; we also notice that whenever we do have orgasm (inadvertently), we experience *unwelcome* shifts in our energy and outlook over the following days. Instead of finding it endearing when he leaves the cupboard doors open, I grumble. He thinks my ever-so-helpful suggestions are irritating. His touch feels more grabby than soothing. For about two weeks these uncomfortable feelings come and go, like erratic waves. They are usually subtle, but can also be quite intense when they intrude. I sometimes experience the most disconcerting effects near the *end* of the cycle.

Through talking with others, we've learned that this cycle takes many different forms. A full list of aftereffects people have mentioned could fill an entire page. Most often they report restlessness, irritability, dissatisfaction, desire for less contact with others, weepiness, anxiety, fatigue, hostility, fuzzy thinking, feelings of insecurity, emotional neediness, compulsive analysis of self or lover, jealousy, burning desire for escape, relief, or oblivion, cravings for substances or activities that raise dopamine, and—our genes' favorite—attraction to other potential partners. In its extreme form (headaches, debilitating brain fog, exhaustion, muscle aches, severe social anxiety), the cycle has been dubbed *post-orgasmic illness syndrome* (POIS).[123]

Historically, severe symptoms have also been called *post-coital depression, orgastic impotence,* and *spermatorrhea.* The usual "cure" of having more orgasms sometimes offers initial relief but tends to intensify the *next* passion cycle, as we'll see.

Q: Why is air a lot like sex?

A: Because you take it for granted unless you're not getting enough.

Most people don't make the connection between sexual satiety and subsequent uneasiness or emotional friction. For example, no one who is having sex too seldom can even *conceive* of the possibility that sexual satiety could ever occur, let alone cause a problem. To see the truth, people usually have to be in a relationship and remain physically affectionate but avoid orgasm for a while—and then return to orgasm. Even then, it's easy to miss the clues. As one woman said:

> I feel that the post-orgasmic illness syndrome folks are exceptional because they actually correlated their symptoms with orgasm. I was not able to make the connection until its possible existence was pointed out to me. There were just too many other influences stating exactly the opposite—that the more orgasms the better off you will

be! I spent thousands of dollars working through my supposed sub-conscious issues, only to have the same thing happen again in my next relationship . . . just like clockwork.

Instead of looking inward when we feel irritable or uneasy with no obvious cause, most of us project our uneasiness *outward*. That is, we look outside ourselves—and often in our partner's direction—to explain our state of mind. "He used to be so funny; what happened to him?" "Why is she looking at me like that, with that blank stare?" "Why doesn't he put his laundry in the hamper?" "More new clothing? I'll be taking it to a charity next month when she's tired of it." "I've asked him three times to take out the trash. Is he deaf?" "She used to hug me all the time." "He'd rather be with his friends than with me." "She's always talking on the phone." "Something's just not working." These are *not* the lyrics of love songs.

In fact, these insignificant molehills become mountains of distrust when they lead to fights. And even if you're not the fighting type, such feelings (and thoughts) may cause your partner to look a lot like another serving of Hamburger Helper instead of your favorite dish. These feelings can also make you less likely to engage in generous, affectionate contact—such as a surprise kiss or a spontaneous foot massage. As we'll see in Chapter Seven, this decrease in unselfish, affectionate contact delivers an unsuspected subconscious message: *emotional bond weakening*.

Sometimes you project your changed feelings *not* onto your mate, but rather onto your boss, your kids, or some other aspect of your life. Then *that* aspect of your life seems to be the cause of your uneasiness. Sooner or later, however, your mate is likely to feel the withering effects of your shift in perception. If you look for specific emotions, you may not spot them. Just watch for growing distance between you.

> I had a wonderful encounter with a beautiful goddess I had known for some time. I decided to sleep over when invited. I got into bed with her, wearing some clothing, and spent the night in a full body snuggle. I woke up so refreshed. It was invigorating. When we did get back together, conversation flowed just as easily. This time we did a full body massage, and ended up having intercourse, with ejaculation.

We have not repeated another physical encounter. For a variety of reasons, we are not meant to be together. But that is OK, and we know we can still be great as friends. Hangover? I don't think I had one. Because the sexual encounter was sharing- and connecting-focused, and not riding the rails to orgasm as a goal. I think my body relaxed and released more than exploded. However, the difference after the encounters was marked. After just snuggling I felt refreshed, awake, alert, and alive. I could not stop smiling for days! After the final encounter, I was anxious.

What happens? Orgasm feels great. If the story stopped there, the mainstream view that "there's no such thing as too many orgasms" would be correct. We would associate only the good feelings of sex with a lover—and stay in love indefinitely.

To comprehend how orgasm can change your feelings toward your lover, it helps to understand the physical reality behind your mammalian mating program. This program is being played out in your brain, though it feels like it's happening only in your genitals. It disguises itself extremely effectively—as perfectly logical reasons why your partner is a jerk, a witch, unsuitable after all, or uninteresting as compared with some hot new person.

WHAT GOES UP MUST COME DOWN

You've probably bumped into the concept of homeostasis. It's the principle that the body maintains ideal levels of oxygen and blood sugar, an ideal temperature, and so on. If you get cold, your muscles shiver and blood vessels constrict to warm you up; if you get hot, you sweat and your blood vessels expand to cool you down. Keeping in mind this simplified concept that your body strives for optimal conditions, let's look at the brain and neurochemicals.

Remember those cocaine addicts whose dopamine receptors (the tiny hands that grab neurochemicals) decreased after repeated drug use? Cocaine blasts the reward circuitry so that it pumps out massive amounts of exciting dopamine. This accounts for the high. Then two things happen simultaneously. First, the high begins to fade as the brain disposes of the extra dopamine.

Second, because so much excess dopamine can damage or kill nerve cells, the cells protect themselves by reducing the number of dopamine receptors (little "hands") on their surfaces. If a thunderstorm rolls in, you close all the windows and wait for it to pass. That's what the cells do, except they assume that another storm is on the way, and stay closed up for a while. The addict has lowered her sensitivity to dopamine—a substance that helped give her the high.

Now our addict feels rotten. She has two choices: Take more cocaine to jack up her mood artificially by saturating the remaining dopamine receptors, or suffer withdrawal symptoms. Withdrawal symptoms arise when the reward circuitry is starving for dopamine. Whether you have too few receptors for dopamine, or too little dopamine circulating around the nerve cells, you get the same result. Your reward circuitry batteries are low, leaving you with an acute desire to feel normal again. In this state, anything that promises rapid relief will cause an intense craving. Ironically, this craving is the result of a *spike* of dopamine. Contentment would be a return to *balanced* dopamine sensitivity—but that takes time, and will power.

I'm male, 33, and wonder why the majority of times after sex I feel depressed. It could be the greatest sex ever, but afterwards I'm depressed and can't wait to get away from her.—Don

---

The dopamine drop happens to a lesser extent even without drugs. For example, if you have a big Thanksgiving meal, you probably experience a slump afterward. Dopamine rises when you're hungry and drops after you eat, its mission accomplished. Now is when guests traditionally reach for coffee, more alcohol, another dessert, or a cigarette—in order to get their dopamine back up and remain alert enough to make conversation.

Both cocaine and the feast produce an initial pleasurable effect, followed by a less pleasant hangover. The bigger the blast of dopamine in connection with the initial event, the more uncomfortable the aftereffects. After overeating you tend to sit around feeling like a slug for a few hours. Shoot up on methamphetamine and you stay awake for hours, and later sleep for four days.

Dopamine equals anticipation and *wanting* rather than gratification itself. It is the promise of that juicy roast pig at the end of a long hunt, or a kiss at the end of your first date. Stoked on dopamine, we can waste hours visiting stores (what's around the corner?), playing video games, fantasizing about someone, clicking to the next porn image (maybe it's even hotter), or gambling (could be the big one), even if we end up with nothing beneficial to show for it. Dopamine anticipation equates with "the grass is always greener ... someplace else."

The ultimate reward, if any, appears to be related to neurochemicals called opioids, such as endorphins (the body's natural morphine). Yet, whatever the destination, dopamine is driving the Reward Bus. It fires up in anticipation of whatever our brain perceives as a possible path toward those fleeting feel-good sensations.

A big part of the thrilling rush up to climax is a sharp rise in dopamine levels in the brain. Indeed, pursuit of orgasm is the biggest legal blast of dopamine that we can engineer at will. After all, our reward circuitry didn't evolve so we could get hooked on cocaine or gambling; it's there so we will pursue mates and orgasm (among other things). Not surprisingly, when Dutch researcher Gert Holstege scanned the brains of men ejaculating, he commented that the scans resembled brain scans of those shooting heroin.[124] In case you're wondering, the men had fifty seconds to climax, holding their heads completely still while lying in a narrow MRI tube as their female partners assisted. Not surprisingly, researchers reported that much home practice preceded the experiment.

Dopamine spirals upward as you become sexually aroused. Interestingly, a female rat raises her dopamine by playing hard to get, that is, by running away from a potential mate several times before copulating. Her dopamine rises even higher if she receives her preferred rate of copulation (vigorous).[125] Apparently her heightened anticipation causes other neurochemical changes that prime her for pregnancy. Might women's brains have similarities that explain their frequent requests for more foreplay? As we've seen, mammals have surprising similarities in their underlying mating programs.

In both sexes, there comes a point where the momentum of rising dopamine may push the person over the edge of climax. Bang! Dopamine drops.[126] Other neurochemicals surge, and changes in receptor levels are also set in motion. These adjustments set dopamine levels on an erratic course, preventing it from bouncing back to its ideal baseline level right away. These fluctuating dopamine levels have much to do with changes in libido, outlook, and behavior. (It may also be that sensitivity to dopamine rises and falls in the brain during this time.) Sexually active adults typically go in and out of these dopamine highs and lows frequently, without, of course, realizing that their perception, desire for closer contact, and moods are also flickering.

DOPAMINE—THE LYNCHPIN

At ideal levels, dopamine equates with feelings of well-being and healthy decision-making. We feel optimistic and open, much like pre-pubescent children, who have not yet buckled themselves onto the dopamine roller coaster, and are delighted by everything from bugs to Barbies.

Why do we care if dopamine fluctuates? The three lists on the next page show conditions that researchers have connected with dopamine levels in the brain. (Other neurochemicals can be at work, too. Yet research reveals that changes in a single neurochemical can profoundly alter behavior.) The left column shows some effects of excess dopamine and the right column shows what happens when there is a deficiency. The middle column lists the states of mind and behaviors associated with balanced levels of dopamine. (Think Goldilocks.)

Unusually high or low dopamine can *both* be crazy-making—or at least perception-distorting. At high levels, dopamine is the "I've got to have it, whatever the repercussions" signal that lights up the brain's reward circuitry. We can become as single-minded as someone clutching a betting stub during a horserace.

Scientists know that high dopamine can drastically alter behavior because of its unexpected effects when given as a drug to treat restless leg syndrome and Parkinson's symptoms. Mayo Clinic researchers reported that a number of patients taking dopamine agonists (drugs that mimic dopamine) developed uncharacteristic compulsions, including gambling, compulsive eating, increased alcohol use, and hypersexuality.

EXCESS	HEALTHY	DEFICIENT
More wanting—less liking	Healthy bonding	Inability to love
Sexual fetishes and compulsions	Healthy libido	Low libido
	Feelings of well-being	Erectile dysfunction
Addictions	Pleasure in accomplishing tasks	Addictions
Impulsive sensation-seeking	Energy and vitality	Depression
	Motivation	Anhedonia—no pleasure
Unhealthy risk-taking	Healthy risk-taking	Lack of ambition
Gambling	Sound choices	Withdrawal
Aggression	Realistic expectations	Low energy
Delusions	Good feelings toward others	Social anxiety
Schizophrenia		No remorse

"When our neurologists tapered the patients off the medication, several reported a dramatic resolution of their problem," a Mayo spokesman said. "One patient said it was like a light switch going off."[127] Since this side effect has been publicized, hundreds of surprised patients have come forward admitting to uncontrollable addictions that gripped them after taking their prescribed meds.[128]

In contrast, with very low levels of dopamine, we have no drive and no desire to interact. Indeed, recent research confirmed that low dopamine is closely tied to social anxiety (the urge to avoid healthy contact with others).[129] Life seems joyless and pointless. We can feel miserable, as if something just isn't right. Consider the experience of this healthy young medical student whose dopamine was artificially lowered using drugs:

After 7 hours, Mr. A felt more distance between himself and his environment. Stimuli had less impact; visual and audible stimuli were less sharp. He experienced a loss of motivation and tiredness. After 18 hours, he had difficulty waking up and increasing tiredness; environmental stimuli seemed dull. He had less fluency of speech. After 20 hours, he felt confused. He felt tense before his appointment and had an urge to check his watch in an obsessive way.

After 24 hours, Mr. A had inner restlessness, flight of ideas; his ideas seemed inflicted, and he could not remember them. He felt a loss of control over his ideas. After 28 hours, he felt ashamed, frightened, anxious, and depressed. He was afraid that the situation would continue. At that time, blepharospasm [spasm of the eyelid], mask face, and tremor were noted. After 30 hours, he was tired and slept 11 hours. After 42 hours, he had poor concentration. In the next hours, he returned to normal.[130]

Compare this with the experience of Web site visitors, who suffer a dramatic low after orgasm. Keep in mind that post-orgasmic symptoms, whether mild or severe, are part of a longer cycle, and that dopamine is only one of the players (more in a moment).

After I ejaculate I have brain fog, low energy and I'm tongue-tied. I feel mentally and physically exhausted for a week or longer. Last spring I started experimenting. After two weeks without masturbation, I had incredible drive to do things, think clearly, talk to people easily. I simply felt normal. I can destroy that with one or two masturbations.—Rolf

I suffered from depression since I was about twelve until this year (age twenty-four). My depression was part of bipolar disorder. It has completely gone away since I stopped masturbating. I'm taking some herbs too, but abstaining from orgasm definitely helps a lot with my mood.—Andrea

By now it won't surprise you to learn that nearly all mood disorders implicate the reward circuitry and related structures. For example, bipolar and schizophrenic psychiatric drugs affect dopamine levels or the reward circuitry. Also, common anti-depression medications appear to act by making the reward circuitry more sensitive to dopamine.[131] Unfortunately, when doctors tried to treat addictions by suppressing the reward circuitry, the drugs caused severe depression and even some suicides.[132]

We need a little caution and a little humility when we're messing around with our brain chemistry. We are still learning things that are relevant to safety.
—Martha Farah,
  neuropsychologist

ADDICTION—QUEST FOR MORE MISERY

Notice that addictions are listed above in connection with both high *and* low dopamine. How can this be? When your dopamine is already high, it's driving you toward a goal—come hell or high water. That's when you open another bottle of wine, place that bet you cannot afford, or pursue orgasm to utter exhaustion. When dopamine is low, you easily fall prey to any activity that will raise it again, such as ripping into some junk food or clicking to a porn site. Indeed, a 2006 study showed that low dopamine leads to poor, emotion-based decision making characterized by shortsightedness. Subjects with lowered dopamine had difficulty resisting short-term reward, despite long-term negative consequences.[133]

The point? Balanced dopamine can keep you from doing stupid stuff.

Also notice that ideal dopamine levels (neither high nor low) are absolutely necessary for healthy bonding. If interactions with your partner don't produce adequate dopamine (and oxytocin, more on that later), you've lost that loving feeling. Both

> "Aw c'mon. Who the @#$% is going to find out?"
> —Bill Clinton, 1999

addicts, whose intense cravings equate with dopamine surges, and the clinically depressed, whose emotional flatness—and susceptibility to seeking quick relief—equate with low dopamine, tend to behave in very self-centered ways. Neither group has a good mindset for healthy romance.

People suffering from extremes in dopamine levels can be strongly motivated to self-medicate, or use others, to alter their uncomfortable moods. Often they pursue rapid relief at the cost of setting off another cycle of discomfort—in the form of a minor, or major, withdrawal period. Those with high dopamine can feel jittery and anxious, and be looking for something to take the edge off. Healthy choices might be affectionate touch, meditation, or yoga. Less healthy choices might be liquor, Valium, or marijuana.

What are two of the most potent quick fixes when discomfort strikes on the dopamine roller coaster? Anticipation of a new potential mate or another orgasm. Could this explain the commercial success of romance novels, pornography, and racy magazines teaching seduction and promising better sex? Your reward circuitry—calibrated to react to all things sexual with great fireworks—has trouble distinguishing a virtual mating opportunity from a real one. Even if you do seek your fix from your mate, you may temporarily perceive him or her largely as a collection of body parts beckoning with relief—and not as your beloved.

BALANCE AND BONDING

Dopamine levels matter. They influence us without our conscious awareness. It's probably evident that the perennial search for sexual satiety pushes lovers back and forth from dopamine excess to dopamine deficiency. When our dopamine is soaring, we see "Mr. or Ms. Right," or at least someone who looks really hot. But when sensitivity to dopamine drops, we may feel flat, apathetic, dissatisfied, fatigued, or irritable (and especially susceptible to substances and activities that promise quick relief). Dopamine fluctuations can cause mood swings and perception shifts. Even when subtle, they can make intimacy bewildering. We may be looking at each other through rose-tinted glasses one day, and long, dark tunnels the next.

A period of intense [sexual] love was followed by a long period of anger; a period of mild love induced a mild irritation. We did not understand that this love and this hatred were two opposite faces of the same animal feeling.

—Leo Tolstoy, in *The Kreutzer Sonata*

In our experience, how we make love definitely influences our moods and perceptions of each other. I had figured that out years earlier, as recounted. Now it was Will's turn. When we met, he was secretly abusing alcohol, taking antidepressants for chronic depression, and climaxing about four times each week. Depression and alcoholism ran in his family—his therapist mother had suffered from both. His father taught sex education, and as far as Will was concerned, orgasm caused no problems at all, but he was willing to test karezza-style lovemaking.

As we experimented, Will remarked repeatedly that he was feeling normal—for the first time as far back as he could remember. Within months he had stopped using alcohol. A year later he was off his depression meds and doing better than ever. These changes were gradual, but made his life far more enjoyable.

It bears repeating that a major theme of this book is that the intense pursuit of orgasm tends to raise dopamine sharply. In fact, a preliminary study with normal subjects showed that brain activity associated with sexual arousal looks like that accompanying drug consumption.[134] High dopamine then makes it urgent to find comfort via climax (or else experience severe frustration). The usual relief—orgasm—triggers fluctuations of dopamine over the next two weeks or so. Whenever dopamine or dopamine sensitivity drops, it can register as an even more urgent need to escape the misery. Inflamed libido is thus a function of events in the brain, not the genitals—a theme we will return to in the next chapter.

As noted, the Taoists (among others) observed this phenomenon long ago. They discovered that the way to restore equilibrium is not more orgasm—or abstinence—but, rather, a different approach to sex altogether. Its goal is to ease sexual frustration (that is, to avoid dopamine fluctuations) and stay balanced naturally by means of lots of gentle lovemaking. (We'll see why careful, affectionate lovemaking can lead to *less* frustration, not *more,* when we look at another neurochemical, oxytocin.)

In this way lovers escape their mating program's uncomfortable seesaw of highs and lows. By altering their behavior, the Taoists altered their neurochemistry. Greater inner balance turned out to be the best way to prevent the buildup of sexual frustration in the first place. In other words, bonding-based lovemaking offers lovers a strategy for tapping greater feelings of well-being and remaining in that healthy column of the above lists.

Although the moment after orgasm *feels* like it is a return to equilibrium, it is not. The body will return to homeostasis in its own time—at the end of a longer, intricate neurochemical cycle, which we'll look at next.

SCIENTIFIC EVIDENCE OF
LINGERING CHANGES AFTER ORGASM

The complete passion cycle is more complex than the simple highs and lows of dopamine. It is difficult for scientists to obtain the full picture because they cannot slice up and examine the brains of lovers over the weeks following orgasm. Also, researchers haven't been looking for this cycle—because of the prevailing belief that orgasm is purely beneficial.

What little is known is quite new. It comes via brain scans (MRIs) and blood tests on humans, and experiments on rat brains—primarily with a view to developing new sexual enhancement pharmaceuticals. Despite the obvious differences between rats and humans, rats have been called "guiding flashlights" for understanding the neurochemical and genetic mysteries of the more primitive parts of the human brain.[135]

Based on these recent discoveries, we think that a simplified graph of the return to homeostasis after sexual satiety would look something like this fractal pattern. No two recovery periods would have identical ups and downs or duration, yet all would conform to a recognizable cycle.

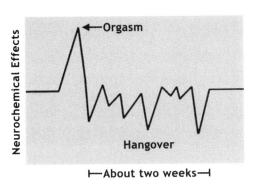

We are ignoring for the moment other factors we suspect affect the sequence, such as degree of sexual surfeit, whether a partner and loving affection are present, the type of sex (intercourse or not), and individual sensitivity to pertinent neurochemicals. Here we'll just highlight some of the known neurochemical events in the mammalian brain during the period after sexual satiety, and discuss some of their theoretical roles in our unconscious mating program. (The actual picture will prove more complex. There is much still to learn.)

DOPAMINE SUPPRESSION

In 2014, scientists discovered that ejaculation causes key dopamine-producing cells to shrink for at least two weeks, presumably reducing dopamine output.[135a] Also at orgasm, dopamine drops and another neurochemical sharply rises in both men and women: prolactin. These changes are like a foot on the brakes, sexual satiation signals.[136] Men may experience them as the "I'm going into a coma now—good night" phenomenon. Interestingly, prolactin rises four times as much after ejaculation during intercourse, as compared with ejaculation during masturbation.[137] Our genes know when a man has done his fertilization duty.

Clearly not everyone has precisely the same immediate reaction to every orgasm. Women often report that the first orgasm just makes them feel ready for the next one. Is this a vestige of some mammalian forebears' program to gather sperm from as many donors as possible—while satiated sperm donors snooze? In sperm competition, "you snooze, you lose."

Could this be why a man would more often be knocked out after sex than a woman? Among our close genetic relatives, the chimpanzees, a female chimp typically has sex with as many partners as she can manage. This means that she doesn't feel fully satiated by her first partner (or perhaps by any partner). Remember, genes don't care if Ms. Anna Nicole Chimp is *ever* satisfied, as long as her behavior results in genetically successful offspring.

From her genes' perspective, post-copulation restlessness is a perfect mechanism, a way to make sure that her precious ovum is not wasted on guys shooting blanks.[138] A woman's work may never be done, but apparently a gent can take a well-earned

> Orgasm may induce changes in the hypothalamus that overwhelm prolactin inhibition [thus, allowing prolactin to rise dramatically]. . . . Prolactin is an important sex hormone with potentially far-reaching daily consequences. It has a fundamental role in sexual activity, and may be the first candidate for a circulating molecule with the capacity to regulate sexual feelings and preparedness.
> —Jeremy Heaton, urologist

break after copulation—unless a novel partner rouses him to action, as we'll see in the next chapter. In any case, male chimps cope with their "fidgety female" reality with enhanced gene-making machinery (bigger testicles). Less-promiscuous primates have relatively smaller testicles. Human testicles are right in the middle, relative to our size.[139] Looks like we are wired to go either way.

Multi-orgasmic people appear to be able to keep going *because* prolactin levels do not rise after their initial orgasms.[140] Based on our experience, and that recorded by others who have experimented with karezza, we suspect that easing sexual tension without orgasm sidesteps the post-orgasmic damper, leaving lovers feeling more lighthearted and refreshed—and less knackered, or restless—after sex.

> *After ejaculating I experience clouded thinking, lack of interest in things I love (including people), fatigue, difficulties sleeping, and short attention span. The symptoms go away slowly after a week. Seeking relief, I took fenugreek [an herb that either encourages production of prolactin, or imitates it]. My symptoms disappeared, but my orgasm was not insanely intense like usual. Maybe people who experience*

severe symptoms have stronger orgasms. If so, orgasm could be compared to drugs or alcohol. The more intense the rush/high/orgasm, the worse the recovery/low. Incidentally, I've gone eleven months without ejaculating. I felt terrific!—Duncan

In the usual situation, neurochemical changes after orgasm tell you that you're done—at least for the moment, although they may soon have you looking around for more. One way they accomplish all this is by suppressing dopamine. Have another look at that three-column dopamine listing on page 109 to see why changes in dopamine matter.

Evidence suggests prolactin *may* be a greater influence on women's post-orgasmic perception shifts than on men's. For

Post-orgasm Effects?

Russ returns from a doctor's visit having learned that he has only twenty-four hours to live. Wiping away his wife's tears, he asks to make love. Of course she agrees. Six hours later, Russ goes to her, "Maybe we could make love again?" They make love. Later, Russ is getting into bed, "Honey? Please? Just one more time before I die." She agrees. Four hours later he taps his wife on the shoulder. "Honey, could we . . . ?" She sits up abruptly, turns and says, "Listen, Russ, I have to get up in the morning. You don't."

example, vigorous copulation will stimulate a female rat to begin producing twice-daily surges of prolactin for *two weeks*, even if she did not get pregnant. These surges seem to be an automatic mechanism to prepare the rat for possible pregnancy after intense sexual activity.[141] (Prolactin, like most neurochemicals, does many jobs in the body depending upon which cells it stimulates. Thus it is not only a sexual-satiation hormone but also a major pregnancy hormone.)

This research suggests that vigorous sex can set off a domino effect that drops dopamine whenever prolactin shoots up. Could some vestige of this same mammalian program affect women during the weeks after sexual satiety? Perhaps prolactin surges were behind the bothersome mood swings and perception shifts that both Anya and I observed after orgasm. I notice these effects more in the second week after orgasm, and they seem most intense just before I return to equilibrium. Even forewarned, Will was stunned when he experienced this neurochemical cycle secondhand—with open eyes. I morphed from his beloved into a scary-looking "Miss Here's-a-Piece-of-My-Mind," and then back into a loving, supportive mate—all in the course of two weeks, and probably more than once.

[From online forum] Man: My wife turns into a major bitch on occasion the morning after a night of really great sex. I'm talking multiple orgasms and a 2–3-hour session. And the next morning I am the anti-Christ!

Woman: This happens to me, too! I wake up in the morning after a great night with my dear husband and feel like the bitch from hell sometimes ... really irritable and moody. Normally I'm a very even-keel kind of gal. Things feel better when orgasms are more spread out. I have personally noticed a significant decrease in my attraction and warm fuzzy feelings toward my spouse when the "O" is on a constant, regular basis.

In 2012, German neuroscientists got the bright idea to check whether sex also initiates a lingering neuroendocrine "memory" in women (possibly dampening their libido). Lo and behold, sexual intercourse with orgasm indeed produced a prolactin "echo" a day later in the women they tested![141a]

Next, the German scientists plan to see if post-orgasm prolactin blips are related to lack of desire (suppressed dopamine). What additional hormonal events are involved? How long do they linger? Might they affect some women more than others (think PMS)? How would these events interact with a menstrual cycle? It's too soon to say.

Intriguingly, however, UK and Australian researchers[142] ended up baffled when they analyzed women who report recurring depression, irritability, or tears after sex (eight percent of women, in the UK study). Researchers expected to find that childhood abuse/marital distress correlated strongly with symptoms. Not so. Some unknown factor produces those pronounced postcoital mood swings. Might it turn out to be a neuroendocrine cycle with the potential to alter both mood and sexual desire? Are the eight percent simply at one end of a bell curve, and thus conscious of neurochemical fluctuations the rest of us disregard or misconstrue?

Needless to say, I once again bypassed all of the loving exchanges, had orgasmic hot sex (with a few successful runs of sex without orgasm). I feel no attraction to him at all now. He is disoriented and confused. It looks to me like he is obsessed with authority, prestige, and the question of his potency as a male. Forgiving, supportive, yin energy? Not sure that I have it in me.—Shana

In further support of the idea that orgasm increases uneasiness in women, an earlier study linked masturbation with greater depression and relationship dissatisfaction—as well as less physical pleasure.[143]

Is prolactin behind such shifts? It's too soon to say. However, intriguingly, patients who have elevated prolactin (for various reasons) report a lot of the same symptoms as lovers do when their honeymoons end. For example, men with high prolactin levels sometimes report low libido, headaches, erectile dysfunction, and anxiety. Women report similar symptoms. In one study, three-quarters of women with unexplained high prolactin levels were suffering from depression, anxiety, and hostility.[144] What subtle, or maybe not-so-subtle, effect would a sudden squirt or two per day of prolactin in a key part of her brain do to a woman's mood? And is the usual attempt to ease these symptoms with more orgasm just keeping women on an unnerving roller coaster?

It has been a year since my husband's death and I decided to see if I was still capable of orgasm. (My husband was very sick for several years before his death, so it has been a while.) The very next morning I woke up slightly depressed. Each night I masturbated again, trying to shorten the time to climax. Each morning I woke up a bit more depressed. After a couple of weeks of this I made the connection, and stopped. The depression is now completely gone, but I'm still horny from all that masturbating. (I wasn't at all horny before starting to masturbate.)—Lorene

---

Prolactin has many jobs. High prolactin also appears to be part of the mammalian repertoire of stress responses. It is more associated with long-term anxiety and despair than fight or flight—which is mainly associated with heart-pounding adrenaline.[145] Perhaps over time one of its functions is to convince mates that their unions are just not working, so they seek out new partners.

If these kinds of mood changes sound extreme, keep in mind that the effects of the orgasm cycle are often muted in new lovers. They are under the temporary influence of highly stimulating, yet also perception-protecting, honeymoon neurochemicals.

My relationship is going so well, and I know a lot of it has to do with this approach to relationships. I feel great. I feel in love and I am not confused or scaring men off anymore.—Nora

---

TESTOSTERONE AND FRIENDS

There's evidence of a two-week orgasm cycle in male mammals, too. Male rats typically copulate about eight times before losing interest in a mate—that is, becoming satiated. (Whose job is it to count these things?) Surprisingly, after he reaches sexual unresponsiveness, a male rat needs up to *fifteen days to return to normal* levels of sexual responsiveness.[146] One of the mechanisms that suppresses libido involves changes in testosterone (androgen) receptors in the brain.

One reason males typically have such dependable sexual desire is that they produce far more testosterone than females. Testosterone increases dopamine levels in the reward circuitry.[147] (Aha! Another influence on dopamine levels.[148]) Result? A man can usually pursue sex at the drop of his trousers. Women also produce testosterone and it contributes to their sexual desire, too. In fact, a pharmaceutical company unsuccessfully sought FDA approval for a testosterone patch to increase women's libido. Among other hazards, it produced beards, acne, and extra weight.[149] The patch has been approved in Europe, although it offers women little more than one extra episode of sexual activity a month, compared with a placebo.

After copulation a rat's testosterone receptors decrease in a part of his reward circuitry known as the hypothalamus. This means he's less sensitive to testosterone's effects in this key part of his brain. If he continues copulating to the point of sexual satiety, he experiences a *drastic* reduction in testosterone receptors here.[150] The hypothalamus shrieks "enough already!" This suggests that the greater the sense of sexual satiety, the more a mammal may suffer uncomfortable ripples in its reward circuitry over the following two weeks. (Reminder: You are a mammal.)

Testosterone levels in the rat's blood haven't dropped, even though he's sexually disinterested. (Testosterone has other jobs to do in the body.) Yet he is likely to *feel* like his testosterone has decreased, because his reward circuitry can't fully respond. His sexual desire for his female cage mate drops off. In fact, he will not copulate at all with her for up to four days. His testosterone receptors actually recover before then. This suggests that other, as-yet-unknown, neurochemical events are also occurring, which retard his return to full steam for fifteen days.

> We had sex, and he told me instantly afterwards that I had to leave (seconds post-coital). He was cold and disinterested in me for fourteen days ... and then for a further fourteen days slowly changed and tried to woo me again until.... This went on for years. He is normally a nice guy and none of this ever made sense. I charted the pattern for a while and was at a complete loss to explain its rhythmicity.—Mia (who happened to be a German medical doctor)

Various other neurochemicals showed changes during sexual exhaustion in rats, too. Opioids suppress sexual desire. One rat study compared the rise in opioid levels after a single copulation with the rise after sexual satiety. In both cases, levels had not recovered forty-eight hours later.[151] In other words, ejaculation appears to kick off a neurochemical cycle, even if a mammal does not *exhaust* himself sexually. Females also produce opioids after energetic sex, which seem to inhibit sexual activity and induce prolactin surges over several days.[152]

Serotonin is another possible link in the post-sexual satiety chain of neurochemical events. It's released right after orgasm. Like prolactin, it appears to inhibit dopamine (once again, affecting that key neurochemical). Most of us think of serotonin as a good-mood neurochemical, but its effects depend upon which nerve cells it signals. Researchers know serotonin can flatten sexual desire because patients taking antidepressants, which increase serotonin in the brain, often report lower libido. One doctor has even experimented with using SSRIs to ease post-coital depression,[153] but might it not be wiser to emphasize soothing bonding behaviors instead of decreasing sexual responsiveness artificially?

WHAT ABOUT MEN?

In human males it is, of course, impossible (or at least fatal and unethical) to map out post-orgasmic changes in the neurochemicals and receptors deep in the mammalian brain. Nevertheless, scientists have already found unmistakable evidence that the human orgasm cycle extends for at least seven days in men. When they sample the levels of testosterone in men's blood during the days following orgasm, they see a predictable spike at the seven-day mark.

> The results showed that ejaculation-caused variations were characterized by a peak on the 7th day of abstinence; and that the effective time of an ejaculation, is 7 days minimum.[154]

In short, a man's orgasm kicks in a reproductive program, not unlike the reproductive program ovulation triggers in a woman. Menstrual cycles vary, but seldom by much, and they feature distinct hormonal spikes (of progesterone and estrogen). Predictable neurochemical surges are not purposeless. For example, it is a spike of testosterone that signals the bones to *stop* growing in adolescence.

What does a man's surge of testosterone at day seven signify? Testosterone increases dopamine. Does it make him more susceptible to novel mates—so he doesn't pester his previous, possibly pregnant, mate? Is it but one domino in a longer neurochemical program? Neither? Both? No one yet knows. One thing is certain: During their counterpart of this cycle, male rats only bother to get it up and get it on for *novel* females. Past hook-ups just don't raise their dopamine. This is the Coolidge effect—a form of habituation in which a mammal experiences low dopamine in response to an existing mate, and a thrilling surge of dopamine in response to a novel mate. The neurochemistry that urges us on to additional mates is our genes' secret weapon—the poison on Cupid's arrow.

Incidentally, no one knows what testosterone levels do in men practicing karezza (intercourse without orgasm). However, abstaining from sex, and engaging in less sexual activity (orgasm), actually *elevate* men's testosterone levels overall, compared with those who are more sexually active.[155]

After three weeks of abstinence from orgasm, I'm feeling mighty surges. My self-image, never low, is becoming borderline self-admiration. My body is hardening, stomach muscles are showing again, without exercise, even after living off of holiday desserts since Christmas. Where the orgasm-craving urge was a weak sit-in-a-dark-room urge, the testosterone urge is a strong one driving me out the door to meet real women. I read that the testosterone levels of men in 1940 were twice as high as they are nowadays. What's up?—Stephen

Although the picture is rudimentary, the neurochemistry of our mating behavior may one day disclose why lovers sometimes see each other so differently during the weeks after sexual satiation. One day he looks like Dr. Jekyll, the next day like Mr. Hyde. One day she looks like Aphrodite, the next like Medusa with live snakes for hair. Given the fact that researchers aren't yet seeking evidence of a post-orgasmic passion cycle (extended recovery cycle), it's fascinating that there's already so much hard evidence of one.

Sexual problems don't always bespeak deep, dark psychological problems. They may be nothing more than a quirk in the neurobiology of sex.
—Richard A. Friedman, psychiatrist

THE PERCEPTION GAME

Now that we've examined some possible neurochemical underpinnings of our mating program, let's return to the question of how the feelings evoked by this program may be interfering with our love lives. Imagine you are well past the honeymoon period in your relationship, and that you are also in the two-week return to homeostasis following orgasm. Due to involuntary neurochemical events, two things are happening. First, your dopamine is low—at least in relation to *your* lover. He or she has lost some luster in your eyes. Second, your inner alarm system may be on red alert and looking for trouble. (More on its role in the reward circuitry in Chapter Eight.)

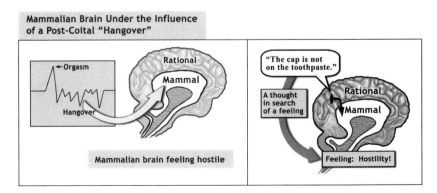

You may not feel exactly like a rooster looking for his next hen, or a chimp looking for her next sperm donor. Yet you are hearing neurochemical whispers from your mammalian brain. You could be feeling restless and irritable—perhaps desirous of vigorous sex, but unenthusiastic about affectionate foreplay, or the reverse. Without your conscious awareness, your rational brain has already begun scanning for reasons to justify your very real, but otherwise unreasonable, feelings. It can easily find them.

> Another's wife is a white swan, and ours is a bitter herb.
> —Russian proverb

In effect, your rational brain and your mammalian brain are playing a form of ping-pong—and your mammalian brain has a much stronger serve. This is because the brain pathways by which the mammalian brain communicates with the rational brain are like superhighways, while the pathways that the rational brain uses to talk to the mammalian brain are like dirt roads in the wilderness, slow and sparse.

When an observation comes to the attention of the rational brain, it connects it with your feelings in the mammalian brain, and then analyzes it further. Through this process you rationalize your feelings. The series of images below shows how a random feeling of hostility—a perfectly normal occurrence during the low points of the passion cycle—can cause chaos. Your mammalian brain is coloring how you see your lover during this cycle, and the color can be very unflattering.

Suppose that after climax you experience suppressed dopamine (or decreased sensitivity to dopamine) as a period of low energy or absent-mindedness. How will you see your lover at such times? Probably as demanding or a control freak. Even your mate's most reasonable, diplomatic

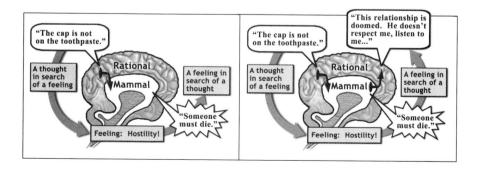

request will feel like nagging. On the other hand, suppose an orgasm triggers subsequent waves of insecurity in you. How will you see your lover? As selfish, insensitive, or flirting with others. No matter what your mate does (or *doesn't* do), it won't be enough to reassure you.

No partner, however tolerant or attentive, can consistently soothe our discomfort, or fill a "hole" inside us, which we are experiencing because our behavior—although perfectly natural—has disturbed our neurochemical balance. Like it or not, sex pursued to the point of satiety has the potential to filter our perceptions of each other, especially after the neurochemical honeymoon has worn off.

When under the influence of post-orgasmic mood swings, we tend to see a very imperfect partner. She or he may seem high-maintenance, self-absorbed, inadequate, annoying, unable or unwilling to meet our needs, lazy, critical, boring, demanding, threatening, selfish, greedy, irrationally jealous—or all of the above. It's hard to adore a beloved while feeling defensive or disappointed. Instead, we tend to resort to subconscious thought patterns and behaviors learned on those occasions when loved ones let us down as children. This is when romance can wither like a rose under a prism in the sun. And we never suspect that our self-generated mood changes are a big factor in our changing perceptions.

Shifts like these underscore the brutal clash between our evolutionary bonding program and our evolutionary "binge on sex until we feel compelled to add a novel mate" program. The wreckage virtually guarantees that we tangle up love and fear in our subconscious, especially with respect to intimate relationships.

You have two choices in life: You can stay single and be miserable, or get married . . . and wish you were dead.
—W. W. Renwick

Attempts to address the symptoms of this built-in separation mechanism with therapy, communication skills, negotiating skills, or artificially enhanced passion often get results, but they do not address its biological source. New rationalizations for distance arise. We humans will continue to get the same results, on average, as long as our wily genes call the shots. Those results are lots of babies and lots of broken or limping intimate relationships. We are caught in a genetically inspired dance of wanting connection—and yet wanting those things that break it up. And from our genes' perspective, this tension is a strength, not a weakness.

We need not habituate to our partner in this way. By changing our behavior we can raise our sensitivity to our partner and continue to see him or her as rewarding. Indefinitely.

TAINTING LOVE WITH FEAR

If you continue your current habits, you may eventually find that your built-in cycle of attraction and repulsion can cause subconscious uneasiness between you and *every* new lover. Perhaps this is the work of the amygdala—the part of your reward circuitry (pictured again here) that records emotional memories. One of its chief jobs is to protect you from repeating painful experiences by encouraging you to avoid things that hurt you in the past. If it begins to associate intimacy with fights, nasty comments, feelings of depletion, the need to escape, and recurring anxiety, then it will react to intimacy as if to a snake or predator.

Indeed, the amygdala can snap shut like a rusty, but fully operational, bear trap. It issues its warnings chemically and so quickly that it can activate your body's defense reactions before your rational brain even has a chance to evaluate your circumstances.[156] At that point, it is easy to fall into one of three stress responses: fight, flight, or freeze.

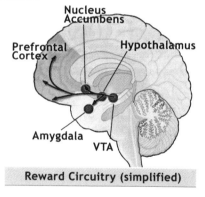

Reward Circuitry (simplified)

Your amygdala does not realize that fallout from sexual satiety is a major source of your distress. After all, orgasm feels great—especially with a new partner. Instead, it may register the problem as *relationship,* because that is where the friction usually shows up during the weeks after orgasmic sex. The amygdala's motto then becomes: Orgasm is good, relationship is dangerous. Know people operating on this motto? If so, they are right where their genes want them. Yet, as we will see in later chapters, this maxim is poor guidance indeed—unless our ambition is to serve *only* as gene machines.

[Within days of passionate lovemaking in a relatively new relationship] I thought this relationship was going to be good for me, for us, but ... now I'm done. Can't do it anymore. Something inside is saying, "Get rid of that woman. She doesn't listen. She has too much stuff. She's too critical of my driving. She thinks I do things too slowly."
—Eric

In some people these messages arise immediately after a first encounter with a new partner. Eventually this protective mechanism may flip on when you even approach anyone with whom you could form a real relationship. While your amygdala is "saving" you from ongoing intimacy, stable, generous partners just will not turn you on. And you will not even bother to question your verdict. "Oh, there was no spark between us." Mysteriously, however, you will find unavailable, incompatible partners (those with Exit signs flashing behind their heads) ever so attractive. Again, even if you determinedly stay married and faithful, these warning signals can make you uneasy about close contact long after the end of any passion cycle.

The fact that you're allowed to marry another woman, in addition to your wife, makes you hesitate about having an affair with another woman.
—Muhammed Sha'alan, Muslim

It's probably evident that there can be no harmony except when the defensive response of the amygdala is deactivated. The amygdala is our sentry, our security guard. If we want to bond we have to quiet it at the same time we activate our reward circuitry. Otherwise our partner can register in our mammalian brain as "disagreeable"—and to be avoided. (Passionate sex temporarily turns off the amygdala, which is one reason couples can fall into a pattern of hostility punctuated with hot sex—for a while.)

Tolstoy once concluded that in marriage, "Love was exhausted with the satisfaction of sensuality." In fact, he had it backward. The uneasiness during the days after sexual satiety temporarily mask loving feelings with stress, and the rational brain can begin to formulate lasting convictions that love is a delusion.

The way I make love reflects immediately on the overall emotional atmosphere between us. When I have a "normal" orgasm I experience loss of the ability to feel the beauty, loss of the enchanting sense of life, and lack of subtle tenderness and completeness. After ejaculation I feel depleted not only hormonally, but also emotionally and spiritually. For partial recovery, I need at least three or four days. For complete recovery, about two weeks are needed. In fact, I am astounded to see confirmation of my own observations in your material. During this time, one's partner becomes the mere reflection of one's inner state of mind. It's terrible!—Serge

When you do not perceive your beloved as a safe harbor and reliable source of rewarding feelings, you can begin to feel wary. Indeed, your nervous system may no longer be *able* to sense what it was like to be in love with your mate—until you turn off your warning bells. You can retire your sentry (and reverse any habituation) by mutually reinvigorating your innate bonding program.

In fact, as we'll see later, a variety of other primates frequently soothe themselves with bonding behaviors (both non-genital and genital), even though they often don't climax. Perhaps, like them, we evolved to seek contentment through lots of friendly connection with occasional climax rather than constant pursuit of mutual orgasm

Before we look more closely at the gifts of bonding behaviors, let's examine how the dopamine mechanism behind the orgasm cycle leaves us susceptible to excess.

MALE CONTINENCE

Beginning in the mid-nineteenth century, a series of American social pioneers spontaneously rediscovered the principle of making love without orgasm, and its power to make relationships happier. One might assume they were hypnotized by the sex-as-vice viewpoint of their era. However, the three whose insights we will consider in this Wisdom section and the next two were unambiguously sex-positive. Their frank discussions of orgasm and masturbation rival those of today's sex therapists, even if their message challenges current thinking.

Around 1850, a spirited Yale Divinity School graduate named John Humphrey Noyes (1811–1886) happened upon the concept of sex without orgasm due to events in his own marriage. Ultimately, he violated the fundamental principle of his own discovery, made a fool of himself, and was relegated to the annals of comic historical figures. Yet his initial discovery was insightful, and his findings enabled later explorers to fill in essentials he had not taken into account.

Noyes made his discovery because he nobly determined to put the welfare of his wife before his own sexual desire. After watching her suffer through five pregnancies, only one of which resulted in a living child, he pledged never again to cause her such torment and vowed to abstain. Yet he missed the intimacy of intercourse and, being a scientifically minded fellow, it dawned on him that sex served two independent functions, which he called the "amative" (spiritual, loving) and the "procreative." He experimented with making love calmly, without the "propagative crisis," and found:

> ... the self control which it requires is not difficult; also that my enjoyment was increased; also that my wife's experience was very satisfactory, as it had never been before; also that we had escaped the horrors and the fear of involuntary propagation. This was a great deliverance. It made a happy household. I communicated my

discovery to a friend. His experience and that of his household were the same.[157]

Two years later, Noyes and others founded what grew into a communal organization of 300 people. They ultimately lived together in an elegant mansion in upstate New York, supporting themselves by farming and making traps. Members practiced "male continence," as Noyes christened his discovery. Inspired by Noyes's unique conception of Christianity, they ultimately viewed marriage as idolatrous and developed "complex marriage," an arrangement by which all adult men were married to all adult women.

Lovers scheduled time alone by mutual consent in rooms set aside for that purpose. Young men perfected their continence skills with post-menopausal women. As funds were tight at the outset, the community used male continence as a very successful form of birth control for many years. (Don't try this at home!) At last the prospering community changed its policy and determined to meet the internal demand for more children. Due to his scientific bent, Noyes tried to plan for superior offspring. That's when all hell broke loose.

Like any alpha male, Noyes concluded that his sperm were some of the finest to be had. He also wished to disprove the earlier predictions of medical men that male continence would imperil reproductive health—an objective he definitely achieved. Predictably, however, engaging in orgasmic sex distorted his thinking without his awareness. He continued to select himself as sire despite his advanced age, and it seems that a lot of young virgins were on his scientifically prepared list of ideal potential mothers. Noyes eventually departed, and the community collapsed.

In 1872, before things disintegrated, Noyes published his pamphlet *Male Continence*, in which he defended the principle of sex without ejaculation with great flair, highlighting its power to "bring about a true union of the sexes." Here are some passages:

> The objection urged to this method is that it is unnatural, and unauthorized by the example of other animals. I may answer that cooking, wearing clothes, living in houses, and almost everything else done by civilized man, is unnatural in the same sense, and that a

close adherence to the example of the brutes would require us to forego speech and go on all fours!...

In the normal condition, men are entirely competent to choose in sexual intercourse whether they will stop at any point in the voluntary stages of it, and so make it simply an act of communion, or go through to the involuntary stage, and make it an act of propagation.

The situation may be compared to a stream in the three conditions of a fall, a course of rapids above the fall, and still water above the rapids. The skillful boatman may choose whether he will remain in the still water, or venture more or less down the rapids, or run his boat over the fall. But there is a point on the verge of the fall where he has no control over his course; and just above that there is a point where he will have to struggle with the current in a way which will give his nerves a severe trial, even though he may escape the fall. If he is willing to learn, experience will teach him the wisdom of confining his excursions to the region of easy rowing, unless he has an object in view that is worth the cost of going over the falls....

It is seriously believed by many that nature requires a periodical and somewhat frequent discharge of the seed, and that the retention of it is liable to be injurious. Even if this were true, it would be no argument against Male Continence, but rather an argument in favor of masturbation; for it is obvious that before marriage men have no lawful method of discharge but masturbation; and after marriage it is as foolish and cruel to expend one's seed on a wife merely for the sake of getting rid of it, as it would be to fire a gun at one's best friend merely for the sake of unloading it.... But it is not true that the seed is an excrement like the urine, that requires periodical and frequent discharge. Nature has provided other ways of disposing of it. In fact it ... is in its best function while retained.... The community has had no trouble from retention of seed; but on the other hand, has nearly exterminated masturbation by the reflex influence of Male Continence....

Another apprehension suggested by medical men has been, that the avoidance of the crisis in sexual intercourse would so increase and prolong the excitement as to induce excesses, which would lead to various nervous diseases.... [T]he general experience of the community has not confirmed it ... [and] it was shown by careful comparison of our statistics with those of the U.S. census and other public documents, that the rate of nervous disorders in the community is considerably below the average in ordinary society.

Noyes admitted that there had been a couple of cases of nervous disorder in the community, which he attributed to misuse of male continence. As he pointed out, over-excitement can be as much a problem for women as for men. Significantly, perhaps, the women of the community were not enjoined to avoid orgasm. By the time he wrote *Male Continence,* it is possible he was rethinking this very issue.

To cultivate self-control in respect to the seminal crisis, but neglect it in other sexual indulgences, is evidently Male Continence in a spurious and dangerous form.

CHAPTER SIX

THE ROAD TO EXCESS

Our environment has dramatically changed, but our reward circuitry and mammalian brain have lagged behind. The capacity to binge on food and sex evolved when sugary foods and sexual opportunities were scarce.

Now we face an array of superstimuli, which tamper with our reward circuitry, leading to withdrawal symptoms, cravings for more stimulation, and, sometimes, more permanent brain changes.

Low dopamine is behind withdrawal symptoms, but it spikes when we see a cue we associate with relief. Intense cravings, and often compulsions, can result. They make the return to equilibrium very challenging.

We have lost many of the rewards of close companionship that our ancestors enjoyed, which makes us more susceptible to overindulging, addictions, and compulsions.

I n the last chapter we looked at the normal, often subtle, two-week passion cycle, which follows masturbation or intercourse. Now we shift from those ordinary highs and lows to the sexual equivalent of a supersize roller coaster—with mind-buzzing heights and unnerving drops. Extreme erotic stimulation carries a special risk: compulsion. Once we begin whizzing around on a monster coaster, we may need longer than two weeks to restore equilibrium.

The difference between sexual roller coasters is entirely subjective. One person may find glimpses of something forbidden more exciting than someone else finds a threesome. What matters is how intensely something gets *you* going, whether it's fine footwear, viewing erotic combos you hadn't realized were humanly possible, or sex with prostitutes. The only constant is the dopamine soaring, and plummeting, in the mammalian brain.

YESTERDAY'S GENES

As we have seen, mammals are programmed to mate like mad as dopamine surges—and then, when it drops, go about other activities until their libido recovers naturally. However, males are equipped to override this natural cycle automatically under a single set of circumstances: exposure to a novel mate.[158] Dangle a receptive female before a sexually satiated male rat, and he will valiantly rise to the occasion. (Female mammals also appear to perk up around new sperm donors.) This is the Coolidge effect, but you may want to think of it as "the Sooty effect":

Romeo Guinea Pig Causes Baby Boom:
A guinea pig called Sooty enjoyed a night of passion with twenty-four females after fooling his way into their cage in south Wales. Sooty wooed the lady guinea pigs, one by one, and has now become the proud father of forty-two baby guinea pigs.... "He was absolutely shattered. We put him back in his cage and he slept for two days."[159]

Think some vestige of this program is still encoded in *human* brains? What about polyamorous hunter-gatherer men and women, sultans with harems, porn users in search of the next novel image, and today's revolving-door marriages?

Where is this program pushing us these days? Not only where our genes want us to go—exploitation of the occasional chance to fertilize multiple mates—but often beyond, into empty compulsion. And all because times have changed.

The mammalian brain is designed to capitalize on short-term opportunities. This is why we have the dubious ability to gorge when presented with high-calorie food—and store it as spare tires and thunder thighs. In the days before refrigerators and reliable food supplies, it made sense to binge and convert surplus food to a bit of extra fat for easy transport.

Similarly, if, like Sooty, you find yourself in a cloister of lonely hearts, you could (theoretically, of course) amaze yourself with your prowess. Or, if female, your ability to gather competing sperm. Think mating season.

Speaking of getting it while you can, both the fat-storage and sexual satiation-override programs evolved when high-calorie food and novel potential mates were Big Events, not daily occurrences. Our ancestors' reward circuits lit up brightly and our genetic programs are the result. One reason that intense "go for it!" signals once worked in humanity's favor in the case of high-calorie food and sexual opportunity is that our stark environments *also* regulated us.

Chantek is a smart, lovable orangutan who lives at the Atlanta zoo. Trained in sign language, he has a vocabulary of more than 150 words, and he is considered a decent artist....

Growing up in this human setting, Chantek became REALLY FAT, weighing in at five hundred pounds, roughly three times his ideal size. Afraid that the massive bulk would collapse his lungs, scientists placed him on a strict diet. Formerly five hundred pounds of fun, he became four hundred pounds of anger. During the diet, his favorite sign language symbol became "candy." He refused to draw and instead ate the crayons given for his artistic use.

While on his diet, Chantek even pulled off an escape.... He was eventually found sitting next to the up-ended food barrel, using all four limbs to stuff monkey chow into his mouth.

Chantek is unique, not only for his human contact and his linguistic and artistic abilities but also for his weight. You see, there are no fat orangutans outside zoos and research centers. Wild orangutans, despite sharing Chantek's genetic zest for a fine meal, maintain a svelte 160 pounds or so because food is relatively scarce and difficult to obtain in the jungles of Borneo.[160]

As Terry Burnham and Jay Phelan explain in *Mean Genes: From Sex to Money to Food, Taming Our Primal Instincts,* our environment has changed, leaving our reward circuitry very vulnerable. Like Chantek, we are *molded to meet conditions that prevailed during our brain's millions of years of development.* Honey and ripe fruit were rare sources of concentrated sugar, and cave girls were no doubt cute, but their erotically posed images weren't airbrushed to perfection and projected over every visible surface. There was less opportunity for hooking up with exciting new mates you barely knew. No singles bars, no tantra weekends, and no schools with hundreds of cute strangers of the opposite sex.

Here's the danger in our modern circumstances: When a mammal's brain hasn't adapted to the intensity and quantity of a stimulus, that stimulus registers as a *superstimulus.* The examples at the end of the preceding paragraph can be superstimuli for our hunter-gatherer brains. Internet porn is an *extreme* superstimulus. It's on tap twenty-four/seven, free of social constraints, always novel, and ever kinkier.

Exposure to supranormal, i.e., above-normal, stimulation evokes *especially powerful "This is great; pay attention!" signals* in the brain, thanks to surging dopamine. Next, brain changes urge us to override our satiety mechanisms, so, like Sooty the guinea pig, we don't miss an apparent golden opportunity. Alas, a potent "Focus on this!" command doesn't guarantee that the activity or substance is actually worthy of our exaggerated attention (and our consequent *inattention* to other things or people in our life).

MEMORIES THAT PACK A PUNCH

Intensely stimulating activities and substances are easy to sell. That's why they're big business. They give our reward circuitry a buzz, and we easily say "yes!" to them without using our rational brain to weigh their long-term value to us (if any). Our brains are actually more tuned for *wanting* than *liking.* Researcher Kent Berridge summed it up this way: "We all are inherently susceptible to wanting more than we'll actually enjoy, at least in certain situations."[161] Dopamine is the "wanting," or craving. It's why we can still eat dessert when we're full, and fantasize about another partner when we're happily married.

Opportunity may knock only once, but temptation leans on the doorbell.
—Anonymous

Our brain is also designed to remember—and react to—everything *associated with* intense stimulation. Scientists call these associated things *cues.* Do you think Sooty, the Romeo guinea pig, will ever forget the location of the ladies' cage, how he broke into it, or their welcoming squeals of delight? Do you think his genes *want* him ever to forget any of the cues related to a bonanza like that? Certainly not. He stores this type of information by linking it to surges of dopamine in his reward circuitry. When next mating season rolls around, Sooty will find that every cue related to his Big Night is burned into his brain.

The mammalian brain reacts powerfully to cues associated with past rewards. This is how squirrels remember where their acorns are buried, and how bears recall which streams have salmon runs. It's also how our nomadic forebears remembered where they found food and resources. Today, MacDonald's golden arches are a cue for the reward of a quick, flavorsome snack—and the image of a naked stranger in heels is a cue for the excitement of sex with a novel partner.

Of course, we don't always react by dropping what we're doing to pursue such things. Yet we are sometimes *very* susceptible to cues, even when we know something is not in our best interests. Why? Here's a clue: Even if an alcoholic can't find her car keys or checkbook, she always remembers where she hid her bottle.

"WHERE'S MY TRIBE?"

The more intense the stimulation, the greater the subsequent discomfort. Most of us learn this fairly early by drinking too much alcohol. So why do we keep reaching for empty temptations that leave hangovers? Usually because we aren't getting enough of the other rewards our brain finds gratifying. Let's look at what we're missing.

While we can't know exactly what our hunter-gatherer ancestors' daily lives looked like, we have some idea based on anthropologists' accounts. Typically, we would have spent our lives among one, or two, relatively small groups of people whom we knew well. Although courtship and sex would have been two of life's most intense pleasures, we would also have enjoyed other rewarding activities: the thrill and satisfaction of a successful hunt, eating simple foods with no refined sugar, interacting with others through ceremonies and daily tasks, and, of course, bonding with our parents, offspring, and extended family. As children we would have received on-the-job training (and teasing) from our friends and relatives.

There was also probably a good bit of leisure time. For example, Africa's Bushmen hunt and gather for only a few hours a day. They spend the rest of their time hanging out socializing.[162] As we will see in later chapters, social interaction with those we trust is one of the best forms of health insurance.

Contrast that lifestyle—the one for which our brain is well equipped—with today's. At every turn we are confronted with intense stimulation. There are millions of diverse Web sites, thousands of stores, and hundreds of TV channels clamoring for our attention. We're constantly tempted with empty-calorie, high-sugar snacks, risk-taking opportunities, high-action video games, sexually stimulating images, and, often, opportunities to hook up for orgasms without emotional ties. All promise exciting dopamine surges, which means that many of us suffer withdrawal symptoms, mild or severe, a lot of the time.

Is it any wonder that porn use is growing exponentially? Or that obesity in the U.S. has increased to the point that, for the first time, our life span is predicted to be shorter than that of our parents?

Sexual stimulation for its own sake sounds good, and the urge to grab it when it's offered is certainly natural. But one reason it's *so* enticing these days is that many of life's *other* rewarding pleasures are hard to come by. Those age-old rewards of playing, working, learning, and facing challenges with lifelong companions are both comforting and healthful.

Food has replaced sex in my life. Now I can't even get into my own pants.

In contrast, today's parents often have little time for social rewards. Mothers return to work soon after a child arrives. Many do not live near extended families, so kids are separated from their clans and placed in daycare, then school, with strangers. There they face the stress of sitting all day, testing, worrying about grades, bullies, cliques, social rejection, and even violence—all without their natural companions or lifestyle. For example, recent research suggests that ADHD is not a pathological condition—for a hunter-gatherer. He *needs* to be impulsive, energetic, and easily bored.[163]

As adults we're glued to computers in cubicles or factory slots, and seldom have the satisfaction of working face-to-face to meet common challenges. Ceremonies may be few, and there is often little time for chewing the fat with friends or helping each other with life's trials. Tasks that would once have registered as enjoyable, such as preparing our children for adulthood, now register as exhausting. At the same time, our inherent tendency to find novel mates compelling is resurging—due to greater opportunity and, often, shorter, less comforting relationships.

How well suited are we to this lifestyle of lots of stress countered by so little reliable affectionate interaction? Our mammalian brain is designed to seek what is pleasurable and avoid what is (harmfully) stressful. What pleasures can it find today? Not many of the once familiar, life-enhancing, comforting connections with others. Instead, we often believe we have to seek pleasure among the more selfish, often solitary, thrills of high-calorie snacks, shopping, pursuit of orgasm, and chances to win money. Also, companionship must be cultivated, while many solitary indulgences seem to offer easy pleasure—until we overdo them, and want off of the roller coaster.

Q: How did Pinocchio discover he was made of wood?

A: His hand caught fire.

No wonder many of us grab for available pleasures with such determination. But there is a hidden risk. Research suggests that the absence of friendly interaction makes us *more susceptible* to addiction.[164] In this chapter, we'll look at this phenomenon from various angles.

THE AGONY OF EXCESS

Imagine a "stimulation gauge" that looks something like a tachometer (the instrument in your car that registers revolutions per minute, or RPMs). After dopamine surges into the "red zone" during intense stimulation, receptors for it drop even lower than normal. Dopamine sensitivity can then fluctuate for a while during the return to homeostasis—as your tachometer does when you shift through the gears.

Every deep dip can leave you aching for relief—and ready to pounce on any promising activity or substance. When is your mouth most likely to water in response to the smell of something appetizing? After a big meal? No, your gauge won't budge. If someone offers you more, you're likely to say to yourself, "no way!" But what about when you work late, skip dinner, and smell a grilling burger? Your body lets you know (with surges of dopamine) that you need to make eating a *top priority*.[165]

The more uncomfortable you are, the more urgently your mammalian brain scans for something to relieve your misery. When it lights on a cue it associates with relief, it sends your dopamine needle into the red zone of your inner gauge. You experience an intense craving. A candy bar may look so vital to your reward circuitry that your rational brain will temporarily ignore your expanding waistline. This mechanism worked fine for your distant ancestors. All their options for relief were reasonably healthy ones, and their frugal environments made bingeing a rare occurrence.

In contrast, our lifestyle doesn't protect us from overindulgence. Too much stimulation, followed by frequent lows, means we are riddled with unusually intense cravings for relief. Superstimuli keep us *out of balance,* making us better consumers, but less satisfied overall. Our recurring, urgent sense of lack heavily influences the choices we make—without our conscious awareness.

SACCHARIN AND THE SHAKES

Consider the following experiment. Researchers withheld food from rats for twelve hours and then gave them nutritionally balanced food, plus a heavy dose of sugar (glucose) water. This created a cycle of bingeing. When researchers cut off the sugar water after only ten days, the rats showed signs common to drug withdrawal, such as anxiety, chattering teeth, and tremors, as well as craving and relapse (evidence of long-lasting effects in their brains)[166]

Scientists then measured the rats' dopamine levels. They found that the levels were "qualitatively similar to withdrawal from morphine or nicotine," which suggests that the rats were indeed addicted to sugar.[167]

What does this tell us? That we are really mean to little white rats. But it also tells us that mammals can become addicted, and suffer withdrawal (hangovers), from *natural* substances and experiences—if they indulge in a way that throws their dopamine levels out of kilter. Unlike alcohol or nicotine, glucose (sugar) is not a drug. The body automatically keeps blood glucose within rather narrow ranges no matter how much sugar you eat, or don't eat. In other words, a "sugar high" (and low) comes from activation of your reward circuitry when you taste (or later crave) something intensely sweet. It doesn't come directly from the sugar itself going into your blood and acting on your brain.

Glucose itself can't create a long-tailed glucose junkie; dopamine highs and lows can. Intense stimulation (sweetness) is the key factor. We know this because scientists repeated the same experiment using the artificial sweetener saccharin, and guess what? They ended up with rat saccharin addicts (yuck).[168] It is the superstimulation of *excess* that sets up the potential for addiction by dysregulating the reward circuitry. In the case of saccharin, a fake substance with no nutritional value, the intake of which does not increase our chances of survival, fools the reward circuitry—leading to addiction and withdrawal misery. Obviously the mammalian brain associates sweet with "ripe." It never had to contend with saccharin. Eventually the body figures out that saccharin isn't as satisfying as sugar, which is why you may reach for even *more* food than usual if you use artificial sweeteners.[169] But the cycle that can lead to withdrawal symptoms is triggered by sweetness, not sugar.

Let's see. How else can our reward circuitry become highly activated by a natural reinforcer without any payoff for us or our genes?

A new study found that male monkeys will give up their juice rewards in order to ogle pictures of female monkeys' bottoms. The way the experiment was set up, the act is akin to paying for the images, the researchers say.[170]

Pornography!* And which is strongest: the urge to eat ripe fruit, or the urge to fertilize a novel mate? Blast your built-in sexual eagerness with images, videos, and activities that *you* find intensely arousing, and you can slip into a sexual binge. Porn is as empty as saccharin, in that there's no real value, no one to impregnate, and no rewarding, comforting interaction with another human being.

After your dopamine shoots up in response to a superstimulus, key dopamine receptors drop. Frequent orgasm (even without porn) can *also* lead to a numbed pleasure response, because you aren't waiting out the recovery period of the passion

A lot of addiction is the result of experience ... repetitive, high-emotion, high-frequency experience.
—Howard Shaffer, psychologist

---

*Much of this chapter applies to any habit of seeking intense sexual stimulation detached from the balancing properties of trusted companionship.

cycle. (Remember how fried Sooty was after his night of passion?) Withdrawal symptoms, such as restlessness, irritability, frustration, desire for isolation, and apathy are signals your full vigor hasn't yet returned.

So why the massive libido? During recovery, you're very susceptible to cues that promise rapid relief from your discomfort. When you spot one, your reward circuitry starts yapping and bouncing around like a crazed Jack Russell terrier. It's hard to ignore, so you want to "feed it," just to shut it up. Yet if you climax now, you can easily remain in an accelerating passion-cycle orbit, medicating yourself with orgasm every time you get especially uncomfortable or see an exciting cue.

> *Within about ten minutes after orgasm I am cloudy-minded, light-headed, disoriented, and anxious, although the duration and intensity of the different symptoms has varied quite a bit over the years. Orgasm was not only the cause of these problems but also seemed like the CURE. I would have orgasm when feeling affected. Sometimes I would do it twice if the first one didn't work. But after awhile, I found I needed to do it more and more often to relieve the symptoms. Eventually I was up to five times a day. This was exhausting, and cutting back had strong withdrawal effects.—Dustin*

Strapped onto this roller coaster of peaks and drops, you may forget entirely what balance feels like. (And if circumstances caused you to start masturbating early enough, severe mood swings may be part of your self-image.) However things went out of kilter, you unfortunately have to go all the way through the passion cycle to experience balance again. There are no shortcuts, and if you're seriously hooked, you may need longer (more on that in a moment). When back in balance, you can contemplate sex without feeling horribly deprived ... or manic. However, like the rest of us, you will not be immune to the post-orgasm passion cycle in some lesser form.

> *When I was growing up Playboy was porn, but the "new thinking" about masturbation was very much in vogue. It made my escalating porn/masturbation addiction seem "normal" to me for years. I can't imagine the long-term effects on society brewing in the generations behind me. What if Internet porn had been available to me when I was*

fourteen? I shudder to think of the consequences of being exposed to such things when your sexuality is developing. Ugh. I, at least, formed healthy crushes during my teen years and experienced romance. I don't think I would have had those experiences if I had had easy access to Internet porn. It's a few months since I quit masturbating, and I am just getting back in touch with those romantic feelings I had as a young man. But what if I had never had them to begin with? That is what makes me feel bad for younger people facing this problem.—Glen

PORN'S SURPRISING LESSON

Mere orgasm can set off a cycle of discomfort, so it shouldn't be a surprise that bingeing on porn, a limitless supranormal stimulus, can create intense withdrawal symptoms. Yet I learned this by accident. I was all for freedom of speech, and a staunch member of the "to each his own taste" club. However, I had created a Web site that discusses the highs and lows of sexual satiety in terms of the highs and lows of the typical addiction cycle and the parallel wisdom found in historical texts.

To my surprise (and theirs, I'm sure), men from all over the world showed up in *my* Web site's forum complaining of addiction to porn/masturbation, and seeking to regain their free will. They were stuck on a dopamine elevator going between penthouse and basement, without ever being able to explore the floors in between. It seemed that information about how orgasm can become compulsive was so scarce that even a site grounded in ancient wisdom about managing sex was filling a void. (Gee thanks, Google!)

At first it was painful reading their stories. These guys were constantly overheated—due to the many virtual mates that their mammalian brains perceived as genetic opportunities. Unlike Sooty, however, they could *never* rest. Their fertilization duties were never done. There was always another enticing image just a click away, and their mammalian brains were determined to leave no picture unfertilized. Their issue wasn't shame; it was addiction. When they tried to unhook themselves, they faced intense withdrawal symptoms that fluctuated in intensity for weeks:

First guy: Today the whole day I have been shaking with jitters similar to how it felt when I quit smoking. My body has been jolted with what felt like unusually intense energy, especially in my spine. I feel tense and stiff for a while and then as if my spinal bones are being popped and a big relief and then tension and then relief. It just came out of the blue and has been subsiding.

Second guy: Here are the withdrawal symptoms I have experienced: intense bouts of anger leading to interpersonal difficulties, aggressive demeanor, easily stressed out (I'm inexperienced confronting the real world without that soup of post-orgasmic chemicals sedating me), suicidal ideation, severe depression, violent dreams while sleeping (I actually enjoyed these, however others might consider them nightmares), insomnia, hallucinations (jumped out of bed screaming because I felt a "presence"), felt like insects were crawling all over me when going to bed, shakes, mania (energy far in excess of my ability to use it constructively), and inability to concentrate.

Third guy: *Bored?* Masturbation. *Angry?* Masturbation. *Sad?* Masturbation. *Stressed?* Masturbation. I went from being the first of my class to the very bottom, until I dropped out for good. I ended up working on the Web, making good money and having my porn one click away. This was my life, and I didn't recognize I had an addiction until I had surgery and masturbation was out of the question for fifteen days. On day three, I was literally shaking, and I began to connect the dots. My other symptoms are: irritability, inability to focus ("staring at walls syndrome"), mood swings, headaches (sometimes quite strong), sense of pressure in my genitals, pictures of movies/starlets popping out in my mind, paranoia, self-defeating thinking, depression, sense of hopelessness ("I lost so many years of my life". One example: I painstakingly created 250 DVDs with twenty to thirty porn scenes each, meticulously cataloged ... and now destroyed.), and fear that I will never be able to have sex because I have not learned any social skills since I delved into porn eight years ago as a teen.

My husband, Will, and I thought we were the only ones making the connection between experiences like these and the addiction cycle of high-low dopamine. Then we found the words of Princeton's longtime reward-circuitry researcher, the late Bartley Hoebel:

> Highly potent sexual stimuli [and junk food] are the only stimuli capable of activating the dopamine system with anywhere near the potency of addictive drugs.[171]

"TOO MUCH OF A GOOD THING … IS EVEN BETTER!"

So said the witty Ms. Mae West. However, too much intense stimulation of the reward circuitry is not better. It's worse. As we've seen, the risk isn't hairy palms or going blind. It's ending up on a high-speed treadmill, trying to stay ahead of withdrawal symptoms. Incidentally, too much ejaculation also has physical repercussions beyond changes in the reward circuitry. When men engaged in a "ten-day depletion experience," ejaculating an average of 2.4 times per day, their sperm output remained below pre-depletion levels for more than five months.[172] What other subtle changes might accompany this measurable one—especially in the brain, where the experience of orgasm occurs, and where the controls for testosterone and sperm production lie?

One unwelcome side effect of frequent supranormal stimulation is that normal pleasures—the kinds of simple things that would have delighted our ancestors—gradually lose their capacity to delight us. As biologist Robert Sapolsky remarked:

> Unnaturally strong explosions of synthetic experience and sensation and pleasure evoke unnaturally strong degrees of habituation. This has two consequences. As the first, soon we hardly notice anymore the fleeting whispers of pleasure caused by leaves in autumn, or by the lingering glance of the right person, or by the promise of reward that will come after a long, difficult, and worthy task. The other consequence is that, after awhile, we even habituate to those artificial deluges of intensity.... Our tragedy is that we just become

hungrier. More and faster and stronger. "Now" isn't as good as it used to be, and won't suffice tomorrow.[173]

Recovering cocaine addicts report that they do not feel pleasure in anything for a while after they stop using.[174] Their pleasure response is numbed. Porn addicts report similar experiences:

> Porn was easy excitement. I didn't interact with others because it took too much work, I had to think too hard, and interaction was "boring." I was numb and my senses were dulled. And I feared they would continue to be that way even after I quit using porn.
>
> I'm dating a woman now for the first time since quitting (months ago). It's amazing! I am finding her so attractive, just as she is. She's in her thirties, has two kids, and an average body. She's not supple and "perky" like the girls in the videos, but I'm more attracted to her real body than I ever was to porn. I never imagined that would happen, and it is so exciting. I had to stop orgasming, and keep off of porn for an extended period of time. That got easier. Eventually I looked around and realized that the colors were back in my life!

Porn users also complain that sex with a partner just doesn't seem as exciting as it once did (perhaps accounting in part for the rise of sexual enhancement aids). What is going on? The situation can be compared to that of heavy cocaine users who, when responding to sexual stimulation, show measurably less brain activation than control subjects.[175]

Even though we're designed to find relationships rewarding, their subtler, healthier rewards don't generate the supranormal stimulation of an afternoon of vivid erotic imagery—especially not after we have dulled our senses. Pursuit of supranormal stimulation can change perception. A recent study showed that mere exposure to images of sexy females could cause a man to devalue his real-life partner. He rated her lower not only on attractiveness, but also on warmth and intelligence.[176] Other experiments show that porn causes men to devalue marital fidelity and makes them more likely to believe that women like rough sex.[177] These shifts set off a downward spiral, making partners less likely to engage in the generous affection that actually bonds them and lets them enjoy each other.

CROSS-TOLERANCES

Another risk of supranormal stimulation is what scientists call *cross-tolerance*. That is, one kind of intense stimulation (or its aftermath) can make someone more likely to reach for *other* potent stimuli, such as recreational drugs, alcohol, gambling, junk food, or reckless shopping. Stimulation primes the pump, or in this case, the reward circuitry. Potent sexual stimulation, gambling, and cocaine can all offer an addict short-term relief, because they activate dopamine production.

> *I feel like this addictive impulse has mass, like a balloon, and when I squeeze it in one place by cutting back on porn, it grows larger elsewhere, as in drinking or using drugs.—Matt*

Since one addiction lowers the threshold for developing another, sex addicts are more likely to have problems with other addictive behaviors (alcohol, gambling, and so forth).[178] Interestingly, teens who are sexually active also use more recreational drugs than those who are not.[179] One might argue that teens make these choices due to personality, parenting, or other factors—and they may. However, researchers also found that *hamsters* that have previously mated are more likely to use amphetamines than are virgin hamsters. Something about sexual activity made the little critters more likely to dabble in drugs, without any peer pressure or lousy parenting.[180] Sexual experience, like repeated drug use, produced long-term changes in their brains,[181] and sensitized dopamine pathways.[182] In fact, the more sexual encounters they had, the more their dopamine rose during sex.[183]

Sugar, by the way, can also affect the brain this way, producing cross-tolerance with drugs of abuse.[184] Feed rats oodles of sweets for weeks and they become more sensitive to other psychostimulants, such as alcohol, amphetamine, or morphine, than rats on a normal rat diet. Changes in dopamine (and opioid) receptors are thought to be the culprit. Similar changes are seen in the brains of rats on cocaine and heroin.[185]

Our work provides links between the traditionally defined substance-use disorders, such as drug addiction, and the development of abnormal desires for natural [stimuli].
—Bart Hoebel, neuroscientist

Whatever the precise mechanism, an excessive reward stimulus primes your brain for a second experience or substance. Your reward circuitry is on that escalating neurochemical roller coaster, seeking satisfaction, but too shortsighted to realize that more stimulation will soon leave you profoundly *unsatisfied*. In contrast, affectionate social interaction, which *also* activates the reward circuitry—meaning it, too, feels good—does just the opposite. It is soothing enough to help *protect* you from the urge to reach for another stimulating fix. Friendly social interaction therefore leads to greater satisfaction. We'll look at how it does this in later chapters.

Unfortunately, as we saw in Chapter Five, low dopamine is associated with social anxiety. Thus frequent masturbation can keep you from pursuing your healthy longings for the good feelings of socializing. Orgasm's greater intensity seems more valuable to your mammalian brain, because it responds so unerringly to supranormal stimulation.

> *The interesting part is the* mind-shift *that is taking place since I cut back on masturbation. I've gone three to four weeks now. I feel I'm working with a "new neurochemistry," in which I interact with other people on a whole new level, because I NEED to. I absolutely NEED to. Exercise, low-key healthy diet (no hormone-polluted beef, etc.), and meditation helped ease the transition, but the "cure" is human contact, showing love and receiving it back. I admit that during the recovery period, I sometimes felt like, "Okay, now I have to ejaculate, or semen will either pour out of my ears, or I'll go crazy." But somehow I resisted, and the craziness and depression of the first couple of weeks have changed to a calm, serene state of mind. The urge has dissipated, and my satisfaction from interacting with people is much greater.—Max*

Could achieving balance in our sex lives be especially helpful in soothing all cravings? Was Freud right that masturbation addiction is close to the heart of all addictions?[186]

THE PLASTIC BRAIN

In a moment we'll consider the experience of the men who left their compulsive porn use behind in more detail, but first let's look at why it is so challenging to change directions.

Your brain is not a machine or a computer. It's as malleable as clay, not only when you're young, but also long after your hair turns gray. You constantly construct new brain circuits. This is both bad news and good news. It's bad news because you can reinforce unhealthy behaviors until they become bad habits, or even compulsions. It's good news because you can leave those habits behind and consciously steer for behaviors you want. In fact, each memory, experience, and insight leads to a corresponding change in the structure and functioning of your brain.

As you will recall, a neural pathway, or circuit, consists of a group of interconnected nerve cells. Some pathways are hardwired, such as the reward circuit and reflexes. Place honey on a human tongue and the reward circuit lights up. Shine a beam of light into an eye and the pupil is bound to constrict. These pathways are pretty much the same in all of us.

We form other pathways from scratch as we learn and create memories. Climb on a bike for the first time and the nerve cells throughout the brain that control movement and balance come alive with electrical impulses. They spurt neurochemicals into the synapses with the message "Let's form a strong pathway!" Relevant nerve cells sprout branches, which reach out to each other and create efficient communication at their synapses. The more you work at balancing on two wheels, the stronger the connections between the intertwining vines of nerve cells. Years later you can jump on a bike, activate that circuit, and zip down the road without thinking. As the saying goes, "Nerve cells that fire together wire together."

Learning and memory are pathways of connected nerve cells—whether they consist of a few connected nerve cells, or millions. When enough neurochemicals are released into the synapses between cells, communication between nerve cells can become a scream: "Tighten up these connections. We have to remember this. It's important!"

Some learning does not involve repetition. A circuit will form instantly if an event has a lot of significance or emotional impact. If a child burns

The same surge of dopamine that thrills us also consolidates the neuronal connections responsible for the behaviors.... [Internet porn users get] massive amounts of practice wiring these images into the pleasure centers of the brain, with the rapt attention necessary for plastic change.
—Norman Doidge, *The Brain that Changes Itself*

her hand on a hot stove, the synapses are so overwhelmed that the event is etched into her brain. As the saying goes, once is enough. Other examples might be a birth, a car accident, or sexual abuse.

Habits are at first cobwebs, then cables.
—Spanish proverb

For our purposes, however, we can imagine circuits in the brain as footpaths. If you decide to take a shortcut to the movie theater through a field of tall grass, you may find it heavy going at first. Yet if you keep trampling down the grass, you need less and less effort. Eventually the path is just dirt, or maybe even a rut (if you're watching too many movies). These pathways are the memories, skills, and habits we cultivate.

IN A RUT

The significance of the brain's plasticity is that consciously or unconsciously, we are always learning behaviors that strengthen neural connections and mold our brain. It matters where we seek our stimulation in the present, because those things automatically direct our *future* attention.

Learning is great when we use it constructively to master a skill we want to have such as playing an instrument or learning a language. However, we can use the same process to lay down damaging pathways, such as chewing our fingernails when nervous, cutting ourselves when anxious (it releases endorphins, an opiate-like substance), or smoking a cigarette after every meal.

Pathways can lead to other pathways. For example, if I'm walking with a friend and we meet a panting Doberman, I may freeze with my heart racing and turn pale, while she runs up to the dog and pats it. My "Doberman pathway" leads to my innate *fight-or-flight* pathway because I once had a bad experience with a Doberman. In contrast, her childhood pet was a Doberman, so her "Doberman pathway" leads to her *reward* circuitry. Our individual neural "ruts" can thus trip the switches of our fundamental drives.

The mammalian brain's job is to seek what is pleasurable and link it with a reward response, and avoid what is potentially harmful by linking it with a defensive response. It is always asking the basic question, "Is this agreeable or disagreeable?" The rational brain helps to shape the answers to that question by analyzing our circumstances. Trolling the shopping mall might not connect with my husband's reward circuitry at all (except for the lingerie store display). Yet for some shoppers, even the thought of a trip to the mall activates a string of neurons firing right into the reward circuitry.

In essence, addiction is merely learning. (So is recovery!) The phenomenon of addiction is complex, but dopamine and the reward circuit are central to understanding it. Some things, such as cocaine, methamphetamine, or an electrode, act directly on nerve cells in the reward circuit. Other experiences and behaviors activate circuits that have formed strong connections to (and light up) the reward circuit. Each "stream" flows into its specific river. Heavily reinforced pathways—and the sensory cues that turn them on, such as hearing slot machines for gamblers or spotting a suggestive image for porn addicts—flip on intense desire via the reward circuit.

As we have seen, overstimulation can set off a lingering, or recurring, drop in dopamine , a decline in receptors, or both. The addict's reward circuitry is stuck idling when it needs to be in gear for him (or her) to feel normal. Very little electricity is flowing along this critical circuit.

How did the addict get to this point? His brain initially registered a behavior as intensely rewarding and created pathways to remember the actions leading to it. The more enticing or exciting (extreme or shocking) his destination, the bigger the brain's motivation to get out the weedwhacker and mow a path, and then wear down a rut, so he visited as often as possible.

At some point, the addict's rut became the path of least resistance. His mammalian brain had learned that it led to an infusion of dopamine, but it couldn't factor in the ultimate cost of that short-term relief (withdrawal misery). Only his rational brain could do that, and he could hardly hear it over the "noise." Especially when tired, angry, bored, lonely, under stress, or suffering from withdrawal discomfort, his mammalian brain automatically shoved him back on the coaster.

Now, paths that once led to other rewarding aspects of his life—such as time with family and friends, playing ball, or even leisurely

Once the brain becomes less sensitive to dopamine, it "becomes less sensitive to natural reinforcers" such as the "pleasure of seeing a friend, watching a movie, or the curiosity that drives exploration."
—Nora Volkow, Director of the National Institute on Drug Abuse

foreplay—fell into disuse, because his inner compass had increasing difficulty resisting the ready relief of his addiction. Grass and weeds filled those other paths. The connections between relevant nerve cells weakened. *His priorities rearranged themselves without his conscious choice.*

Addiction results from persistent changes in brain structures and function. Both drugs and behaviors can create ruts. What matters is not *type of stimulus,* but rather *strength of pathway.* So gambling and porn use can be as addictive as abused substances if the pathways are strong enough.[187] In short, addiction is a brain disease that shows up as compulsive behavior.[188]

Again, once your "beast brain" registers something as valuable, it hijacks the rational part of your brain to rivet your attention on associated cues. When most of us walk down the street, we notice the people we pass, the dogs, or the red Corvette. When an alcoholic walks down the street, she notices the bar. If she hears familiar sounds (cues) as she nears it, the pathway to her reward circuitry lights up and she may think "Just one drink won't hurt." She is in a slightly altered, high-dopamine state, as heavily reinforced neural pathways fire up.

I don't need to look at pornographic images; they are all hardwired into my brain. Even though I haven't used porn for weeks, I still see vivid images when I close my eyes and it makes abstinence from masturbation very difficult. Still having wet dreams, too.—Victor

A minority of us are especially sensitive to the signals that encourage excess. Greater impulsivity, novelty-seeking, fewer dopamine receptors in different parts of the brain, and childhood stress are all associated with susceptibility to risky behavior and/or addiction.[189]

However, it looks like the vast majority of us can get hooked on superstimulating versions of natural reinforcers like food and sex. Two-thirds of Americans are now overweight. How many can't resist unlimited access to Internet porn? A nationwide 2014 poll revealed that twenty-three percent of adult men ages 18–30 believe they may be addicted to Internet porn. Another ten percent are unsure. (The corresponding percentages for women are six percent perhaps addicted and one percent unsure.)[190]

DECEPTIVE CUES

So it is that the more often you pursue supranormal stimulation, the harder it is to change course. After all, your brain is literally rewiring itself to focus more and more of your future attention on it.

The real danger of cues is not their power to grab your attention; it's their power to grab your *controls* with a spike of dopamine in your reward circuitry. High dopamine can put you in a sort of altered state of strong motivation—but impaired judgment. (More on that in a moment.) Cues are especially powerful when your brain is in the low part of the passion cycle. If you're feeling miserable, and you get wind of an apparent way to feel good again, your dopamine will flare even higher than it did during the stimulation that initially hooked you.[191] This makes sense. When you first flirted with your superstimulus, you were merely seeking pleasure, right? Now you're downright uncomfortable, too, and your brain seriously wants *relief.*

> Sensitization [change in the addict's brain] makes dopamine-related brain systems overreact to cues subsequently, and this can persist for years.
> —Kent Berridge, biopsychologist

If you now feel like engaging in a frenzy of orgasm, don't assume your underlying libido has actually increased. More likely, your mammalian brain is just screaming for "medication" (which will ease the short-term symptoms, but trigger another cycle). In short, your addiction is escalating. It may seem hard to believe, but you won't remember what balance feels like until you step off of the roller coaster for an extended period.

The low part of the passion cycle is the biggest barrier to both unhooking from compulsive orgasm and learning karezza. Confusing mood swings are common and each cue (spike in dopamine) will convince you that you are unbearably horny. It takes enormous will power to ignore these urgent messages, and wait for your body to return to equilibrium naturally.

> *Boiling loins. Battle is joined in earnest now. Constant "home movies" in my skull. The withdrawal is really intense. I am physically ill right now. I have averaged maybe four hours or less of sleep a night since beginning the process of kicking this habit.*—Gavin

Cues are the reason that addicts who are trying to change direction have to avoid anything that reminds them of their former habit. What happened to Pavlov's dogs when they heard that bell? They salivated—whether or not the food showed up. Cambridge University addiction neuroscientists have shown that porn addicts' brains respond to porn cues much as drug users' brains respond to drug cues.[191a] Anyone determined to overcome a porn/masturbation addiction, will make more progress by avoiding both orgasm *and* porn for a while. Each is a cue for the other. Would a recovering alcoholic find it easier to avoid alcohol by staring at open bottles or hanging out in bars? Talk about white knuckles and sweaty palms.

DOPAMINE AND DISTORTED PERCEPTION

Are You Hooked?

This test, known as the 'Three Cs,' highlights the signs, symptoms and behaviors that signal addiction:

1. **Craving** and preoccupation with obtaining, engaging in or recovering from the use of the substance or behavior;

2. Loss of **control** in using the substance or engaging in the behavior with increasing frequency or duration, larger amounts or intensity, or in increasing the risk in use and behavior to obtain the desired effect; and

3. Negative **consequences** in physical, social, occupational, financial and psychological domains.

A liaison with Monica Lewinsky no doubt seemed to Bill Clinton's mammalian brain like an excellent idea. His rational brain probably had an entirely different view—just like the rational brain of a retiree who, in an altered state of intense anticipation, feeds her scarce resources into a slot machine.

The dramatic power of dopamine to interfere with free will and create sexual (and other) compulsions became clear when patients took drugs that imitate dopamine. For example, a Frenchman who took such a drug to control Parkinson's symptoms recovered a large settlement from a pharmaceutical company after the medication temporarily gave him compulsive homosexual urges. (He was straight when not on the meds.)[192] Another Parkinson's patient suddenly found himself cross-dressing after seventy years of uneventful heterosexuality. When doctors decreased his dosage of the dopamine-like drug, the urge to put on his deceased wife's clothing evaporated.

The researchers hypothesized that excess, or sensitivity to, dopamine may be behind both paraphilias (fetishes) and hypersexuality (including an abrupt yen for anal sex).[193] Scientists also found that fruit flies will attempt to mate with other males if their dopamine levels are raised.[194] Yes, even the lowly fruit fly experiences startling behavioral changes when his dopamine is jacked up.

Maybe men like U.S. Senator Larry Craig, who insist that they aren't gay, yet engage in homosexual sex, are simply hooked on risky, high-dopamine encounters. (For the ultimate thrill, maybe Craig should try it while skydiving!) As one man explained, bathroom sex isn't really about gender orientation.

> The transgression and fear of being caught add an extra thrill to the experience ... and no one cares about your "orientation" in a lavatory—in there, it's all business.... Having a secret, perhaps double, life gives you a sense of importance, of life as drama, a sense you'll probably relish if you find yourself elected governor of New Jersey. Sex feels otherworldly, forbidden and scary, like you've gone so deep into the closet that you've arrived in Narnia.[195]

Although we may *choose* the behaviors that cause us to become hypersensitive to cues, once that happens, we're captive. When we experience sex as a superstimulus, we give our mammalian brains the power to override

Inordinate desire takes possession of the sensory forces of the body. It is habit forming.
—Edgar Cayce, healer

our free will, and set our priorities in ways that may even shock *us*. In New York City, HIV cases in gay men under thirty have jumped thirty-three percent since 2001.[196] The cause is widespread "barebacking"—sex without a condom. Their reward circuits have learned to value risky sex more highly than safety, at least while dopamine is flaring. Sadly, as we're about to see, many people—straight and gay—have had help in becoming highly sensitive to intensely stimulating erotic cues.

JACKING UP DOPAMINE

As we've seen, it's possible to jack up dopamine quite unwittingly—simply by pursuing superstimulation to the point where the cues for it begin to rule us (especially when we're feeling low). But a lot of us have *help* in training ourselves to become oversensitive to sexual cues. Such "help" comes in forms such as "laced" porn, teachings about the "sinfulness" of sexual stimuli, and sexual abuse as a youngster.

Guys like looking at girls, and I found it endearing when a male friend once said to me, "When I saw my first picture of a naked woman I thought, 'this is just wonderful!'" However, a lot of today's porn is different. Just as cigarette manufacturers sometimes add extra nicotine to their products to make them more addictive, so porn makers spike their products to increase their drug-like effects. They know what overstimulates the mammalian brain, and they steer right for the images that send dopamine flares skyrocketing. Today's porn doesn't just supply an instant harem; it supplies a harem trained to cause rapid sexual surfeit using the most shocking videos porn makers can conjure up.

This combination constitutes a stimulus that did not exist in a hunter-gatherer environment, which means we have not necessarily inherited the fortitude to resist it easily when exposed to it. And bingeing leaves us even more defenseless.

Not only does your mammalian brain increase dopamine when you come across something novel or erotic; it gives you a similar dopamine jolt for "shocking," "painful," and "risky." Domination themes also arouse the mammalian brain, perhaps because of their effects on testosterone (which raises dopamine). Such images excite the brain in a way that images of cuddly affection do not. This is why so many television shows and films revolve around sex and violence.[197] Such images put you in an altered state that makes you more susceptible (to advertising in the case of TV, or to compulsion in the case of porn). They induce cravings because they raise dopamine.

I'm twenty-five and started watching porn when I was eleven years old, masturbating up to five times daily. During all this time, I was easily aroused and always excited to have sex with women. Gradually, though, my porn tastes escalated to extreme fetishes. Sometimes I felt I was even forcing myself to watch it because I needed a new "kick" or "thrill" to my porn habit. I didn't really have any problem with these new tastes until I began losing sexual interest in real women. This has destroyed my confidence and sense of identity since I always thought I would marry a woman.—Bruce

In effect, porn sites don't just cater to colorful tastes; they, like advertisers, *create* them. They also exploit users' innate tendency to move from one novel image to the next in search of more stimulation for the brain. The brain produces more dopamine and stronger brain pathways in response to novelty.[198] (Think slot machine.)

There's a second way to make images register as more outrageous (that is, make the peaks of the roller coaster higher). Paradoxically, it is well intentioned. Religious authorities often attempt to protect their followers against reckless sexual behavior with the use of guilt, shame, or moralizing. Inadvertently, they are making the challenge *more* difficult for many.

You can tell someone you are an alcoholic or a drug addict, and people may feel sorry for you or want to help you—but if you admit publicly to a PORN addiction, the pitchforks come out. Somehow you must be a deviant, a perv, and maybe even a sex offender or child molester! It is easier to shun, than to comfort, a porn addict.

Add to that the fact that before people can fully recover, they have to admit their addiction, that they are powerless with regard to it, and "give it up" to a higher power to pull them through. This process is accompanied by great shame, disgust, and self-loathing. "How did this happen to me? I'm normal (?). I can handle this by myself! No one can find out. I need to stop this NOW! How gross am I? How pathetic am I that I can't just turn the computer off????" and on and on. It is just easier to give in.—Wilt

---

Few things can make sexual stimuli more risky and exciting (and more stirring at a neurochemical level) than a conviction that their use is "forbidden," "sinful," or will lead to eternal damnation. In fact, someone who is coached to believe that potent sexual stimuli are a path to the Fiery Furnace may find them even more dicey (and thrilling) than condomless anal sex. "Erotic + risky" increases both dopamine and adrenaline *(fear)*. Adrenaline is an especially powerful memory-enhancer (neural pathway creator). A dangerous, frightening event, in effect, burns the brain. This may be why philandering church leader Ted Haggard raised his dopamine with methamphetamine use *and* sex with a male prostitute—when he wasn't railing against homosexuality from the pulpit.

Folks who want to stay on the straight-and-narrow can do so a lot more easily if they understand how supranormal stimulation can pull their strings, and which activities do a better job of promoting lasting good feelings (more on those in the next two chapters). Meanwhile, if one chooses to step off of the roller coaster onto solid ground, it is more effective to view an unwelcome habit as a soon-to-fade brain pathway than as a "sin," and set about retraining the brain.

A third way to create hypersensitivity to sexual cues is through unusually intense sexual stimulation early in life. Young brains are especially plastic and eager to wire up sexual cues in order to enhance later reproductive success. By adulthood they have pruned back unused neural connections, making it more difficult to alter sexual proclivities. This is why adult-child sexual contact and widespread youthful use of extreme porn are both problematic.[199]

My older brother would look at our dad's porn magazines and then come into my room and lie on top of me. I was about five or six. When I eventually announced my homosexuality, he called me a "fag."
—Jerome

Unusually intense sexual stimulation may, of course, come about quite innocently (as by stumbling upon an adult porn cache, or receiving tuition from an older sibling who can't wait to demonstrate). However, eighty-one percent of sex addicts seeking treatment reported having been sexually abused.[200] It may be that, in addition to all the other damage child sexual abuse does, it can also sensitize victims to particular cues, such as risky, kinky, or forbidden sex. This brain training then shapes future choices in unsuspected ways, and makes the search for superstimulation more likely in the future.

Psychiatrist Wilhelm Reich spoke of witnessing the family's maid having intercourse with her boyfriend, and later asked if he could "play" the part of the lover. He said that, by the time he was four years old, there were no secrets about sex for him.
—Myron Sharaf, *Fury on Earth: A Biography of Wilhelm Reich*

Plain old vanilla masturbation or intercourse, which are normal and have only short-term repercussions, take on lives of their own with long-term consequences when supranormal stimulation enters the equation. However it comes about, a neural pathway that negates our free will, or even impairs our judgment, changes the picture. The revealing question is, "Does this activity or substance—the way I'm using it—absorb my attention in such a way that it is dictating my choices?"

REWARD CIRCUITRY OVERLOAD

Frenzied orgasm to the point of sexual exhaustion (followed by full recovery) is normal, in the sense that Sooty's once-in-a-lifetime escapade was normal, or gorging at a feast is normal. We have the capacity for excess, but excess as a steady diet is more than just good fun. Today an Internet user or adult-store patron can encounter more nubile virtual females (or whatever gets him going) in a few minutes than a hunter-gatherer would have met in his entire lifetime. We hear a lot about how the human brain is not equipped to handle "information overload." Today's erotic stimuli often constitute "reward circuitry overload." Our nervous system may simply not be designed to handle this deluge—apart from any debate about free speech.

Pornographers promise healthy pleasure and relief from sexual tension, but what they often deliver is addiction, tolerance [the need for more extreme stimulation], and an eventual decrease in pleasure. Paradoxically, the male patients I worked with often craved pornography but didn't like it.
—Norman Doidge, psychiatrist

Of course, individuals are not all equally susceptible to addiction, but the fact remains that given the way our brains learn, the risks of supranormal stimulation are real—and largely unacknowledged. As psychiatrist Norman Doidge recounts in *The Brain that Changes Itself*, adults have no sense of the extent to which pornography reshapes their brains. His patients report increasing difficulty in being turned on by their actual sexual partners, spouses, or girlfriends, though they still consider them objectively attractive. They try to persuade their lovers to act like porn stars, and they are increasingly interested in "fucking" as opposed to "making love."

Humanity is running a massive, uncontrolled experiment, and we don't yet know the results. However, there's increasing evidence that there's no free lunch. Prolonged elevation of dopamine not only rewires our desires; it also appears to promote depression and anxiety (low dopamine). Mice exposed to protracted elevated dopamine later behaved like they were depressed in response to stress, and became desensitized to certain drugs.[201]

Similarly, rats that have been bingeing on sugar show signs of anxiety and brain changes (decreased dopamine).[202]

A visitor to our site suggested another possible long-term effect of chronic overstimulation:

> I believe there is a correlation between porn viewing and erectile dysfunction. I am sure that if a study were actually done with honest men, we would see significant results. This is the type of issue people don't talk about. I think the porn industry takes advantage of the uninformed public and makes billions. Then the pharmaceutical companies sell us costly sexual enhancement drugs to treat the side effects and make billions.

Not only are pharmaceutical companies selling sexual enhancement drugs; they are also proposing drugs we can buy to attempt to treat porn addiction itself.[203] (Maybe it will turn you on only when your computer is turned off.) Yet why buy a drug that is likely to have unintended side effects rather than learn how to manage the brain's reward circuitry naturally? We can retrain our brains to delight again in less extreme forms of pleasure.

BRAIN TRAINING

Our reward circuitry is a primitive, subconscious apparatus. It can't perceive its limitations as an inner compass. It only knows how to urge us to seek pleasurable stimulation or avoid pain. Once we're in an addictive cycle, that simplistic formula backfires. We can't "medicate" our pain without initiating more.

The men who visited our site figured this out for themselves. They realized that if they didn't give up orgasm *and* porn entirely for long enough to return to equilibrium, they would continue to suffer severe withdrawal symptoms after every orgasm. They already knew withdrawal was hell, and they only wanted to go through it *once* more.

I have given up orgasms for about six weeks, and the withdrawal, as it turns out, was harder than cocaine, opiates, booze, or nicotine. I spent a solid week weeping every night after returning from the uni-

versity where I teach. I couldn't sleep, and I had almost zero appetite. The thought of dating made me want to curl up into a ball and quit. But here I am. I feel free.

[Six months later] I have fallen in love just this month. We are taking things slower than I've ever done before in my life, which is totally rewarding on all levels of my being!—Andy

Most of the men had to make several attempts, and some haven't made it yet. For those who persevered, however, the worst was over in four to twelve weeks of consistent abstinence from porn/porn-fantasy and little or no masturbation. Interestingly, an addiction researcher has found that a protein called Δ-FosB sticks around in the reward circuit for a month or two after repeated exposure to a stimulant. It causes brain changes that persist after a user stops, and renders mammals more prone to addiction by making them more sensitive to cues. If injected, it can induce relapse.[204] Δ-FosB also works its "spell" in the case of compulsive behavior (nondrug addictions),[205] which may explain why porn addicts need so long to recover, and remain sensitized to cues for a long time.

For most, the initial weeks were hellish, but there were joyful moments, too.

The withdrawal symptoms are incredible; it's incredible how real this is and how it MUST be an addiction if the symptoms are like this. Yesterday (day twelve) I was all shaky and anxious and feeling fidgety like a crack addict. I lay down on my bed and just wrestled with my covers out of frustration, burying my head in the covers and mumbling incomprehensible gibberish while rocking

First Aid

One measure that can help whenever compulsion strikes is to tell yourself that you won't act on your urge for at least five to ten minutes. Take some deep, slow breaths. Now, turn your *rapt* attention to a pre-selected activity. Choose something constructive, such as a breathing exercise, a stretching routine, gardening, pet training, practicing a skill, vigorous exercise, or recording thoughts in a journal. Can't? Then simply *visualize* yourself engaging in such an activity, vividly picturing the details. Also imagine how it *feels* to exercise your will, and what it is like to have a whole team of people you admire congratulate you on your success. When you consciously redirect your attention, you make it easier to do so again in the future. You are rewiring your brain—strengthening the new pathway and weakening your former compulsion.[206] Prepare your mind in advance so you are ready for recurring crises.

—Mary Sharpe, *Sharpe Thinking*

back and forth. An hour later I felt better. For the most part, though, my life feels totally different. I treat people differently. Things are MUCH, MUCH, MUCH better socially for me now. It's easier to joke around with people at work. I'm becoming popular—that's how different things feel for me all of a sudden! I'm happy ALL DAY LONG instead of just for a few minutes each day.

To the men's relief, the once-familiar feeling of having "both feet on the ground" began to resurface. As they returned to balance and their true (calmer) libido levels, these guys were noticeably happier. At that point the occasional orgasm didn't (usually) throw them back into compulsion—even if they did experience the effects of the passion cycle. When they made love again, they could do so in search of mutual pleasure—not simply in search of relief by the fastest route. They were actually reassured that they didn't *need* all those orgasms, which had once been the center of their world.

Every time porn thoughts intruded, I rapidly substituted a neutral movie of myself configuring a computer modem. I concentrated totally, actually imagining my arms touching the cables, typing into the keyboard, and so on. Within ten seconds I lost the erection and the image was gone. There was no "will power" involved. I worked with the natural processes of my brain, not against them. It always succeeded.
—Takahiro

Reaching out to others and receiving encouragement helped those in recovery as much as anything else. Caring contact registered as rewarding—and therefore soothing. (We even set up a Courtly Companion program on the site to recruit anonymous pen pals for them.) They taught themselves to value contact with others above using superstimulation to shift their uncomfortable feelings. In fact, in the process of recovery, they actually became stronger, wiser, and better mates. Many found that exercise, creative projects, and meditation also helped.

As the grass grew over their disused compulsion pathways, earlier pleasures were vivid again. Their sparkle and optimism returned. Some were joyful:

I'd always just accepted that I was below average socially. It wasn't even an issue anymore, but turns out, after two weeks without orgasm, my voice has gotten bigger and richer, I've been laughing and cracking jokes almost nonstop, and talking to people has been fluent and easy. Now I'm the chatty one. It's something to get used to.

These visitors have brought many gifts in addition to their humor, honesty, and courage. They've also confirmed that the passion cycle can profoundly influence perception and make healthy discipline extremely difficult:

My counting of days suddenly got a whole lot easier as I now am back to "day one." Did I invent a time machine, you ask? NO, I just deactivated the higher functions of the brain and let my mammal brain show me its moves. Impressive as they may be, they are not very suited for this semen-retention business. In the aftermath, I can appreciate how much difference these last six days [of abstinence] made. My urge to masturbate now is WAY more intense then it was before the "slipup," and my apathy has worsened a great deal. I don't feel like doing my tai chi; I just want to find some nasty porn and get on with it. All feelings and thoughts point in the wrong direction.

My visitors have also taught me that sexual compulsion isn't a character defect. Nor is it healthy. The monster roller coaster is simply another destination on the Dopamine Superhighway. All you have to do to end up there is allow your mammalian brain to set your priorities. What would the world look like if the men currently hooked on porn were once again operating on free will?

There are plenty of people who can masturbate in moderation. I am just not one of them, so I made the decision to stop entirely. After six months, I could write a book on how much better my life is. The amount of time I wasted each week was substantial—not just jacking, but staring at the tube, worn out. Now I am doing all the things I only thought about, and it is awesome. Hobbies, reading, social contact. I even have a dog. With the money I saved, I just bought a new iPod as a "reward." The best change is a far improved self-image and much better self-esteem. People ask me what have I changed because I am so much more outgoing. I have never, NEVER been more confident or motivated about approaching and engaging actual women. (And I'm actually getting real sex now!) The severe performance anxiety I had during sex, while consuming porn and beating off, is gone. Steps I took:

 - Cancelled my "porn" credit card
 - Cleaned my computer with an adware removal program
 - Deleted all links
 - Purchased and installed a comprehensive porn blocker
 - Kept a journal for the first three months, just typing my feelings and logging improvements
 - Called friends and family nightly, even old friends. Engaged people socially. Went to a corner coffee shop. Stopped watching the tube or biting my nails and did something!

 After a few days I noticed increased energy, increased attention, and higher self-esteem. After a month—although it took several tries to get there—those improvements were all through the roof. And before the second month was over, I had had real sex for the first time in ages. The porn I used is all a blur now. It is nice to get aroused by little things, like a revealing blouse or just a woman's flowing, shiny hair and fragrance. All this makes my complete abstinence from "burping the worm" SO WORTH IT.—Jed

As William Blake aptly put it, "The road to excess leads to the palace of wisdom ... for we never know what is enough until we know what is more than enough." Men who voluntarily leave porn behind have been through boot camp, and if they choose to add karezza to their repertoire they will find it easily achievable. (And should they find that extensive overstimulation has left indelible brain changes,[207] which make orgasmic sex a trigger for unwanted flashbacks and cravings, karezza offers an alternative for maintaining a satisfying, harmonious love life.)

Meanwhile, no one should be made to feel shame for being attracted to casual pursuit of orgasm—any more than one should feel shame about wanting sweets or petting a dog. All are predictably appealing urges, given the way our brains evolved over millions of years. Yet superstimulating versions of food and sex have the potential to become unhealthy addictions because of our primitive reward circuitry. We can easily begin to undervalue healthy foods and live companions. In short, supranormal stimulation is not necessarily harmless even when it's arguably natural.

Using porn and engaging in risky or kinky sex are like jumping on a bike with no brakes. Maybe you can stop, maybe you can't. One thing is certain, the longer you coach your brain to seek relief through intense sexual stimulation, the harder it will be to stop. Your brain is always in training.

A few words on how life is after almost a month without orgasm. I am amazed! I feel more confident than ever especially at work, with its many demands and stress. I have been able to keep lucid and cool, despite a heavy workload and pressure recently. I manage to socialize effortlessly, while normally doing so is effortful for me. In general, I feel as if the world at large is nicer to me; people tend to respond to and interact positively with me.—Stan

---

HOW DOES IT FEEL TO BE A GUINEA PIG?

Oxford evolutionary biologist Richard Dawkins says the content of our genome (our full DNA sequence) is information about how our *ancestors* survived and reproduced successfully. Past genetic success, however, is no guarantee that our preprogrammed instincts serve *our* well-being.

> To the extent that present day conditions are different from ancestral conditions, the ancestral genetic advice will be wrong.[208]

Conditions *are* different. Our distant ancestors weren't battered on all fronts with abnormally stimulating triggers goading them to binge on food or sex and throw their subconscious decision-making circuitry out of kilter. Sure, they liked orgasm and high-calorie treats as much as we do, but their less abundant lifestyles dictated a degree of restraint that we cannot count on to regulate our neurochemistry.

In a radio interview, Dutch scientist Gert Holstege said: "We are addicted to sex as you know, as everybody is." He pointed out that people who are injured, so that their rational brain isn't working right, go for orgasm all the time.[209] Without our ancestral scarcity to protect us, we have very little between mammalian impulse and action except our rational brain. For decades our culture has pushed us to let our rational brains interfere with our pursuit of sexual satiety as little as possible.

If love is blind, why is lingerie so popular?
—George Carlin

Many of us have ended up on the Superstimulus Roller Coaster. Remember the rats that were addicted to sugar? The researcher pointed out that withdrawal symptoms and dips in dopamine levels aren't evident when meals are moderate and regularly scheduled—that is, no sugar-dopamine flares.[210] This suggests that regular occasions of gentle intercourse, without orgasm-dopamine flares, may help us restore balance. In the next few chapters we'll look at how this can be experienced without a buildup of sexual frustration.

Karezza—Alice B. Stockham, MD

Alice Bunker Stockham was a practical Quaker, born in 1833, on what was then the western frontier of the United States. She was one of the first women admitted to medical practice in the States. Married to another doctor and the mother of two children, she was both an active physician and a highly respected author. Several years before she wrote her book on sex, she authored a popular text entitled *Tokology* ("Obstetrics" in Greek). It was translated into French, Finnish, German, and Russian (with a foreword by Leo Tolstoy).

Tokology[211] was far ahead of its time, and written for lay readers. In it Dr. Stockham recommended natural childbirth, eating a high-fiber diet, exercising during pregnancy to promote a pain-free childbirth, and doing away with corsets. Many of Stockham's patients were exhausted from too many pregnancies and unable to give their children adequate attention. She boldly advocated the use of Noyes's discovery (sexual continence) during pregnancy and to discourage pregnancy, which brought her into conflict with laws prohibiting promotion of birth control. Stockham responded that the widespread conviction that women should be legally forced to participate in ejaculatory sex—lest they go to any length to avoid the travails of childbirth—was nonsense.

In 1896 she self-published her first edition of *Karezza: Ethics of Marriage*,[212] in which she explained that making love without orgasm is strengthening for both husband and wife.

Stockham's thoughts on sex were frank and guilt-free. In fact, she insisted that the sexual urge is not only pure, but that it emanates from spirit. She viewed sexual desire as a signal that a greater power is tapping one for some larger endeavor. Sexual energy, she wrote, is creative energy. When contained, it can be used to regenerate the body, increase the gift of healing, and give birth to great inventions, humanitarian pursuits, and works of art—which she characterized as nonphysical offspring. Unlike

Noyes, Stockham clearly advised *both* partners to contain their sexual energy, and explained that it increases harmony.

> Karezza so consummates marriage that through the power of will, and loving thoughts, the crisis is not reached, but a complete control by both husband and wife is maintained throughout the entire relation.... satiety is never known, and the married are never less than lovers; each day reveals new delights.... The common daily sarcasms of married people are at an end, the unseemly quarrels have no beginnings and the divorce courts are cheated of their records.[213]

Stockham investigated tantric concepts. She recorded a visit to India, where she stayed with a matrilineal caste of hereditary warriors allegedly of Brahmin descent, on the Malabar Coast. Known as "the free women of India," Nayar women chose their own husbands, were well educated, and all property descended through them—until the British put an end to that custom.

Stockham used the word *karezza* for the practice of controlled intercourse. She saw it as a form of spiritual companionship. She believed there are deeper purposes to our reproductive faculties than are generally understood:

> In the physical union of male and female there may be a soul communion giving not only supreme happiness, but in turn [leading] to soul growth and development.[214]

She advised thoughtful preparation for karezza by means of readings that exalt the spirit, "reminding one of the power and source of life." She also recommended meditation on giving up one's will and preconceptions in order to allow cosmic intelligence to guide the process.

Here is a taste of her work:

> The ordinary hasty spasmodic method of cohabitation, for which there has been no previous preparation, and in which the wife is passive, is alike unsatisfactory to husband and wife. It is deleterious both physically and spiritually. It has in it no consistency as a demonstration of affection, and is frequently a cause of estrangement and separation....[215]

During a lengthy period of perfect control, the whole being of each is merged into the other, and an exquisite exaltation experienced. This may be accompanied by a quiet motion, entirely under subordination of the will, so that the thrill of passion for either may not go beyond a pleasurable exchange. Unless procreation is desired, let the final propagative orgasm be entirely avoided. With abundant time and mutual reciprocity the interchange becomes satisfactory and complete without emission or crisis. In the course of an hour the physical tension subsides, the spiritual exaltation increases, and not uncommonly visions of a transcendent life are seen and consciousness of new powers experienced....[216]

Men who are borne down with sorrow because their wives are nervous, feeble and irritable, have it in their power, through Karezza, to restore the radiant hue of health to the faces of their loved ones, strength and elasticity to their steps and harmonious action to every part of their bodies. By manifestation of tenderness and endearment, the husband may develop a response in the wife through her love nature, which thrills every fiber into action and radiates tonic to every nerve....[217]

Be patient and determined; the reward will come in happy, united lives, in the finding of the kingdom of heaven in your own hearts.[218]

Stockham died in 1912. One repercussion of works like hers was that the Vatican condemned the entire concept of karezza. In 1952, the Sacred Congregation of the Holy Office issued a Monitum, or "solemn warning," published in the *Acta Apostolicae Sedis,* which noted that several contemporary writers, in discussing married life, had described, praised, and even ventured to recommend something they termed "a reserved embrace."

Citing an express mandate of Pope Pius XII, the Sacred Congregation seriously admonished all such writers to refrain from these suggestions and forbade priests and spiritual directors ever to suggest that there was, in the light of Christ's law, nothing objectionable about "a reserved embrace." Nevertheless, as we have seen in the Wisdom section on Christianity, there's a strong possibility that the Pope was misled about Christ's law in this respect.

CHAPTER SEVEN

LEARNING TO STEER

We could not fall in love without changes in a specific part of our mammalian brain's reward circuitry.

This reward mechanism is not gender-specific; it evolved to bond us to our parents—and our children. It does not operate on words or logic, but rather on specific, frequent behaviors.

We can use these behaviors at any age to strengthen emotional bonds and keep them strong. As we drift away from them, bonds weaken.

Karezza is relaxed, gentle sex. It is a simple approach if couples move toward it gradually, with lots of generous bonding behaviors.

As pair-bonding mammals, we're programmed for both reproductive urges (mating) and a desire for physical and emotional closeness (bonding).

I remember when I was a teen and being driven crazy for want of a girl. Had I known what I know now, I would have realized that sex wasn't (only) what I wanted. It was touch, someone in my arms.
—Dylan

From our genes' perspective, bonding is all well and good—to a degree. In our species, bonds contribute to our genes' goal of getting more of themselves into the future, because children with two caregivers have a greater chance of surviving to reproduce.

Yet even if we often fall in love before we have sex, bonds are secondary in our sexual relationships. Those bonds need only last long enough (on average) for caregivers to bond with their *offspring*. In our genes' view, bonds must not interfere with the genetic goal of encouraging infidelity. Evolution's solution? Our mammalian mating program leads to recurring sexual satiety. As we habituate to a lover, we view him or her as less rewarding (less dopamine). Over time, weakening emotional bonds free us to fool around (or simply fuel unnecessary resentment and discouragement).

We are programmed for this tension. Parents who stay in love are best for children. If lasting love were also best for our genes, we'd be great at it already. (And if promiscuity were best for our genes, we'd be as promiscuous as bonobo chimps.) Instead, we're programmed for a tug-of-war between mating and bonding. Even so, once we know how to regulate both programs, we can steer for harmony over habit.

Our capacity for emotional bonding with our mates, friends, and pets arises from the same mechanism in the brain that allows infants to bond to caregivers. Reptiles generally just lay eggs and wander off; baby mammals need strong emotional ties to survive. Evolution works with what it has, modifying existing mechanisms to perform slightly different functions. Bonding between mates (pair-bonding) is known as an *exaptation* because it uses a mechanism that originally evolved for another purpose (infant-caregiver bonding), and expands it a bit.

Yet this evolutionary stepchild can serve as the basis for harmonious, lasting union if we choose to use it for this purpose. How do we know this? One clue is that parents can continue to love their own children,[219] even if they end up as murderers. In other words, we have the means to find another person rewarding indefinitely—if we activate this bonding mechanism, keep it activated, and combine it with lovemaking that soothes our "mating" hunger without causing sexual satiety.

Our mammalian bonding program does not operate on words or logic; it runs on a *mutual exchange of specific behaviors*. Yet it can only succeed—even between infants and caregivers—when both parties activate and sustain it using those behaviors (also called *cues).*[220]

This means that you can maintain and deepen your emotional bond with your mate by continuing to exchange the right signals. Typical bonding cues would be eye contact, hugs, and skin-to-skin contact. A more complete list is provided below. As recounted in Chapter Three, my husband and I worked some of this out by acci-

Wife: Why don't you tell me that you love me?

Husband: I told you I loved you thirty years ago when I married you. If I change my mind, I'll let you know.

dent. We noticed that when we drifted too far into self-centered, hungry touch, we needed to stop and tune up with a few nights of conscious, generous affection. Without realizing it, we were signaling our mammalian brains to renew our bond. After only a few days, we looked adorable to each other again (except during low points in inadvertent passion cycles). Now we exchange these cues daily, even if only for a moment or two.

The rational brain can't fall in love, however much it would like to. Bonding cues, like the addiction cues we looked at in the last chapter, work directly on the mammalian brain. It may be that those rare couples who somehow avoid habituation are regularly using these cues unconsciously to help counteract the fallout from sexual satiation.[221]

My parents just celebrated their fifty-eighth anniversary. I now realize that they do a lot of affectionate touching. If they are standing next to each other, chances are they have their arms around each other. It's a habit. They hug and kiss a lot. They always went to bed together at the same time, and have always slept in the same bed. When I asked, Dad said, "I have experienced those post-orgasmic feelings, although we didn't split up. Now that we're physically old, caresses bond us even closer than before."—Lorenzo

The strategy of consciously exchanging these cues may feel a bit artificial at first, but it soon becomes automatic. It also becomes increasingly pleasurable for two reasons. First, male or female, you are wired to find these behaviors rewarding. Your early survival and the survival of your children both hinge on this built-in pleasure response.

Though it was after 11 PM, we cuddled. For about two hours. Ecstatic cuddling. Two hours. Ecstatic. Hours. I had experiences last night that

I do not have immediate words for. Rich, deep, full. Subtle. Powerful. Moving. Meaningful. Pointing to greater connection with all life. We were in connection. In the same wave, as she put it, like a flock of birds wheeling in the sky as if with one mind.—Brian

Second, as you engage in these behaviors, you awaken a neurochemical ally: oxytocin. The "cuddle hormone" has a special property that distinguishes it from dopamine. As we've seen, dopamine induces excitement and puts you into high gear. When stimulated with too much dopamine, your nerve cells decrease their sensitivity to it. What goes up must come down. Your mood changes. Typically, you feel less alive—and very susceptible to suggestions that send up a dopamine flare.

Oxytocin is unusual in that it can have the opposite effect. Not only does it induce a calm, warm mood that can increase tender feelings and openness, but also the more oxytocin produced, the *more* sensitive some nerve cells become to it (because they activate additional oxytocin receptors on themselves).[222] What goes up stays up, or goes a bit higher—as does your sense of satisfaction.

This may be why daily bonding behaviors can produce increasing feelings of well-being over time—rather than boredom (habituation). Oxytocin may also help us "unlearn" the items on our ideal-mate checklist—as well as our attachments to previous mates. By increasing brain plasticity, oxytocin apparently even rewires our aesthetic sense.[223] If you want your partner to look adorable (to you) forever, keep snuggling!

If it feels odd to use infant-caregiver cues in an adult relationship, realize that you're already using them. Caressing a woman's breast is an obvious adaptation of infant-caregiver bonding behavior, and kissing seems to have evolved from the way primates feed their infants solid food. These activities feel good because your reward circuitry is the same one you arrived with. That warm glow you get from a kiss can only come from one place: your mammalian brain. You can't command it to fall in love and stay in love, but you can use your rational brain to feed your mammalian brain the signals that encourage that result—or not.

My wife and I had visitors for three weeks. The downside of being busy and polite was that kissing, cuddling, complimenting each other, and making love took a backseat. Now we're on our own again, and it's proving a bit of a slog to restart the sparkle. It's like we're partial strangers. However, we have learned from experience that even as little as a minute a day will rekindle our attraction.—Wes

According to the late Ashley Montagu, author of *Touching: The Human Significance of the Skin,* we adults tend to drift toward using these cues exclusively to pursue tension release in the form of orgasm. Yet, if we used them more consciously as tender acts of communication, they could relieve stress more effectively. (More on *why* in the next chapters.) Montagu cites research in which rats that had been handled frequently and gently could withstand stressors that rapidly proved fatal to ungentled rats. The handled rats were also strikingly calm and friendly, unlike their wild cousins.[224] Selfless touch is a powerful source of inner peace and well-being, so go on, handle your rat!

THE SURPRISING GIFTS OF BONDS

A strong emotional tie, grounded in the frequent exchange of these simple bonding behaviors, has beneficial repercussions throughout one's life. For example, children who have an opportunity to benefit from these bonds are more resourceful and resilient when coping with stress and trauma. They also have less difficulty managing their impulses and emotions. They show greater trust and reciprocity, and more compassion and empathy. They can see themselves more objectively, and they are more confident.[225] As already noted, when my husband and I first explored affectionate karezza he experienced similar changes (overcoming addictive impulses and depression). Again, Taoists observed long ago that one outcome of lovemaking without orgasm was the "cessation of cravings and impulses."

Just doing touch without an expectation of either reward or rejection has made an enormous difference in both our comfort levels. My spouse is opening to a newer and higher level of comfort in her own sensuality. I am feeling more relaxed and at peace in the relationship than I thought possible. There's a constant buzz of sexual energy, which for me feels like I have had a couple of double espressos—not bad or uncomfortable but different in some way. I walk around with a kind of quiet clarity.—Ryan

Any of us can harness this bonding mechanism at any age—not just to make our relationships more sane and loving, but also to improve our confidence, resilience, and empathy. Consider the experience of Daniel Solomon, a thirteen-year-old suffering from reactive attachment disorder (impulsive rage resulting from absence of early parental bonding).

An orphan, Daniel spent seven years in a shared crib in a Romanian orphanage. His adoptive parents tolerated years of his random, explosive anger, physical violence, and the creation of more than a thousand holes in his bedroom walls. In desperation, they at last experimented with bonding cues. They held Daniel's adult-sized body for twenty minutes a day, in their laps, on the couch, while looking into his eyes, feeding him ice cream, and listening to what he had to say.

He resisted the process at the beginning (hence the ice cream bribes). Yet after three weeks his behavior improved, and he finally began to register that his parents loved him. A secure bond with them freed him to develop normally elsewhere in his life. He began making friends his own age, and even received an award from the temple that had previously banned him for his intolerable behavior. His acceptance speech, in which he thanked his parents for their determination to connect with him, exemplifies the power of bonding cues in action.[226]

It's never too late to have a happy childhood.
—Berke Breathed

THE LOOPHOLE IN OUR GENES' PLAN

One reason that we all enjoy the idea of connecting with a mate (apart from all that racy honeymoon neurochemistry) is that it feels good to bond deeply with another person. Our pair-bonding mechanism (like our mating program) has the power to light up our reward circuitry.[227] (Those dopamine urges to eat food, drink water, and connect with others are all necessary for survival.) In fact, one reason addicts become addicts is that they are seeking the neurochemical rewards that they have not found through comforting emotional bonds.[228] This is a key point, to which we will return.

Remember those smiles of delight, kisses and hugs, and lingering gazes of your earliest romance? Sweethearts, like parents and infants, instinctively exchange subconscious bonding cues. These exchanges feel so good that we would continue to engage in them—if it weren't for the aftereffects of too much stimulation. Orgasm can flatten our neurochemical sensitivity and distort perception for approximately two weeks. In some of us it makes any activity, including affection, seem pointless, unless it is geared toward intense stimulation. This cheats both partners, because non-goal-oriented bonding behaviors are perhaps the most efficient way to restore balance, and therefore sensitivity to life's subtler pleasures.

Meanwhile, if you just trust your instincts while experiencing the sub-conscious effects of the passion cycle, you may believe you have fallen out of love—or are justified in meeting your heightened cravings for intense stimulation elsewhere. The prospect of an affair can feel like neurochem-ical medicine when you have allowed your mating program to dampen your responsiveness to your mate. You may be hypersensitive to any hot prospect who seems to promise to restore your "aliveness."

Even the healthiest relationships depend on lovers continuing to find each other rewarding at a subconscious level. If you want to outsmart your conniving genes and keep the sparkle in your relationship: (1) learn to relieve your sexual

There's nothing like new pussy to clear the mind.
   —Chris Rock, comedian

tension without resorting to orgasm to the extent possible (more on that in a moment), and (2) exchange bonding cues with each other often. These are the two pedals that allow you to drive *around* your genes' deep-seated relationship roadblocks.

I would recommend keeping a daily mood journal. It can give you a clear picture of how well this works. My partner and I started down this path about 18 months ago. I was sure the hangover wouldn't be real for me, but I learned I'm definitely critical and more emotionally unstable after orgasm. I also feel more alone and misunderstood, and ready to blame my partner for any slight. Recently, someone com-mented about how happy we seem all the time, now. Always smil-ing and laughing together. And it's true. I can't remember the last time we had an argument.—Carrie

BONDING CUES

The beauty of bonding signals is that most of them don't require words, and many are so effortless that they can be done even at the end of a long day. Yet they are potent signals for contented closeness. Here is a list, adapted from caregiver-infant cues. You can no doubt add some of your own.

> ▷ Smiling, with eye contact
> ▷ Skin-to-skin contact
> ▷ Providing a service or treat without being asked
> ▷ Giving unsolicited approval, via smiles or compliments
> ▷ Gazing into each other's eyes for several moments
> ▷ Listening intently, and restating what you hear
> ▷ Forgiving or overlooking an error or thoughtless remark, whether past or present
> ▷ Preparing your partner something to eat
> ▷ Sharing a meal, or a walk, with your attention on each other
> ▷ Synchronized breathing
> ▷ Kissing with lips and tongues
> ▷ Cradling, or gently rocking, your partner's head and torso (works well on a couch, or with lots of pillows)
> ▷ Holding, or spooning, each other in stillness for at least twenty minutes to a half-hour
> ▷ Wordless sounds of contentment and pleasure
> ▷ Stroking or hugging with intent to comfort
> ▷ Massaging with intent to comfort, especially feet, shoulders, and head
> ▷ Gentle intercourse (more on this later)
> ▷ Lying with your ear over your partner's heart and listening to his or her heartbeat for several moments
> ▷ Touching and sucking of nipples and/or breasts
> ▷ Gently placing your palm over your lover's genitals with intent to comfort
> ▷ Making time together at bedtime a priority (even if one partner has to get up and work on something afterward)

The desire for, and rewards of, these behaviors are deeply rooted in millions of years of evolution. Enjoy!

How curious that we don't all do them all the time. Very little effort and zero expenditure! My favorite is "wordless sounds of contentment and pleasure." We both do that already; but I'm up for doing it a whole lot more. I think I felt it was something infantile and therefore not to be indulged in too much.—Colin

---

SELFLESS TOUCH VERSUS HUNGRY TOUCH

All of the bonding behaviors listed above are powerful, but touch can be tricky until equilibrium reigns. On the one hand, communication transmitted through touch is the most powerful way to establish a human relationship,[229] a life-enhancing gift. On the other hand, not all touch is caring, as any victim of child abuse well knows. Touch always has a "charge" to it. As a friend said: "Hungry touch is not about wanting *somebody*, but *something*. It's incompatible with mutual giving."

Hungry touch (which is quite normal during a passion cycle) can be a drain, and even an invasion—and can easily activate the "bear-trap" reaction of the amygdala (as we saw in Chapter Five). Grabby touch is welcome only when *both* lovers feel a lot of sexual tension and want to use each other for mammalian mating fireworks. In a moment we'll consider how lovers can find relief from sexual tension without putting their precious emotional bonds at risk.

The goal of bonding-based touch is to stimulate each other's subconscious bonding program *without* activating the amygdala (the inner sentry). You can easily accomplish this by making your touch totally *unselfish*. One person said that to get in the right mindset, he imagines the loving feelings he has when lying together, naked and relaxed, with his lover. Then he calls on these feelings when touching his mate, and his touch becomes a gift. Another told me she touches her partner with the same nurturing, unconditionally loving energy she would use to comfort a family member.

The need for tender, caring touch never goes away and is a large part of the sexual caress for me. It's the need for comfort and security in a loved one's arms.—Graham

---

You might also try Will's technique of touching each other's entire body as if one part were no more important or arousing than the other. Has your mate been complaining about something hurting or feeling fatigued? Think about sending healing, comforting attention to that body region. Try to sense your partner's response to your touch instead of concentrating on your own sensations. Sometimes it helps to imagine that energy is flowing out of your hands into your partner as you touch.

Trust your intuition. Whenever you feel your partner's generous energy flow toward you, show your pleasure with sounds of contentment. Be patient, too. It sometimes takes a while to figure out if one's touch is based on *giving* or *getting*. After all, traditional foreplay is usually hungry touch, and it may be a habit by now. The good news is that, as you get more oxytocin flowing with those bonding behaviors, it produces an especially generous state of mind. It may also allow you to unlearn past associations and reconfigure former habits with unexpected ease.[230]

BACK UP WHEN NECESSARY

When the post-orgasmic hangover puts mates out of sync, touch can cause a lot of confusion and hurt feelings. If you feel like you "need space," you may believe that your partner—who now bears a peculiar resemblance to a starving octopus—is intentionally ignoring your signals of disinterest. Hungry touch at the wrong time can bring up surprisingly powerful feelings of aversion and resentment. Think of one mammal approaching another mammal for sex when it is *not* mating season, and you understand why it sometimes feels like you get a hoof in the gut when you suggest sex.

On the other hand, if you are suffering from uncomfortable sexual tension, and orgasm is the sole option you see for relief, then hungry touch with the goal of heating up your partner seems your only possible path to relaxation (the sudden drop in dopamine after orgasm). You are also likely to imagine that your partner—or *any* potential partner—can't wait to rip off *your* clothes.

Whichever role you've fallen into for the moment, resentment and defensiveness are natural—and extremely strong anti-love potions. The less responsive one partner is, the more irritable and grabby, or manipulative, the other can easily become.

Let's suppose you have inadvertently tripped the switch on your beloved's amygdala and you are now being regarded through a filter that is making you look more like a cobra than a comforter. One solution is to back up a bit and reactivate your mutual subconscious desire to bond. Use *less intimate* cues (avoiding breasts and genital touching), which will feel so safe and nurturing that they will not trigger defensiveness.

> *I have been practicing the suggestions. I can say from personal experience that they work. I am impressed with the simplicity and natural "heartfulness." I find that they open the heart and enliven the exchange of energy between the two of us throughout the day as well. The extra calm and attentiveness we feel naturally overflow onto the kids.—Thomas*

Touching your lover with intent to comfort does two things. First, it creates a space of coziness and safety, which will allow your lover to open up to you again over time. Second, it can actually ease *your* sexual tension. This paradox is at the heart of karezza, and likely related to oxytocin's unique power to soothe and reduce cravings. (More in the next chapter.)

Once you and your partner have "rebooted," you might try taking turns requesting a favorite intimate activity. One mate might choose taking a walk, holding hands or exchanging massages. The other might choose snuggling on the sofa or intercourse. At least every other day, you'll be enjoying an activity you like—without having to negotiate. You may find this simple approach increases your appreciation of, and appetite for, both sexual *and* nonsexual intimacy.

This strategy also circumvents the pain that builds up when the choice becomes "sex with orgasm, or nothing." In this familiar scenario, both parties tend to treat *all* affectionate contact as foreplay for orgasmic sex— and one may avoid it while the other gets hungrier. This cheats them both of the daily bonding behaviors they need to thrive, and keep their union rewarding.

Before we leave the subject of touch, let's review how Western culture lost sight of the crucial importance of comforting touch and its power to nourish and bond. We can regain lost ground more quickly if we see where we went astray.

TEARS IN THE NURSERY

Did you know that for the first half of the twentieth century, psychologists and other mental health professionals argued vigorously *against* cuddling babies when they cried, in the mistaken fear that it would creating demanding, needy children? Most physicians sided with them "to prevent the spread of germs," and newborns were walled off behind protective curtains. These neglected children may still be lurking in your family tree.

Government-printed pamphlets warned mothers against the character damage they could do by hugging, kissing, or even holding their own children. The head of the American Psychological Association, John Watson, said, "There are serious rocks ahead for the over-kissed child." Even when children in orphanages withered and died due to lack of physical contact, the experts clung to their prejudices. As author Deborah Blum explained, there was an attitude of "affection is wrong; love isn't real, and 'trust us; we're scientists.'"[231]

It took renegade researcher Harry Harlow to point out that well-being in primates is dependent upon lots of comforting contact with a parent figure. In his lab he created two "mothers" for his baby monkeys. One was made exclusively of wire, but it contained the milk. The other was terrycloth, and it had no milk. The logic of Harlow's peers dictated that the babies would prefer the milk-giver. Instead, the baby monkeys bonded with the figure that they found most comforting, spending up to nineteen hours of each day hugging and grooming the terrycloth figure. As long as "she" was in the cage, they were noticeably more curious, adventuresome, and active.

I have rare sexual fantasies, but constant longing for the maternal soft, deep acceptance I never experienced from my mother.—Ted

---

As Harlow demonstrated only half a century ago, touch and connection are higher priorities for primates than food (also vital). At long last, psychiatrists and others were convinced of the importance of comforting touch and bonding (at least for infants). As we will see in the next chapter, science has more recently begun to demonstrate benefits from comforting touch and connection *between mates*, too. We are beginning to acknowledge that we are, actually, pair-bonding mammals.

In the meantime, however, a lot of damage was done—for generations. Children who never develop the fundamental bonding they need to thrive are often unable to bond securely with their own children. One way to break this cycle is to engage in lots of bonding behavior within the confines of safe relationships—not just with our children, but also with our mates. We are all wired to relearn bonding and benefit from it. We have only to make a conscious effort to exchange those bonding behaviors.

My wife and I have learned that when we're avoiding orgasm it is really important to enhance our skills of being sensual through loving touch, such as exchanging massages or cuddling. It's like being on a first date that lasts for weeks. I start to experience a sense of bliss. I get more sensual joy just from being alive. It becomes clear that the only means I have for being really deeply satisfied is through the heart.
—Scott

MATES CAN STRENGTHEN EACH OTHER

Bonding cues of the kind listed earlier create solid feelings of completeness rather than fostering co-dependency or helplessness. They naturally ease the nagging sense that something is missing, which is so common in modern life. Having endured other relationships in which we didn't practice karezza, Will and I are convinced that the unhealthy dynamics that so often enter relationships arise in part from subconscious feelings of depletion, irritability, neediness, and insecurity.

Sexual satiety naturally exacerbates such feelings, which then trigger old memories of feeling insufficiently loved, as well as old reactions. Projecting anxious feelings onto each other, lovers overreact. This is how the passion cycle can cause partners to become uncharacteristically possessive, jealous, judgmental, needy, or demanding. These feelings may contribute to unhealthy co-dependency as well.

In contrast, bonding-based intimacy *not* geared toward sexual satiation discourages co-dependency because it engenders feelings of wholeness and centeredness. It appears to shift brain chemistry away from extremes and longings, toward balance. It is an exchange of gifts, not "fixes."

Will and I have noticed greater confidence and productivity—as well as increased sensitivity to each other, more willingness to accommodate each other without feeling resentful, increased trust in the fundamental goodness of each other's motives, a flirty energy that continues even outside of the bedroom, livelier interactions, more kidding around, a willingness to help with each other's projects, and random acts of generosity and kindness. We can even give each other advice without triggering resentment.

We also relish the fact that we continue to find each other cuter than ever, even though neither of us is movie-star material. And it's a relief to be able to tease each other and speak frankly about anything, without feeling a need to tread on eggshells, or negotiate constantly.

Our relationship is not "clingy," however, and when professional and family demands temporarily part us, we both function quite well on our own.

THE OTHER WAY OF EASING SEXUAL TENSION

Now that you understand the importance of bonding behaviors and how easy they are to use—as long as you keep *giving* and *frequent* foremost in your mind—let's return to the question of how lovers can meet their needs for relief from sexual tension. Many people regard this challenge as more of a male issue, with good reason. On average, men produce ten to twenty times the high-octane testosterone women do. Testosterone increases dopamine, that craving neurochemical. One result is that men tend to be *proceptive* (willing to initiate sex) a lot of the time. Women tend to be most proceptive around ovulation, thanks to their own sex hormones.[232]

Whatever your gender, you probably experience sexual frustration as the strongest weapon in your genes' arsenal. If you can't resolve your sexual tension in a relationship, you are keenly motivated to add a lover on the side (real or two-dimensional), or move on to a relationship where you *can* resolve it—at least temporarily. Sadly, as we've seen, the harder you try to resolve your frustration through better or more frequent orgasm with *any* partner, the more you trigger the sexual satiety that can push mates apart. You are programmed to be *unable* to find lasting sexual satisfaction that way with a mate, because you have evolved to see a sex partner as less and less rewarding over time.

If you've realized that heating things up throws you onto biology's script, and avoiding sex leads to frustration, or the stagnation of a sexless union, you may want to try karezza, that is, bonding-based lovemaking. You ease your sexual tension completely (intercourse included), without resorting to orgasm. It is simple, but very different.

One way to decide if you want to add karezza to your lovemaking repertoire is to try it for a while—and then return to fertilization-driven sex. In fact, my husband and I often remark that we learn the most about karezza from our inadvertent orgasms. During the two weeks after an orgasm, we notice a temporary dimming of good feelings, and we are always delighted when, like clockwork, we come back into sync at the end of the cycle.

When I began learning bonding-based lovemaking, my habits around sex were so ingrained that they got in the way without my realizing it. It's not so easy to leave behind all those familiar landmarks of foreplay geared toward orgasm. I remember thinking to myself that it is no wonder humanity easily forgets about this gentle, affectionate approach despite its benefits. Initially it feels *all wrong*. Also, I just couldn't believe how effortless karezza was.

> *For a long time I'd been doing Taoist-style sex with my wife with good results—using exercises, lovemaking techniques, and energy visualizations. However, I decided to set it aside temporarily to learn more about karezza. The first thing I noticed was that karezza got the same results as my old Taoist practices. But karezza required no specialized energy work. All I did was to slow way down, with periods of near stillness while engaged in sex and breathed slow, deep breaths. I did nothing else. Anyone could do karezza.*
>
> *I soon started to sense another feeling that I didn't recognize—a deep, satisfying feeling. I guess it was the oxytocin, the cuddle hormone. It feels like peace and love all mixed up together—a sensation of being in love with life.—Larry*

Eventually I realized that karezza is indeed simple and effortless (though certainly not *easy* at first). Its real challenge is that it does not produce rapid, obvious results (as, for example, a new foreplay technique might). Karezza's effects are cumulative. I needed several weeks of pleasant, but patient, consistency to see why I had made the effort to try it. During that time, I experienced a growing sense of empowerment, optimism, and connectedness with others. I felt as if I were "in the flow." Yet these changes seemed

so *natural* (and well-deserved), that it was easy to miss the link between cause and effect.

In sharing my experience, I'll draw not just on my time with Will, but also on my earlier efforts—which were a lot rockier. Ultimately, I backed into the power of subconscious bonding cues, even though I didn't realize *what* I had discovered, or why they worked.

BALANCE FIRST

The effects of karezza show up first as a return to balance. If you haven't felt a sense of equilibrium in a while, you may find it odd. For example, a girlfriend once tried gentle intercourse without orgasm with her busy executive sweetheart during a weekend away. Initially, it caused him to sleep far more than usual. He felt great at the end of the weekend. Yet he clearly found his uncharacteristic behavior disturbing. In fact, he asked if she had given him a sleeping pill!

In contrast, those who are feeling sluggish begin to shift toward a renewed zest for life. A friend in England who experimented with bonding behaviors found that she soon enthusiastically initiated sex with her husband, which he relished. For years she had grimly endured intercourse, which she found painful, just to hold her marriage together. "And," she confided in her colorful Cockney accent, "'E *loved* 'is foot massage. In twenty-foive years of marriage oi'd never even *seen* 'is feet!"

Moving toward karezza *during* the passion cycle (after orgasm) can be a bit like watching paint dry at first—albeit with the added benefits of a companion and an increasing sense of well-being. This was especially true when I was pumped up on honeymoon neurochemicals and feeling passionate. Incidentally, at first I thought it was karezza's job to keep the neurochemical illusion of the honeymoon going indefinitely. It's not. Honeymoon neurochemistry is like a feeding frenzy—exciting, exhausting, and intended for maximizing genetic success.

The mind-altering buzz of new love is not sustainable without continual artificial life support. When we rely primarily on dopamine for our thrills, more and more stimulation (or a longer interval between trysts) is generally needed to attain the same orgasmic intensity. After a while, mastering additional G-spot geography or seeking novelty by having sex on the kitchen table or tying each other up can feel like work. It becomes far more efficient to add a novel partner, with whom passion will be effortless—for a while.

Karezza let me off of the carousel, but it took some getting used to. It didn't squelch the honeymoon effect, but it shifted it from "edgy" to "lighthearted." In fact, karezza was sweet sanity by comparison.

Initially, I wondered if I would be attracted to my partner without that exciting "love sickness" I was hooked on. I was relieved to realize that our mutual magnetism remained. There just wasn't a desperate, "rip your clothes off" quality to our attraction. With or without clothes, it felt more like two dolphins frolicking. We tended to laugh a lot, to

> Our bodies are simply not equipped to sustain for long periods the physiological arousal associated with passionate love, desire, and other intense emotional experiences.
> —Pamela C. Regan, psychologist

find just the right times to make love, and to enjoy hugging or touching each other at other times. Our attraction was reliable. It didn't come and go, as it did when I ran my love life on the passion cycle. When issues came up, we were in a better place to address them, because our interior weather wasn't as stormy.

I began to see passion and love in a new way. For as long as biology had orchestrated my love life, passion always seemed intensely real, while love appeared depressingly ephemeral. Now the situation reversed itself. I experienced love as increasingly solid and reliable. Passion, however, fluctuated in a surprisingly predictable pattern. How had I missed this for so many years?

> *Now that I'm in this goody-goody phase of life, in which all my pleasures are so bloody innocent, I wonder how I can ever go back to the psychodrama, the abandonment issues, the jealousy?—Ellie*

RELAXATION VERSUS PERFORMANCE

It is probably clear by now that karezza depends on the rewarding feelings that come from relaxed mutual adoration and generous touch (bonding behaviors). As we'll see in the next chapter, karezza seems to be associated with a neurochemical cocktail that's a lot heavier on the "cuddle chemical" (oxytocin) than on passionate surges of dopamine. Karezza definitely does *not* rely on the rewards that come from approaching one's own orgasm or inducing it in a lover. This makes it radically different from most tantric or sex magick approaches, in which partners work hard at revving each other up to achieve mind-altering intensity.

Both approaches can be pleasurable, but they lie in different zones of the sexual pleasure spectrum. Sexual techniques based on climbing toward orgasm employ performance and the excitement of sexual tension. In contrast, karezza is effortless. When I first explained it to Will, he couldn't believe his ears: "A woman who is asking me to do *less?*"

Sometimes karezza is just pleasant, gentle intercourse that leaves us refreshed and more balanced; sometimes it's an amazing, heart-opening experience for which we can hardly find words. The outcome is not in our control. All we can do is keep our biologically driven habits out of the way, and enjoy what bubbles up.

> *My partner and I have just clicked over two and a half weeks practicing the Exchanges, and have spent the past two days connected at the mouth and looking deeply into one another's eyes, like we were when we first met. The level of connection just keeps on surprising us, it's so beautiful.—Mark*

The Taoists distinguish the two fundamental approaches to sex as "valley orgasm" and "peak orgasm," but that terminology confused me mightily. In my mind, "orgasm" sounded like a clear goal, something to strive for, an unmistakable line to cross. Since I wasn't experiencing a tension-release response resembling a conventional orgasm with karezza, I first assumed I was doing it wrong. I also imagined that the valley orgasm must lie somewhere near the peak orgasm. It doesn't. You flow into the valley when you're feeling relaxed, safe, and loving. As soon as you engage in effort, you have your hiking boots on, and you're headed for the peaks again. Striving is counterproductive.

I understood the distinction better once Will explained that the human nervous system isn't meant to strive and relax at the same time.

Karezza apparently activates the body's relaxation response more than orgasmic sex does. Perhaps you learned in school that your nervous system has two fundamental responses to stimuli: parasympathetic and sympathetic. Comforting stimuli activate the parasympathetic nerves, allowing your system to focus on regeneration, digestion, healing, sexual arousal, and general housekeeping.[233] Karezza, with its emphasis on relaxed, non-goal-oriented affection, seems to rely heavily on activating these nerves.

Reiki and Quantum Touch employ quiet touch of at least a half-hour with beneficial results. In my experience the extended hugs in the quiet periods of karezza are healing in the same way as these therapies.
—*Warren*

Although sexual *arousal* is a parasympathetic (relaxation) activity, the actual drive to orgasm invokes your body's sympathetic nerves (the ones that enable the fight-or-flight response). Hot sex is an athletic exercise. Your heart rate increases; you perspire. It's like any other goal-directed activity, particularly when your survival is at stake. Indeed, biologically driven sex is exactly that. You are in performance mode, doing what needs to be done to survive (through passing on your genes).

The body "reads" bonding behaviors as signals for feeling safe and getting closer. It may be that it does *not* "read" performance-oriented lovemaking as a bonding signal, but rather as something more akin to a fight-or-flight activity. This powerful drive may produce orgasms, but not profound feelings of safety or a desire to remain close. This could explain why certain types of sacred sex practices, which call for vigorous lovemaking, do so little to bond partners over the long term.

Paradoxically, the more exhausting your daily demands, the more appealing hot sex can seem. It fires up the exciting fight-or-flight response, making you feel alive and vital, and then it provides the temporary stress release of a sudden drop in dopamine. It's a coping mechanism, but it means you relax through using each other in a way that can cause *subsequent* feelings of depletion and apathy toward your partner. In contrast, karezza is fulfilling and reassuring because you both continue to feel energized enough to nurture each other attentively.

> *When I was eighteen, I had a girlfriend with whom I began practicing intercourse without orgasm without even knowing techniques, just by intuition. Without realizing it our bodies and minds were healed in a profound way. Later, we experimented with books that were teaching something similar to what we experienced, except that they were talking about orgasms without ejaculation, and promised more physical pleasure. We soon broke up and things changed a lot for both of us—for the worse.*
>
> *One thing I use to compare that happy time with the present time is the fact that my sister and I used to wait in hiding and then jump out to scare each other. In those days my mind was so clear, focused, and in the present that she could never scare me. Today any dog's bark can make me jump, and now I suffer from insomnia. What have I learned? "Throw away your tantra books, just send the energy to the heart." That's simple enough to follow. Just do it; don't try to figure it out before the actual experience.—Miguel*

With karezza, you ideally stay away from the edge of orgasm. However, if you sense yourself slipping into performance mode while making love, you can pull yourself back into parasympathetic with deeper, longer breaths. The buildup to orgasm coincides with an increase in muscular tension and an urge to restrict your breathing. Therefore, if you want to switch over to your relaxation response, rest your abdominal muscles and slow your breathing. Shift your attention to nurturing your partner.

The ultimate goal of karezza is to remain in relaxation mode, yet fall into a heightened state of dynamic stillness. It's not a tense state of hyperalertness, but more like the "flow" that artists and athletes report. The unfamiliar emphasis on relaxation may be why karezza feels so foreign at first.

One benefit is that there is absolutely no performance anxiety—unless you create it for yourself (as I did) by imagining that there *should be* a simple cause and effect, leading to a predictable, repeatable result.

As I learned more about my neurochemistry, I also realized that "striving" equates with "craving," which entails high dopamine—and self-serving behavior. Slow learner though I was, I finally grasped that I would never experience karezza's full potential while striving for any kind of experience.

I personally don't think that there is any sexual tension in what you call bonding-based sex. If there is, then it is fertilization-driven sex. I think of sexual tension as passion, desire, fire, horniness—like a volcano that can only ease itself with a flow of lava (climax or orgasm). Bonding-based sex is connection on a deep level. It's union with each other in harmony with the goal of becoming one. There's no sexual frustration, just a subtle, powerful sexual energy.—Katrina

---

BIRTH OF THE ECSTATIC EXCHANGES

Even after I stopped struggling toward some confusing valley orgasm, I was still somewhat perplexed. I knew that the kind of lovemaking I was trying to learn involved avoiding orgasm. Yet trying to *avoid* orgasm wasn't any more relaxing than striving *for* it. In fact, making love as usual, but without orgasm, was like walking along a knife's edge. It never succeeded for long, and it also led to frustration and irritability at times—perhaps because of high dopamine.

During this point in my learning curve, I was also noticing that the effects of orgasm lingered for about two weeks—and that it was harder to stay on the nearside of orgasm during that recovery period. If my partner and I saved intercourse for when we were back in balance after the passion cycle, it was definitely less frustrating and more satisfying.

Yet what were we supposed to do while we were passing up the rewards of conventional sex, and awaiting karezza's soothing benefits? Like Scheherazade of *One Thousand and One Nights,* I realized that I would have to come up with entertaining activities that would give us something to do with our powerful sexual attraction. I also realized that I'd have to do it without relying on habitual foreplay. "Heat 'em up" foreplay, such as oral sex, that didn't culminate in orgasm was a recipe for crankiness. To resolve this dilemma, I began to come up with ways to pamper each other that would leave us feeling satisfied.

Thus the Ecstatic Exchanges were born—a three-week program of sensual, lighthearted activities for adults, which can be found at the end of this book. Why three weeks? I had heard somewhere that it took about three weeks to solidify a new habit. Later I learned that, according to neuroimmunophysiologist Monika Fleshner, your brain will register more eager anticipation for a new regime (that is, start to produce a healthy amount of dopamine in response to it) if you force yourself to change your behavior for at least two weeks.[234]

Meanwhile, of course, you also have to avoid your usual habits. In fact, the more radically and thoroughly you alter your behavior when creating a new pathway in the brain, the easier it is to create one.[235] And don't worry. Weeds will never grow over your brain pathway for fertilization-driven sex; it's wired into all of us. You can easily reactivate it when you wish to compare your karezza results with conventional sex.

In my efforts to rival Scheherazade, I designed the first two weeks of activities *without* intercourse. (Talk about radically different behavior!) I had discovered that it was useless to attempt non-goal-oriented intercourse while contending with lingering flares of sexual frustration due to a passion cycle. Whenever I had tried it, my devious genes came out on top.

I also figured out (the hard way) that nakedness is a loud signal to the mammalian brain that a fertilization opportunity has arrived and requires urgent attention. The presence of underwear and a shirt (if female) tends to mute that signal. In established relationships, even this scanty garb helps re-establish a mini-courtship during this two-week interval. It creates a fresh, even virginal, mindset in which it's easier to forget past resentments and gain a new emotional start.

With all this in mind, I gathered a series of playful, affectionate activities—consisting of all my *other* favorite things about sexual intimacy. That list turned out to be a lot longer than I first thought possible: head rubs, back-scratching, gentle stroking, gazing into each other's eyes, hand and foot massages, back massages, and so forth—followed by snuggling, kissing, and sleep.

My partner and I were amazed at how much we enjoyed two weeks of this mutual pampering. By the end of that time we were effortlessly seeing each other's wings and halo. True, if a lot of honeymoon neurochemistry was flying around, we sometimes spent the first few nights more awake than asleep. Yet within about three days, that racy feeling started to shift, leaving us both refreshed, sleeping better, and still eager to spend time together. In this way, a lover and I could transition from the usual way of making love to karezza—and still relish every moment.

We are awed by what is happening. We're into the Exchange just before the one with actual coupling. Wow. I lay there on the bed at one point this morning, and after a long, long stretch of pranayama-type breathing, all I could do was laugh out loud for a while. I felt so high and so grounded at the same time!!!—Lance

Over time, I learned that this two-week period, with lots of affection and absolutely no goal of sexual intercourse, was excellent balm for two, quite different, afflictions. With a new lover it helped keep our fiery honeymoon neurochemistry from galloping off with us. On the other hand, when a passion cycle had erupted into emotional distance, this two-week refuge allowed us to come back into harmony while nurturing each other safely. It seemed to snap us out of any habituation blues and give us a fresh start. In both cases, when we added intercourse in week three, we were more likely to find karezza-style lovemaking deeply satisfying.

Another gift of the first two weeks of the Exchanges is that couples who are not ready for intercourse, or incapable of it, can still experience how fulfilling bonding activities alone can be.

INTERCOURSE

It becomes evident, after a while, that the more profound karezza experiences are not dependent upon genital intercourse at all; they could be enjoyed by two paraplegics with open hearts and a desire to merge. This means that intercourse—although very enjoyable, and a profoundly nourishing bonding behavior—is, in a sense, an added luxury when practicing bonding-based intimacy. A lot of whatever benefits us from intercourse also benefits us during intimacy without it.

Mind you, I'm an intercourse kind of gal, so I highly recommend it. But I now realize that it's not The Goal of karezza. Intercourse is one more way my partner and I can nurture each other and move toward a sense of wholeness or completion. Generosity toward each other and a desire to get closer are more important than genital friction.

Most lovers don't start the Ecstatic Exchanges with hearts unguarded, and that's fine. The process itself gently moves lovers in that direction without any effort required—due to the power of those subconscious bonding cues I had unwittingly woven into the Exchanges. Sometimes lovers discover that they have fallen into a timeless, joyful reverie with each other, while doing nothing at all.

> *After half an hour or so of relative inactivity, I experienced an extraordinary merging moment, where I could no longer sense the boundary between my wife and myself. It felt supremely peaceful and I could have remained like that indefinitely.—Roger*

That being said, the third week of the Exchanges includes intercourse—for us sex fiends. Clothing comes off, too—phew! But I learned that we had to begin intercourse in a position that did not allow for much movement or we inevitably ended up racing for the finish line. (Possible positions are pictured in the Exchanges.)

At this point, it was extremely easy to escalate into goal-oriented sex. One strategy Will and I used, once we realized its effectiveness, was to make sure we put "snuggle nights" in between "intercourse nights." Snuggle nights are useful refresher courses for the nervous system. Even a little bit of cuddling offers a taste of relaxed satisfaction with no goal whatsoever. The next time we have intercourse it is easier to stay in that tranquil mindset. If ever we feel frustrated after lovemaking, rather than satisfied, we simply put on our underwear again (or our "underwear mindset") and tune up with a few days of simple bonding behaviors. We both seem to sense when we are back in the groove.

> *When I visited a woman I met online in her hometown for a day, I felt an overwhelming sexual tension the whole time. But when we hugged at the end of the date to say goodbye, I felt all the tension just dissolving in her gentle, friendly caress. It lasted for quite a while too.... I guess we males need this intimacy and touching. Actually, we both need to give and receive this love that relieves tension. Men even more so, as we tend to suffer the greater urges.—Salim*

TENDER TANGO

As far as actual intercourse goes, we move *far more slowly* than we did during conventional sex. A sacred-sex teacher once shared this simple exercise, which helps her students understand how they could feel more pleasure with slow, rather than vigorous, intercourse.

> Lightly, slowly run your thumb and index finger up and down your other index finger. Feel the tingles? Now use your thumb and index finger to grab that same index finger, and rub it quickly and vigorously for a moment. Do you notice a degree of numbness setting in?

Not only do we actually *feel* more when making love slowly, it also seems that gentle intercourse helps prevent mood swings in me. Remember the female rats in Chapter Five, for which brisk copulation set off two weeks of hormonal surges to prepare them for possible pregnancy?

In addition to making the most of the less-is-more insight, we fall into *total stillness* frequently while making love. Some of the most gratifying and profound experiences occur when *not* moving. As a result, our lovemaking goes in waves, somewhat like breathing. Erections also come and go—and arise again when we start kissing after a pause.

I don't think that we have been this close in the ten years we have been partners. I still have my doubts about abandoning orgasm absolutely, but so far, the last six weeks have been the best, consistently loving, time period of our relationship. If anyone has any doubts about trying it, don't. Instead of going crazy from the lack of release, I think maybe we have become sane.—Leo

---

We kiss and gaze into each other's eyes a lot. We also let each other know how loved we feel with wordless sounds of pleasure and reverent, or playful, touch—depending upon our mood. Sometimes we make a conscious effort to diffuse the sexual energy from our genitals throughout our bodies by tightening the muscles of our pelvic floor and breathing the energy up. Sometimes when we close our eyes we notice flashing lights in the third-eye region of the forehead.

We make love in very comfortable positions, where our weight is supported with a minimum of tension. Side-lying position, with my legs wrapped around Will, is a favorite. We also sometimes fall asleep connected, which makes waking up especially enjoyable. Because we never "finish," we've noticed that a flirty energy continues to flow outside the bedroom. This helps stave off habituation. In fact, my husband says he feels like a human "Pepe Le Pew," the amorous cartoon skunk whose love always remained unconsummated—and undying.

As for the dynamic between us during sex, we try to stick to the Taoist adage that "the man is the pilot, the woman is the boat." Women often find it a delicious experience to fall into that space of trust—knowing they have attentive, safe pilots. The men find it equally gratifying to be trusted completely. However politically incorrect, this dynamic seems to bring out men's nobility and women's relaxed responsiveness. At the same time, both partners want to focus *within,* on what each is individually experiencing. That is, the pilot steers intuitively, but not with a view to making his partner respond in a particular way.

One paradoxical outcome of falling into the boat-pilot roles in the bedroom is that both of us have become more flexible outside of the bedroom. For example, Will and I find that in our daily lives we fluidly switch back and forth between typical gender strengths—such as intuition and sensitivity on the one hand, and efficiency and the ability to make things happen on the other. At the same time we have a greater appreciation of how our strengths complement each other.

In daily life I'm a bit of a speedboat; I steer myself all over the place. Yet inside the bedroom I find the boat role very natural. Will is also an instinctive pilot—both relaxed and somehow courtly. We also suspect that the balance we achieve through karezza makes us more attentive and relaxed.

We are happily sticking to our non-orgasmic lovemaking, and finding the new way very easy for us actually. A lot easier than I thought. He's a total natural and because of that, I have no need for regular sex anymore. It's amazing.—Marta

When I described the boat-pilot dynamic to a friend, he begged Will and me to attend his tango class. "It's exactly what you're describing, except that we're dancing," he said excitedly. He was right. In tango, one partner leads with great sensitivity and gentlemanly attentiveness, and one follows. Yet there's always an enlivening, mirroring dynamic also going on between the dancers, with lots of eye contact—and unmistakable electricity. The woman is not so much passive, as *magnetic*. She is certainly not pushed around like a cardboard box on wheels.

My friend says that tango is a form of karezza—although I suspect he believes that karezza is actually a form of tango. Either way, like karezza, tango ideally produces a blissful altered state of union, in which the music dances the dancers. Even when my friend is without a sweetheart, he says that nourishing current on the dance floor soothes his sexual frustration.

Will and I have both commented that historical descriptions of, and recipes for, karezza seem vague. This is because technique is virtually immaterial. It's a practice about *not doing,* about getting your mating program out of the way long enough to fall into a state of relaxed union. It's more of an *experience* than a *practice*. It shifts your outlook as you go—perhaps by restoring your reward circuitry's ideal sensitivity. However, if you have questions about your specific circumstances, have a look at Chapter Nine, and visit the Habit to Harmony forum at www.reuniting.info. Also, Chapter Ten, The Path of Harmony, recaps the practice.

IS HISTORY REPEATING ITSELF?

Today we face a similar challenge to the one Harlow faced. The experts of his time insisted that infants didn't need touch and that they must be failing to thrive for other reasons. Harlow's research finally opened their minds. Comforting touch leading to a solid bond proved to be a most vital ingredient for well-being—with implications that extend throughout adulthood.

These days we have a similar blind spot. Our experts assure us that sexual gratification is vitally important, even if we need sexual enhancement drugs, arousal gels, vibrators, or porn to achieve it. We're also told orgasm is an essential ingredient for relationship harmony—even *more* important than non-goal oriented affection.

After only a few decades of this mindset, cracks are appearing—cracks that would

"Many boys [on university campuses] spoke openly about how they masturbated at least once every day, as if this were some sort of prudent maintenance of the psychosexual system." . . . The danger is that [their addictive need for increasing stimulation] will carry over into relationships, as it did in my patients, leading to potency problems and new, at times unwelcome, tastes.

—Norman Doidge, psychiatrist (quoting Tom Wolfe)

have caused an ancient Taoist sage to nod knowingly (based on his self-scrutiny and study of hundreds of years of carefully recorded observation). As I discovered in my own love life, it's very difficult to emphasize orgasmic intensity and frequency *and* maintain satisfying, harmonious togetherness. As it turned out, my relationships were fragile because I had my foot down too hard on the accelerator, and virtually no awareness of the critical importance of true bonding behaviors.

The belief that only passion will keep marriages together can throw us onto an uncomfortable treadmill. For example, *Kosher Adultery: Seduce and Sin with Your Spouse* by Rabbi Boteach advises couples to promote gut-wrenching fear and raging jealousy to keep their marriages together.[236] Our fellow primates don't have to work so hard. Tamarin monkeys, which, like humans, are socially monogamous, increase oxytocin using frequent cuddling, grooming, stroking, and sexual behavior.

Curious if tamarins ever practice "monkey karezza," I asked lead researcher Chuck Snowden if they generally ejaculate when they mount. He answered, "I'm almost positive [ejaculations] did not occur on every mount, but I can't make even an educated guess on what the proportion might be since tamarins don't show anything like an orgasmic response." If sexual activity without ejaculation strikes you as odd, consider that macaque male monkeys ejaculate in scarcely half of their copulations. And that even the infamous bonobo chimps engage in "rather casual and relaxed" sexual activity for social bonding, frequently without climaxing.[236a]

Could this common primate behavior help explain why people who try karezza (frequent affection and intercourse, infrequent climax) claim romantic bonds are easier to maintain? Today, as the objectives of intense passion and lasting union prove harder to yoke, we often seek well-being in orgasm alone. Yet without the soothing properties of close connection, many of us pair-bonders are not thriving—even if we are orgasmic. Unlike the few other "monogamous" species with both pair-bonding *and* mating programs, we humans can consciously steer toward one—or the other. Even if some of us are more neurochemically inclined toward monogamy than others, we all possess both programs. To the extent we emphasize mating or bonding, we tend to find long-term relationships more challenging—or more rewarding. Let's see why.

Karezza—J. William Lloyd, MD

J William Lloyd (1857–1940) was known as the "drugless physician." In addition to *The Karezza Method, or Magnetation: The Art of Connubial Love,* he authored various unpublished writings on the subject of ideal relationships.[237]

The Karezza Method is a beautiful, practical little volume. In it Lloyd, a medical doctor, addressed such concerns as the question of semen buildup:

> That the semen can be and is absorbed [if not ejaculated] I think is satisfactorily proven by the numerous instances where men have been sterilized by accident, disease, or intentional operation in such a way that the testicles are left unharmed, but the semen is cut-off from its natural outlet. After being once secreted only two things are possible—either it must be absorbed or it will form a swelling. It does NOT form a swelling; therefore it certainly is absorbed.[238]

Lloyd openly questioned the trend toward viewing orgasm as purely beneficial:

> A school of physicians has arisen which claims the orgasm as a most important function, beneficial, and justifiably attained by artificial means if natural ones are not available, including with apparent approval, masturbation, and the use of mechanical and chemical contraceptives [to make casual sex possible].
>
> [This teaching leaves] the reader of little experience with the idea that orgasms are practically harmless, that excess is unlikely, and that if no immediate bad results are noticed the practice may be indulged in to about the limit of desire.
>
> [Yet] that orgasms are weakening is easily proven.... To get facts about the orgasm go to the stockbreeder. Business has no sentiment

or prejudice. Every stockbreeder will tell you that to permit a bull or stallion to serve too many or too often is to devitalize him.[239]

Lloyd observed that karezza offered health benefits. For example, he said he knew it to "act like magic in painful menstruation," and as a remarkable nerve sedative, even curing nervous headache. He also found it one of the best agents "for the benefit and cure of ordinary sexual weaknesses and ailments, including urethritis [urinary tract infection] and prostatitis [inflammation of the prostate gland]."

> In successful Karezza the sex-organs become quiet, satisfied, demagnetized, as perfectly as by the orgasm, while the rest of the body of each partner glows with a wonderful vigor and conscious joy ... tending to irradiate the whole being with romantic love; and always with an after-feeling of health, purity and well-being. We are most happy and good-humored as after a full meal.[240]

However, he was "willing to concede that where the intercourse is of such a nature as to cause a congestion that is not sublimated, or where sexual congestion occurs and sublimation and [karezza] are not available, the orgasm may have a necessary place."

In Lloyd's day, some people objected to karezza on the grounds that it would encourage excessive indulgence in sexual relations. He responded:

> Those who do not use Karezza are vastly more liable to excess, and this usually from too frequent and intense orgasms, too frequent pregnancies, or too coarse, cynical and invasive an attitude. Where there is merely a physical itch or craving gratified, with no mutual tenderness or kindness, or perhaps actually against the desire or protest of one party, sex is always excessive.[241]

Lloyd offered many practical, inspiring tips for successful karezza, including the need for lovers to *give* in order to benefit from controlled intercourse. "Try to feel yourself a magnetic battery," he advised.

> As you acquire the habit of giving your sexual electricity out in blessing to your partner from your sex-organs, hands, lips, skin, eyes and voice, you will acquire the power to satisfy yourself and her

without an orgasm. Soon you will not even think of self-control, because you will have no desire for the orgasm, nor will she.[242]

Karezza, said Lloyd, is the greatest beautifier because it increases and makes enduring heart love. He advised that to increase sexual control, "keep the spiritual on top, dominant—loving is the first thing, and at-one-ment ... of your souls, your real end." "Sex is very close to soul.... [It only satisfies] when it unites souls, not merely copulates bodies for a thrill."

In a chapter called "Does the Woman Need the Orgasm?" he even had the courage to explain why she doesn't. (Brave man.)

> The ordinary husband-and-wife embrace is purely sexual, and based on his demand to get rid of a surplus. There is little or no thought to make it esthetic or affectional—it is merely animal. If the husband stays long enough and excites his wife sufficiently to have an orgasm, then she has a gushing out of fluids that relieves the congestion brought on by his approaches, and on the physical plane, at least, she is relieved and satisfied, the same as he....
>
> But what happens in Karezza? Here, if she really loves her partner, her whole nature is attuned to his, in delicious docility, expectation and rapport. Every nerve vibrates in sweet gratitude and response to his touch. There is a marvelously sweet blending and reconciliation of the voluptuous and the spiritual that satisfies both her body and her soul at once.... [When] his magnetism is flowing through her every fiber, uniting them as one, such a heavenly ecstasy of peace, love and happiness possesses her that she "melts" (there is no other word for it), her whole being wishes to join with his, and though there is no orgasm in the ordinary definition of the word yet her fluids gush out in an exactly similar manner and all possible congestion is utterly and completely relieved.[243]

A mystic at heart, Lloyd surmised that lovers' experiences of oneness represent the re-creation of the divine androgyne at the heart of so many esoteric thought systems. He wrote that the full magnetic rapport of *karezza* occurs when:

> Two souls and bodies seem as one, supported and floating on some divine stream in Paradise.... This is the real ideal and end of

Karezza. You will finally enter into such unity that in your fullest embrace you can hardly tell yourselves apart and can read each other's thoughts. You will feel a physical unity as if her blood flowed in your veins, her flesh were yours. For this is the Soul-Blending Embrace.[244]

CHAPTER EIGHT

Science That Binds

Oxytocin is the primary neurochemical that enables us to bond with others.

Emotional bonds require both oxytocin and dopamine to stay strong. Orgasm causes dopamine to fluctuate in the reward circuitry, which can destabilize bonds.

Bonding behaviors are protective of health because they counter the effects of stress.

Fights with a loved one can put the amygdala, or "inner guardian," on alert, which erodes bonds. Bonding behaviors (oxytocin) calm the amygdala.

Proud parents go gaga over their wee infant, taking hundreds of pictures of the most miraculous creature ever to hit the planet. A teen spends hours composing an e-mail to his new love. An elderly woman puts a sweater on her Chihuahua as she kisses it on the nose and offers it a treat. What do all these people have in common? Their reward circuits are lighting up.

As we have seen, none of us can fall in love unless dopamine activates our reward circuitry. Our ability to fall in love, or bond with another, differentiates us from reptiles. A reptile's reward circuitry lights up for sex, eating, and drinking, but it has no use for sweethearts or pets—and has often been known to snack on younger models of itself.

While we humans require the release of dopamine and activation of our reward circuitry to fall in love, we obviously don't fall in love every time our reward circuitry lights up. For instance, we don't bond emotionally with a chocolate truffle. After the thrills, we turn off the computer or leave the casino, just as most animals mate and then move on. Dopamine cannot be the entire story. Something else is going on when we bond emotionally, and that something else is oxytocin.

Oxytocin and dopamine work together. Think of it this way. Dopamine makes the *activity* of pursuing sex rewarding. The addition of oxytocin makes the particular *person* rewarding. In a pair-bonding mammal, it produces that heartwarming sensation of "I'd do anything for you."

> *Six weeks ago I wouldn't have thought it is possible to avoid ejaculation, but even though it is frustrating at times, it is possible for me and feels good most of the time. And would you believe, I actually met someone this past week and I was intimate with her without ejaculating? It felt so good holding her for the last two nights. I feel great.*
> —Dietrich

THE NEUROCHEMISTRY OF MONOGAMY

A few years back, scientists got a good look at the intricate dance between the mammalian programs of mating and bonding, courtesy of voles—mouse-like rodents that come in two flavors: monogamous and promiscuous. After mating, promiscuous montane voles scurry off, muttering "I'll call you," while monogamous prairie voles are so enchanted that they stick with a partner for life (with a little fooling around on the side).

Prairie voles are socially monogamous. That is, they raise their pups and bunk together, while their montane-vole cousins keep adding notches to their belts, and single montane moms raise the pups. Even among prairie voles, however, many males never find a permanent partner—and remain on the prowl. They make it their mission to persuade female voles living with other males to fool around. Sound familiar?

Scientists wondered what accounts for such a striking variation between two otherwise iden-

That woman speaks eighteen languages, and can't say "no" in any of them.
—Dorothy Parker

tical species. They discovered that it comes down to the difference in their reward circuitry. As in all mammals, dopamine surges in the voles' reward circuitry when they have an opportunity to mate. That makes pursuing sex rewarding—they've "got the lust thing happenin'."

Yet prairie voles are also heavily influenced by oxytocin. A squirt of "cuddle chemical" in their reward circuitry gets "the *love* thing goin' on." As a result, prairie voles register each other as very rewarding to hang around with.[245] Like humans, they can even fall in love through physical barriers, without mating.[246]

Why do most mammals get on, get off, and get home, while prairie voles sit around snuggling as they wait for the arrival of their peewee voles? In a nutshell, these monogamous voles have more nerve cell receptors for oxytocin, or, if male, vasopressin. The additional receptors make prairie voles much more sensitive to the effects of oxytocin and/or vasopressin.[247] Voilà! They form pair-bonds.

Vasopressin is a neurochemical cousin of oxytocin. It's so similar that it can bind to the same nerve cell receptors. It also gives males an extra boost of "Don't step in my burrow, buddy!" That is, they are inclined to guard their mates from those eager gentlemen callers mentioned earlier. In moms, oxytocin also plays a dual role. It's behind the "Touch my kids and I'll chew off your paw!" reflex.[248] Don't stick your fingers down a vole hole.

This rare, and imperfect, mammalian monogamy mechanism apparently survived millions of years of evolution, and is even found in some primates. Research on the monogamous titi monkeys of South America shows mating-related activity in the same regions of the brains as prairie voles.[249] In humans, brain regions activated by seeing beloved people also appear to correspond to regions with oxytocin, vasopressin, and dopamine receptors.[250]

> The biochemistry [of bonding] is probably going to be similar in humans and in [socially monogamous] animals because it's quite a basic function.
> —Sue Carter, neuroendocrinologist

Like prairie voles and titi monkeys, humans are considered socially monogamous—that is, we like to pair-bond, even if we stray. Obviously, most of us aren't still cuddled up with our first lover, so it's apparent that our brains aren't organized exactly like those of prairie voles and titi monkeys. (Or, despite similarities, we often do something to override a potential for lifelong bonding.)

Yet oxytocin is vitally important in our social interactions, and those of all mammals, whether it's monkey-grooming or hanging with the pack. Mice genetically engineered to produce little or no oxytocin couldn't recognize any mouse they had previously met. Perhaps when oxytocin is inhibited or low, we, too, have trouble remembering how important someone is to us—or at least we have trouble remembering our anniversary. Preliminary research shows that oxytocin plays a powerful role in human social bonds, behavior, and how we perceive ourselves and our world. For example, unusually high or low activity in the oxytocin system is associated with autism, as well as social phobia, depression, anxiety disorders, obsessive-compulsive disorder, eating disorders, addiction, schizophrenia, and post-traumatic stress disorder.[251] Some claim oxytocin imbalance plays a role in obsessing over a departed mate. We suspect that dopamine dysregulation also fuels such cravings.

WARDING OFF THE HABITUATION BLUES

With oxytocin's bonding properties in mind, let's return briefly to the passion cycle discussed in Chapter Five. Both oxytocin and dopamine—at ideal levels—are necessary to keep an emotional bond rewarding. When researchers blocked either dopamine *or* oxytocin in the reward circuitry of monogamous voles (and rodent mothers), the same thing happened—or, rather, didn't happen. Prairie voles remained footloose and fancy-free, and moms didn't bond with their pups.

Now, suppose, like most folks, you and your lover engage in frequent orgasm. This makes the ideal balance of oxytocin and dopamine tough to maintain, especially in relation to each other. Dopamine temporarily fluctuates (or sensitivity to it changes) during each passion cycle. If you've exceeded your allotment of "honeymoon uppers" (that extra helping of temporary new-relationship "obsession" neurochemicals), your relationship is likely to suffer when dopamine levels bounce around. Engaging in sex will probably bring initial relief, but also push you farther toward habituation to your partner. You may begin to feel irritable, resentful, needy, or fatigued. Even if you feel none of these things, you may notice yourself engaging in annoying (separating) behaviors—or find that your partner has mysteriously become insufferable.

Think of oxytocin and dopamine as the yin and yang of bonding and love. There's even evidence that these two neurochemicals stimulate each other's release, so if one is low, it affects levels of the other.[252] This means that the neurochemical changes after orgasm, which cause dopamine levels to fluctuate for a while, may well interfere with our oxytocin-based feelings of love. Ouch.

Whatever the combination of mechanisms, habituation is a definite risk. A mate (unlike a potential *novel* partner) can start to look like a movie we've seen too often, or a food we've eaten too much, or one of those really annoying "Top 40s" hits—even though we still like movies, food, and music.

Although you and your beloved enjoyed a strong emotional bond in the past, you may not find your interactions very juicy while your dopamine is low. Your honey, who registered a "9" on your brain's dopa-mine scale before all that hanky-panky, is now sometimes registering a mere "4." A "9" was worth the effort of generous affection. A "4?" Not so much. You may feel less like snuggling each other using those oxytocin-producing bonding cues listed in the last chapter. You may even morph from a doting prairie vole into a disinterested montane vole. It could seem like you and your partner have different levels of commitment to the relationship.

And all this misery is normal. A similar neurochemical phenomenon occurs with regard to food. Both animals and humans will turn to a new food rather than eat one that they've already gorged on. That's why you can still eat an ice cream sundae even when you can't face another helping of grandma's famous stroganoff.[253] Just as our genes want variety in our diets, they want variety in our sex lives.

Adam was walking around the Garden of Eden feeling very lonely, so God asked, "What's wrong with you?" Adam replied that he didn't have anyone to talk to. God said he was going to give him a companion . . . a woman. "This person will cook for you and wash your clothes. She will always agree with every decision you make. She will bear your children, and never ask you to get up in the middle of the night to take care of them. She will not nag you, and will always be the first to admit she was wrong when you've had a disagreement. She will never have a headache, and will freely give you love and passion whenever needed."

Adam asked God, "What will a woman like this cost?" "An arm and a leg," replied God.

"Well," hesitated Adam, "what could I get for a rib?"

I have absolutely noticed his post-orgasmic behavior changes: drained sense of being, food and tobacco cravings, etc. In the first few days after our reunion the connection was so beautiful. Now, three weeks down the track, when I ask if he would like to breathe into the heart to connect more deeply, he says "yes," but shuts his eyes (says he's tired) and I can't feel him at all.—Mira

Ever notice that the first slice of pizza is much better than the fourth? You produce less dopamine in response to that last slice. Same thing with the mate with whom you've repeatedly sexually satiated yourself. You can't feel gushy while experiencing low dopamine in response to someone's presence. Neurochemically, it's out of the question.

Ideal levels of oxytocin and dopamine may also make mates more tolerant and likelier to accommodate each other. Certainly during the honeymoon period, things that normally bother people, don't, and lovers find it harder to be unhappy.[254] By avoiding habituation, my husband and I continue to experience uncharacteristically high levels of tolerance and contentment. We suspect both (balanced) dopamine and oxytocin are at work.

Stronger bonds, increased flexibility, and greater happiness are good reasons to master lovemaking that leaves you contented—but not *finished* (sated). Think of karezza as the equivalent of having two or three slices of pizza. Afterward you're not hungry, but you're also not stuffed. In fact, by emphasizing the bonding behaviors in the last chapter, you can continue to find each other delicious, which may lead to a bit of nibbling. And you sidestep the dangers of your built-in "too much pizza" program.

As J. William Lloyd once wrote:

It is the wine of sex that gives love its enchantment and divine dreams. This is easily proven by giving lovers unrestricted license to express their transports. No sooner have they wasted the wine of sex by reckless embraces—often a single orgasm will thus temporarily demagnetize the man—though they love each other just the same, as they will each stoutly assert—the irresistible attraction and radiance and magnetic thrills are gone, and there is a strange drop into cool, critical intellection or indifference, or perhaps dislike.... To have frequent orgasmal embraces, as most married lovers do, is to keep the wine in the sexual beakers low by constant spilling, to thus kill all romance and delight and finally starve and tire out love itself.[255]

HOW DOES COMPANIONSHIP PROTECT HEALTH?

The benefits from deep connections are very real, and often underrated. Yet you may be wondering *how* affection and close companionship protect your well-being. Physiologically speaking, oxytocin appears to be a big part of the short answer to that question. However, it's worth looking at the longer answer, too, so you understand what a gift harmonious companionship is, and how important it is to your health and outlook.

The fact is, disharmony is very hard on us. Putting out the "desire fire" in the usual way may not be worth the high price of unnecessary emotional friction, or fragile relationships. As we'll see in a moment, those popular "sex is good for you" articles, which seem to imply that the benefits of sex come from *orgasm*, may be mistaking sex (intercourse) benefits for orgasm benefits. Sex is one event where you don't have to cross the finish line to get the prize.

So, how can the oxytocin that *bonds* us also *benefit* us? The exact mechanisms are not clear, but one key seems to be oxytocin's ability to counteract the negative effects of stress. This has huge implications, and to understand them you need some background. You also need to know a bit more about that very important part of your reward circuitry: your inner guardian, or amygdala. The amygdala is the core of your emotional brain. It channels your brain's activity down one of two paths: *love* or *fear*. Armed with this knowledge, you will see why relationships are good medicine, yet how easy it is to overreact to a lover. Like us, you may decide that you want to protect your relationship against needless emotional friction—whatever it takes.

OLD BRAINS + MODERN
RELATIONSHIP STRESS = ILL HEALTH

The mammalian brain evaluates things as agreeable or disagreeable, and it does so very quickly, thanks to the powerful amygdala. Soothing or reassuring stimuli (receiving a massage or a gentle kiss) are associated with a neurochemical mix that includes oxytocin, while stimuli perceived as threatening (a growling dog or arguing with your mate) cause an increase in stress hormones. Information about your environment travels to both the mammalian and rational brains. However, it hits the amygdala first, because the amygdala is the shortest, quickest pathway to launch your stress response. In an emergency, you are molded to react first, think later.

Your speedy amygdala therefore acts on far less detail than your slower, rational brain receives. The amygdala gets only the headline: "Object rustling grass—left." You jump to the right, heart racing, breath bated and pupils dilated. A split-second later your rational brain analyzes the rest of the story: "Four-legged, long-tailed lizard scurrying off. Encountered many times. Harmless." The rational brain sends this amendment down to the amygdala, which turns off your stress response. Your agitation gradually subsides as the body disposes of circulating stress hormones.

What works great in the jungle can create problems in your love life. Stress responses are as old as animals, and roughly the *same* in all mammals. This means that your stress responses are ancient—shaped for the threats that animals encountered. Those stressors were chiefly physical—such as running from a predator or subduing your next meal. In most cases, events were quickly over and done with, and didn't involve much emotional processing.

For our ancestors, the most common chronic stressor involved long periods without food, not financial worries or relationship drama. Events such as drought, long migrations, and holing up away from possible threats after critical injury, all entail physical strain, the need for mental alertness, and low food intake.

When stress is chronic, adrenaline takes a backseat, and the hormone cortisol takes the wheel. Cortisol helps animals cope with extended physical or emotional stress—and affects virtually all body systems. It mobilizes energy reserves for the brain, while also turning down less essential activities, such as reproduction and digestion. It keeps an animal alert, hypervigilant, or even paranoid. This is beneficial when entering new territory or hiding from predators. Today we humans still experience high cortisol—as anxiety, insomnia, and agitation.

If a stressful situation continues, cortisol remains elevated. When threats remain, the body seems to assume that starvation is a risk. Therefore, to ensure that the brain and other vital organs are fed, higher levels of cortisol begin to *break down non-essential organs and tissues* to maintain blood sugar levels. Like an inner ghoul, cortisol starts to digest bones, muscles, and joints to obtain key nutrients to feed vital organs.

This is good for an injured deer, hiding in the bushes. After weeks without food, our recovering deer has a working brain and heart, and functional kidneys. However, its bones are thin and it has less muscle. It's still alive, though—which it wouldn't be without the miracle of cortisol.

Today, our biggest long-term stressors are emotional and mental, not physical. In effect, today's humans are a new scientific experiment. The lasting threats we face typically show up as turmoil in a marriage, potential job loss, economic woes, the pressure of commuting in heavy traffic, and a barrage of fear-producing media—perhaps all in the same day. Instead of dealing at once with physical threats, we tend to anticipate threats and imagine all sorts of gruesome outcomes. (In comparison, our dog Spot *maybe* worries about the location of his bone.)

Even though ongoing relationship friction is not a physical threat, your body reacts like you're an injured deer. Its automatic response is *more cortisol.* Cortisol can put you on hair-trigger alert, making you irritable and subject to outbursts. As time passes, changes in your brain can lead to depression or apathy. Cortisol is also very hard on your body when it stays high for a long time. In a seemingly paradoxical result, it depresses your natural immunity to disease, which can lead to innumerable disorders. It causes elevated blood fats and sugar, which are related to diabetes, heart disease, and stroke.

Like dopamine, cortisol is not "bad." You could not get energy from food without it. And when the going gets tough, cortisol keeps you going—allowing you to accomplish more than you normally could. You may pay for it later, though, just like that deer. The damage will show up where you're weakest, not in all your muscles and bones.

Oxytocin, and the behaviors that produce it, are your best defense against damaging, unproductive stress. In fact, research shows that oxytocin actually counteracts the effects of cortisol on the body, also reducing psychological stress.[256] You feel more optimistic, relaxed, and confident. We'll look at some interesting findings about oxytocin's power in just a moment. First, let's turn to your amygdala's role in evaluating the safety of your relationship, and why you might want to soothe it consciously to protect your union.

> *The other night my boyfriend told me I was more effective than Ritalin at calming him down. I was like, "Score! I can't be replaced by a pill."*
> —Janet

"ATTENTION—ACTIVATED AMYGDALA"

As we just saw, the amygdala is your inner sentry, the gatekeeper. As a key component of your reward circuitry, it scans every experience and colors the way you see it. It stores links to memories of what it perceives as threatening—or rewarding. You use it constantly in deciding what is good or bad. Without it your life would be stripped of personal meaning. It's the reason that you never stuck another paperclip in an electrical socket. It's why you won't miss the great buys at next year's White Sale (heaven forbid).

Yet the amygdala has trouble with nuance. It is like a scale, always tipping toward fear or love—and cortisol or oxytocin. Having a "bad hair day"? It could just be a "bad amygdala day."

Why do events in the amygdala matter to your relationship? Because *everything* going on in your life matters to your amygdala. It helps decide whether your relationship is safe or threatening—and its assessment is subject to change. Being in love deactivates it, thanks to good old oxytocin. Oxytocin turns down the amygdala so you feel safe enough to unite. Otherwise, you would always be on guard, unable to connect deeply with anyone. Remember that temporary, giddy honeymoon neurochemistry we talked about? One of its risks is that it turns the volume on your amygdala down so low that you can't see any flaws in your beloved. That's why your family may be unable to appreciate the magnificence of your new sweetheart's body piercings the way you can.

All passion depends on the amygdala, but so do tears and sobbing. How can you stop someone's sobs? Calm that ruffled amygdala with an extended hug.[257]

Thanks to your amygdala, your guard is either down—or you're on guard. So what happens after that temporary, mind-altering buzz of honeymoon neurochemistry wears off? Let's say the lows of the passion cycle cause you to see your partner as unbelievably selfish, or needy, and you two have a fight. When your amygdala perceives a threat, it activates your adrenal glands and the production of cortisol. It doesn't care if the name of the threat also appears in that heart-shaped tattoo on your bum. It sees your mate as *dangerous*—even when your mate is just having a bad day (or recovering from an especially passionate night). If you allow your cortisol to remain high instead of soothing yourselves with bonding behaviors, your health can eventually suffer.

In short, your amygdala is like a ticking bomb in your subconscious. It is waiting for that moment when a passion cycle leads you to imagine that your

Make love not war. Hell, do both. Get married!

post-orgasmic discomfort is not just random, but *due to your partner.* The moment this projection of uneasiness causes you to see your partner's fundamental character as a threat to your well-being, your relationship can easily begin to deteriorate. Obviously, repeated relationship dramas can set your amygdala on hyper-alert. This is one of the hidden costs of sexual satiety: fragile relationships. We can become fearful (often unconsciously) of the very unions that could best protect our health.

On the bright side, mates who *are* able to make their spouses feel loved and cared for live longer than those who give no emotional support.[258] This is why we would be wise to forgive errors as "just human," or "just mammal," rather than analyze each other's characters each time discomfort arises. We can train our amygdala to be wary—or loving. An amygdala that is low on oxytocin is a grumpy amygdala, often seeing enemies where there are none. Even a short, daily snuggle can help turn this situation around with important implications for better health and lasting harmony.

Unfortunately for relationship harmony, the amygdala has a much stronger influence on the rational brain than the reverse. The brain pathways running from the amygdala to the rational brain are like high-speed optic cables. In contrast, the rational brain communicates with the amygdala using the equivalent of dial-up. This is why intense emotions can be hard to control. In a tug-of-war, the amygdala wins. On the other hand, if you count to ten when angered, your rational brain has a fighting chance of influencing your reaction—at least for as long as you are counting.

When that stray toothpaste cap causes you to see red, it happens before you've really thought about it. Worse yet, even thinking about it may be of limited use, because the amygdala sometimes links memories with events or situations that your rational brain cannot recall. When you later say "I don't know why I overreacted that way," you're telling the truth. Your rational brain may have *no idea* why you flipped out. Your amygdala's script may now be "You did something to me, although I'm not sure what it was." Or "You just irritate me, even though I can't put my finger on why." Or "I don't really trust you." The scale has tipped to low oxytocin and high cortisol.

"Honey, when we were together, you always said you'd die for me. Now that we're divorced, don't you think it's time you kept your promise?"

Now you see how you can project the discomfort of a passion cycle onto a lover and find him or her hopelessly annoying or threatening, without realizing that you're projecting your own inner turmoil onto your hapless mate. Even if you do recognize why you are overreacting, it can take time to calm down. The amygdala's high-speed alarm messages tend to be much more intense than the rational brain's plodding reassurance. The bottom line is that your rational brain is not in control once a spat triggers your amygdala. Think involuntary manslaughter.

OXYTOCIN TO THE RESCUE

You have a built-in defense against alienation from your mate, although you may need to change your habits and employ lots of those mammalian bonding behaviors on page 178 to muster it. The key is oxytocin—nature's antidepressant and anti-anxiety hormone. It is the basis of your relaxation response. It deactivates the stress response in the amygdala. It creates feelings of calm and a sense of connection, so it actually filters how you see the world—and even your lover. When you feel peaceful, the world looks like a better place, and your lover looks like a better person. Oxytocin also improves your health and your ability to bounce back from stress. In effect, nature rewards you for bonding—with greater well-being.

Couples in a recent experiment—who, in effect, duplicated some of the effects of bonding behaviors by sniffing oxytocin before arguing—listened better and laughed more than couples who did not. (The latter more often interrupted, criticized, or degraded each other.) Importantly, the cortisol levels of those who received oxytocin were lower after the conflict. Said Swiss researcher Beate Ditzen, oxytocin may explain "how close relationships—and particularly couple relationships—have a positive effect on our health."[259] You can harness your rational brain in this effort, too, by being willing to forgive a mate's "amygdala flares" when they occur in situations that are not, in fact, threatening.

Without these countermeasures, each quarrel may strengthen a defensive response, and your relationship could start to feel like a minefield of chronic stress. If stress levels rise whenever you're together, you can perceive your mate as you would a competitor, or worse, a predator. Stressful feelings and an overheated amygdala can show up as inability to trust, self-centeredness, irritability, anxiety, decreased libido, putting one's own needs first, depression, addiction, an us-versus-them mentality, paranoia, insomnia, and fatigue. You may feel stressed just *reading* that list! In any case, it's hard to earn the "Mate of the Year" award haunted by such feelings. Yet when our mate suddenly resembles a skull-and-crossbones to our ruffled amygdala, such feelings are understandable. Been there?

Finally, as if cortisol's effects weren't enough, stress also decreases dopamine. Now your partner may appear quite unappealing. No wonder you find yourself looking around desperately for anything, or anyone, who will raise your dopa-

A Woman's Rule of Thumb:

If it has tires or testicles, you're going to have trouble with it.

mine—preferably someone your amygdala hasn't yet managed to associate with subconscious fear. The good news is that a happy, oxytocin-rich amygdala keeps dopamine in the reward circuitry—making your mate look *good* and improving your mood.[260]

If you want to become less reactive and enjoy a more harmonious relationship, choose daily oxytocin-producing behaviors to shift the neurochemistry of the amygdala and turn down its volume. This tactic can also restore your bruised perception of each other. Yet oxytocin does even more.

IS THE "BIG O" OXYTOCIN?

If you listed all the conditions and diseases related to stress, or aggravated by stress, you'd have to list nearly every known condition. Less stress means increased immunity and faster recovery, so soothing oxytocin (bonding behaviors) helps to heal them all. Feeling depressed? Anxious? Overactive stress response and amygdala activation are key factors in depression, and oxytocin relieves both.[261] When you feel peaceful, the world looks like a better place.

Isn't it nice to know that you can tap the benefits of oxytocin and increase your well-being without pharmaceuticals? For example, just ten minutes of warm, supportive touching between couples who live together causes a marked increase in oxytocin in the blood.[262] The more supportive those couples, the higher their blood levels of oxytocin. Massage and other supportive and caring touch lower stress hormones and blood pressure, particularly among young married men, while also releasing oxytocin.[263] Want more proof of the power of bonding behaviors to supply stress relief? When facing a dreaded public-speaking gig, try hugging and watching a romantic film. It lowers blood pressure and heart rate better than resting quietly together.[264] Who needs Toastmasters?

Notice that supportive touch alone makes the difference. "Talking about it" may be of limited use when a mate is anxious or irritable. Talking uses the rational brain, while holding your partner instead—preferably in silence—soothes the "problem child" itself, the amygdala. (Guys will appreciate the "in silence" part.) The time to talk will come later when perspective is restored.

We sleep in separate rooms; we have dinner apart; we take separate vacations. We're doing everything we can to keep our marriage together.
—Rodney Dangerfield

Since Will and I have been using bonding behaviors more consciously in our marriage, we've noticed that discussions about who didn't clean up a mess or take out the trash occur much less frequently, and even thornier discussions leave virtually no emotional wake. Best of all, we don't have to "create space" from each other.

Speaking of good reasons to snuggle, did you know that hugs might reduce late-night attacks on tubs of ice cream? Oxytocin appears to limit consumption of both sweets[265] *and* addictive substances. It also reduces drug withdrawal symptoms.[266] Your brain knows that you're getting the affectionate connection with others that nature intends, and it registers satisfaction. (Social animals got their oxytocin through interaction before scientists thought to pump it into their brains.)

In contrast, if you isolate yourself, or take shortcuts to good feelings, such as using superstimulants, your system penalizes you with dysfunction. In the long run, it knows what's real.

Obviously, oxytocin is likely to be behind the benefits of *all* affectionate intercourse because touch and intimacy produce this "cuddle chemical." Not only that, oxytocin often surges briefly (at least in the blood) at orgasm and drops off soon thereafter. This has lead to an urban myth that we can fix our tendency to habituate to a lover simply by having more orgasms, and thereby producing more brief surges of oxytocin.

However, before you rush off to get your "relationship glue" via orgasm, you should take into account that the brief oxytocin spike at orgasm apparently signals the post-orgasmic rise in prolactin, that sexual satiation hormone we examined in Chapter Five.[267] Prolactin, as you will recall, suppresses dopamine (desire and mood). You need dopamine to feel bonded, so you might want to get your oxytocin in a way that *doesn't* result in lower dopamine. This oxytocin-prolactin mechanism may help explain why more orgasmic passion can actually speed habituation to a lover.

In any case, when you don't wait out the passion cycle, and instead use hot sex to "bring back those feelings" while dopamine is suppressed, the subsequent crash can feel even worse (lower dopamine), pushing you farther apart. Evidence of this phenomenon is seen in the fragility of romantic relationships as compared with friendships—especially as the contrast between the highs and the lows becomes more apparent. It's hard not to conclude that "something's really wrong," even though this deterioration is perfectly natural, and much of it would pass if lovers gave themselves time to recover while engaging in soothing, daily affection.

If you're ready to get around the passion-cycle problem entirely, give bonding-based sex a try. It emphasizes oxytocin-producing affectionate touch *without* triggering subsequent feelings of "enough already." Amazingly, oxytocin also plays a key role in both sexual receptivity in females[268] and erections in males.[269] In other words, oxytocin may go far in explaining why bonding-based sex is viable. It makes us feel sexy *and* it decreases the intensity of our cravings (sexual frustration), all at the same time.

In *Love and Survival,* Dean Ornish wrote, "If love and intimacy came in pill form, doctors who failed to prescribe it would be guilty of malpractice."[270] (Let's see *that* advertised with its side effects!) Here's one more sampling of what companionship and touch can do. Happily married women in a threatening situation show signs of immediate relief when holding their husband's hand, and this has been observed in brain scans.[271] As mentioned earlier, companionship also makes wounds heal faster and has been linked directly with higher oxytocin.[272] Companionship increases longevity. HIV patients with a partner live longer and develop AIDS less rapidly.[273] Givers of both sexes benefit, too. Providing care for your spouse for more than fourteen hours a week significantly decreases your risk of death.[274] Giving also lights up the reward circuitry.[275] Learning to make giving the focus in relationships is excellent health insurance. No one can cancel your policy either!

My morning glucose readings were higher than most physicians would like to see.... 150s, 160s. My A1c tests have always been good, 7.0 or less. My last orgasm was July 4. During July my glucose morning readings were still in the high 140s and 150s. For the last three weeks (since entering the second phase of the Exchanges, with intercourse) I have been seeing readings in the 110 to 130 range, which is right where they should be for long-term good health. Suffice it to say I am pleased with these results for myself, and it is wonderful to experience the subtle changes in my relationship with my wife.—Calvin

---

As my husband and I learned more about the many gifts of oxytocin, we couldn't help asking ourselves whether it was behind the benefits we had noticed when we experimented with karezza. Were we producing more sustained levels of oxytocin with our generous, non-driven lovemaking as we went through the Ecstatic Exchanges (at the end of this book)? Perhaps increased oxytocin was strengthening my immunity, keeping yeast and urinary tract infections at bay. Oxytocin also offered a possible explanation for Will's ability to overcome his long-term addiction and chronic depression. Recently, scientists uncovered evidence suggesting that vasopressin, the neurochemical brother of oxytocin, which plays an additional role in pair-bonding for males, *also* helps inhibits alcohol use.[276]

Maybe there is something to that old saying "The more you give, the more you get"—at least when it comes to generous bonding behaviors.

OXYTOCIN ISN'T A "LOVE DRUG"

You may wonder how researchers did most of the oxytocin experiments related to bonding. They piped it (or drugs that neutralized it) directly into rodents' brains—onto spots no larger than peppercorns. However, even if you could pipe it into an unloving mate's brain, you'd have to squirt it in every time you were together. Bonds are only created when oxytocin is consistently released *in response to a particular person.*

Next time you read about the wonders of oxytocin, keep in mind that the only feasible way to deliver it to anyone's brain today is by way of a nasal spray—and that is not such a good idea. Such sprays have been used for a long time to induce milk letdown, but the oxytocin ends up all over the brain and circulating in the blood.

In contrast, your body delivers neurochemicals in just the right amount, precisely to the places they are needed, for as long as they are needed, and then quickly disposes of them. A shotgun approach can cause unintended consequences and alter the brain itself. A rise in oxytocin in a minuscule part of a mother rat's brain causes her to guard her young fiercely. The same rise one-tenth of an inch away makes her passive.[277] Manipulating humans with oxytocin is also dodgy. When scientists tried to relieve symptoms of obsessive-compulsive disorder long-term, using oxytocin nasal spray, it caused severe memory disturbances, psychotic symptoms, and marked changes in blood sodium levels.[278] In another experiment it brought on high blood sugar (diabetes).[279]

At present researchers only use oxytocin nasal sprays for short-term experiments—to learn the kinds of behaviors it influences. In this way it became evident that oxytocin increases trust—by calming the amygdala.[280] Spraying your brain is a fine tactic if you want to trust everyone, including Wall Street bankers, used car salesmen, and politicians. For example, in one experiment, those who took the placebo did not reinvest with a trustee who betrayed them, while those who had inhaled oxytocin continued to do so.[281]

The upshot? Oxytocin is probably at the heart of karezza's benefits, but it won't work as an artificial love drug regardless of those headlines you see—or the advertising claims. (Nor will blocking oxytocin work as an innocuous "love vaccine," as one journalist proposed, apparently in pursuit of casual sex without strings. For one thing, oxytocin facilitates erections and female sexual receptivity, advantages he would probably not care to sacrifice even to ward off emotional ties.[282])

Long-term manipulation of oxytocin via nasal spray could be quite dangerous. Oxytocin spray cannot cause a connection with anyone in particular. Moreover, higher blood levels of oxytocin alone do not guarantee that you experience its benefits. When researchers measured how oxytocin-producing behaviors affected women, they were surprised to discover that the women who got the most benefit were in stable relationships—even if their oxytocin levels were not as high as the women without relationships.[283] Like it or not, you'll have to snuggle (not spray) your way from habit to harmony.

The good news is that we don't need artificial oxytocin. Neurochemicals don't just control us. We can choose behaviors and thoughts that encourage the neurochemical responses we desire. If you sense more oxytocin would be a positive influence in your life, choose the behaviors that release it *naturally* in the quantities and locations for best results. Are you giving and receiving generous, affectionate touch? Focused on comforting someone else? Engaging in spiritual devotion? Singing in the shower?[284] Or spending time with trusted companions?

> When someone loves you, the way they say your name is different. You know that your name is safe in their mouth.
>
> —Billy, age 4

Feeling too shy to get started? Petting a dog and massage both release oxytocin, and can therefore make you more comfortable with human companionship.[285]

IS IT LOVE, IS IT ORGASM, OR IS IT INTERCOURSE?

Could the benefits of affectionate intercourse actually be at the heart of the benefits currently ascribed to orgasm? Based on the increasing understanding of oxytocin's health-giving properties, this seems a reasonable line of inquiry. Researchers can't yet do studies on bonding-based sex in which orgasm is deliberately avoided, for reasons we'll explain in a moment. However, one bold psychologist has already demonstrated that intercourse furnishes unique benefits when compared with orgasms without intercourse.

For example, sexual activity in the form of masturbation and oral sex did not reduce stress as much as penile-vaginal intercourse (PVI). Nature treats you better if you link up those reproductive organs.

Volunteers who had intercourse, but none of the other kinds of sex, were least stressed when doing public speaking, and their blood pressure returned to normal faster than those who'd only masturbated or had non-coital sex. The effects lingered for over a week. Don't skip your karezza though—or at least your bonding behaviors! Those who avoided all sexual activity had the highest blood-pressure response to stress.[286]

This study implies that intercourse is a more healthful bonding behavior than other orgasmic activity. It also leaves open the possibility that the health gains from sex are coming from the nurturing intimacy of intercourse rather than orgasm. Close contact matters. For example, in men, low testosterone levels normalize with the resumption of coital activity—irrespective of which therapy method used for erectile dysfunction.[287] And another study suggests that, despite its obvious risks, condomless sex is protective of women's *psychological* health,[288] perhaps due to greater intimacy, trust, or chance of pregnancy (happy genes)—or even the neurochemicals in sexual fluid.

Since the time of Kinsey it has been asserted, but never supported by evidence, that all sexual behavior is equivalent. That has been more an assertion of ideology than fact.
—Stuart Brody, psychologist

However, in the absence of actual data about where the benefits of sex originate, there has been a tendency to assume that they derive from orgasm or semen, rather than intercourse or affectionate closeness. In all fairness, the discoveries about oxytocin's life-giving properties, its connections with touch and bonding, and the health benefits of supportive union are fairly recent—so it has been easy to overlook such factors.

A "CATCH-22"

It would be great if studies had been done that reveal which aspects of intercourse offer the most benefit to lovers. Sadly, in the last century a trend began that has tied sex researchers' hands. We'll see its roots in the next chapter. One result of this trend is that today's researchers *cannot* study karezza because they assume it is a paraphilia—like a bondage fetish or a hankering for rubber garb. Apparently, some folks actually get off on *not* getting off. True fetishists have been studied, and their activities are associated with unusually high dopamine.[289] Karezza would not be.

Even though other primates frequently copulate without climax, more than one researcher told us that it would be unethical to ask study volunteers to engage in making love without orgasm for a few weeks. On the other hand, to our amusement, an ethics committee willingly approved an experiment that required a mechanical device to be surgically implanted in the spines of eleven women to produce orgasms using a remote control.[290] (Imagine if their kids picked it up to channel surf by mistake. "Uh, sorry, Mom.")

As a consequence of their rigid definitions, researchers can't separate the effects of intercourse from the effects of orgasm. They cannot determine the degree to which each is protective of health. Therefore, current research is producing an incomplete picture. It's quite possible that people who have trusted companions, balanced lifestyles, and regular intimate contact live longer, healthier lives *in spite of,* rather than because of, orgasm. As my husband quipped, "If orgasm was the magic bullet, porn addicts would be the healthiest people on the planet."

At the moment most sex researchers study orgasm by having subjects masturbate in the lab—on the assumption that all orgasms are the same. This assumption appears to be flawed. Already we have seen that the neurochemistry of orgasm with intercourse is different than the neurochemistry of orgasm with masturbation. The first produces four times as much prolactin in men, and less stress in both partners.

The different stress responses between penetrative sex and masturbation suggest the biology of one person affects another.
—Simon Crowe, neuropsychologist

Intangible factors like trusted companionship and generous affection are far more difficult to study in sexual relationships than indications of sexual performance (orgasms). As a result we hear a lot about the latter, and the former generally remain beneath the radar. Yet the fact that science can't yet tell us much about these factors doesn't mean that their effects are negligible.

WHAT DO WE REALLY NEED FROM SEX?

Let's look at a sprinkling of the research often cited in those popular "why sex is good for you" articles, which journalists love to write. The following items are common to most such lists.

  ▷ Sex relieves stress
  ▷ Sex improves cardiovascular health
  ▷ Sex boosts self-esteem
  ▷ Sex boosts immunity
  ▷ Sex burns calories
  ▷ Sex reduces pain
  ▷ Sex helps you sleep better
  ▷ Sex is an instant cure for mild depression
  ▷ Sex is the perfect beauty treatment

All of these benefits can be achieved through bonding behaviors, loving intercourse, reduced cortisol, and consistent levels of mutually generated oxytocin. In fact, it's quite possible that you can achieve these benefits *better* with bonding-based intercourse than with a few minutes of friction and seconds of orgasm. It's true that vigorous friction might burn a few more calories (although lovers tend to make love longer with karezza), but if you need orgasms to keep from developing a spare tire, you just might want to think about getting out of bed more often.

What about support for the claim that orgasm itself improves health? The Caerphilly Cohort Study is often cited for this proposition.[291] Its authors consider it proof that more frequent ejaculation prolongs men's lives. The study reported that men who had sex twice a week had a risk of dying half that of men who had sex once a month. The query was one of many intake questions asked of men (ages forty-five to fifty-nine) in a Welsh town between 1979 and 1983. (The examiners dropped the question halfway through their interview series because men objected to it.)

Unless lovemaking is preceded by enough touching, it is seldom, if ever, fully satisfying.
  —Bernard Jensen, MD, author of *Love, Sex & Nutrition*

Was ejaculation indeed the critical factor in longer lives? As another researcher pointed out:

It is likely that those men who had regular sexual activity in late middle age were either married or in long-term relationships. The greater longevity of married compared with unmarried people has been shown repeatedly and this might be an important confounding factor.... If the authors were mainly interested in the health effect of orgasm, as a purely biological phenomenon, surely masturbation should not have been ignored. Thirdly, it is unlikely that sexual behavior is static.... Sexual activity is influenced by age, health factors, and psychopathology. To these might be added changes in relationships, loss of spouse etc.... Given these shortcomings, the authors should have been more cautious in their conclusions.... Inventing new health promotion slogans with numerical imperatives would be premature and should certainly be withheld.[292]

In other words, the Caerphilly gents may have benefited from intimacy with trusted companions more than orgasm.

Even so, claims about sex abound. They make great headlines; here's just one: "Lots of Sex May Prevent Erectile Dysfunction: It's the 'Use It or Lose It' Principle at Work, One Expert Says."[293] We agree. Intercourse is good exercise for genitals. However, these headlines are right up there with "Walking Helps You Walk Better" and "Breathing Uses Lungs." Such observations are no doubt valid, as far as they go.

Alas, readers of such headlines are likely to conclude that men could engage in unlimited orgasm via intercourse or masturbation with no effects beyond fitter penises and longer lives. When we read articles about sex research, we try to keep in mind that the doctors quoted are often trying to help sexually dysfunctional patients. Their advice does not automatically translate into healthy formulas for everyone else. Flashy headlines make no such distinctions.

The Caerphilly study described above is often cited in conjunction with another study showing that women who are satisfied with their sex lives are healthier.[294] Yet what really satisfies them? Is it mutual magnetism, trusted companionship, harmonious intimacy, male pheromones (airborne chemical messengers, which have been shown to evoke healthy physiological responses in women),[295] or mere orgasm? Surely, if frequency of orgasm were the key factor, then men would have outlived women for centuries, instead of the reverse.

I did not have morning depression after orgasm during the decades I was having orgasms with my husband. I now think that all the affection that filled our lovemaking smoothed out and covered up the negative effect orgasm seems to have on me as a widow. And I also think that climaxing with a loved one is very different from climaxing with empty lips and vagina.—Lynn

---

PROSTATE HEALTH

One place it would be especially helpful to have definitive research on karezza is in the important area of prostate health. Here scientists have measured many factors and their relationship to prostate cancer: ejaculation, intercourse frequency, marital status, and number of partners. (Bonding-based sex itself has not been evaluated, of course.)

So far, study results conflict with each other on almost every factor, and a more likely culprit appears to be infection. Yet the popular press has made a lot of noise about isolated aspects of results that make good headlines. For example, in one study men who remembered ejaculating more during their twenties had lower rates of prostate cancer.[296] This is touted by the press—not the researchers—as proof that "frequent masturbation will prevent prostate cancer." Before you go (get?) off to improve your health, check your date of birth. The beneficial correlation was only seen in relation to frequent masturbation in one's twenties. Moreover, a 2009 study found the reverse correlation: Those who were most active while younger had *more* chance of developing cancer later.[297]

It seems likely that any practice that either discourages affectionate intercourse or puts a strain on the prostate gland is unwise. However, karezza is a very gentle form of intercourse—unlike tantra or some Taoist practices, in which forceful breathing and muscle-contraction techniques are often employed to resist orgasm. Trying to stay near the edge of orgasm is risky for lots of reasons.

With karezza, lovers tend to make love for longer periods of time, and more often (over the long term), without fighting to control themselves or going near the edge of intense arousal. Also, erections come and go, which gently pumps blood throughout the entire prostate region.

A recent study on prostate health suggests that holistic lifestyle changes can turn off disease-promoting genes, and activate beneficial ones. In the study, the prostate health (of patients *with* prostate cancer) responded dramatically to stress management techniques (participation in a weekly support group, yoga-based stretching, breathing techniques, meditation, and daily guided imagery), walking thirty minutes per day, and dietary supplements.

After three months, researchers repeated a biopsy of normal tissue in the subjects' prostate. They found that genes associated with cancer, heart disease, and inflammation were down-regulated or "turned off," while protective, disease-preventing genes were "turned on."[298] Researchers suggest that similar lifestyle changes may benefit all men, as the biopsies were of healthy tissue. Might soothing bonding-based lovemaking someday prove to be one such beneficial lifestyle change?

I asked my urologist about ideal ejaculation frequency. He said that, in the absence of the "irritation of frequent masturbation," a man's wet dream interval is a good guide. He advised me to wait until I had two wet dreams, without disrupting the cycle by climax, and use that interval as a guide. He explained that glands are not muscles and do not need exercise. Glands secrete fluids all on their own (e.g., wet dreams), and manual intervention is not needed. Since I have not had a wet dream for a decade or more (always masturbated) I asked, "What if I don't have a wet dream?" He replied, "Well then, you no longer need to ejaculate."—Nathan

---

UNLIMITED BONDING VERSUS UNLIMITED MATING

Overall, the evidence that orgasm itself is a vital source of benefit is surprisingly weak. Upon close inspection, one could responsibly hypothesize that the benefits of sex are better explained in terms of intimacy, touch, trust, emotional bonding, *and* resolution of sexual tension. None of these gifts of sex are dependent upon orgasm—if one masters karezza. More-over, with karezza, couples don't risk bleeping each other recurring sub-conscious mammalian signals that say "Something's just not right."

> *It is quite true that one undergoes a PROFOUND change in percep-tion after orgasm and I am certain this has evolved in order to moti-vate us males to seek out additional partners. Nonetheless, I can say that nothing compares with prolonged lovemaking without ejacula-tion; the feelings that can well up are beyond the ability to describe in words. For the first time, you know how it really feels to "be in love," if I can call it that; you start saying silly, romantic things to your part-ner because you simply feel SO GOOD! The pleasure I get from mak-ing love this way is orders of magnitude greater than what I experience from simply "having sex."—Dirk*

At the moment, because of our culture's general unwillingness (and professional powerlessness) to consider the benefits of intercourse apart from orgasm, we may grow up persuaded that orgasm by any means, as frequently as possible, is vital to happiness. In fact, we're often told that anyone who questions this assumption is "anti-pleasure" or "anti-sex." Yet if karezza offers longer-lasting, if less intense, pleasure than fertilization-driven sex, who is to say which is "most pleasurable"? And if a focus on orgasm intensifies the drive to seek ever more stimulation or novelty—thus pushing partners apart or toward private porn use—is it not, in some sense, "anti-sex"? Are we focused on the trees, but missing the forest?

Eleven percent of women and five percent of men are taking antidepressants. A generation or two ago, the age of onset of depression purportedly occurred on average at age thirty-four or thirty-five. Today the mean age for the first bout of depression is fourteen.[299]
—Charles Barber, psychiatrist

If I were a young man with a computer or a young woman with a vibra-tor, and the standard view, I would conclude that frequent masturbation is "good medicine." And if I needed relief from the (unacknowledged) pas-sion cycle's dopamine lows, I might eventually conclude that antidepres-sants and anti-anxiety drugs are my only options for relief. Are they? Or could I regulate my mood and keep my body healthy by exploring bond-ing-based sex and the mood-elevating gifts of affectionate connection?

We pair-bonding humans have unlimited bonding potential—and lots of good reasons to make the most of it. We can employ simple, comforting bonding behaviors to sustain our attraction to each other, and reap the benefits of oxytocin. Moreover, unlike many mammals, we're not constrained by mating seasons (going into heat). We can use karezza lovemaking as a bonding behavior as often as we like.

There are a number of mechanical devices which increase sexual arousal, particularly in women. Chief among these is the Mercedes-Benz convertible.
—P. J. O'Rourke

Consider the pair-bonding tamarins from Chapter Seven. The researcher focused on their oxytocin levels. Although pairs varied widely, when one mate had a high level of oxytocin, so did the other. Those with high oxytocin engaged in more cuddling, grooming, stroking, and sexual behavior, while those with low levels spent less time on these relationship-building activities. The high-oxytocin monkeys seem to know how to soothe their partners by supplying what the other needed.

Interestingly, when sexual behavior was removed as a variable and the pairs were ranked using only huddling and grooming frequency and duration, the correlation with pair oxytocin rank was still highly significant. In short, sexual behavior is good, but other bonding behaviors may be vital to keep oxytocin high. Said researcher Snowden, "Here we have a nonhuman primate model that has to solve the same problems that we do: to stay together and maintain a monogamous relationship, to rear children, and oxytocin may be a mechanism they use to maintain the relationship."

Unfortunately, human capacity to engage in unlimited *bonding* behavior is not the same thing as the capacity to engage in unlimited *mating* (fertilization) behavior. The latter has hidden costs. It may be that confusing the two has led us to set the wrong benchmark for "normal" sexual performance. Even folks whose libido has gone south can benefit from bonding behaviors.

Have we mistaken hypersexual behavior stemming from intense pursuit of orgasm for normal libido? Recovered porn addicts and others discover that their natural libido is quite different from their frenzied libido while prisoners of the passion-cycle roller coaster. Perhaps we're rushing toward risky artificial remedies for forcing erections and orgasms without sound justification. Not only that, in an effort to meet this dubious benchmark, we may be throwing couples out of sync sexually—thereby speeding the deterioration of their relationships. It is not uncommon for some satiated lovers to experience an urgent need for more sexual stimulation when an enticing cue sends up a dopamine flare, while others experience a growing distaste for an exclusive focus on sexual stimulation. (Have you noticed that mates from these two groups invariably seem to find each other?) Will and I find intercourse such a nurturing bonding behavior that we highly value remaining in sync sexually.

Only when I am feeling lustful and want sex with my husband do I feel sexual hunger. I can see it in the way I make love to him, which basically is fertilization-driven. It is a different experience from when I am just in his arms feeling that time has stopped or when we are looking in each other's eyes and wanting to become one. I don't feel any sexual hunger then. We can stay connected sexually for hours, with the least movement possible. There is no effort to avoid orgasm. On these occasions, everything is different from the start.—Natalia

In the next chapter we'll review the historical reasons for our culture's current convictions about sex as we consider how to move toward experimenting with karezza. We'll also look more closely at what it means to be a pair-bonding mammal, and how our unfulfilled longings may be healthy signals that we need to make generous touch and long-term companionship higher priorities.

BUDDHISM

Recently, two well-known Buddhist teachers living in the United States shocked many of their fellow Tibetan Buddhists by making public the fact that they live together as a spiritual practice. One is a monk, one is a nun, and both consider themselves celibate. Their relationship is physical, but sexually chaste.[300] They say they chose this practice because they felt that if Tibetan Buddhist ideas were to spread in the West, those ideas would have to be more inclusive of women as equals.

This partnership between equal mates is foreign to Buddhism—which sprang from Hindu roots and tends to be androcentric (male-centered). However, the idea that controlled sexual union between male and female can be a spiritual practice definitely lurks behind the scenes of Tibetan Buddhism. For example, female Buddha Lady Yeshe Tsogyel became enlightened through ritual sexual union with her guru more than a thousand years ago.[301]

Today, many Buddhist teachers seem the very picture of contented celibacy. Yet some Tibetan Buddhist holy men still quietly take consorts for the purpose of ritualistic lovemaking, without ejaculation. The Dalai Lama himself teaches that "the best opportunity for further [spiritual] development is during sexual intercourse" without seminal emission:

> The reference here is to the experience of entering into union with a consort of the opposite sex, by means of which the elements at the crown are melted.[302]

He explains that the penis is utilized, but the energy movement taking place is fully controlled and is never let out. It is eventually returned to other parts of the body.[303] The principle of controlling the sexual energy applies to women, too.[304] He notes that because of the need for avoiding orgasm, "there is a kind of special connection with celibacy."[305]

Some of today's Tibetan Buddhist-inspired tantra teachers include orgasm in their courses—after an intense buildup of sexual energy that produces a drug-like state of mind. However, the Dalai Lama teaches that orgasm cannot lead to enlightenment. He says this belief is a "root downfall,"[306] a mistaken practice, perhaps based on distorted, selfish values. He also explains that it is not intercourse, but state of mind that matters.

> Mere intercourse has nothing to do with spiritual cultivation. When a person has achieved a high level of practice in motivation and wisdom, then even the joining of the two sex organs, or so-called intercourse, does not detract from the maintenance of that person's pure behavior.[307]

Teachings like these reveal an uneasy tension between celibacy and intercourse. Perhaps this is why some Buddhist holy men keep their sexual trysts behind the scenes. Such unions are not between equals, as a young Scottish woman found when she was recruited to participate in this type of concealed liaison.[308] As she pointed out, the *tulku* system, by which a lama symbolically gives birth to himself through reincarnation as another male, forestalls equal spiritual partnerships between men and women. It also works a hardship on young boys, who are raised away from daily contact with loving women in an all-male environment. The result of this practice is a male monastic tradition that regards women as potential pollutants and obstacles to religious practice, while at the same time revering them (during sexual ritual) as goddesses who are essential to a man's enlightenment.[309]

All of this means that the couple mentioned at the beginning of this section are engaging in quite a different practice than the traditional one, even though their approach is very consistent with Buddhism's loftiest principles. This may be why the Dalai Lama expressed his disapproval of them, publishing a statement that this "unconventional behavior does not accord with His Holiness's teachings and practices."

The tension between celibacy and ritual sex in Buddhism may go as far back as Gautama Buddha himself. Some even suggest he taught that enlightenment resides in the sexual parts of women *(Buddhatvam Yosityoni-samasritam),*[309a] a disquieting maxim for his many celibate disciples. He also urged his disciples not to continue the cycle of suffering by fathering children.[310] These two suggestions dovetail in the practice of sex without ejaculation, yet few Buddhists choose this path despite their traditional emphasis on compassion, self-control, and retention of semen.

The Tibetan Buddhist myth *The Legend of the Great Stupa Jarungkha-sor*[311] sheds some light on the tension between celibate purity and sex as a spiritual practice, by suggesting that there are actually *three* paths to enlightenment (which may support each other, of course). All address the power of sexual desire to distort spiritual perception, because this source of distortion is believed to be at the heart of humanity's worst problems (and spiritual blindness).

The first two paths are the *Mahayana* and the *Hinayana*. The Mahayana is the neutralization of passion through selfless service and dedication to releasing all life from the bonds of emotional distortion and limited vision. It is open to a wide range of personalities. In contrast, the Hinayana is *not* suited to all personalities. It prescribes total rejection and renunciation of passion (celibacy), and is characterized as safe, sure, and slow.

According to the *Great Stupa*, one's best chance for freeing oneself from the chaos of mankind's spiritual dark age is to tame the passions using the third path of *controlled indulgence,* or *Vajrayana,* a homeopathic method in which one uses sexual desire, but carefully, by avoiding orgasm and drawing the sexual energy upward. Vajrayana is open to all, and is a means of overcoming humanity's impulsive nature. "We rise by the same way that we fell" is a Tibetan Buddhist adage, meaning that if sex and emotions have brought humankind down, they are a means by which it can heal and restore itself.

The path of controlled indulgence is considered the fastest, yet most risky, of these paths. Interestingly, the legend suggests that the service and celibate devotion paths—although excellent, beneficial disciplines—won't get the job done during the chaos of humankind's spiritual dark age.

The late scholar Mircea Eliade explained that for a Tibetan Buddhist, sex holds the key to regaining the Light:

> So long as man practices the sexual act in instinctual blindness, that is to say like any other animal, the light remains hidden. But ... by checking the seminal ejaculation one defeats the biological purpose of the sexual act.[312]

Controlled indulgence is thus a means to move toward the androgyny of a divine state. According to Eliade, some tantrics seek an experience of gnosis, or nirvanic consciousness, while some speak of yogis who realize immortality in the body. According to tradition, they do not die; they disappear into heaven clothed in "spirit-bodies," "divine bodies," or "bodies of Pure Light."

This experience of androgyny may, in some cases, require the spiritual synergy of both sexes. An earlier Dalai Lama (the twelfth) apparently resisted the insight about the power of such union, to his peril. He recorded a vision in which the famous male guru of the Lady Yeshe Tsogyel (the female Buddha mentioned above) spoke the following words:

> If you accept the practice of secret mantra by
> Relying upon a Knowledge Lady [a woman he had met,
> Rigma Tsomo],
> Tibetan Buddhism will thrive
> And the Dharma Protectors will act.
> But if you do not rely upon
> The siddhi [extraordinary power] of karmamudra [sexual yoga],
> You will soon die.

That Dalai Lama died at the age of twenty.[313]

CHAPTER NINE

BRIDGING THE GAP

As we humans have lost the rewarding companionship that is the perfect "mood medicine" for our mammalian brains, compulsions have increased. Oxytocin-producing behaviors ease these compulsions.

We can use karezza to meet our longing for a pair-bond, soothe sexual frustration, counter habituation, and compensate for our missing tribal companionship.

Even without the cooperation of a mate, you can observe the orgasm cycle in yourself.

Inflamed libido is not due to a physical surplus in the body. It is often due to oversensitivity to stimulating cues. Unconsciously, the sufferer may actually be seeking relief from withdrawal symptoms—and the comfort of a pair-bond.

B y this point, you may be ready for a fresh start. You're armed with a new understanding of how your underlying mammalian mating program has an ongoing mandate to screw up sexual relationships, and hopefully the explanation makes some sense to you. You also know about the power of subconscious bonding cues, and how to keep that underlying mating program in check. All in all, you may even be feeling a growing optimism about romance.

On the other hand, you may also feel a bit lonely—as if you're the only one at the party who took the hallucinogen. Chances are, there's a modern consensus in your culture that "there can be no such thing as too many orgasms," and that "one can't pass up orgasm without risking a debilitating fear of sex (sexual repression)." If you don't yet have a partner, how the heck are you supposed to explain a radical new concept when the right moment arrives? If you do have a partner, how is she or he going to react to such an unfamiliar idea as making love without the goal of orgasm?

Moreover, if you are drawn to the concepts in this book, the chances are good that you value relationships, would like to cherish a mate, and, generally speaking, are willing to accommodate your partner when you can. It is stressful to realize that accommodating your partner in this instance means adhering to biology's script. You sense that may not be a sound strategy.

My boyfriend and I are close and the sex is good. But I have noticed a strange cycle that occurs after we both reach orgasm. We're more easily aggravated, and even more so if we orgasm often. An odd "distance" between us stays around for a while. And when we don't orgasm for a while, or we make love in a more relaxation-oriented way, things are much better and calmer.

These days a lot of couples are breaking up. As he said, "I don't understand. Some people have it so good, and have been together longer than we have. Yet things just fall apart due to too many fights or affairs." We don't want anything to come between us, especially if it can be prevented. Sadly though, we differ as to what to do about it. His latest solution is the excitement of "group sex" online, using avatars. This doesn't feel right to me.—Petra

Before we consider concrete steps for introducing these ideas to another, let's pull the key concepts of the book together by examining some history that has been clouding our understanding of sex, bonding, and orgasm. Without this perspective, you may hesitate to propose karezza to a partner because you fear that you would be asking someone to deny herself or himself an essential ingredient for well-being: orgasm whenever the urge arises. After all, there's a widespread belief that orgasm is one of the best "mood medicines" available to us. And there's no question that we need mood medicine today—more than ever. It's also true that making love *can* be great mood medicine.

MAMMALIAN BRAIN PAIN AND THE CASE FOR KAREZZA

To understand why generous bonding behaviors and karezza are likely to be even *better* mood medicine than orgasm, we need to peer back into our distant past. Warning: We're going to cover a lot of history very quickly. Yet without this history, it's difficult to understand why moving to karezza is a loving act, and not an act of deprivation.

To recap, our brains evolved over millions of years. During much of that time we lived in small primate bands. Survival depended not just on enthusiasm for reproduction, but also on mutual support and willingness to engage in close companionship with others. Living alone meant death (for our genes, too). Our mammalian brain rewards us for touch and companionship—meaning they *make us feel good*. This is important information, because we're stuck with this brain. Ten thousand years is scarcely the blink of an eye—evolutionarily speaking.

What happened about ten thousand years ago? The march away from our hunter-gatherer lifestyle toward modern civilization began. Despite cell phones, books on relationships, and roller blades, civilization has hidden costs. One cost is that our mammalian brain has lost its ideal lifestyle. Important sources of rewarding feelings have slipped away, steadily increasing our levels of stress and anxiety. "Something is missing" feelings make the search for mood medicine increasingly urgent. Some of us have naturally used orgasm to medicate our distress (in addition to other mood-altering activities and stimulants).

Primate brains are molded to find friendly touch, personal relationships, and hanging out with others both rewarding (dopamine) and comforting (oxytocin, endorphins). Why? Taking pleasure in close contact favors the survival of a tribe (or troop), as well as the survival of infants. If Africa's Bushmen and arctic Eskimos are any indication, we devoted much of our day to this source of mood medicine for most of human existence. Indeed, today's wild primates still spend much of their time grooming and, in the case of bonobos, rubbing genitals on each other. These activities are rewarded because of their power to maintain vital social bonds and reduce stress. For example, low-ranking males spend a lot of time grooming to reduce the stress of being picked on by the big boys.

Maybe our ancestors' bonds with mates proved only temporarily fulfilling. After all, there was probably no selection pressure for lifelong unions because of the evolutionary advantage of having offspring with different partners. But our forebears' supply of friendly, or otherwise rewarding, interaction was all around them. (Think hunts, years of nursing each infant, tattooing one another, elaborate hairdressing, celebrations, and rituals.)

Ten thousand years ago, these health-giving aspects of daily life began to dry up. Most of us gradually settled into agrarian lifestyles, which led to insular families. We lost our tribes, and the healthy emotional transparency and conflict resolution skills of tribal life. Then, three to four hundred years ago, we began migrating into cities. As we grew more mobile, many of us also lost our extended families and our roots (our comforting sense of belonging, or connection with others).

We also forfeited hours of daily contact with our kids, who often went into factories themselves or boarding schools. This decreased both their opportunity to engage in bonding behaviors with familiar, trusted family members *and* their future tendency to engage in bonding behaviors themselves. Monkeys that lack comforting caregivers as infants make terrible parents.

If psychological well-being is linked with having deep intimate contacts, being a valued member of an enduring social group, and being enmeshed in a network of extended kin, then the conditions of modern living seem designed to interfere with human happiness.
—David M. Buss, psychologist

This trend may explain how Harlow's peers came to undervalue comforting touch, and why we have trouble recognizing the power and importance of bonding behaviors in our relationships today. Bonding behaviors don't come naturally to us if we didn't learn them as children. This unfortunate trend continues with fragile relationships, working moms, single-parent families, and kids who aren't receiving enough bonding contact to build the resilience they need to cope with stress later in life.

NEW LIFESTYLE, NEW COMPULSIONS

When we moved off the farm, our use of mood-altering stimulants gained sharp momentum—particularly in the direction of *self*-stimulation. Now, for the first time in history, stimulants, old and new, became widely available: tobacco, chocolate, rum, gambling, shopping, and financial speculation. (These can still be found at your neighborhood convenience store, of course.) It is perhaps significant that there was no term in the English language for "addiction" prior to this time.

We also began to medicate our moods with pornography, novels about passionate romance—and frequent masturbation. Obviously, masturbation wasn't a new idea, but, prior to the eighteenth century, no one saw it as likely to lead to a troubling addiction, except for the occasional sexually segregated cleric. Now people noticed that more folks were becoming hooked on all sorts of behaviors that were not serving them, single-minded pursuit of orgasm included. The resulting compulsions were unfamiliar and scary because they were not easy to overcome. There weren't any Twelve-Step programs either.

It's useful to keep in mind that the panicky cultural reaction to sexual compulsion began *not* because sex and masturbation were seen as "sinful." Indeed, the Church was a relative latecomer to the debate. It began because people were deeply concerned with stemming the sharp rise in habit-forming, harmful excesses.[314] Masturbation was by no means the only one, but it was the easiest for children to fall prey to. Hence the understandable, if misguided, admonition that sex was to be used only for procreation. Keep in mind that without a clear understanding of how orgasm interacts with the brain, there *was* no comprehensible justification for moderation.

Fears about compulsive masturbation were first publicized in regard to kids in boarding schools, many of whom were already anxious due to unnatural deprivation of contact with families and peers of the opposite sex. One reaction—with truly tragic results—was a virulent outcry against "self-pollution." Generations of lonely, displaced children were raised to view the search for relief from sexual urges via masturbation as a *moral* failing, rather than as a natural activity that merits foresighted management. Unfortunately, if they later found partners, the link between sexual desire and "vice" didn't always magically vanish. One unhealthy outcome was fear of sex itself, which, as we have seen, can make sexual stimuli abnormally compelling.

FROM FRYING PAN TO FIRE

Another unforeseen result of self-righteous finger wagging about sexuality was the equally extreme backlash it has caused in the past century. Instead of a relaxed, inquiring attitude toward orgasm and masturbation, we're now saddled with an unexamined belief that we must pursue both by whatever means, and as frequently as possible—or risk unhealthy sexual repression.

It's not clear that the resulting slippery slope is any better for kids than making them feel guilty about sex. For one thing, both schools of thought (making-sex-wrong and encouraging-pursuit-of-more-orgasm) tend to undervalue the benefits of trusted companionship and bonding behaviors *independent of orgasm*. Both extremes can deter kids from sufficient wholesome contact with their peers, and turn the pursuit of orgasm into a superstimulus. Either can thus increase the risk of isolation and compulsion.

Our current mindset also veils key evidence that would deepen our understanding of both our sexuality and superstimuli such as porn and risky behavior. We tend to ask only, "Is this behavior *normal?*" As we saw from Sooty's night of passion, excess upon occasion *is* normal. Yet the wiser question may be, "Is this behavior satisfying or does it increase my frustration overall?" Or even, "Whether or not someone says it's normal, is it causing me to act like someone I know I am not?"

Adolescent exploration is one thing. Sure, it's natural to masturbate when you are fifteen. But if you are a forty-year-old beating off daily to Internet porn, that is not "natural," and it certainly isn't "healthy." With all the ridiculous pro-masturbation propaganda out there, it took me years to recognize I had a problem, and months to get my life back.—Luke

---

Wondering how we ended up with today's conviction that we can't apply the brakes without causing worse problems? Let's take a brief detour to look at the work of two seminal thinkers in this field: Freud and Kinsey.

Sigmund Freud assumed that repressed sexual desire was behind most ills—not an unreasonable thesis in his day. However, he supported his conclusions with only six full case studies, including patients who were not his.

Since his lifetime, scholars have unearthed letters and contemporaneous case notes that demonstrate Freud did not produce the dramatic cures in these cases that he claimed.[315]

Freud experienced the death of passion in his own marriage, although he couldn't have been more fervently in love while engaged. (Cocaine may also have heightened his ardor.) In his forties he informed his (now) wife that they would live a life of celibacy, because he needed to sublimate his libido in order to have more creative energy. (There have always been rumors that he channeled his carefully hoarded energy into an affair with a novel mate: his sister-in-law.)[316] It's our loss that he did not to turn his brilliant mind to the question of why sex with his wife depleted his energy, or why they became sexually estranged.

A few decades later, Alfred C. Kinsey asserted that "orgasm is merely an outlet." He boldly jumped aboard the Superstimulus Roller Coaster—and experienced precisely the results that a more in-depth understanding of his reward circuitry would have predicted. He pursued orgasm compulsively with partners of both sexes and fell into escalating sadomasochism. Tragically, he never realized that sexual satiety was only the initial phase of a longer cycle with the power to push him around. This gap in his knowledge caused him to assume that his own out-of-control sexuality was normal and healthy, a belief he confidently

> Kinsey's book takes sexual behavior out of its interpersonal context and reduces it to a simple act of elimination. . . . It suggests no way of choosing between a woman and a sheep.
> —Margaret Mead, anthropologist[319]

projected onto his society as a whole.[317] Kinsey even maintained that non-violent sexual contact between adults and children was harmless sex play.[318]

As someone who grew up very much persuaded by "Kinsey-think," I was startled to learn that his proof was as wobbly as Freud's. He claimed his statistics reflected valid cross-sections of the U.S. population, but, in fact, they significantly over-represented prison inmates, homosexuals, college students, and, apparently, prostitutes.[320] Interestingly, his *Sexual Behavior of the Human Female* assumed throughout that frequency of orgasm was very important to, and closely associated with, marital success. Yet his sample indicated almost the opposite. The women reporting the most orgasms more often either failed to marry or divorced.[321]

My dad told me always to make sure my lovers orgasm, but, looking back after many years of dating, the women I had the "best sex" with were also the most moody and unfaithful. Seems like most of them never speak to me anymore, while the ones I never had sex with for various reasons, or was not very sexual with, have become good friends and still love me to this day.—Doug

Since Kinsey kicked off the sexual revolution half a century ago, fatherless families have been on the rise. In 1968, the United States became the world leader in fatherless families. Between 1950 and 1996, the percentage of children living in mother-only families climbed from six percent to twenty-seven percent.[322] The percentage of father-only families is also mounting. This trend reflects various developments, but perhaps we should also examine its concurrence with our increasing emphasis on orgasm and superstimulation—given that sexual satiety speeds habituation to a partner and fosters attraction to novel mates.

Commendably, Freud and Kinsey did their best to stamp out sexual repression based on moralistic finger wagging. After all, shame can *itself* transform sexual stimuli into risky supranormal stimulation. They also reminded anyone who didn't already know it that sexual pleasure is a good thing.

Yet it may be time to fine-tune their conclusions about where the most pleasure lies, now that we have the tools to understand how orgasm can set off an unwelcome passion cycle, and even rewire the brain. We don't *have* to choose between dangerous suppression and risky, untrammeled sexual expression. In fact, there may be more overall sexual pleasure to be found in balance, trusted companionship, and an approach like karezza, than in the brief, mind-altering highs and merciless lows of the Superstimulus Roller Coaster.

I am sure of one thing: The kind of behavior I've been through isn't healthy sex. It is not "sexual repression" to stop compulsive sexual behavior.—Martin

Incidentally, karezza offers an effective way to reverse a Kinsey-type progression toward sexual compulsion because it does not lead to the rewarding payoff of orgasm. Without the reinforcing payoff, neural pathways that connect such behaviors with reward (cues) steadily lose strength.

One can speed the rewiring process by substituting a new, unfamiliar behavior—such as gentle intercourse with lots of relaxed stillness.

ADDICTION AND CIVILIZATION

Back in the eighteenth century, when attempts to self-medicate with substances and activities began their ominous surge, observers referred to compulsions as "diseases of civilization." In the sexual arena, they pointed to the distinction between sex with a person and sex with one's imagination. The participation of a partner naturally set a brake on excess in the form of partner availability, family demands, financial constraints, or the burden of arranging trysts. Do-it-yourself sex, on the other hand, had no inherent limit, and could more easily become compulsive. Some realized that one solution was not to tamper with nature, and keep the emphasis on union. Intercourse based on "natural needs" (and mutual agreement) was thought to be more beneficial than intercourse, or orgasm, produced with imagination or other self-stimulation.[323]

In short, our assumption may be wrong that humans have generally used orgasm as mood-altering relief, happily climaxing to satiety whenever aroused, alone or with a partner, and without ill effect. Indeed, anthropologist A. Ernest Crawley records that tribal cultures all over the world believed that temporary abstinence from sex was appropriate in connection with many activities. These included hunting, warfare, planting, fishing, harvesting, wine preparation, shamanic deeds, pilgrimage, the first days of marriage, pregnancy, lactation, menstruation, and so forth. Often believed to increase abundance as well as male invincibility and vigor, such periodic abstinence was so widespread that Crawley characterized temporary chastity as an "infallible nostrum for all important undertakings and critical junctures."[324]

The modern, nonstop pursuit of orgasm may be a fairly recent loop in a spiral we've only recently recognized. Neurohistorian Daniel Lord Smail points out that one can view the entire history of civilization as an accelerating trend toward greater use of mood-altering (psychotropic) substances and activities, including shopping sprees and gorging on empty calories. Pursuit of frequent orgasm is one among many—although a particularly compelling one.[325] In keeping with Smail's observation, libido (or novelty seeking) is one area where our brains have been evolving unusually quickly in the last ten thousand years.[326] The key point is that this dreary historical trend toward self-medication with stimulants isn't just bad luck. It arose as our reassuring connections with others eroded, and we lost the neurochemical balance those connections afforded.

THE IDEAL MOOD MEDICINE

Hijacking the reward circuitry of our brains in search of our missing comfort has become such a familiar habit that we have lost sight of that circuitry's true purpose. It's there to urge us closer to deeply gratifying contact with our fellow humans. Unlike grizzlies, we don't thrive on solitude. Research reveals that too little friendly contact with others increases our susceptibility to addiction.[327]

Yet on the bright side, the mammalian brain is molded to function contentedly *without* extra stimulation when adequate rewards come from daily activities. For example, rats that exercise a lot can't be bothered to work hard for the reward of cocaine, while sedentary rats pursue it however much effort is required.[328] In the case of our ancestors, daily rewards probably included not only friendly interaction and feelings of support, but also exercise, closer contact with nature, and the satisfaction of mastering skills and crafts.

I think what is erotically charged has double and triple power in a culture increasingly disconnected from the senses. When I feel sexually starved it is not that I am really starved for sex per se, but that I miss being connected to the world through every sense. I feel amputated. I could be compulsive and just hook up with someone, but I know this would sate nothing. My agitation (which shows up as sexual frustration) is due to the fact that I am increasingly pulled into a lifestyle that denies my sensual side.—Charlene

---

Eventually two doting caregivers became a survival advantage—as human babies came to be born "prematurely" so their bigger brains could pass through Mom's pelvis. Our brains changed to promote pair-bonding, becoming more sensitive to the highs from sex and love. While all kinds of wholesome activities that once improved our ancestors' state of mind also no doubt improve ours, a harmonious pair-bond became one of the most important determinants of happiness.[329] In fact, trusted companionship does more to protect our well-being than increased exercise, better diet, our individual genetic blueprint, stopping smoking, or prescription drugs.[330]

In contrast, loneliness throws the body and brain of both men and women out of balance. It can become a downward spiral according to *Loneliness* authors John Cacioppo and William Patrick. For example, people with few ties to others are more likely to die from restricted flow of blood to the heart, brain, and other parts of the body. Loneliness predicts changes in our gene activation, which shift our cells' sensitivity to cortisol, dampening our ability to turn off the body's inflammatory response (a cause of cardiovascular disease). This means the lonely person is actually less able to absorb the stress-reducing benefits that others derive from the comfort and intimacy of their human contacts. Resilience and recovery also suffer. Even when the lonely got the same *quantity* of sleep as the non-lonely, their *quality* of sleep was greatly diminished.

Men and women with few ties to others were two to three times more likely to die in a nine-year follow-up period than those who had many more contacts. They died not just from cardiovascular disease, but from all causes of death. In short, social isolation is on a par with high blood pressure, obesity, lack of exercise, or smoking as a risk factor for illness and early death.[331] Did you get your hug or pet your cat today?

[Comments of two recovering porn addicts] Days when I have had much communication with other people are usually days with a pretty calming end, where I do not need porn. Days when I have little contact for whatever reason, porn is harder to resist, as if I can make up for a lonely day by watching some porn or having a quick wank.
—Kyle

On days when I am purposefully engaged in the service of others I am less likely to do porn. So now I realize that I should be focusing on participation in wholesome activities, not simply on abstaining from porn.—Adrian

---

In some sense, the history of civilization has been the sad story of our descent from the trusted companionship and sensual connection we need to thrive—into an escalating search for substitute mood medicine.

I lost thirty pounds with very little effort while I was in a relationship. Since it ended two years ago, I've gained back fifteen, and have a very hard time shedding any of it.—Chantal

One substitute "mood medicine" is pursuit of casual sex. It's easy to miss the potential stressfulness of brief flings, because they offer temporary, mood-altering relief. They *feel* like the cure for anxiety, because they are, in fact, steps on a healthy trajectory. Yet using encounters purely for sexual relief naturally accelerates the tendency to undervalue each connection in favor of pursuing a novel one.

58 percent of women and 23 percent of men regretted their one-night stands.[332]

If loneliness is lethal, then sexual encounters that are empty of sustained bonding behaviors—and still interspersed with periods of stressful loneliness—may do little to reduce our overall levels of anxiety.

Loneliness is damaging within relationships, too. For example, a study was done of almost ten thousand married men with chest pain (angina). Among those with high risk factors—elevated cholesterol, high blood pressure, age, diabetes, and irregular heartbeat—there was almost twice as much angina in the group of men who answered "No" to the question "Does your wife show you her love?"[333]

PAIR-BONDING MANDATE

Love is a need—at least for pair-bonders like us. In contrast, ninety-five percent of mammalian species are cheerfully promiscuous. They don't get much buzz from pair-bonding. They just get the usual dopamine surge from mating (and other survival activities, such as eating and drinking). Mating casually doesn't leave them with a nagging sense that something is missing. We, however, compose love songs and line up at the box office to watch romantic films.

The world's most reliable solo-orgasm supply won't completely satisfy the average human. Even if he firmly believes he doesn't *need* a mate, and even if she thinks she is as happy as a fish without a bicycle, there's an empty hole at a neurochemical level. Our brain is flashing uncomfortable "something is missing" signals. For us, mating is ideally *a pair-bonding exercise,* because it improves the chances of survival of any offspring. We're wired this way, all things being equal.

For example, a large 2006 study of German-speaking Swiss found that most of the singles were only without partners because they hadn't found a suitable one. More than half stated that something is missing and almost two thirds wished for a fixed relationship.[334] Roughly three-quarters already lived in a fixed relationship, although partnership duration was declining with each generation. Shorter, more casual romances do not constitute a healthy trend for pair-bonding mammals like us because of the inevitable gaps between partners.

Recent research suggests that pair-bonding mammalian species are more susceptible to depression[335] and addiction[336] than promiscuous species. The same neural circuitry that governs pair-bonding also governs susceptibility to these disorders, and pair-bonders seem to have a *more sensitive* version of it than

Women in steady relationships, according to a study published in the December 2008 issue of *Current Sexual Health Reports,* are far more likely than their single peers to feel comfortable with their natural appearance below the belt—and that comfort translates into higher scores on six separate measures of satisfaction between the sheets.
—*Time* magazine

most mammals. Scientists saw this recently when they compared the effects of amphetamine on two types of voles: pair-bonding prairie voles and promiscuous montane voles. Dopamine rose significantly more in response to the drug use in the pair-bonding voles than in the voles who were not wired to seek long-term mates. The monogamous voles were inclined to find certain dopamine-based rewards *more rewarding* than their promiscuous vole cousins.

This suggests that lonely pair-bonders have a greater risk of becoming addicts than would mammals with no built-in urge to form a pair-bond. The "neurochemical hole" described above appears to be very real indeed.

The neural mechanism common to both bonding and substance abuse didn't evolve for addictions; it's there for love (pair-bonding).

Alas, we humans do not necessarily interpret this craving as a "go forth and bond" signal. Unlike other pair-bonding mammals, we are quite likely to jam a square peg into a round hole by seeking out a substitute, healthy or unhealthy. Some of us do this with lots of friends. Some with therapeutic massage or tango classes. Mother Theresa did it her way. But all of us have to address this "little hole" somehow. Nature abhors an aching heart.

It seems likely that these pathways and genes evolved not for drug abuse, but for mediating the motivational aspects of social interaction, including pair bonding.
—Thomas R. Insel, MD,
behavioral neuroscientist

The situation is risky because our reward circuitry has one fundamental way to motivate us: dopamine surges. It's therefore easy for us to conclude that the more our chosen substitute stimulates our reward circuitry, the more comfort we have found. We're therefore easily tempted by alcohol, drugs, and emotionally empty sexual stimuli—especially if we have come to associate intimacy with pain, or we don't yet know how soothing bonding behaviors can be.

Could this help explain why single men are more than three times as likely as married men to die of cirrhosis of the liver, and why seventy percent of chronic problem drinkers are either divorced or separated?[337] Conversely, emotional bonds help ward off cravings for addictive substances and behaviors. In a seven-year study of 800 young adults, depression and alcohol abuse declined more significantly for those who married during that time.[338] Cohabitors, too, enjoy significantly lower levels of psychological distress than individuals with no partner or those with a partner living outside the household.[339] Benefits may stem from lower cortisol.[339a]

The bottom line is that our compulsions spring not just from our mating program (drive to fertilize), but also from our built-in longings for a pair-bond. It's ironic that if we were *truly* a promiscuous species, instead of pair-bonders who fool around sporadically, we would likely be less susceptible to addiction. We wouldn't have this added sensitivity—that is, this emptiness to fill. (We would probably also still have brains small enough to enable one parent to rear a healthy child without disadvantage. After all, pair-bonding evolved because it offered the evolutionary advantage of permitting offspring with larger brains.)

The important point is that the majority of us are *supposed* to be uncomfortable when we are without mates. Just as we're supposed to be hungry or thirsty when we need to eat or drink. Few of us are wired for a life of isolation or one-night stands, however convenient it would be if we were. Our discomfort is a signal that we need to reach out to potential companions not just if they look like alluring genetic opportunities—but because they are "good medicine" when we cultivate them as trusted, long-term companions. If we don't connect, we risk being powerfully drawn to other sources of stimulation in our search for comfort.

Yesterday my boyfriend said he always seemed to feel less need to masturbate when in a [pre-sex]relationship. He was like, "although, you'd think in some ways the desire would be greater." I was like, "No, I feel the same way."—Suzie

In recent decades many of us have been trying to fill our longing for love with mere sex, or even mere orgasm. Alas, neither addresses our subconscious need for a pair-bond. In fact, it can easily carry us *away* from nourishing connection with a mate by speeding up the habituation effect. (Of course, many of us got it just right with a sensual, loving relationship, and then watched in dismay as our underlying mating program eventually shattered our mutual source of well-being despite all efforts to preserve it.)

The most effective solution may be right in front of us: mating behavior that *doesn't* trigger habituation and the desire for a novel mate. Contented union employing karezza could be the most reliable way to satisfy both our built-in "I need sex" signal *and* our built-in "I need ongoing companionship" signal.

KAREZZA AND MONOGAMY

Loneliness is stressful and, as we have seen, an unhappy mammalian brain sends out distress signals that are louder than the thoughts of the rational brain. Happily, we can relieve our mammalian brain pain and promote greater inner equilibrium by harnessing our intimate relationships—albeit in an unfamiliar way.

Karezza is just the thing for pair-bonders like us. It converts a *mating behavior* (intercourse) into a *bonding behavior,* so it addresses our inherent neurochemical longing to bond. At the same time, it retains the aspects of intercourse that increase our well-being (intimate, caring union with another). Tribeless karezza lovers are, in effect, substituting bonding behaviors *in sexual relationships* for some of the rewarding activities their ancestors once gleaned partly from abundant nonsexual contact in daily life. Karezza also helps lovers elude the biological undertow that so often makes mates lose their luster.

Can humans safely make this transition? Even though we pair-bonders willingly dabble in polygamy thanks to our underlying add-a-mate program, most of us actually live some form of monogamy. This is true even for eighty percent of those in polygamous societies. We are flexible creatures, and can certainly *adjust* to harmonious monogamy, without doing ourselves harm. In any case, as Barash and Lipton point out in their book *The Myth of Monogamy:* "Biology is neither overweening nor even a worthwhile guide.... There is very little connection, if any, between what is natural or easy and what is good."[340]

There is no human moral imperative to obey evolution.
—Julian Savulescu and
  Anders Sandberg, ethicists

Karezza offers a way to make the zest for monogamy authentic—from within. When bonds are deeply satisfying, a transformation occurs. Uncomfortable, demanding sexual urges, which would normally lead to satiety, habituation, and a powerful hankering for variety, change into warm readiness. We can make love when the opportunity naturally arises, and feel at peace and affectionate the rest of the time. Perhaps this is because other *kinds* of contact become more thoroughly satisfying. As we've seen, in other pair-bonding mammals, "sexual behavior is neither especially frequent nor especially fervent." Many interactions between mates take the form of resting together, mutual grooming, and "hanging out."[341]

Is our propensity for frequent orgasmic sex a search for the deeper satisfaction that only dependable, generous bonding behaviors could supply?

All of this is a long way of saying that lovers who experiment with karezza are not denying each other what they need for well-being by sidestepping orgasm. On the contrary, by promoting feelings of wholeness and satisfaction, they are supplying each other with the best mood medicine available—short of a tribe and a reserve of willing, trusted, long-term mates who are indifferent to being swapped for novel models.

As individuals, and as a society, we have everything to gain, and everything to lose, in how well or how poorly we manage our need for human connection.
—Caccioppo and Patrick,
  authors of *Loneliness*

WHAT TO DO?

If you want to try the karezza approach for yourself, you obviously need a partner. Perhaps you are fortunate enough to have a partner who has read this book and is open-minded about trying the ideas. If so, you have some options. You may want to design your own program based on all you have learned, and especially the tips and bonding cues in Chapter Seven. Here's what one couple came up with after several failed compromises:

> *Late last year we decided to have orgasms on the first of every month and on some special occasions. Now, however, we are in our third month of squirtless loving, "because we do not want to ruin a good thing." Our foreplay includes a half-hour of heart-centered, or breathing, exercises. We schedule our lovemaking, so we can both look forward to a special time together. We end it with a meditation that continues into dreamtime.*
>
> *We comment daily on how cute we appear to each other. We are in our fifties and now the loving flow is ... is ... beyond anything portrayed in movies or literature. It is calm and jewel-encrusted, with a deep foundation. I have been tempted by infidelity over the last eighteen years, but now my attitude is that nothing could ever match what is going on inside our marriage. I just love how attractive we have become to each other. Go for it until you get it. Then it keeps you going.—Alan*

You can also start with the three-week program of Exchanges at the end of the book. It's for couples who can snuggle together every night (or almost every night), and it can help gently reset your thermostat. Its ultimate goal is to give you a taste of what life is like in that third week of regular bonding behaviors, without the influence of the passion cycle. This will put you in position to compare regular sex with karezza.

> *When we first starting doing the practice, ending without ejaculating was difficult for me, although not so much from a physical perspective. There was no congestion in my groin, no blue balls, since I was moving the sexual energy up to my heart. But the mental habit of expecting to ejaculate during intercourse was not so easy to break.*

> *Terminating with a short ritual of gratitude with my wife helps reduce the desire to ejaculate.—Richard*

Be aware that halfway measures—such as asking your partner to alternate between making love with, and without, orgasm—unfortunately won't show you the true potential of karezza. This is because you won't escape the neurochemical fluctuations of your built-in two-week passion cycle, with its perception-altering highs and lows. Even if you have a good experience, you may find the memory of it fades completely on the occasion of your next orgasm. (Biology is *very* persuasive!) In any case, you need daily non-goal-oriented affection as you step *beyond* the cycle.

That being said, if you're in an established relationship (beyond the honeymoon high), you *may* find this man's introductory technique a useful experiment. In his view:

> A program like the Exchanges isn't appealing as a starting point. I can imagine a wife saying "Honey, let's try this program, where we don't make love for two weeks ..." (at which moment the man feels like the room is starting to spin, and he grabs hold of a chair to hang on to) "and then we can make love but don't have orgasms" (at which moment the man becomes stone deaf and catatonic). Instead, the experience could begin with the suggestion that the couple make love in the morning without orgasm (or getting close to orgasm), so he can see how he feels during the day. (If he tries this in the morning he won't be anxious about getting to sleep afterward.)
>
> I'm betting that most men will make the same astonishing, but pleasant, discovery that some of us other explorers have. I felt surprisingly normal a minute or two after getting out of bed. There was no feeling of desperately wanting an orgasm, nor did I feel particularly horny throughout the day. Instead I felt *good*. I had a nice afterglow feeling all day. Once a man experiences this for himself, he may be more willing to try the Exchanges.

If you try an experiment along these lines, take care to keep your lovemaking very relaxed. Racing up to the edge of orgasm with vigorous sex and then slamming on the brakes can create discomfort, frustration, and, if you're male, prostate stress. It is strongly *not* recommended.

Last night was the first time I had sex and—by choice—did not ejac-ulate. All in all it was easier then I thought. Mindset and attitude obviously have more power over animal instincts and desire than I realized. From previous nonvoluntary, nonejaculating sex experiences, I was kind of expecting to be extremely horny and jittery afterwards, but I wasn't. And I didn't have the usual after-orgasm drowsiness either. Actually, I just felt rather good. And from my girlfriend's point of view, the less stimulating intercourse was compensated for by my being more ready for cuddling and affection afterwards, so she seemed to think it was a nice experience, too!—Björn

BE STRAIGHTFORWARD

A goal of the practice of karezza is to help restore trust between the sexes. It is most unwise to seduce a partner with conventional sex in hopes that he or she will wish to change direction later. This is like marrying some-one based on your mutual love of chocolate, and then unilaterally decid-ing that there should be no chocolate in the house.

It's far better to ask a potential partner to read something about these concepts, and then give you his or her opinion. This book is one option for reading material, but your partner may prefer a book by a man, such as J. William Lloyd's *The Karezza Method,* available free online.[342] It's best *not* to try to explain the concepts directly to your partner, because initial resist-ance to the ideas can be high. (Remember, the primitive brain reacts a lot faster than the rational brain!) Your partner needs time to reflect on the ideas, as well as past relationship experience, without any pressure.

If I had stumbled on your Web site prior to getting off the stupid mas-turbation/reward wheel you write about, I would have ridiculed you. In fact, if anyone even remotely invalidated my point of view (orgasm is bliss), I'd have harbored resentment toward them for life.
—Alexandros

If you are already in a relationship based on conventional sex, assure your partner that your relationship and sex life are terrific as they are, and that your only concern is whether your genes are subtly conspiring to strain the harmony between you. Never pressure, or manipulate, a doubting partner to try these ideas. A partner who has mixed feelings about experimenting with the ideas, but does so to accommodate you, won't be convinced of their merits even if those merits are evident to you.

After fifteen years of marriage, they finally achieved sexual compatibility. They both had a headache.

Everyone begins this journey at a different point in the romance cycle, which means that the general remarks in this chapter may not address your specific concerns. If they do not, visit the Habit to Harmony forum,[343] where you can find answers to typical questions and solicit input from fellow explorers. If your questions are about the practice of karezza, see Chapter Ten, which recaps it.

KNOW THYSELF WHILE FREE OF THE PASSION CYCLE

Obviously, you cannot experience karezza without the participation of a partner. After all, karezza is not just about avoiding orgasm. It's also about the nurturing exchange of bonding behaviors. We've also found that either partner's orgasm affects both partners to some degree through some as yet unfathomable process.

Even so, if you don't have a partner, or your partner is not enthusiastic about the ideas yet, you can still use your time to deepen your understanding. That way, if the subject of avoiding orgasm comes up for discussion, you will be able to recount your own experience.

Start with a solo experiment. (This assumes orgasm has been part of your life. If it hasn't, you're probably ahead of the rest of us. Your brain is free of a heavily traveled "orgasm pathway." Read these sections anyway. They may help to reassure you that orgasm is *not* essential for your happiness.)

Go without orgasm for at least three weeks, and see what you observe. If you have a partner, be sure to tell your mate about your proposed investigation. Explain that you are making the experiment in order to find out if your mammalian mating program is affecting your mood for the worse. During this time, use the bonding behaviors in Chapter Seven to nurture you both. Let your partner carry on as usual, without reproach.

Record your experience in a journal, even if you keep it simple. Remember that your greatest discomfort may arise in week two. Here's what one woman learned:

As of tomorrow, it will have been a full month since my last orgasm. I suppose this is long enough to call my experiment finished, although I find little desire to resume my former habits at this point.

I think the results of this type of experiment could largely depend on how one approaches it. I have tried to view it as an opportunity to explore the whole idea of channeling sexual energy, and as such it has been rather interesting. I noticed very little difficulty after the second week. In fact, my level of sexual frustration now seems a bit below average for me, if anything.

I think I could have run into trouble if I had just attempted to "put a cap on" my sexuality. Instead, I allowed myself to experience pleasure and arousal without trying to go anywhere with it. I did a good deal of dancing, singing, laughing, jogging, etc., and I think these all helped. The only thing I tried very hard to avoid is any state of mind that felt like it came from craving-mode. I did engage in a little self-pleasuring, which, it turned out, was as satisfying as trying to get myself off.

I think that the main thing I learned from this experiment is about "energy" in general. We think of having energy as a good thing, but on closer observation, our first reaction to having a lot of concentrated energy (sexually, physically, emotionally, etc.) is often to try to get rid of it as quickly as possible ("catharsis"). This is similar to a principle of physics, actually. High potential energy states are considered "unstable" because there is a tendency to return very suddenly to a low-energy state, resulting in a large release of heat. The energy is more useful if it can be converted in a more controlled manner.

I think that if I want to use my energy to best effect, it entails learning to flow with high-energy states instead of trying to escape them. I can learn to walk the tightrope, or I can keep falling off.

Here's the experience of a man who made a similar experiment:

Here's how I approached my own experiments with abstinence and avoided feelings of guilt or failure. (I think the preaching of religious leaders who exhort their followers to not masturbate, and pile a big guilt trip on them if they do, is cruel, outrageous, and unconscionable.)

Very important: My goal, or reason for trying it, was simply to find out what an extended period of abstinence would be like—how would I feel, physically, mood-wise, etc.? Would I have trouble sleeping? Would I become overwhelmed by horniness and cravings for an orgasm? A more specific goal was to get an idea of what it might be like to practice karezza for an extended period.

I didn't set a definite duration for the experiment. Rather, I just planned to continue as long as I felt like it—as long as it was "interesting." When I "slipped," I did so rather deliberately. In a way, I took the experiment into other phases, for example, masturbating without orgasm (sometimes for several weeks at a time), or masturbating with lots of mini-orgasms (gee, I'm multi-orgasmic—like about 30 times in one day!—but that tends to become rather compulsive behavior). Those were opportunities to see how I felt, compare it to how I felt when being totally abstinent, and observe how hard or easy it was to get back on the abstinence wagon.

Abstinence is still "interesting." There have been several times when I was tempted to get off the wagon, and *some* of those times I've chosen to stay on the wagon. My reason is that I like being in control—I don't want my primitive brain steering me in ways I don't want to go, and basically wasting my time!

Q: What makes people chase partners they have no intention of marrying?

A: The same urge that makes dogs chase cars they have no intention of driving.

NOTE: If you can't make this experiment because you simply *can't* avoid orgasm for two weeks due to excess sexual energy, see "What Do I Do with This Surplus?" after the next section.

KNOW THYSELF DURING THE PASSION CYCLE

Once you have tracked your experience when you avoid orgasm, it's time to go for it! (If you have been addicted to porn, you may want to wait at least three more weeks and then climax without porn images.) Enjoy an orgasm with all the bells and whistles. Then record your experience during the two weeks afterward. This part of the experiment is tricky, because when our neurochemical weather gets stormy, it is very easy to project our disquiet elsewhere. Most of us assume that we are seeing the world just as clearly as we were *before* orgasm, and that any malaise we experience is due to life's unfairness, or someone else's actions or attitudes. Be suspicious of your perceptions. You will see the truth best if you make several experiments at least three weeks apart.

This woman's experience is useful, as she offers practical suggestions for coping with a passion cycle:

> First, I note the date in my diary, and then make a note for two weeks later. As days tick by I notice that no matter how good my external circumstances are, I never feel able to enjoy them fully. I have exaggerated feelings of isolation, loneliness, and irritability. Everyone else seems to be getting on better with their lives, making better decisions, enjoying better relationships, having more promising opportunities. I am losing out, and being taken advantage of. This occurs despite clear evidence that many good things are happening in my life.
>
> I tend to feel vengeful, usually in a petty way. I am likely to say or do something that affects my daily relationships in a negative way. When thinking clearly, I see the mixed reality of any situation. When under the cloud, I have an "us versus them" or "the world against me" perspective.
>
> I definitely have reduced will power and am much more likely to eat foods or drink drinks that I know irritate my system, cause allergic reactions, or pile on the weight. If I go overboard, I try not to beat up on myself. I know I can make it up when I'm back in balance.

I use a variety of techniques to help me deal with what is almost like temporary, mild insanity. I meditate, if possible, for fifteen to twenty minutes every day. Even if it feels like nothing is happening, meditation does somehow help. I also go for a walk to oxygenate my brain. It helps with depression and anxiety. These little steps let me feel I have some control over my life, and am doing something constructive.

These days, I journal my annoyance, instead of whining to my friends or writing long pathetic e-mails. Often I see how unreasonable my thoughts are, or I realize that I feel justified in being annoyed—only to remember that the person behaving badly is probably suffering a post-orgasmic hangover, too. Either way, I can let it go more easily.

When things naturally return to normal two weeks later, it's almost like magic, as if the spell has broken. From one day to the next, I feel much better again. I am usually pleased that I haven't said the nasty things I was thinking to those who now look innocent through my cleared vision. My will power returns. I feel more in control of my time and attention, and am more productive in my work. Sometimes I feel a bit low again in the following days, but it is much milder than before, and within no time I'm back on an even keel.

Q: Why do women want to have orgasms?

A: Gives 'em something else to moan about.

If I wasn't aware of this cycle, I am sure I would be drinking more wine to drown my sorrows, running to the doctor for antidepressants, or getting therapy to blame my family, etc. As it is, I can see light at the end of the tunnel and keep clear enough, for the most part, of artificial stimulants. I know when I'm genuinely feeling well, and not just perky as a result of chemically induced relief. Life takes on more meaning.

Here's what a man noticed, and how he copes:

I feel lethargic, less energetic for the first five days. Slight depression. Somewhat brain-dead. Horniness goes up for about two weeks. I have the definite impression that my mate needs to be felt up a lot more, but I don't feel as close an emotional connection. I feel less cooperative, and I don't have much patience for anything except what I need to get done.

I also notice disconcerting fluctuations until I'm back in balance. Some of the roughest "low points" can show up after some impressive upswings in my mood and outlook. This is very disconcerting to my linear mind. I had to make several experiments to see the cause-and-effect clearly.

Knowing about the post-orgasmic cycle doesn't make its effects easy to ignore, but I watch my perturbed thoughts as objectively as I can. There's definitely more "poor me" thinking, and I'm far more reactive to my partner's rather direct style of communication. I try to take a breath before I snap, and if sparks fly anyway, I try to acknowledge what's really at work—once I remember. "Whoa! I forgot this was week two. Scratch that nasty reply, or that meaningless clash of opinions."

Once you know what you're talking about firsthand, you'll be in a position to describe your own experience to a partner. Experience is far more persuasive than theory. Your discoveries may inspire a partner, or potential partner, to make a similar experiment. (Do not make this request directly, unless you know your partner is ready to hear it.)

Many of us are frustrated with wanting to make love more than our partners, and thus often feel uncomfortably horny, lonely, resentful, etc. I think one of the benefits of karezza is reducing the frequency and intensity of uncomfortable horniness. It took several weeks of foregoing all orgasm before I really noticed, "Hey, the cravings are gone!" Now, regardless of how often my wife may want to make love, I don't have those uncomfortable cravings that I did while caught in the orgasm cycle—yet I'm still always enthusiastic!—Len

"WHAT DO I DO WITH THIS SURPLUS?"

One reason people often believe that orgasm is purely a beneficial outlet is that it seems to solve the problem of *too much* sexual energy—or perhaps too much semen if you're male. This impression seems irrefutable, in part because wet dreams are a natural phenomenon of adolescence. It's logical to assume that the urge to ejaculate is proof that the body is making extra semen with nowhere else to go. However, as Dr. Lloyd pointed out (see the Wisdom section between Chapters Seven and Eight), semen that is cut off from its natural outlet does not cause a swelling.

I've long had a predilection for an "orgasm nightcap" in response to my insomnia (when my wife wouldn't have sex). Two weeks into stopping orgasm and guess what? I am sleeping just fine! More and more, I am less inclined to see my beloved orgasm as the wonderful stress-relieving elixir I once did.—Marc

---

Females (no semen) also experience dream orgasms. All of this suggests that there's more to dream orgasms than excretion of a liquid surplus. Perhaps, in both sexes, such dreams are "dress rehearsals," which also naturally increase libido—due to post-orgasmic cravings in the form of increased sexual tension. Our genes, after all, want us ready for action. Perhaps they're also signals that we need to find a deeply satisfying pair-bond.

The common belief that orgasm is merely a healthy outlet has a hidden risk. It encourages us to solve the dilemma of the phantom excess with deliberate masturbation. Without realizing it, we can, with frequent orgasm, overstimulate a very compelling pathway in the brain. As we saw in Chapter Six, this can lead to an uncomfortable cycle of ever more demanding urges, even though it briefly relieves the pressure. (If you are one of those people, realize that it may be because you haven't been engaging in enough bonding behaviors. It would probably help to reach out and touch someone ... else.)

Excess libido is a *brain* event more than a *body* event. Horniness feels like you're stuck uncomfortably at the top of a roller coaster. However, beneath this restlessness is the genuine need to relieve sexual tension *through intimate contact*. Nourishing, non-goal-driven contact decreases tension, countering anxiety and stress naturally. This means that affectionate contact, not necessarily orgasm, will help most, if longer lasting contentment is a goal. The next most soothing option is friendly, less intimate, interaction with others.

Isolation is one of the root causes of addiction. I don't attend any recovery groups, but what I do attend is social events within my school, and I've also gained a social circle, something I've never had. So, for the first time, I have a group of people I know who actually care about me. Now, I find I'm finally willing to remove every last bit of the negative sexual stuff from my mind. In fact, I've lost my taste for porn and nasty fantasy. To my surprise, I've been clean now for five and a half weeks, and hopefully for the rest of my life.—Nick

To recap, the feeling of excess, or surplus, often arises from an overactivated brain pathway, which is throwing dopamine levels out of whack, as explained in Chapters Five and Six. It's like a faulty keyboard letter that gets stuck every time you hit it and types out the same letter nonstop. Think back to your first orgasms. They probably just happened. They set their own natural rhythm.

The overactivated brain pathway is likely to be *your* handiwork. (Good job!) However it happens, once you begin to force orgasm with highly stimulating activities, you strengthen a brain pathway that automatically seeks the same (or even more stimulating) relief repeatedly.

If you are in this situation, you can't rid yourself of the phantom surplus by means of more orgasms. Despite short-term relief (when your high dopamine drops after climax), this strategy is likely to numb your pleasure response during the remainder of the passion cycle. You will be primed for *any* thought or visual cue that your brain associates with arousal or oblivion. Indeed, your brain may helpfully prompt you with a flashback image at low points in the cycle. This kind of help you don't need. You'll go from uncomfortably *low* dopamine to mind-altering *high* dopamine in a flash. Now you feel like you have a huge surplus of libido and/or semen, and no choice but to find relief by the fastest means at hand (literally).

The bottom line is that a superhuman libido, frequent wet dreams, and hair-trigger orgasms *can* be indications of receptor depletion (and related neurochemcial events)—even though they *feel* like evidence of excess. The Chinese Taoists discovered this paradox and its surprising solution (avoiding frequent orgasm) many years ago.

A year ago (pre-porn use), I could easily regulate my rate of mastur-bation, and thus orgasm, to, say, once a week, and during periods of sustained spiritual endeavor, could even go for a month without it. Now I'm feeling like a wild bull—multiple times every day! I don't understand how I missed it before; this is actually unnatural.—Ross

The solution is not simple, and it may take time—depending upon how intensely you have, quite logically, tried to solve your discomfort with more orgasm. The ultimate solution lies in your brain. Avoid excessive sexual stimuli, and do your best not to initiate orgasm (although it may continue to happen inadvertently while your brain is returning to balance). Three weeks may be enough to restore your equilibrium, but you could need many weeks longer, depending upon changes in your brain. When you have returned to balance, the cravings will be far less intense. See Chapter Six for tips on how to refocus your attention when urges arise. By rechannel-ing the urge to initiate orgasm, you don't strengthen the circuitry in your brain that is tapping out those false "surplus" alerts.

An enjoyable side effect of abstinence from porn and tossing off is the welcome resurgence of electrical energy between myself and real three-dimensional living and breathing women. You know, the kind that look you in the eyes and smile back.... It's harmless, subtle flirting but it feels good to me.—Al

At the same time ease your cravings! Avoid the stressful feelings of with-drawal (low dopamine) to the extent you can, using oxytocin-producing activities. Sharing your favorite bonding behaviors with a sweetheart is ideal for this purpose, but other activities also produce comforting oxy-tocin. Here's a soothing-activity list derived from research on oxytocin.[344] A complete list would no doubt be much longer.

> ▷ Voluntary exercise
> ▷ Harmonious interactions with others
> ▷ Support group meetings
> ▷ Caring for pets
> ▷ Voluntary generosity

▷ Inspiring scenery

▷ Pleasant smells (pine forest, bread baking)

▷ Calming music, singing, and tango dancing!

▷ Warm and supportive touch, therapeutic massage

▷ Companionship

▷ Yoga and meditation

All of these experiences are rewarding, but not superstimulating. Make your own list of things you enjoy; include things that don't throw you into an addictive cycle. (In other words, go lightly on the refined sugar, alcohol, gambling, video games, and so forth.) Refer to your list when your mammalian brain tries to urge you toward another cycle of "relief."

Remember when you loved somebody so much that you would do something to make them happy even if you didn't get rewarded? That feeling is coming back.—Curtis

---

The cure for inflamed libido is much like the cure for poison ivy: "Don't scratch, use lots of soothing lotion (oxytocin-producing behaviors), and turn your intense concentration elsewhere, while you wait for healing to occur."

[Nine days into experiment] Emotionally I am stronger. I have fewer moments where I loathe some aspect of another or myself. I can focus for longer periods. I wrote a six-page paper in a single sitting, and it only took three hours. Wonderful! It was one of the better papers I've written in college, too. I am very much loving this self-discovery. I sum it up as: less moody and self-absorbed, more active and life-loving. —Clark

---

TREASURE YOUR PARTNER, ENCOURAGE YOUR FRIENDS, BE SLOW TO JUDGE

As you can see from the above material, whether your partner is prepared to try karezza or not, your presence in each other's lives is a health-giving, mood-medicating benefit. When possible, show your appreciation with bonding behaviors from Chapter Seven.

If you have single friends, comfort them with more social interaction. Introduce them to prospective mates without worrying about what may go wrong. If something goes wrong, it's to be expected. After all, our scheming genes win most hands in the mating game. At least you improve your friends' chances of finding nurturing companionship.

If you don't yet have a partner, you can still enrich your life and the lives of your friends by increasing the degree of comforting interaction between you. Join groups, encourage spontaneous get-togethers, and attend events together rather than alone.

Don't sit around waiting for "Mr. or Ms. Right." Do your best to nourish anyone you can with encouraging, friendly contact. Your supportive remark or genuine smile may be just the mood medicine someone needs to reach out to a potential mate later that day. Why leave each other with the impression that self-stimulation is the only option for good feelings, now that you know social connections are better medicine?

Offer what compassionate friendliness you can, but be clear about your boundaries. As you reach out, think of yourself as a surrogate brother or sister. You are *not* trying to seduce, or impress, someone. Sometimes it helps to view each new acquaintance as "the person who may introduce me to my next partner," rather than as a potential partner. This lets you stay focused on how you can support, rather than manipulate, someone.

This mindset also lets you see your new acquaintance more clearly. If she or he is self-medicating with substances or activities, and not yet willing to let them go, then she or he may also not be ready for karezza. If you choose to nurture someone who is stuck in this familiar limbo, limit your contact to activities during which the person is not around the substance or cues associated with his or her dependency. For example, suggest a walk, rather than meeting for a drink. If you're in a relationship with someone who is stuck in addiction, you may have to make a painful choice.

It was the hardest decision I have ever had to make in my life. Deciding to split with Peter after living together for two and a half years almost broke my heart, and still causes me pain eighteen months later. However, I knew I could not control his alcoholism for him, and he wasn't ready yet to let it go and really try karezza properly. I had loved him as much as was humanly possible. I had to let him go, and get on with my life.—Rebecca

LOOK BENEATH THE FROGGY COSTUME

Wait to raise the subject of karezza with a new acquaintance until you know him or her fairly well. Talking about sex early on is a cue for *mating* behavior, not *bonding* behavior. Also stick to less intimate bonding behaviors. For example, offer a hand massage, not a full-body massage. If a potential partner shows an interest in bonding-based sex because the subject eventually arises naturally, share some information and wait. If someone is genuinely drawn to the ideas, it is time to give that person careful consideration as a partner. A chance to nurture another safely could be more critical to your well-being and life's work than those items on your "ideal mate" checklist—including financial status.

Be compassionate toward needy behavior (such as whining or staring at breasts). Treat others as compassionately as you want to be treated. Keep in mind that needy, demanding behaviors often arise from a healthy, natural longing for the deep connections upon which humanity is designed to thrive. It is especially difficult to tolerate needy behavior if you are single and feeling a bit needy yourself. After all, two energetic black holes *seem* like a combination to be avoided.

However, keep in mind that both of you have the very medicine the other most needs to perk up. Neediness is not a hopeless personality flaw; it's a temporary state of connection deprivation. With the proper mood medicine from caring interaction, she or he will *look* totally different, and *feel* totally different. (Plus, she will also stop whining or being so pushy, or he will stop staring so hungrily at your breasts.) You may be amazed by what this person has to offer when supplied with the proper mood medicine.

Men and women are different in the morning. We men wake up aroused. We can't help it. We just wake up and we want you. And the women are thinking, "How can he want me the way I look in the morning?" It's because we can't see you. We have no blood anywhere near our optic nerve.
—Andy Rooney

In fact, that wilted plant you're judging harshly as "overly needy" could be your ideal mate, temporarily garbed in a rubbery green frog outfit. All of us have been battered by the isolating ways we've been trying to ease our longings. In many cases, the kindest, most loving people have been hit the hardest. They are the ones who most strongly feel something is missing when they are without a mate.

While we're all thinking with our genitals, we tend to let our mammalian brains target our mates. A mammalian brain lights up for alpha males and fertile young females—as these specimens are the best bets for future genetic success. There are a lot of people who would make terrific partners rather than ideal gene machines. If you're not seeking to have a baby, broaden your mate-selection criteria—and remember that affectionate contact (oxytocin) has the power to change aesthetic perception.

If you *are* seeking to have a baby, do so with utmost integrity. Make sure that your partner shares your goal and wishes to help support a child. Those under biology's spell are programmed to ignore the welfare of others. Two friends come to mind who both ultimately went bankrupt because their lovers got pregnant and insisted on having children against the men's advice. From the outset, the relationships were not stable, and all parties were coping with economic hardship and/or health issues. One of the women had assured her long-term partner that a condom was unnecessary because she believed she could not become pregnant. Both women were pro-choice—until their pregnancy hormones kicked in. Pushing men into fatherhood, even if they would make great dads, is like sexual aggression—a result of biological hypnosis. Do your part to prevent wariness between the sexes.

Learn from others' mistakes. You may not live long enough to make them all yourself.

Finally, don't rule out those who were once caught on the road to excess—addiction to porn, alcohol, or whatever. A recovered addict who has learned to value close connections with others above other mood-mending devices is often a wiser, happier person than someone who has never been obliged to set clear priorities.

Next let's look at another challenge that routinely comes up for those who explore the ideas in this book.

THE MYTH OF SELF-SUFFICIENCY

Face it. The neurochemical changes at orgasm instantly free us of our need for other people—at least for a bit. Dopamine drops. Who needs love? Only when one takes into account the effects, and escalation, of the full passion cycle does the reality become evident. As German writer Ariadne von Schirach lamented,

> People who spend so much of their time sitting in front of a computer with their trousers down or their skirts up have little time or interest left for relationships.... Ninety percent of men and eighty-six percent of women [masturbate] regularly. And, in the last thirty years, masturbation among women has increased by fifty percent.... Women have become a more horrific version of men, readily expressing their displeasure over lack of sexual compliance. Men have become insecure and have fled to the Internet. Both are approaching a state of narcissistic lunacy, and solidarity is something that seems attainable only among friends.[345]

Yet escaping the loop isn't a matter of a one-time withdrawal. We need the comfort of a partner to sustain the balance of karezza. At first, this isn't evident. I frequently hear from people who are enthusiastic about the benefits of cutting back on orgasm:

> My abstinence continues (even without nocturnal semen losses, which surprises me). Now what I miss, more than wild sex, is tender moments with a woman. But I do not need a tenderness *fix*, because tenderness and intimacy are not addictive, while orgasm is. And you do not want to be tender with just anybody, because you need a person who feels right. So now, after a couple weeks of cold turkey, I feel healed. For the first time in my life, I can wait. Does this explain what happened at last night's party? Two women insisted on giving me their phone numbers! In the past I had to do the asking.

With balance restored, this man was soon in a long-term relationship. But what if someone doesn't attract a partner right away? Or what if a mate is unwilling to engage in regular bonding behaviors?

I've been so enthusiastic about abstinence. I could sense exactly what was happening, and the results were/are amazing—the most immediate and substantial results I'd ever experienced. Now, over two months later, I have to report that the loneliness is physically brutal. *Solitary* just isn't an option. (On the plus side, the ache has made the awkwardness of rejection completely insignificant.)

Temporary neediness can be *intense* for anyone who courageously attempts to recalibrate desire. Friendly contact with others helps. Unrealistic ambitions of eluding the passion cycle forever while solo do not. "Stiff upper lip" self-talk is equally useless. It's another version of the faulty thinking that led Harlow's peers to insist that affection would spoil infants. As we saw, mammals with a solid sense of attachment are *more* independent and confident.

In touching and being touched, I see both of us being healed, step-by-step. The key seems to be trust and completely clear boundaries. We manage about 1.5 hours together every other day. Loving touch is reopening my heart and healing some emotional wounds. For a long time after my divorce I couldn't verbally express my affection for a love interest. Now I freely call my new love "sweetheart," "honey," or "darling." She's starting to feel the joy, energy, and optimism that she did nearly two decades ago as a teen. She remains as eager as I am. We're in perfect agreement to not pursue sex yet, which excuses us from the whole fertilization behavior chess game.—Anthony (former U.S. Marine)

The groundwork for healing can be accomplished in a matter of weeks. Consider this evidence: Prolonged-embrace therapy reversed the negative effects of childhood stress in teens as old as eighteen.[346] Another study showed that sensitive care-giving behavior was such a powerful influence that it changed adverse effects in children's genetic makeup.[347]

A strong, solid center arises from the experience of trusted companionship, not from a promise of undying love (or intense passion). Familiarity with healthy bonding can help a person handle everything, including changes in relationship. A healing taste of genuine, unselfish attachment is a lifelong gift, which we have the power to bestow on each other, even if life then carries us in different directions.

INNER WORK

Get professional help if you are feeling hopeless or discouraged. It is obvious why many of us find it challenging to rely on each other for well-being. Giving up the rewards of self-medicating in favor of the rewards of personal interaction can produce initial anxiety. After all, the erosion of crucial emotional bonds has been going on for generations. Our parents, and their parents, likely suffered from it, too. As a result, our childhood memories of intimacy are sometimes fraught with crushing disappointments (and too few selfless bonding behaviors).

It may take time, sustained generosity, and even wise counsel from a trusted source, in order to relax your inner guardian (amygdala) to the point where an experiment with karezza would be appealing.

EVOLUTIONARY COLLISION?

Are mankind's increasingly restless urges pushing us back in the direction of our non-pair-bonding ancestors? Such a transition could result in more than just added excitement. Habituation between lovers is painful. Humans without affectionate companionship (and two early caregivers) are more vulnerable to imbalance and infirmity. For those of us who jam the accelerator, compulsive sexual behavior can deaden sensitivity—and not just to union.

There's another direction, which may let us harness the powerful pair-bonding neurochemistry of sex and love for an ancient end. Echoes of it can still be heard. A few years ago, a Gallup poll of more than a thousand young people found that an overwhelming majority were seeking, and expected to find, a marriage that was a spiritualized union of souls. (Only sixteen percent said the purpose of marriage is to have children.)

Three-fourths of those polled also agreed that if they met a person with whom they could have a long-term relationship, they would try to postpone sex until they really knew each other.[348] Unfortunately, delay may not inoculate them against Cupid's poison. The little fellow shows scant respect for marriage vows.

Lofty aspirations are good, but pursuing a larger goal can mean leaving habit behind. Let's see what karezza's mutual devotion can do.

RAINBOW SERPENT TRADITIONS

Author Merilyn Tunneshende writes that the Nagual shamanist practices of Mexico and surrounding regions hint at a hidden potential in union based upon carefully controlled and refined sexual energy. Just as in the right-hand path of Hindu tantra, the teachings advocate solo cultivation of one's sexual energy as well.

Men are advised to avoid expelling the sexual energies "just to relieve the pressure," as this angers the serpent, or sexual energy. According to Tunneshende's shamans, self-mastery enhances longevity and wisdom, and enables men to make love as much as they wish and yet be energized afterward.

Women are taught to avoid conventional orgasm, which weakens them, in favor of true orgasm, an ecstatic energetic experience that is not dependent upon physical stimulation. Like men, they are counseled to pull the energy upward and circulate it throughout the body. The rising serpent energy is said to be regenerative. It fuels healing work and, when sufficiently refined, is said to permit spiritual revelation. If, instead, the energy remains in the sexual center, it creates exhaustion and imbalance.

Tunneshende's teachers advised that casual sex increases sexual desire, but does not increase energy.

When partners have refined their sexual energy sufficiently, they can learn to engage in intercourse that is purely energetic, for which penetration is optional. Here is a description of energetic intercourse, in which the partners only touched foreheads:

> In that moment I felt the most incredible, indescribable feeling of peace and love, beyond anything I have ever felt. Everything vanished and, beneath my closed lids, we and all around us were one, and filled with golden white light.[349]

According to those who claim to have preserved this tradition, sexual energy, when refined, ignites a central column in the body, which embodies both male and female energies. This rising energy, resonating with purity, truth, love, beauty, strength, and wisdom, is necessary for the highest spiritual revelation to occur. It fuels both service to others and humility.

One of the most intriguing aspects of the inner fire, or rainbow serpent, practices is the possibility that they stem from a pre-Tibetan and Siberian shamanic tradition more than 40,000 years old. Wherever that tradition originated, traces of it can be found in Australia as well as Asia and the Americas.

> Knowledge of the Rainbow Serpent fire is found in pieces within the tradition of Kundalini Yoga, in the Tibetan development of the Rainbow Body, within Taoism as the immortal body, and among the Sioux and other native peoples as the Spirits of the Rainbow World. The Australian aboriginals refer openly to the Rainbow Serpent as the primordial life energy and many of their ancient rock paintings represent the energy.[350]

Today's lovers are finding their own rainbow experiences. Perhaps this ancient tradition describes a reality that is accessible to anyone willing to meet its conditions.

> Every time we made love, I had an out-of-body trip. It was like moving through a tunnel at warp speed, moving through space, passing stars and planets until I seemed to be at the center of the cosmos. The universe opened up to me.... All the beautiful colors of the rainbow would pulse through me at times.... I experienced such love the whole time and was awestruck and in loving tears during our lovemaking. My love enveloped everything from the microscopic to the most gigantic galaxies.[351]

CHAPTER TEN

The Path of Harmony

Karezza makes it easier to forgive others and oneself for past relationship craziness. It also increases optimism.

Karezza is based on relaxation and generous bonding behaviors. It does not call for either suppression of orgasm or demanding sexual performance.

Karezza heightens sensitivity to subtle pleasures, so life and gentle intercourse both become increasingly pleasurable.

The Ecstatic Exchanges are a way to move beyond the habit of using sex as a mood-altering device that leads to satiety, and focus on the comforts of harmony.

My husband and I have experienced many gifts from our ongoing karezza experiment. The most empowering one is a clear look at how different our attitude is when we're consistent with the practice, compared with when we aren't (due to an inadvertent orgasm). The differences make me think of white-water rafting. When we stick to karezza, life is as energizing and satisfying as zipping downstream on a brisk current. We negotiate its challenges more like skilled rafters, laugh a lot more, and feel good about our accomplishments. We also enjoy the times when we can allow the current to carry us while we relax and take in life's wonders.

During a passion cycle, however, we generally have the sense that our raft is hung up on unseen rocks and tree roots, or that no matter how hard

The power to make love, which man alone possesses, ... distinguishes him from the rest of the animal species. However, when he misuses this unique creative gift ... he taps back into his animal past, into the mechanical animal drive, and masturbates or mates without love. He is then unhappy.
—Barry Long, tantra teacher

we paddle we are being diverted out of the main channel into backwater, or even that we've flipped over in the rapids. Uneventful periods feel more like doldrums than opportunities to reenergize.

It never *seems* like these very different impressions have a connection with our sex life, but after years of experimentation, the correlation is evident. Long ago, Taoists recorded that the practice of careful lovemaking is a path to greater harmony, not just with one's partner, but also with all of life. It seems they knew what they were talking about.

After sixteen months of karezza, my wife agrees we are more affectionate and more openly in love. A few weeks in, we noticed that we go into a zone during sex; I am still discovering exquisite new feelings.—James

INNOCENT ERRORS

Now that we know how different it is to be in—and out—of the passion cycle, we see everyone's behavior from a new perspective. For example, it's hard to hang on to hurts from past relationships. After all, relationship craziness is a perfectly normal outcome—thanks to the clash between humanity's breeding and bonding programs. Our pasts would have been quite different if we, and our sweethearts, had known how to manage our mammalian brains for better results.

My partner and I have practiced bonding-based sex for several months. It was a new relationship, so we had never engaged in ordinary sex. Getting to know him in this new way has been the most continually beautiful and intimate meeting with a man I have ever experienced.—Ingrid

We can also look back at our own less noble maneuvers and forgive ourselves. How were *we* to know that quelling sexual desire in the usual way was the signal for habituation and seeking more stimulation? Or that it could make a lover uncharacteristically clingy, irritable, insistent, or moody? We didn't realize that the fallout after orgasm was pushing us away from those soothing bonding behaviors—the very gestures that would have *strengthened* our unions.

No wonder we had trouble staying in integrity with our highest ideals! I often hear a comment from people as they stop using orgasm compulsively as a mood drug: "I feel like my real self." Bad dreams of the past begin to fade. It becomes natural to nourish others lovingly and protectively. And, should orgasm occur, one can more easily overlook the bad feelings and overreactions during the weeks afterward, seeing them as the passing clouds they are.

Sex is like fire or water. Fire and water can aid a man . . . or kill him.
—Taoist proverb

Will and I also have a better appreciation of our parents' struggles. After all, they were struggling with the same stressful mating pressures that we *know* make us miserable. Their errors were understandable. In fact, upon reflection, they did a better job of coping than we gave them credit for.

The only tragedy I now see is human ignorance. Why didn't someone tell us that we have the love potion for protecting and renewing romance as handy as Dorothy's ruby slippers? Oh, that's right, they did. We mammals just have trouble hearing this particular message.

My wife and I have been on the non-orgasmic journey for 12 years. I never tire of her, and pretty much can never get enough of her. I appreciate and enjoy her feminine way much more than when I was ejaculating. Women used to be a kind of aggravation; I'd fluctuate between the extremes of desire and "You're driving me nuts."—Tim

---

NO WONDER THINGS ARE CRAZY

A related gift of our karezza experiments is that the current friction between the sexes makes sense. Not only is it comprehensible, it's reparable. I see it with compassion, and even a touch of humor.

Of course sexual relationships are chaotic at the moment. We overcame the dangers of sexual repression, but in the process taught ourselves to use sex as a mind-altering superstimulus that makes it easy to undervalue our pair-bonds. The resulting frailty of relationships has tangled up love with fear. Love seems treacherous, and it's natural to use and mistrust each other, berate ourselves, seek relief in isolation, or be unhappy a lot of the time. Today, humans are increasingly bold about seeking sexual stimulation, but often fearful of the enduring relationships that would best support their well-being.

Our culture's enthusiasm for limitless orgasm is reminiscent of an infant discovering its genitals. A baby's delight in its potential for unrestricted sexual arousal (without the interference of its rational brain) is understandable, but unrealistic. Our bodies (and brains) may simply not be designed for so much unusually potent sexual stimulation. At the same time, the media's sexual promises, combined with the relationship stagnation that Cupid's poison often causes, leave many of us feeling like we're missing out on something vital if we *aren't* determinedly pursuing orgasm.

Because over the past few years, more money has been spent on breast implants and Viagra than is spent on Alzheimer's Disease research, it is believed that by the year 2030 there will be a large number of people wandering around with huge breasts and erections ... who can't remember what to do with them.

—Andy Rooney

Whether we're chasing orgasms or simmering with resentment, by defining ourselves as pathological unless we're having orgasms spontaneously and frequently, we've opened ourselves to manipulation by powerful pharmaceuticals that would "cure" us of our "dysfunctions" at the cost of risky side effects. For example, Viagra is still on the market despite substantial evidence that it can cause sudden, irreversible blindness.[352] By 2001 it had also already been blamed for hundreds of deaths worldwide. Viagra-type drugs affect only circulation and erections, not the reward circuitry directly. Yet other drugs are already available that seek to jack up desire by tinkering with dopamine levels in the brain.[353]

Because women, especially, don't tend to orgasm in the way sexologists have defined as normal,[354] researchers are working frantically to come up with an "orgasm pill." Such a pill would be unbelievably profitable. It could also be very addictive if it triggers its own passion cycle. Moreover, as we saw, the neural circuitry that governs pair-bonding may make us especially susceptible to addiction.[355] This suggests it would be tricky to design drugs that will safely enhance sexual desire. One possibility, a nasal spray[356] that quickly enters the brain, just narrowly missed being approved due to a dangerous short-term side effect (increased blood pressure). Had it been approved, developers intended to combine this spray with Viagra for a super-substance.[357] In the meantime desperate doctors prescribe off-label use of Viagra and even Ritalin for women with low libido.[358]

> *If people have the right to be tempted—and that's what free will is all about—the market is going to respond by supplying as much temptation as can be sold. Market incentive continues well beyond the point where a superstimulus begins wreaking collateral damage on the consumer.—Eliezer Yudkowsky*

Are forced orgasms and sexual performance the best solution? Might less trigger-happy lovers simply be better suited to a gentler approach that relies chiefly on the rewards of bonding behaviors and trusted companionship for pleasure and satisfaction? Can we make ourselves more comfortable, sensual, and fulfilled just by changing how we soothe each other's mammalian brains?*[359]

While we're waiting for everyone to get the memo on the importance of pair-bonds and alternative approaches to lovemaking, watch out! America's experience with cigarettes and fast food[360] suggests that humans are very good at researching and exploiting what excites the reward circuitry of their fellow humans—and very bad at acknowledging the disorders that follow from the resulting excess. As portrayed in the documentaries *Super Size Me* and *Adult Entertainment: Disrobing an American Idol,* when big business caters to the profitable cravings of the mammalian brain, we can anticipate heavy marketing of, and lobbying for, the addictive and the unhealthy.

Human beings, who are almost unique in having the ability to learn from the experience of others, are also remarkable for their apparent disinclination to do so.
—Douglas Adams, author

---

* Might we also end the practice of circumcising infant males? Circumcision became popular decades ago in America to reduce sensitivity to sexual arousal—and, theoretically, the need to masturbate. It s a brutal practice, in addition to the fact that it hasn't worked.

KAREZZA REVISITED

Now that you have a broad picture of how we ended up with our current mating and bonding priorities, and why we might want to master a second way of making love for use when procreation is not the goal, let's review some of the key principles of karezza. To begin with, it works because bonding behaviors work. In fact, karezza is itself a delicious, intimate, soothing bonding behavior. There is nothing mysterious about this, even though its effectiveness in relieving sexual tension may strike you as remarkable after you master it.

> There was a warm glow in the area between our navels and pubic hairline that just demanded that we lie there together motionless to feel the gentle warmth it was radiating. This went on for twenty to thirty "timeless" minutes. Then slowly we inched toward nuzzling in the genital area. Very slowly we got to having intercourse sideways and it was amazing—lots of wetness to make it easy, and lots of control so no frenzy by either. We were both amazed and so loving in the stillness. It is a truly incredible experience. R. is delighted and feels so pleased that he didn't feel the need to come, which has been a big concern for him. It was such a powerful, loving experience.—Gina

With bonding-based lovemaking, the focus is on comfort, not hunger. Instead of diving in and swimming toward each other like barracudas, lovers hold hands and stroll leisurely into the ocean together. They allow the rewards of deep connection to ease sexual tension. In *The Karezza Method,* Lloyd wrote that karezza leads to complete dissipation of congestion, complete discharge of nervous surplus, complete relief from sexual tension, and more complete satisfaction than orgasm. He contrasted it with orgasmic sex, which tends to create local congestion and which must find relief in orgasm, or create distress.[361]

Using karezza's gentle intercourse, lovers discover that they can make love for as long as they need to until any sexual tension melts away entirely—as long as they don't fall back into hungry behavior. During lovemaking, the emphasis is on stillness and heart-centered feelings. If the energy begins to build into goal-oriented sensations, lovers simply relax back into stillness. The feelings during these quiet periods can be especially profound, as if the couple has entered a timeless cocoon of delighted contentment.

> *I have learned to release my sex energy without losing it through ejaculation by choosing to end our lovemaking with a long hug, instead of in the "reproductive" way. I used to have sensations during these periods of stillness, which I thought of as "emotional releases." They felt good, and left me energized, but they were still a version of the reproductive orgasm. I was consciously pulling the orgasmic energy upward (instead of releasing it through ejaculation), and I remained somewhat horny afterward.*
>
> *Now I experience what I think of as a "soul orgasm." It isn't connected to reproductive sex in any way. It can be produced even without sex, although sex is a great way to produce it. As we gently make love, I imagine us both in a glowing ball of light. I feel as if our spirits have merged. For hours after this kind of sex session, if I think of my wife, the feeling of deep love refills me, just as if I were back in bed having sex.—Todd*

You might imagine that lots of natural proceptivity (horniness) would make karezza *less* viable for you. This is not so. Those with the greatest proceptivity also more easily experience ecstatic states during the wave-like periods of stillness.

TAKING IT EASY

With karezza you never suppress orgasm. You allow yourself to relax as often as necessary instead. If some aspect of lovemaking is too stimulating, you back up to a less stimulating position or motion—even if that means terminating intercourse for the time being. (A Taoist manual even advised the extreme measure of keeping a bowl of ice water by the bed for the man to dip his penis in. Not recommended!) The most satisfying feelings arise during the relaxation phase—*not* near the edge of orgasm. Intense arousal just produces frustration. The fact that deep satisfaction can be found in stillness means that sexual performance is irrelevant. Also, as my husband points out, there's no need to wonder about comparisons with former lovers, because karezza lovers are on an entirely different playing field. Even intercourse is optional. Couples have experienced profound feelings from ecstatic touch or gazing into each other's eyes, alone.

During intercourse with karezza, there's no good reason to go near the edge of orgasm. Indeed, there are good reasons *not* to. Flirting with "the edge" is a return to the habit of substituting a mind-altering buzz for the joy of shared experience. It can increase frustration, even if no one climaxes. Frustration equates with high dopamine, but when dopamine goes too high, further changes may numb the pleasure response, producing tension, resentment, and cravings. Going too close to orgasm can also build congestion in the genitals, which may cause sharp pains. If you are fighting yourself, you are going too close to orgasm. If you are male, you are also putting unhealthy stress on your prostate gland. Relax!

Good ways to relax are to take deep, full breaths, and to turn your attention to the root of your penis, or your breasts (if female).[361a] This helps you avoid the trap of using your encounter as a self-stimulating rush, and increases your production of comforting mood medicine.

Your mammalian brain may be telling you that you will feel more frustrated the longer you avoid orgasm. Yet if you experiment carefully, using lots of bonding behaviors, you are likely to find that this is not true.

I have experienced great feelings of well-being after non-orgasmic sex over long periods of time. The contact with the person becomes the orgasm, the sexual contact becomes the orgasm, and then there is no need for orgasm.—Mike

---

What best facilitates karezza? Loving feelings. As Lloyd observed more than seventy years ago:

Karezza is easy and successful just in proportion to the abundance of mutual love—hard and difficult just in proportion as mere sex-craving dominates love. If the woman loves her mate so much that his mere presence, voice, touch, are a heaven of joy to her, so much that the sex-relation is only an adjunct and she could be happy if entirely without it, then, by a sort of paradox, not only does she enjoy it twice as exquisitely as her merely sex-craving sister, but can let it go at any moment without a pang. On the other hand the more the man rises above mere sex-hunger in delicious perfection of romantic love, the more easy and natural and effortless becomes Karezza-control, and the less likely is he to [ejaculate].[362]

Be willing to fall into a reverie with your partner in between cycles of gentle lovemaking. Shift from *doing* to *loving,* and see what you feel. Erections come and go, which is fine. Eventually you may find that your attention moves beyond your bodies entirely, or that you experience a timeless, blissful sensation that has been described as "dynamic stillness," or a sense that your bodies are dissolving or melting.

> *We lay close together, entirely relaxed, delighting in this bodily contact. And then, after about half an hour, something indescribable began to flow in us, making us feel that every single cell of our skin was alive and joyful. This produced in me rapture and delight such as I had never before experienced.... I had the impression that a million sources of delight merged into one and streamed to the skin of those parts of my body that were in contact with her. My body seemed to dissolve; space and time dropped away; and all thoughts disappeared, so consumed was I by a voluptuous rapture that I could find no words to describe. Her words for it were "superhuman," "divine." We both lost at that moment all fear of death. This, we felt, must be a prevision of the afterlife; we were already on the bridge between the material world and the spiritual universe. We had tasted heaven.*
> *—Rudolf*

SUBTLE HARMONY

As you come into a more harmonious flow with life, lovemaking rhythms may also change. Lovers sometimes discover that their true libido is quite different from their earlier, orgasm-chasing libido. One woman said she let go of her attachment to her cherished self-image as "always ready for sex." Others, whose libido had tapered off, found that lovemaking became enjoyable again, and therefore more frequent.

There can be a sense of regaining one's balance and finding a happy middle ground. Lovers may find they both "know" when it is time to make love, and that, in between times, neither feels a nagging longing for sex.

Their lives move toward a more harmonious flow in other ways, too. Each person experiences this phenomenon differently. Perhaps problems with no apparent solution mysteriously untangle themselves. Maybe there's a welcome perception shift, which allows someone to see something with compassion that she formerly saw with black-and-white thinking. Career opportunities appear unexpectedly. Abundance arrives or financial demands decrease.

If I choose to avoid orgasm, it is because I very much prefer it. I feel healthier, more in love, and closer to God. For me, this is not a matter of universal truth or whether this method is the best for everyone. For me, avoiding orgasm is not a way to say "NO" to the exciting pleasure of my body. It is a way to say a great "YES" to a more fulfilling pleasure, one that is deeper, more exciting, and more harmonious.—Raúl

---

The best thing about this "flow" phenomenon is that lovers need do nothing to move toward it—except avoid triggering feelings of lack, depletion, and neediness while they benefit from each other's affection. As mates drop into quiet harmony with one another, they often discover that a creative, playful, ecstatic, healing energy seems to be more present in their lives. Real or imagined, this sensation increases optimism, willingness to take constructive action, and awareness of our common humanity. As balance returns, both cynicism and preoccupation with evil fade. Currently, sex can leave lovers feeling very different: dispirited and defensive or cared for and whole. Perhaps as lovers master karezza, their different philosophical bents will no longer cause them to see "proof" of conflicting metaphysical "realities." Projection makes perception.

Sex is one of the nine reasons for reincarnation. The other eight are unimportant.
—Henry Miller

Whether or not a sense of aligning with a higher power arises, karezza offers lovers other gifts. Some report that they begin to *see* each other differently. When you love someone unconditionally (not for your own ends), it shifts your perception of that person. This loving perception appears to be heavy on the feel-good neurochemistry of oxytocin, endorphins, and ideal levels of dopamine.[363] When in this loving state, it is easy to see a reflection of your own open heart in another. (This same state of mind may explain why devotees see a divine glow around their spiritual teachers.) By keeping subconscious uneasiness out of lovemaking, lovers can begin to sense a glow in each other.

It seems that my vision itself has changed substantially, because I seem to see the divine in my partner on a regular basis. In fact, I think (I KNOW) I could see the divinity in anyone when I "have eyes for it." I wonder if lovers realize that by embarking on this practice, they are actually hurling themselves down the rabbit hole? It seems the longer I keep practicing (Zen and whatever else), the fewer places I have to hide. The Great Mystery creeps in everywhere and stares me in the face.—Leia

---

Karezza lovers may also notice that they have more energy for helping others. Alice B. Stockham, who coined the term *karezza*, referred to this process as "higher procreation for the good of the world."[364] She viewed this phenomenon as a profound transmutation, quoting Édourd René de Laboulaye (the man behind France's gift to the United States of the Statue of Liberty):

> The passions take the place in the soul which the will does not occupy, and there may yet be discovered a process by which passion may be transmuted into intellectual fiber. This is, indeed, the last and highest possibility of human culture.[365]

Finally, some lovers find that karezza becomes a spiritual path, based on experience, not doctrine. Others report that it dovetails perfectly with their chosen spiritual tradition because it gives them a simple way to be at peace with their sexuality.

One friend remarked that for her, without the spiritual element, any version of sex would be just one more idea. She happens to be committed to kosher sex (which calls for mates to avoid all physical contact for approximately two weeks of every menstrual cycle). She and her husband observe this ritual "because God said so." She treasures the fact that their lovemaking is part of a larger

> Sex is a sacred privilege— both the cause of man's downfall and a means to purification and oneness.
> —Edgar Cayce, healer

devotion, a willingness to align with God's will. According to her, the happiness in her love life is not a "personal happiness"; it has an aura of holiness around it.

MAXIMIZING PLEASURE

Once I transitioned to karezza, I required less stimulation to enjoy every aspect of my life. By avoiding the intense peaks of orgasm, I had enhanced my sensitivity. Simple pleasures were all around me, such as the glory of a sunset, the fun of watching dogs playing, the satisfaction of raising a flowering or vegetable-bearing plant, or the moving harmonies of live choral music.

The practice actually increased my daily *pleasure* quotient, even as it decreased the intensity of my lovemaking. This outcome is hard to imagine while hooked on orgasm (or any stimulus). Passing up those peaks at first seems like too big a sacrifice to make. Yet if the goal is more overall pleasure, then letting go of intense stimulation, with its hangover and pleasure-numbing effects, is a sound strategy.

My partner and I continue the Exchanges, now in the second phase, and it has been marvelous, in the strictest sense of the word. We had intercourse last Friday night, and it was a golden moment for both of us. We were sexual for at least six hours on and off and nobody had an orgasm ... although altered states seemed to abound.—Brad

Eventually, I realized my technique hadn't just changed. *I had changed.* I was more balanced and therefore more sensitive to every pleasurable nuance. I was also more tolerant (yet more likely to act on my convictions), lighthearted, generous, and resilient to stress.

Best of all, karezza did not require me to fight my sexual desire or bite my nails with sexual frustration. It didn't even call for much in the way of will power (other than sticking to a program like the Exchanges for the first three weeks). In our experience, there was surprisingly little inner conflict while learning karezza, as long as my husband and I took a gradual approach and remembered to wallow luxuriantly in the soothing pleasures of touch and connection.

Orgasm changes the focus because it's goal-oriented. Karezza is different; there's nothing to achieve. Almost Zen. Instead of knowing where you are going, you follow the thread of the experience, which may take you somewhere else, and usually does if given time.—Emily

Overall, I have experienced more pleasure as a karezza lover than as a conventional lover—perhaps because bonding behaviors increase my sensitivity, while my former intense orgasms tended to desensitize me over time. Certainly, I have done a lot more giggling and enjoyed a lot more harmony. Will says that, for him, karezza's most remarkable effect is that he can be together with me 24/7 without the burning desire to get away that he experienced in past relationships. He adds, "Contrary to what you'd expect, there's no sexual frustration or feeling of missing out on something. It's quite the opposite. We make love a lot. My life is immeasurably better as a result of being in love and staying in love."

Spiritually, [karezza's] lesson is clear and makes a great deal of sense: To attain the most exalted state of happiness and fulfillment, it is necessary to help someone else get there, too.
—Bernard Jensen, MD, author of *Love, Sex & Nutrition*

I'm glad I know why my relationships were once so fragile. The learning curve has been long, but the insights worth the effort. There may be no shortcuts, but lovers *can* transform themselves into "swans" if they're willing to restore their equilibrium with generous affection.

FLEAS IN A JAR

I once read that if you put fleas in a jar and put the lid on, they will try to jump out. After they hit the lid a few times, though, they adjust the height of their jumps to a level just short of the lid. Then, when you remove the lid, they continue to restrict the height of their jumps to just short of where the lid was. In other words, they will not escape, even though they are free to go.

Our genes have successfully convinced us that we are fleas in a jar. Fertilization-driven sex causes us to bang ourselves repeatedly on the painful lid of habituation between lovers. It is no wonder we make choices as stifling as those hopeless fleas do. Maybe we withdraw from relationships altogether and substitute other stimulants, or race toward climax, compulsion, and novel partners, or settle for deadening, but less draining, relationships.

By allowing those calculating genes of ours to lead us around by our mating impulses, we have unwittingly conspired with them to create the illusion of a prison. Modern efforts to spring the trap by using sex as a superstimulus have instead made relationships even more fragile. Without our ideal mood medicine in the form of harmonious pair-bonds with trusted companions, many of us have grown unnaturally despondent and cynical. Yet by learning to preserve and strengthen our unions, we can fortify our well-being and restore our much needed enthusiasm, creativity, and caring to the world.

While we're at it, let's find out if there's any truth in the Wisdom rumors of a transcendent path of relationship. Certainly loving intimacy can be a potent health enhancement and an aid to psychological well-being. Combined with karezza, it may also improve the chances of lasting harmony and ease the modern angst of "never enough." Increased subconscious feelings of wholeness may have major implications for human contentment. What other potential does bonding-based sex offer?

Why not take the hand of a willing partner and jump as high as you can? At the very least your efforts can help you avoid the poison on Cupid's arrow. And, who knows? There may not *be* a lid on the jar.

To cultivate the mind, body, or spirit, simply balance the polarities. If people understood this, world peace and universal harmony would naturally arise.—Lao Tzu

TRANSORGASMIC SEX

Transorgasmic sex is not a tradition. It's a model developed by Chilean psychologist Francisco Moreno Téllez. I include his remarks here because he offers a modern approach to an expanded understanding of sexuality.

Transorgasmic sex is based in thermodynamics, and heavily influenced by the work of C. G. Jung. I use the term "irreversible expansion" (for example, an atomic explosion) for the orgasmic experience, and "reversible expansion" (for example, a nuclear reactor) for the transorgasmic experience.

Transorgasmic consciousness has existed in all cultures. It does not belong to sexuality only. In sports and other physical or aesthetic disciplines we also find "flow" experiences similar to the transorgasmic experience.

With transorgasmic sex, there is a profound difference from the ordinary way of making love. The difference is felt in the body, in all the senses. It also is felt at the emotional and mental health levels. After you make love, when you lie next to your lover, you feel both energized and relaxed; you feel loving; your mind is clear, silent. You don't feel pain or anxiety. You look at your partner and you feel magnetism, attraction. When this way of making love becomes a habit, this harmonious sensation of power and light begins to accompany you throughout your day.

Transorgasmic experience is very different from regular sex because lovers surrender to the pleasure of lovemaking, yet conserve the sexual energy. There is a transcendent and alchemical process of transmutation. We can create a new consciousness; we can move energy and insights from the unconscious body. One feels better and more alive. This is not a theoretical thing.

In contrast, if the ego cannot hold the tension, this energy is discharged. The energy returns to the unconscious without being integrated. The gap between conscious and unconscious widens. The individual has less energy and more confusion. Addiction, compulsive behavior, violence, and other meaningless activities are examples.

My experience is that sex with orgasm tends to follow this same pattern. Of course, there are different degrees, because couples also have emotional resources, and these help to lessen the effects of the loss from the discharge. "Love is all that matters" is thus a partial truth.

Our current models of sexual response are limiting what we perceive. For example, the Masters & Johnson model implies that *all* sexual experience falls into a four-stage model of excitation, plateau, orgasm, and resolution. It implies that masturbation and intercourse are the same, and that sexual response always entails restricted breathing and severe muscle tension, and has been the same throughout history.

This model leads people to think of sex as an *evacuation* mechanism for the body, instead of a source of mutual energetic nourishment. They remain trapped in a linear vision of sexuality, focused on orgasm as the *sine qua non* of every sexual encounter. This blinds them to a broader range of experience. If someone simply burns petroleum for heat because he believes that is its only possible use, he may never discover its many other uses.

Transorgasmic sex helps us to understand the true link between sex and spiritual paths. Spiritual practices are also energetic practices. Their goal is to help us use our energy in the service of self-development. Sex can further this goal if lovers use it in a way that does not leave them feeling that they have dissipated their energy. Ancient sages cultivated, channeled, and harmonized their sexual energies in order to enhance their cognitive abilities and improve their emotional states. Spiritual experience is not contrary to sexual experience; it's just contrary to *orgasmic* experience.

Freud and Reich assumed that energy could not be contained without "repressing" it. This is a misunderstanding. Again, I compare transorgasmic sex to the activity of a nuclear reactor, which performs many mini-reactions leading to an extended, and emotionally more exquisite, pleasure. Instead of reaching climax all at once and in an irreversible way, the couple can enjoy many less intense sensations, which, together, produce boundless joy and pleasure. This reaction doesn't happen in an explosive way, but rather in an implosive fashion. That is to say, there is a feeling of internal liberation, with no ejaculation or violent discharge of energy.

The process is centripetal, not centrifugal. The energy moves inward, nourishing the lovers. The difference does not take place only in the mind. Transorgasmic sex is experiential, practical, and deeply transformational. It affects our consciousness and the biology of our relationships. It catalyzes vital emotional and cognitive processes. By learning to use sex sustainably and creatively, we can feel more lucid and inspired and have more energy, vitality, and love for our partner. In this way, erotic love can be compared with religious devotion or artistic creation.

The transorgasmic model is a new tool for exploring an ancient, rich alternative approach to sex. I hope it will help couples who want to find new meaning in their relationships.[366]

"How Do I Explain This Book to My Friends?"
A SYNOPSIS OF KEY IDEAS

Our mammalian *mating* and *bonding* programs are like two pedals that drive our intimate relationships. The mating program (the urge to exhaust ourselves sexually as often as possible) is the "habituation pedal," because it so often causes partners to get fed up with (habituate to) each other. The bonding program, on the other hand, is the "harmony pedal," because it increases balance and makes togetherness more deeply satisfying. With this simple knowledge, we can more consciously steer toward whatever results we choose.

MATING—THE "HABITUATION PEDAL"

▷ Our mating behavior is driven by a very old part of the brain, which we have in common with all mammals.

▷ Unlike the rational part of our brain, our mammalian brain can't "think"; it operates on impulses.

▷ It is the seat of our reward circuitry, which is the mechanism that governs our drives, desires, and emotions. It is where we fall in—and out of—love.

▷ Falling in love causes neurochemical changes in the reward circuitry. Exciting honeymoon neurochemicals normally keep us slightly addicted to our lovers for as long as two years—although they can wear off at any time. On average, they last long enough to ensure that our children have two caregivers.

▷ No mammals are 100 percent monogamous, and very few pair up for life. Adding mates improves our genes'

291

chances of getting copies of themselves into the future. This, not our happiness, is their top priority.

▷ Sexual satiety (that "I'm done!" feeling) is a mechanism for causing mates to tire of each other. As the honeymoon neurochemistry wears off, the emotionally distancing effects of exhausting sexual desire become more apparent.

▷ Neurochemical fluctuations in the reward circuitry occur after orgasm. They can make a mate look less "rewarding," and we may feel that we are falling out of love—at a gut level (habituation).

▷ At the same time, potential novel mates appear very attractive, because we receive a neurochemical jolt for turning our attention to them. This phenomenon— tiring of a mate with whom one sexually satiates oneself, but finding novel partners very attractive—has been observed in both male and female mammals.

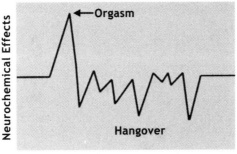

▷ The neurochemical fluctuations that follow sexual satiety last for approximately two weeks. They can cause changes in our feelings toward a mate.

▷ This two-week *passion cycle* is sometimes very subtle, but it can make lovers feel unusually needy, anxious, drained, or irritable from time to time.

▷ Due to recurring discomfort during the passion cycle, we can begin to perceive our lover—or ongoing intimate relationships themselves—as a source of stress. Orgasm, however, will still register as a great idea.

▷ Especially in the case of superstimulation, such as Internet porn, risky sex, or forbidden sex, the low part of the passion cycle can be so uncomfortable that it causes a person to seek another orgasm in order to self-medicate.

▷ When repeated stimulation causes repeated lows, the search for relief via orgasm can become habitual, leading to oversensitivity to sexual cues and compulsive behavior.

▷ Reversing this process and restoring equilibrium can require abstinence from sexual stimuli and orgasm because of semi-permanent changes in the reward circuitry caused by a protein called Δ-FosB.

▷ Such things as bonding behaviors, contact with others, visualization techniques, exercise and meditation all ease the return to balance.

BONDING—THE "HARMONY PEDAL"

▷ The mammalian brain also governs emotional bonding. We could not fall in love without changes in a specific part of our reward circuitry.

▷ This mechanism is not gender-specific. It evolved to bond us to our parents—and our children.

▷ The bonding mechanism operates on specific behaviors, which include eye contact, skin-to-skin contact, soothing touch, attentive listening, and so forth. Anyone can use these cues (preferably daily) at any time in life to strengthen emotional bonds.

▷ As these behaviors decline, bonds typically weaken.

▷ Humans rely on an adaptation of this infant-caregiver bonding mechanism to form, and sustain, romantic relationships (pair-bonds).

▷ A pair-bond is one of the most important determinants of human happiness.

▷ The feelings that follow sexual satiation often leave us less enthusiastic about engaging in bonding behaviors. As a result, romantic bonds tend to weaken over time, so that we find novel partners attractive.

▷ Bonding behaviors are associated with a neurochemical called oxytocin.

▷ Oxytocin naturally counters stress, anxiety, depression, and defensiveness. It also soothes cravings. It is probably the reason that close, trusted—and especially, harmonious—companionship is associated with increased longevity, faster healing, and lower rates of illness, depression, and addiction.

▷ We can manage our mating program, keep our bonds from weakening, and gain more of the benefits of oxytocin, when we do two things: (1) consciously use bonding behaviors to keep our subconscious bonding program activated, and (2) avoid sexual satiety as often as possible by learning to make love differently using *karezza,* or bonding-based sex.

▷ Karezza, or bonding-based sex, calls for gentle intercourse interspersed with periods of stillness and lots of generous affection—but no orgasm.

▷ Karezza converts a *mating* behavior (intercourse) into a *bonding* behavior. This allows lovers to stop sending the "I've had enough" signal that triggers habituation, while amplifying the signals that strengthen their emotional bond.

▷ Lovers often attempt to use orgasm (or other addictive behaviors and/or substances) to medicate the discomfort resulting from modern life's dwindling rewards of close companionship and satisfying intimacy. Bonding behaviors, including karezza, would be better mood medicine.

▷ A good way to learn about bonding-based sex is to experiment with it for at least three weeks (perhaps using the Ecstatic Exchanges in the next section of this book), and then return to sex with orgasm to observe the effects of the passion cycle for the following two weeks. Such experiments help lovers choose the ideal balance of mating and bonding behavior for them.

▷ Variations of bonding-based sex have been recorded in various spiritual and other traditions for thousands of years. Benefits include reduced cravings, improved health, and greater harmony between couples.

THE ECSTATIC EXCHANGES

All the joy the world contains has come through wishing happiness for others. All the misery the world contains has come through wanting pleasure for oneself.

—Shantideva, ninth-century Indian mystic

THE ECSTATIC EXCHANGES

The twenty-one Exchanges are intimacy builders that speak directly to the only part of the human brain that can fall in love or *stay* in love. In both men and women, this primitive part of the brain finds touch, eye contact, and attentiveness more conducive to bonding than discussion or even passion.

Often we humans base our intimacy on seeking stimulation for ourselves. The Exchanges are a chance to see what arises when you and your sweetheart leave that habit behind for a few weeks, and base your intimacy on generous pampering instead. They create a nourishing cocoon of comfort and safety so you can sample the benefits of bonding-based sex.

These activities are for partners who can snuggle every night. Missing a night or two is not a problem, but long gaps allow sexual frustration to build, and decrease the effectiveness of the bonding behaviors. If you and your sweetheart can't be together for three weeks, save the Exchanges until you can. That way they'll be fresh and new when you want the structure of a three-week program. In the meantime, refer to the bonding behaviors listed in Chapter Seven, and use them to deepen your intimacy.[367] If you are in an established relationship, you can also try the introductory experiment described on page 252.

I find the prospect of the Exchanges a bit overwhelming, but I whole-heartedly recommend the bonding behaviors. They are like donning a pair of rose-colored spectacles, but gradually, rather than all at once. The hardest part is probably agreeing upon the need for action. Once the ball is rolling, things seem to progress of their own accord.—Gordon

NOTE: You can pose your own questions relating to the Exchanges online in the Habit to Harmony forum.[368] If you're looking for things to do with a sweetheart, browse through some of the "Exchange of the Day" activities online, too.

STRUCTURE

Please read the rest of the book before attempting the Exchanges. It's very helpful to know why you're trying something so unfamiliar. If you don't know why, your subconscious mating program will continue to pull your strings.

Each Exchange begins with a short pep talk, followed by a "Yin" exercise and a "Yang" exercise. Both partners do each one together. Yin exercises are based on bonding behaviors. Yang exercises tend to be more active and playful. Except as noted, it doesn't matter if you do Yin or Yang first.

Even if you're exhausted, or haven't enough time to do both, do a Yin activity as that day's Exchange, so you engage in some bonding behavior each day. It can be done before falling asleep—or, usually, *as* you fall asleep. Just skip the Yang activity, or find another time to do it.

The first fourteen Exchanges do not include intercourse. Attire yourselves in comfortable chastity belts—in the form of shirts and shorts or modest underwear. Experiment with this even if you have been sleeping together in the nude for years, as it helps create an aura of courtship. Thongs or boxers that promote peeping or overstimulated genitals defeat the purpose of covering up. If too warm, he can remove his shirt.

Some of the later Exchanges include (optional) intercourse, so if you need to resolve birth control issues or arrange for medical tests, it is time to do it.

At the beginning of each Exchange, choose a "guardian." The guardian's role is to suggest a break in the action if either of you begins to use the encounter to stimulate yourself rather than focusing on generous touch.

When it is time to sleep after an Exchange, relax in each other's arms. Try spoon position, with the person who most wants to be held taking the inside position. The person on the outside comforts the other. For example, if he is feeling overstimulated, she can hold him and rest her hand lovingly on his penis, even over his clothes, without stimulating him. This is surprisingly calming and satisfying, and can help him get comfortable with loving contact even when he doesn't have an erection.

DETAILS

There is no need to read all of the Exchanges before beginning, but as you go forward together, read each new Exchange aloud. A few require massage oil. Grapeseed oil is a good choice for those who don't like perfumed oils.

The Exchanges call for a spirit of innocence, which flowers in complete privacy, without interruption. Whatever time of the day you choose to do them, ensure that children, pagers, pets, phones, and visitors will not lead to distractions. Take turns preparing the environment with gentle music, pleasant scents, extra pillows, and non-alcoholic natural beverages. Natural lighting, such as a candle or open fire, enriches evening experiences.

If you are accustomed to drinking a bit of alcohol or smoking marijuana, try cutting back or avoiding it. As explained, the same brain circuitry that you have been activating with substances actually evolved to help you find nourishing contact with your fellow human beings rewarding. This is a rare opportunity to find out what bonding behaviors can do. Also, substances that alter clarity can sabotage the best of intentions, so they tend to slow progress.

What if you feel like snuggling when you are not officially doing an Exchange? Enjoy! Just avoid disrobing or genital contact ahead of schedule. Also resist vigorously rubbing your genitals on your partner or reaching into your partner's clothing. Feeding-frenzy behavior will leave you hungrier than ever. Even lying on top of your partner can increase frustration at first. If you focus instead on your gratitude for having your partner in your arms, and genuinely pamper one another, you may find your contact surprisingly fulfilling.

ORGASMS

Do not masturbate before beginning the Exchanges. It is logical, but mistaken, to assume that if you release your sexual tension with an orgasm you will be more at ease during the Exchanges. Instead, put the bonding behaviors in the Exchanges to the test for a few days. See if they indeed soothe sexual frustration.

What if one of you has an orgasm during the time you're experimenting with the Exchanges? Enjoy it, and trust that it is part of the learning curve. Congratulate yourselves on the time that you *were* able to experiment with Exchanges. Discuss any insights you may have gained from the experience.

Decide what you want to do next. Realize that you're likely to feel out of sync with each other during the next two weeks (off and on) because the post-orgasm passion cycle is at work. Bonding behaviors may also feel less fulfilling during this time. One option is to set the Exchanges aside for the time being, and return to sex with orgasm (conventional sex) until you both feel inspired to try them again.

Another option is to view the event as a signal that you need to slow down. Stay with the bonding behaviors listed on page 178 for the next two weeks, while you wait out the passion cycle. Then begin the Exchanges again—or, if you have been conscientious about engaging in daily bonding behaviors for two weeks, pick up the Exchanges where you left off.

It is not advisable to ignore the orgasm and keep rolling with the Exchanges. The two-week passion cycle would make it very difficult to compare the benefits of bonding-based sex with conventional sex. You aren't trying to "get somewhere" by using the Exchanges. They are strictly a tool for comparing three weeks of bonding-based lovemaking with conventional sex.

If you and your partner can't make up your minds whether to let the Exchanges go for the time being, or back up, flip a coin. There are advantages to both paths, so be appreciative and generous toward each other, whichever route you travel. Take care never to coerce a hesitant partner to return to the Exchanges. The Exchanges are effective only when both people are enthusiastic about experimenting with them. If you are feeling eager to try the Exchanges and your partner is not, treat your partner as compassionately as you would want to be treated if you were the one with doubts.

LEARNING IS LEARNING, HOWEVER IT OCCURS

Trust the flow of events, and be patient. It sometimes takes people months of generous affection and reflection to be able to complete this experiment. After all, the brain pathway for triggering orgasm can be quite insistent, and it may take time for you to build an alternative one. That time is not wasted, especially if you both engage in as many bonding behaviors from Chapter Seven as possible in the meantime.

Others learn more from hitting brick walls head on (as I did). Here's a friend's experience:

> My first attempt to learn to make love this way ended abruptly, after several false starts. My partner Costas would make love without orgasm and be thrilled with his increasing control (he said he had been a premature ejaculator before). However, he never attributed his increasing sense of well-being to our unconventional lovemaking, and his efforts were erratic.
>
> The final crash came when he joined me on vacation abroad. He insisted I book the most expensive hotel at his expense (against my advice). He had promised that he wouldn't make the trip unless he would honor our agreement to avoid orgasm. Then he chose to ejaculate our first night together, on the theory that "we should do it my way sometimes, and your way sometimes." At that point I snapped and thought to myself, "Fine! You want hot sex? You shall have it." I absolutely wore him out. I think we made love four times. The following morning I demanded more.
>
> When we got out of bed, he was a zombie. After a brief effort to tour the city, he retreated to the hotel cocktail lounge, complaining about how expensive the hotel was, and spent the day there drinking. Our guide confessed that he had never met a more unpleasant person than Costas. When I returned from sightseeing he asked me to pay half of the hotel costs.
>
> We went our separate ways until our flight home. To console myself, I ran up a credit card debt it took me two years to pay

off. Imagine my bewilderment when, only a few months later, I overheard him at a party explaining to others the benefits of avoiding ejaculation during sex.... Life is funny, eh? I, too, learned something. I now take a careful, slow approach after time apart from my mate.

SUGGESTIONS

Make your partner the prime focus of your nurturing. You are helping each other open your hearts. For example, if one of you is regularly chatting on the phone to a former sweetheart, it is nearly impossible to create a space of healthy vulnerability. Whatever the future holds, let the Exchanges be dedicated to creating mutual safety and comfort between you. Even if you are not each other's final partners, your time together can leave you stronger and more open to the rewards of future intimacy.

If you have an argument, try lying together without words, in spoon position, breathing deeply for a time, before attempting to resolve your differences. Do this as soon as possible—even if only for a few minutes. Whoever thinks of it first should invite the other one to lie down, regardless of how *right* the would-be peacemaker may be. Take turns inviting each other, if possible. No matter how self-righteous or discouraged you are feeling, see what bonding behaviors can do.

Intimacy builds rapidly using the Exchanges, but there is no need to spend every minute together. Instead, why not use the good feelings you are creating to do something you have been putting off? Express your creativity, cheer a sick friend, do a brilliant job at work, study with intense concentration, or clean out a closet. Your increasing inspiration and efficiency may surprise you.

RECALIBRATING

For the first few nights of the Exchanges, lovers often require special consideration. Those who have been without a partner for a while can have intense reactions to intimate contact. As one man said about the Exchanges: "I won't be able to sleep next to a woman; I'll be awake all night." And the fact is, he might. Yet if you both stick with this soothing approach, such restlessness will pass within a few days.

Some people swing the opposite way. Before they can reach a balanced state of well-being, their mainspring has to unwind. They may sleep more than usual during their initial adjustment.

Even people who slept poorly on their own (or poorly with a partner) frequently find that they sleep far better with a partner using this approach to relationship—after they come into balance. So, whoever is feeling most centered should willingly put his or her needs aside for a few days. Though it may not feel like it when you are sleep-deprived, your greatest need is for a centered partner. Give him or her "all you can eat" of thoughtful, non-erotic attention, using the bonding behaviors on page 178. Your generosity will return to you in the form of a more stable, energetic, and attentive partner.

— YIN DELIGHT —

Decide who will tap the other at the end of the exercise (and act as guardian for this Exchange). Lie on your backs next to each other, but in opposite directions, either on the floor or diagonally on the bed. (Your head will be near your partner's ankle and vice versa.) Put your hand over your partner's heart (or navel), rest your elbow comfortably, breathe deeply, and send loving energy to him or her for several moments.

— YANG EXPLORATION —

As soon as you recognize that there are two types of touching—giving and getting—you have the key to bonding-based lovemaking. Your intention is far more important than what you touch or how intimate the touch is.

Sit next to your partner on the bed, as he or she lies next to you. Silently, slowly stroke or gently squeeze your partner's muscles from head to toe, without intentionally sexually stimulating him or her. Imagine that your hands are glowing with selfless, healing energy and that you can activate your partner's ability to relax and heal with your touch. Imagine your partner's body lighting up with a healthy glow as you work. When you have finished, gently cradle your partner's head or feet in your hands for at least five minutes. Change roles.

FROM HABIT TO HARMONY

W hen I first began collecting the Exchanges, I didn't realize that they were a prescription for sidestepping our age-old habit of overstimulating our brain chemistry with substances and activities. With such a mindset, we're innocently, but selfishly, focusing on ourselves.

Three such habits are arousing yourself via foreplay, the thrill of causing your partner to become intensely aroused, and the drive toward your orgasm. These are so ingrained that it's sometimes hard to imagine intimacy without them.

Find out what it's like to receive generous gifts of touch from another person (rather than touch geared toward orgasm). Part of your mammalian brain is set up to respond to this selfless touch in very positive ways. Instead of using these exercises as a chance to "get the goodies," let your partner *give* you the "goodies," and vice versa.

If your partner has been feeling especially drained or discouraged, it may take time before he or she feels "full" again. Until then, you may feel like you are both just going through the motions. Be patient. Try putting your attention on nurturing your partner. See if you feel better.

Before beginning, talk about what you experienced following the previous Exchange.

> ▷ Did you have trouble sleeping together? If so,
> experience has shown that it is best not to give in to the
> urge to separate. Just enjoy your nights together and try
> to catch a nap at some other time. Eventually your body
> will adjust to your new intention to let nothing stand
> between you and healthy intimacy.

▷ Do you feel happy? If you do, tell your partner why. Any other emotion coming up? Want to share it?

▷ Are you intentionally stimulating your partner's genitals or rubbing your genitals on your partner? If so, rein in that mammalian brain!

— YIN DELIGHT —

Decide who will squeeze the other's hand at the end of a few moments, and also act as guardian for this Exchange. Sit comfortably, facing each other. Pretend that you have all the time in the world. Now, breathe deeply, let go of all other thoughts, hold hands, and look into each other's eyes for several moments. Can you use your left eye to focus on your partner's left eye? If the idea appeals to you, imagine that you are breathing in and out through your hearts.

— YANG EXPLORATION —

Take turns practicing the following techniques for cooling things down when you're the guardian.

▷ Vigorously scratch or rub your partner's scalp.

▷ Touch the region over each other's heart, and send waves of calm.

▷ Crack a joke, tickle your partner (if she or he doesn't mind), or invent a silly song to halt the momentum.

WHERE IS YOUR ATTENTION?

Here's the experience of a friend:

I've just discovered how vital and real my attitude is during these Exchanges. As we began one I was feeling a whole range of emotions and judgments: boredom, acceptance, avoidance, guardedness, love, stubbornness. His face looked childlike, which was *not* attractive to me. Then I began to wonder if my attitude toward him mattered. I stopped thinking about myself and decided to regard him with appreciation—and as a MAN. Almost immediately, his posture straightened and he breathed in more deeply, became more confident.

My awareness moved to both of us as a unit, a current of energy. It was no longer about him and me, about my judgments or fears. For just a fleeting few seconds, we found a crack in awareness, in which we could bask unencumbered. I realized that my attitude determines the scope of my awareness. When my focus is on myself, we are having separate experiences even as we hold hands. When I broaden my awareness, I can sense not only my energy flowing but also his, and for a split second notions of "me" and "him" are able to dissolve, allowing the current of energy to flow freely.

Before beginning, talk about what you experienced following the previous Exchange.

> ▷ Are you able to ask for comforting hugs without insisting on "let me feel you up" foreplay? Are you able to let your partner sleep?
> ▷ Take a moment right now to think of something *you* enjoy, which you could share with your partner in the next twenty-four hours. Could you make a favorite

snack to share? Suggest a look at the stars to point out your favorite constellations?

▷ Is either of you reaching in the other's underwear while snuggling? (If so, hold off on that.)

— YIN DELIGHT —

Decide who will end this exercise and be the guardian. Sit facing each other and take a couple of minutes to do an Energy Circulation. Close your eyes and tighten the muscles of your pelvic floor. Imagine drawing the energy up your spine to the top of your head as you inhale. (This is the Energy Circulation.) Draw it down the front of your body, through your heart, and store it in your navel. Feel any tingles? After a few of these deep breaths, join hands for a moment and smile at each other.

— YANG EXPLORATION —

Choose to do either of the following activities. Flip a coin if you can't agree.

ROCKING

Have your partner lie next to you, face down, on the bed or on a cover on the floor, and relax totally by taking deep, slow breaths. Imagine your hands glowing with energy. You are sitting or kneeling, whichever is more comfortable. Now, beginning at the outside of your partner's calves, use your palms to gently rock your partner's lower leg with a slow, gentle motion. Gradually move up your partner's side to his or her shoulders and down the arm. Do the other side. Have your partner roll face up, and repeat the process. Breathe your energy into your partner as you work. Change roles.

SOUND PEACE

Sit facing each other, hold hands, and hum or tone together. Continue until you feel a powerful vibration in your forehead. Let it spread throughout your bodies. Keep it up for at least a full minute. Talk about how you feel afterward.

Shaky Compromises

I had a *lot* of experience with the Exchanges, because I was very good at rationalizing "harmless" departures from them. Often I did so in an effort to please my partner. I would think "I can sense we're off the track here, but maybe if I'm especially accommodating this time, he'll be equally generous next time, and will wholeheartedly try this other approach with me."

Wrong. I was not helping my mate learn a new habit by ensuring he received a reward (worse yet, half a reward, if he managed to avoid orgasm) for moving toward his former habit of self-stimulation. Frustration merely increased his search for more stimulation. Not surprisingly, he became resentful and emotionally flat when we had to back up. Eventually, we had to go through a second, very uncomfortable period of withdrawal before we could make progress.

It may not be possible to transition to this new approach while continuing to trigger most of the usual foreplay rewards during lovemaking. After all, our mammalian brain is always there, and it has its own agenda. We can never teach it new songs. We can only teach ourselves (gradually) to listen to the bonding tune more than the mating tune.

Before beginning, talk about what you experienced following the previous Exchange.

> ▷ Did you remember to choose an activity you could share with your partner? If not, do it before the next Exchange.
> ▷ Do you feel at ease? What would make you feel more at ease?
> ▷ Be especially careful of morning erections. They tend not to be heart-centered. If you cuddle in the morning, begin by silently synchronizing your breathing.

— YIN DELIGHT —

Who was guardian last time? The other partner chooses a bonding behavior from the following list, and acts as guardian. If appropriate, take turns.

> ▷ Several moments of synchronized breathing
> ▷ Cradling, or gently rocking, your partner's head and torso (works well on a couch, or with lots of pillows) for at least five minutes
> ▷ Gazing into each other's eyes for several moments
> ▷ Several minutes of hugging with intent to comfort
> ▷ Holding, or spooning, each other in stillness for at least twenty minutes to a half-hour
> ▷ Several minutes of stroking with intent to comfort
> ▷ Lying with your ear over your partner's heart and listening to his or her heartbeat for several moments

— YANG EXPLORATION —

Take turns practicing the following techniques for cooling things down when you're the guardian.

> ▷ Sit next to your reclining partner and lightly stroke his or her torso, arms, and legs, avoiding genitals.
> ▷ Quietly say "Inhale" and then sit up straight, or lie together in each other's arms, breathing deeply and slowly. Do an Energy Circulation by tightening the muscles of your pelvic floor and drawing the energy up to your crown and down to your navel. Repeat until you are both calm and centered.
> ▷ Hold your partner in spoon position and rest a hand lovingly on his penis, or over her heart, until things calm down.

RELAXATION

Biology pushes us toward certain roles, which one guy summarized as "We're the gas, they're the brakes." The man is urged to exploit every possible fertilization opportunity, and resist taking "no" for an answer. The woman is pushed into the role of law officer. She must do whatever it takes to keep the man in check unless she wants to have intercourse. This "keep sniffing till she stops growling" dynamic is perfect for mating dogs, but it doesn't create the safety and trust that relaxes the amygdala (the inner guardian) and facilitates deeply nourishing union.

The Taoists recommended different roles in which "the woman is the boat and the man is the pilot." The woman gradually relaxes into total receptivity, which she obviously cannot do if she has to police her lover. The man maintains a courtly attentiveness, or protectiveness, which allows his partner to become more receptive and helps keep them both at ease. This he cannot do if he is blind with impulsive behavior. Ideally, instead of rowing, he merely steers.

The key to a man's becoming a good pilot rests with his partner. If she is open and loving (rather than seductive), he will find self-control easier. Likewise, the man holds the key to the woman's receptivity. If she knows she is in the hands of a safe pilot who has taken his foot off the gas, she can stop being the brakes, and fall into a relaxed, even ecstatic, state, in which he can join.

If someone is feeling guarded, that person needs time to relax into his or her ideal role. Generous, undemanding bonding behaviors facilitate this process, but it unfolds at its own pace. Be patient.

Before beginning, talk about what you experienced following the previous Exchange.

> ▷ Have you noticed any shifts in the way you feel about
> each other since you have been doing the Exchanges?

- ▷ In the morning, have you tried synchronizing breathing before you move on to other types of touch?
- ▷ Take a moment right now to think of something your partner would enjoy, which you could do for your partner in the next twenty-four hours. Surprise him or her.

— YIN DELIGHT —

Who was guardian last time? The other partner chooses a bonding behavior from the following list, and acts as guardian. If appropriate, take turns.

- ▷ Kissing with lips and tongues
- ▷ Several moments of synchronized breathing
- ▷ Cradling, or gently rocking, your partner's head and torso (works well on a couch, or with lots of pillows) for at least five minutes
- ▷ Gazing into each other's eyes for several moments
- ▷ Several minutes of hugging with intent to comfort
- ▷ Holding, or spooning, each other in stillness for at least twenty minutes to a half-hour
- ▷ Several minutes of stroking with intent to comfort

— YANG EXPLORATION —

What is the guardian's favorite form of nourishing, nonsexual touch? Demonstrate it on your partner for at least five minutes. Now allow your partner to do it for you.

To Have All, Give All

Before I experimented with the Exchanges, it seemed that getting in shape, progress with my career, and spiritual goals hinged on time spent pursuing them at the expense of other activities. With bonding-based lovemaking, however, I left behind the sense of scarcity on which such conflicts rest. It felt like I plugged into a far more effective means of creating balance, well-being, and abundance. It is based on giving.

When I focused on giving, I felt like I programmed my subconscious for abundance. I was convincing myself that I had enough energy (and time) to be generous, and I began to react accordingly. I had to be willing to break some cherished routines to accommodate my partner, but it was worth it.

I realized that all actions count, both in and out of the bedroom. It didn't pay to measure devotion in "I love you's," tears of joy, or hours logged in the sack.

Before beginning, talk about what you experienced following the previous Exchange.

> ▷ Are you noticing that your burning desire to climax is less than you expected?
> ▷ Do you feel grateful? If so, tell your partner why.
> ▷ Have you been crawling on top of your partner and engaging in passionate kissing to heat yourself up? If so, hold off on that.
> ▷ Did you remember to do something for your partner that your partner would enjoy? If not, do it tomorrow.

— YIN DELIGHT —

Who was guardian last time? The other partner chooses a bonding behavior from the following list, and acts as guardian. If appropriate, take turns.

    ▷ Kissing with lips and tongues
    ▷ Several moments of synchronized breathing
    ▷ Cradling, or gently rocking, your partner's head and
       torso (works well on a couch, or with lots of pillows)
       for at least five minutes
    ▷ Gazing into each other's eyes for several moments
    ▷ Holding, or spooning, each other in stillness for at least
       twenty minutes to a half-hour
    ▷ Several minutes of stroking with intent to comfort
    ▷ Several minutes of hugging with intent to comfort

— YANG EXPLORATION —

Choose to do either of the following activities. Flip a coin if you can't agree.

HEAD MASSAGE

Have your partner lie face up in front of you, as you cradle his or her head in your lap on a pillow. Rest your partner's head in your hands without moving for a moment. Now, slowly massage his or her scalp and forehead and temples with firm but gentle, circular motions. Do not just play with your partner's hair; move the skin over the cranium. As you massage, imagine a glow around your heart increasing and expanding. Allow that energy to move through your fingers and nourish your partner.

When you finish, hold your partner's head in stillness for at least five minutes. Change roles.

JOY

Sit facing each other and hold hands. Close your eyes, take a deep breath, release it slowly, and see if you can locate a feeling of joy somewhere in your body. Concentrate on this feeling for several minutes. Allow it to expand as you take deep breaths. The guardian ends the exercise. Describe your feelings to each other.

RULE BENDING

Usually when Will and I bent the rules while easing our way through the Exchanges, it happened because one of us was unconsciously seeking to adjust his or her *own* brain chemistry.

I tended to slide toward seduction, Will toward "let me feel you up" maneuvers. We found ourselves using rationalizations such as:

> ▷ I don't think it will cause a problem if I take my shirt off ahead of schedule.
> ▷ I can't help it—I'm a guy.
> ▷ Okay, I'll try this stillness thing, but I still have to grab your butt.
> ▷ I will show you the power of the feminine with this satin negligee, or equally seductive little move of my hips.

If you find yourselves drifting in similar directions, do your best to move back toward the rewards that come from nurturing your partner selflessly, and a bit protectively.

Before beginning, talk about what you experienced following the previous Exchange.

> ▷ If you are a new couple, how are you feeling about spending every night together? What's good, what's uncomfortable?
> ▷ Do you find that you are more open to, friendly toward other people? If so, what's different?

— YIN DELIGHT —

Choose a guardian who will end this exercise. Now, hold each other comfortably, sitting up if possible. As you breathe deeply, silently visualize the electromagnetic fields around your hearts getting larger and more coherent. Feel yours pulsing. Imagine it coming into synchronization with the rhythm of your partner's heart field. Feel your body producing the neurochemicals that help you bond deeply with each other.

A relaxed, healthy heartbeat (heartbeat coherence) is an indication of inner balance. It means that our body systems are working especially well together. A coherent electromagnetic heart field may be the key to truly remarkable states of union. When we touch while in a loving, coherent state, our heartbeat can even register in another's brain waves.[369]

— YANG EXPLORATION —

Other partner, what is *your* favorite form of nourishing, nonsexual touch? Demonstrate it on your partner for at least five minutes. Now allow your partner to do it for you.

VISION

When you look at another person from a space of caring, appreciation, adoration, or desire to nurture, you see a reflection of your own open heart. That gives the object of your affection a radiance that appears to be missing from those you do not care for in this way. In short, your degree of openheartedness determines whether you see someone as adorable.

For better or worse, we reserve this generous vision for those whom we perceive as being safe to love (usually a child, relative, pet, or spiritual teacher). By changing our habits we can also take the subconscious fear out of romantic love.

There's a huge difference between your hugs and his. When you hug me I feel like you're hugging me for me. You want to comfort me and make me feel loved and lovable. When he hugs me I feel like he's hugging me for him. He wants to get his hands all over me because it turns him on.—Eliza

---

Before beginning, talk about what you experienced following the previous Exchange.

> ▷ Are you reaching into your partner's clothing to stimulate your own brain chemistry? Is so, let it go for now.
> ▷ Can you believe that your sexual partner is totally safe to love? If not, what would make that easier to do?
> ▷ Can you see your partner's glow yet?

— YIN DELIGHT —

Choose who will end this exercise and be the guardian. Sit facing your partner and focus on the area between your partner's eyebrows. Now, soften your gaze and let your vision blur. Can you imagine a radiance around your partner? Do you experience any special feelings? Tell each other what you saw or felt.

— YANG EXPLORATION —

Choose either of the following activities.

FOOT MASSAGE

Have massage oil and towels handy. Fill the tub or a dishpan with warm, slightly soapy water. If possible, soak your feet together in the tub or dishpan. If not, take turns. After ten minutes, tenderly dry each other's feet thoroughly and give each foot a kiss.

Exchange foot massages. The recipient's feet should ideally be at the level of your chest, with legs relaxed and comfortably supported. Now, energize your hands by clapping or rubbing them for ten seconds, and then resting them for a moment, palms up. Sense the heat or tingling in them.

Place your partner's feet on a towel and rub them gently with massage oil. Allow your love to flow through your hands as you massage your lover's feet silently, using your thumbs to press as deeply and firmly as you can without causing pain. Knead each bit of surface area of the sole, penetrating deep below the skin. Then, using circular movements of the thumb and forefinger, give special attention to:

> ▷ The pituitary stimulation point in the middle of each
>   big toe pad
> ▷ The pineal stimulation point, up from the pituitary
>   point and slightly toward the inside of the toe
> ▷ The sexual balancing points (the heel, the areas just
>   below the ankle on both sides of the foot, and the
>   Achilles tendon area, just above the heel)

Change roles.

LOVING GIFTS

Take turns asking each other, "What things do I do that make you feel most loved?" If it is convenient, each of you do one now for the other.

"Harmless" Activities

I'm a very oral person ... and I'm not talkin' about talkin'," said a friend. Sorry, Tiger. Years of experience and frustration have revealed the unwelcome but simple truth: However clear our intentions when we crawl into each other's arms, if we engage in certain activities, our autopilot takes over.

Most of us view activities such as dressing in lacy underwear, crawling all over a partner naked, posing nude, frenzied kissing, rubbing genitals on a partner, oral sex, viewing porn, and so forth as harmless. I, too, assumed that such pastimes must fit into the picture of bonding-based sex somehow.

In fact, they didn't. At least not for us. Innocent and enjoyable as these actions are, they pulled all our attention swiftly toward physical gratification of the urge they awakened in our mammalian brains. In my experience, women can be the most determined to show off the mood-altering skills of their inner temptress. Keep in mind that a dazzling performance will evoke an equally performance-oriented display by your partner. Performance is not relaxing, and therefore, not perceived by the body as a bonding activity.

Before beginning, talk about what you experienced following the previous Exchange.

> ▷ Have you found simple sensual contact more pleasurable since beginning the Exchanges? If so, share your experience. If not, what would make it easier for you to feel greater pleasure from your partner's gifts of affection? Sometimes less is more.
> ▷ Do you feel happy? If you do, tell your partner why. Any other emotion coming up? Want to share it?
> ▷ Have you been crawling on top of your partner and engaging in passionate kissing? If so, hold off on that.

— YIN DELIGHT —

Who was guardian last time? The other partner chooses a bonding behavior from the following list, and acts as guardian. If appropriate, take turns.

- ▷ Kissing with lips and tongues
- ▷ Several moments of synchronized breathing
- ▷ Cradling, or gently rocking, your partner's head and torso (works well on a couch, or with lots of pillows) for at least five minutes
- ▷ Gazing into each other's eyes for several moments
- ▷ Holding, or spooning, each other in stillness for at least twenty minutes to a half-hour
- ▷ Several minutes of stroking with intent to comfort
- ▷ Several minutes of hugging with intent to comfort

— YANG EXPLORATION —

Choose either of the following activities.

APPRECIATION

This activity requires pen and paper. Take a few minutes to write down at least three things you appreciate about your partner. Share your lists with each other. Express your gratitude to your partner with a good, old-fashioned back scratching, exactly to order. Change roles.

ROCKING THE SHOULDERS

Have your partner lie down, face up, and relax. Begin at his or her head, with your hands on his or her shoulders. Gently lean on your partner's shoulders, and shift your weight from one shoulder to the other in a rocking motion. Slowly walk your hands down your partner's upper arms and back up to his or her neck. Then walk your hands onto your partner's pectoral muscles (next to the shoulders), still slowly rocking. Continue for several minutes. When your partner is thoroughly relaxed, place your hands over your partner's heart and be still for at least a minute. Change roles.

BIOLOGY'S RULES

P rogress is not linear. When you're feeling resistance, know that your crafty genes, and your old habit of seeking to alter your brain chemistry yourself, are at work.

Here are some of the thoughts that held us back:

▷ I'm too tired.

▷ What's the rush?

▷ I can't do this—it's too hard.

▷ I'm not spiritually advanced enough for this yet.

▷ How do you know we're not chasing a wild goose?

▷ Why can't I just do it the usual way till I tire of it?

▷ I am who I am and I can't change that.

▷ Maybe I'd be better off with someone else.

These thoughts were like chains—and they had precisely the strength that we gave them. Had we yielded to them, we would soon have been too fearful of intimacy and too discouraged to keep trying.

Gradually we learned to hold our course and wait for the benefits to materialize. The full advantages of bonding-based lovemaking only dropped in as our inner guardians relaxed. They had their own mysterious schedule, yet progress was unmistakable.

Before beginning, talk about what you experienced following the previous Exchange.

▷ Do you have more energy? If so, are you adjusting to being "on" more of the time?

▷ Do you feel safe? If so, tell your partner why. If not, what would make you feel safer?

▷ Do you feel more confident if you are a man? More like relaxing into the role of "boat" if you are a woman (leaving your partner to pilot you safely)? If not, why not?

— YIN DELIGHT —

Who was guardian last time? The other partner chooses a bonding behavior from the following list, and acts as guardian. If appropriate, take turns.

▷ Kissing with lips and tongues
▷ Several moments of synchronized breathing
▷ Cradling, or gently rocking, your partner's head and torso (works well on a couch, or with lots of pillows) for at least five minutes
▷ Gazing into each other's eyes for several moments
▷ Holding, or spooning, each other in stillness for at least twenty minutes to a half-hour
▷ Several minutes of stroking with intent to comfort
▷ Several minutes of hugging with intent to comfort

— YANG EXPLORATION —

Choose either of the following activities.

FIGURE 8

Lie on your backs and place the hand nearest your lover over his or her genitals. Without moving your hand, send loving energy to your partner through your hand with each out-breath. With each in-breath, imagine it returning through your lover's hand, until you are both completely relaxed.

CLEARING

Choose one of the topics from below and talk about your feelings relating to it until you are finished. Allow your partner to massage your hands while you talk. Do not ask for any feedback. Just talk. And remember to breathe deeply.

▷ Your least noble action with respect to the opposite sex. Was it infidelity, emotional blackmail, insisting on having a child over your partner's objections, concealing a secret your partner needs to know, abandonment, aggression? (Never mind what triggered the event.)

▷ Anything you want or need to get off your chest (addictions, herpes, prescription antidepressants you are taking, or whatever).

When the first partner finishes speaking, the second should look into his or her eyes and deliver this message in his or her own words: "These are symptoms and wounds from years on a planet that has been governed by painful separation. There is no blame. The past is over. We can heal best by strengthening each other." Then hold each other silently for as long as you like. Change roles.

Anything shared is off-limits for future discussion, unless the person who raised it wishes to speak about it further.

IT ISN'T EASY BEING GREEN

No matter how froggy you or your partner may look from time to time, you are actually royalty in disguise. For example, Will amazed me. Years of slavery to his mood-altering habits had left him with a deeply embedded impression that he was, in fact, a frog. He had pretty much accepted the dimensions of his aquarium, padded it with a couple of substance dependencies, and hunkered down for the duration. Uncomfortable as it was, it was home. Despite his façade of enthusiasm for trying the Exchanges, he was skeptical about forsaking familiar territory in favor of "some pie-in-the-sky summit."

Yet gradually, but steadily, as we stuck to our bonding-based lovemaking, he metamorphosed from a discouraged addict into a warm, insightful, recovered companion who is still my favorite teacher. The transition took time, but my belief in his power to transform himself was also a factor. These days, he masterfully soothes my ruffled feathers, or gets me laughing when I'm taking myself too seriously. We both feel very fortunate.

Before beginning, talk about what you experienced following the previous Exchange.

> ▷ Do you feel cherished? If so, tell your partner why. If not, what would make you feel more cherished?
> ▷ Are you able to enjoy your partner's gifts of affection, or are you angling to see "what you can get away with?" Try to resist altering your own mood by seeking sensation, and see what it feels like to relax, receive, and give.

— YIN DELIGHT —

Who was guardian last time? The other partner chooses a bonding behavior from the following list, and acts as guardian. If appropriate, take turns.

> ▷ Kissing with lips and tongues
> ▷ Several moments of synchronized breathing
> ▷ Cradling, or gently rocking, your partner's head and torso (works well on a couch, or with lots of pillows) for at least five minutes
> ▷ Gazing into each other's eyes for several moments
> ▷ Holding, or spooning, each other in stillness for at least twenty minutes to a half-hour
> ▷ Several minutes of stroking with intent to comfort
> ▷ Several minutes of hugging with intent to comfort

— YANG EXPLORATION —

Choose either of the following activities.

MUSICAL INTERLUDE

Each of you selects some slow, romantic music. (You can also pick a fast song to use as a warmup, just for laughs and exercise.) When you're ready, put on the first romantic song and dance in each other's arms. Just swaying back and forth to the music is fine if formal dance steps are not in your repertoire. Imagine you are merging with your partner as you dance but do not directly stimulate each other's genitals. Kissing is fine.

Put on the second song. Remind your hips how to move without thrusting. He leads, she follows. If you are feeling playful, stand back-to-back. Keep your buttocks touching as you bend your knees slightly and circle your hips a few times. Change direction. Experiment with slower circles. Try smaller circles. Try hip circles facing each other. Try holding each other's hips while you circle your hips.

HAPPY TOUCH

Spend at least five minutes giving your partner his or her favorite non-erotic touch. Change roles so you can receive *your* favorite touch.

THINKING AHEAD

The experience you are now seeking is not dependent upon sexual performance. Admittedly, this is a radical change from your genes' ideas of what your time in bed is for. With bonding-based love-making, erections come and go, but the exhilarating exchange of affection on which the rewards of this approach depend is unaffected. A powerful sense of connection is already flowing between you, thanks to your increasing relaxation and feelings of well-being in each other's presence.

As you move toward intercourse (not yet!), know that intercourse is a reflection of a deep desire to merge, but genitals do not cause desire—or satisfy it. Rather, desire for true intimacy reaches ideal levels once all uneasiness about deep union is gone. Australian sacred-sex teacher Barry Long taught that a period of sexual unresponsiveness is natural as we move back into our hearts. It passes as we heal any heart-genital split of the past. So let your genitals show you when this split has healed.

If you need to wait for a partner to feel ready, be patient. If you indicate that you want intercourse *now*, he or she will do his best to oblige you, even if not truly ready, and may slip into forcing performance with fantasy or vigorous stimulation. This is counterproductive; it creates stress and uneasiness about getting closer. When the time arrives, simply touch genitals instead (possible positions are pictured later), and imagine a flow of energy between them.

Sex at age ninety is like trying to shoot pool with a rope.
—George Burns

Will once suggested I call this book *No Viagra, No K-Y Jelly* because sexual arousal tends to become effortless. The reason is that you never force it. Ever. Even if your partner was very aroused last time. Even if your partner would respond rapidly to deliberate stimulation. Just wait until another occasion, and reassure each other with loving affection. It is better to stick to non-performance-oriented, loving contact for the full three weeks of the Exchanges than to push forward. Conventional foreplay, Viagra, vibrators, and anything else that artificially stimulates sexual performance slows true union.

While your body is deciding whether intercourse is a good idea, put your attention on the comfort and well-being of your partner. You may discover that performance is *not* essential for fulfilling intimacy.

Before beginning, talk about what you experienced following the previous Exchange.

> ▷ Did you allow yourself to calm down after the romantic dancing?
> ▷ Do you feel that you are being nurtured? What would make you feel more nurtured?
> ▷ If you have had an argument, have you tried lying together without words, in spoon position, and breathing deeply for a time before attempting to resolve your differences?

— YIN DELIGHT —

Choose a guardian who will also end the exercise. Sit facing each other, each with a pillow on your knees to support your elbows. Close your eyes, touch foreheads, and hold each other's elbows. Be still for several moments and with each exhale send your partner loving energy. What do you feel?

— YANG EXPLORATION —

Choose either of the following activities.

FACE MASSAGE

Have some massage oil and a small towel handy. Partner A is the massage therapist, B the recipient. B, lie comfortably with your head face-up on a towel and pillow in A's lap, feet facing away from A.

A, before beginning, energize your hands by moving them apart and then slowly together until they are almost touching. Repeat this motion. Can you feel the energy build between your hands? Meanwhile, B, clench your teeth, scrunch your face toward the tip of your nose in a tight ball, and hold it for at least ten counts before relaxing completely.

A, put a drop of massage oil on your hands. Rub B's cheeks, nose, and forehead gently up toward you and out to the side, using movements that would feel good to you. Allow your love for B to flow through your hands. B, visualize your mask melting away, revealing your true, much-loved self.

Now, A, rub B's temples with a gentle, circular motion. Next, gently stroke around B's mouth. Make tiny circles on the muscles under B's cheekbones. Knead B's scalp and the base of B's skull. Conclude by gently but firmly pressing the top of B's skull for a count of three. Ask B what else he or she would like. Change roles.

PICK A FAVORITE

The guardian chooses an exercise that he or she particularly enjoyed, or one that you skipped.

 NOTE: For the next Exchange you will need two light, comfortable blindfolds or scarves.

SABOTEURS

B e forewarned. It is quite likely that your chief defense to intimacy—whether it is flight, harsh judgments, substance abuse, or compulsive preoccupation with work or childrearing—will valiantly rally to create an ugly crisis or two. It may happen during the Exchanges, or shortly afterward. This defense mechanism's job is to keep you "safe" from intimacy.

When our crises arose, Will and I did our best to see the separation mechanism for what it was. This sometimes required both a cooling-off period and new insight. Lying still, holding each other in silence, was very helpful—when we could manage it.

It was quite a shift to realize that my judgments of Will were as much a product of *my* separation programming as his addictive behaviors were of *his*. Once we had correctly analyzed our challenge, and reminded ourselves of the benefits of union, we returned to generous affection—knowing that it was the best mood medicine available to us. As our inner guardians, our amygdalas, settled down again, and our brain chemistry grew more balanced, our perceptions of each other healed again. Eventually, lighthearted harmony prevailed.

Before beginning, talk about what you experienced following the previous Exchange.

> ▷ What do you like most about your time together?
> ▷ Do you feel that your partner cares deeply for you?
>   What would make you feel more cared for?
> ▷ Have you settled on a birth control method, if needed?
>   If not, see if you can do that now.

For both the Yin and Yang parts of this Exchange, you will need two light, comfortable blindfolds or scarves.

— YANG EXPLORATION —

This time start with this Yang exploration. She is the guardian for this Exchange. When ready, gently blindfold each other. Imagine that you have never before explored the body of a man, or a woman. Rub your hands together for a moment and then let them rest, palms up. Can you feel tingling energy? Now, take turns slowly removing your lover's clothing, except for underwear. Touch your partner as sensitively as you can, noticing the details of what you feel. Also try to communicate how much you cherish your partner. Send loving energy through your hands. Feel your partner's love and warmth flowing back to you. If you like, try keeping your blindfolds until you finish snuggling.

— YIN DELIGHT —

If you feel comfortable doing so, sleep with your shirts off. Take care to caress, rather than devour, your partner. Keep all touch generous and reverent. If at any time, now or in the future, she feels that she is being feasted upon visually, she should replace her shirt.

NOTE: The next Exchange entails time-consuming massages. If you don't have time to do both, the second one can be done during the following Exchange.

INTENTION

F orce of will is of limited use on this journey. So are good but flimsy intentions. Until my intention to change over from an old neuro-chemical reward system to the rewards of bonding behaviors was total and received my full attention, I subconsciously remained aligned with the status quo.

Some spiritual sources speak in terms of two inner voices from which we choose to take direction. It helps me to imagine those voices as two different reward systems. One rewards generosity, tranquility, and closer bonding. The other rewards intensity and fertilization efforts. It took a while, but eventually I determined to hear only the first voice when I made love.

If at any time you feel that your partner is hearing the "fertilization or fear voice," speak up. It is all right to say: "You say you're feeling really satisfied with this approach, but now you're thrusting, or writhing seductively. Have you changed agendas?" Or: "You say you are in the mood to make love, but your body says otherwise. How about holding me for a while, and we'll see how we feel later?"

Before beginning, talk about what you experienced following the previous Exchange.

> ▷ Is your need for "space" less than you imagined it would be? Or have you sometimes felt restless? (Quite normal.) Either way, talk about what would make you more comfortable.
> ▷ If you slept with your shirts off, did anyone slip back into classic, feeding-frenzy foreplay? If you have different answers to this question, share your reasons. Can the frenzied partner (or partner unjustly perceived as frenzied) try touching as if each body part were equally precious?

— YIN DELIGHT —

Choose a guardian, who will end the exercise. Gently, affectionately undress each other to whatever extent desired with lots of kisses. Lie quietly, skin-to-skin, for at least five minutes.

— YANG EXPLORATION —

Have some massage oil and towels handy. Exchange back massages, giving your full attention to relaxing your partner's back, head, and neck muscles, rather than turning yourself on. The partner with the most massage experience should give the first massage.

If working on the floor, and it is feasible to do so, sit astride your lover's back. Take a few deep breaths together while the partner in the therapist role allows loving energy to charge up his or her hands. Using some massage oil, massage him or her in whatever way you would like to be massaged. Your lover can give you feedback with wordless sounds of relaxed delight to let you know what is most satisfying. But do not chat. Lean your weight onto your partner's body (sensitively, but without straining), instead of trying to press harder using your strength. Avoid pressure on the spine itself. End with a massage of the head and some kisses on the neck.

Key concepts for good technique include:

> ▷ Making your movements slow and strong, *or* feathery,
>   but not in between
> ▷ Staying conscious of what you are doing and how you
>   think your actions would feel to your partner

Change roles (or plan to do so after the next Exchange).

NOT YET

I finally had to accept that none of my past learning or great lovemaking skills were of any use, given my new goal. I knew lots about heating a partner up and asking for what I wanted, and virtually nothing about quiet forms of shared ecstasy or conscious nurturing. I felt like an electric bass player who had just been handed a harp. It was awkward, and at first I was not enthralled by the sounds it made, either. Occasionally I got frustrated, grabbed my bass, and got another shocking reminder that it was time to master a new skill.

Slowly I learned that touch based on giving opens the heart in profound fulfillment, and that ecstatic, *shared* stillness does exist. Best of all, I learned that fulfillment can be combined with intercourse. But I did not reach this new territory until I completely abandoned my familiar habits, and made these new activities my sole focus for an extended period of time. Bonding-based union is totally different. It feels different. Its rewards feel different. And I had to be willing to give my nervous system time to reorient before I could accurately judge which form of lovemaking was the most satisfying.

My mate and I learned that we could assess our state of mind by watching our thoughts. When either of us found ourselves saying or thinking phrases like "I just want to swallow you whole," we realized we were draining each other, and needed to refocus. In contrast, thoughts like "I am just so grateful to have you in my life" and "What can I do to help you feel loved?" meant we were right on course.

Before beginning, talk about what you experienced following the previous Exchange.

> ▷ Did you fall back into standard foreplay during the
> massage? If so, return your focus to considerate
> attention for your partner. Don't try to arouse yourself

directly or indirectly. Allow yourself to be pampered instead.

▷ Does your intimate time together feel like inhaling and exhaling, that is, like arousal followed by easy relaxation? If not, what could you do differently to make that experience more likely?

— YANG EXPLORATION —

Do this Yang exercise first. Choose a guardian. Take turns guiding each other into new positions, using only light touch without words. Then, together, choose hand signals for the following:

▷ Asking your partner to stop moving immediately and inhale to relax (this can prevent undesired outcomes, and also allow you to savor the stillness together when you are in a relaxed, loving space)
▷ Asking your partner to hold you in a comfortable position (useful in the middle of the night when you do not feel like talking)
▷ Telling your partner wordlessly how glad you are that he or she is in your life (always useful)

Do you need to finish up the previous Exchange with another back massage?

— YIN DELIGHT —

Kiss and snuggle as much as you like. When you are both adequately relaxed, or if it is evening and you are ready to fall asleep, move into the scissors position (illustrated). Remove your clothing and lie together, forming an "X" on the bed, legs intertwined. He is on his side, and she is on her back. It is fine if you are not aroused. If you are, just enjoy it. If you are uncomfortably aroused, do an Energy Circulation (look back at Exchange Three if you need to remind yourself) until you both relax.

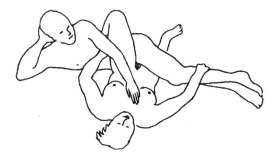

Scissors position

Merely press your genitals together, without intercourse, as you lie in the scissors position. If you wish, circulate the sexual energy between you by visualizing it flowing into her genitals and out of her heart, and then into his heart and down to his genitals, in a circular flow. For at least fifteen minutes try not to change positions or move, except to get more comfortable. When you finish, fall asleep, or get dressed and get on with your day. Do not heat yourselves with classic foreplay. If you awaken in the night uncomfortably aroused, move back into the scissors position with your lover. It will nourish you, while also permitting you to relax deeply.

If ever you suffer from pain in the genitals, you are engaging in too much physical stimulation. The pain is harmless and will go away, usually within twenty-four hours, though it can last longer. You do not need to have an orgasm to help it pass. Wait patiently and accept that you have been given a clear signal that you need to relax and wait for good feelings to arise, rather than trying to produce them yourself. Meanwhile, take care to avoid stimulating each other's genitals.

CLARITY (INTERCOURSE)

Who hen I first became interested in bonding-based lovemaking, I thought it would be all about will power. I learned, however, that it is actually about knowledge. Once I understood that I could not make any progress in learning this while still triggering my old neurochemical reward system, an ancient mystery began to reveal itself in modern, easily comprehensible terms.

Seen from this new vantage point, visual stimulation, passionate kissing, traditional foreplay, and vigorous intercourse were not inferior. They were just especially ... fruitful. That is, over the millennia, those who engaged in them tended to produce more babies—with similar inclinations. So, thanks to all the fun our ancestors had (and all of today's casual erotic stimulation), we have brains that immediately reward us for just thinking about such activities. Even more challenging is the fact that, once stimulated, we naturally crave more and more stimulation, and feel deprived if we do not dance to our mating program's tune.

Fortunately, bonding behaviors, including karezza, offer a way around this mechanism. If you feel your sexual energy rising, resist the urge to seek self-stimulation. Soothe your nervous system by channeling your energy consciously into gratitude and unselfish affection for your partner. Also, pause frequently and be still together. Can you feel pleasure in stillness itself while touching?

Before beginning, talk about what you experienced following the previous Exchange.

> ▷ Did your scissors position feel like a reverent act, a prayer for union? Why? Why not?
> ▷ Could you sense the conscious flow of energy between you? Or did you just fall asleep in protest because you could not rub all over your partner? (Or did you rub all

over your partner??) For this Exchange focus on those subtle energy flows. They may surprise you.

— YIN DELIGHT —

Who was guardian last time? The other partner chooses a bonding behavior from the following list, and acts as guardian. If appropriate, take turns.

▷ Touching and sucking of nipples and/or breasts
▷ Several moments of chest-to-chest, skin-to-skin contact
▷ Gently placing your palm over your lover's genitals with intent to comfort
▷ Several moments of synchronized breathing
▷ Cradling, or gently rocking, your partner's head and torso (works well on a couch, or with lots of pillows) for at least five minutes
▷ Gazing into each other's eyes for several moments
▷ Holding, or spooning, each other in stillness for at least twenty minutes to a half-hour
▷ Several minutes of stroking with intent to comfort
▷ Several minutes of hugging with intent to comfort

— YANG EXPLORATION —

Choose from the following activities, if you're both agreed. If not, do the first one.

EAR MASSAGE

Put your partner's head in your lap on a pillow. Give your partner a slow, sensual ear massage for several minutes. Remember to include some gentle earlobe tugging. Change roles.

INTERCOURSE

Only continue into intercourse if you are both adequately aroused from gentle kissing and touching without deliberate, physical stimulation, sexual fantasy, or sexual stimulants. His erection need not be strong, but she must be lubricating (or enthusiastic about proceeding, if health or age limitations prevent natural lubrication). Feel free to just touch genitals and lie still, if intercourse doesn't yet seem like the right idea to either of you.

Kiss and snuggle as long as you like. When you decide you are both adequately relaxed, or if it is evening and you are ready to fall asleep, move into either the scissors or bridge position (illustrated). Unite genitals as you lie in in this position.

Bridge position

Do not try to kiss while in the scissors or bridge position. Visualize the sexual energy flowing between you from your partner's heart through your genitals to your heart, and back through your genitals to your partner's heart. For at least fifteen minutes, try not to change positions or move, except to get more comfortable (you may find that you have to switch sides or even choose another side-lying position). Express your love with your hands by touching your partner's heart or placing your hand over your partner's hand. Relax totally.

Connect as many times as you wish in these positions. If you are overly aroused, gently disconnect, sit up, and circulate energy together—or use another favorite "cooling off" technique that you have already practiced. Once you fall asleep, or arise, do not have intercourse again until the Exchanges call for it.

VIRGINITY

S acred sex texts sometimes speak of the importance of "virginity" in permitting the free flow of lovers' energy streams. Some believe that it is these streams of energy that build up a magnetic charge between partners, enabling some of the more profound experiences of merging, or permitting a sense that the physical boundaries between mates are an illusion.

What is actually needed is not *virginity,* but rather a *virginal mindset.* This has two aspects. The first is the ability to move beyond any excessive sexual hunger you may have taught yourself, that is, beyond the habit of short-circuiting your sexual arousal via orgasm. Instead, allow your energy to radiate throughout your entire body (and, ultimately, your lover's as well) to the degree possible.

The second aspect of a virginal mindset is an emotional openness, free of past resentments and defensiveness. Even if you still feel resentful, hold the goal of allowing those resentments to dissolve so that your energy can flow freely.

Before beginning, talk about what you experienced following the previous Exchange.

> ▷ Did you avoid vigorous thrusting? If not, why not?
> ▷ Did you feel nothing during intercourse and just fall asleep instantly? If not, what did you feel? If so, why?
> ▷ Did you feel satisfied afterward? If not, why not?
> ▷ During or after the Exchange did you have the urge to say "I love you" with words or touch?
> ▷ Did you have erotic images of conventional sex or foreplay pop into your mind during, or since, the Exchange? (That old brain pathway can be really

powerful. Try to shift your full attention to an image of union that you find inspiring instead.)

▷ Did you feel totally safe? If not, what would make you feel safer?

▷ Did you have an orgasm in your sleep afterward? If so, give yourself a pat on the back, and refer to the introduction to the Exchanges. It's time to back up for a bit.

— YIN DELIGHT —

Who was guardian last time? The other partner chooses a favorite bonding behavior, and acts as guardian.

— YANG EXPLORATION —

Choose either of the following activities.

BATHING TOGETHER

If you have a shower or hot tub, try a long, still hug there. Bathe your lover, not yourself. Let him or her wash you. If you shampoo, do that for each other, too.

SOOTHING TECHNIQUES

Take turns practicing these techniques for cooling things down when you're the guardian:

▷ Meditate together for a moment or silently pray together for inner peace.

▷ Have your partner lie face up, in front of you, as you rest his or her head in your cradled hands without moving.

▷ Stop moving. Look into each other's eyes for a moment.

CONSISTENCY

W hen I trained my dog, consistency was more important than anything else. Otherwise, he naturally assumed that commands were mere suggestions. So it proved with my brain. I was trying to lay down a new habit. And I discovered that the more consistent I was, the more rapidly I got through the uncomfortable period of hypervigilance, and the sooner I could relax into the rewards.

On the other hand, my mate and I got some things right. We slept together loyally, even when suffering from distressing separation hangovers. And we never deliberately climaxed or tried to make each other climax.

Before beginning, talk about what you experienced following the previous Exchange.

> ▷ Do you feel pampered? What would make you feel more pampered?
> ▷ How are you doing with the motionless snuggle in which only energy moves? Trust that something is happening, even if it is subtle.
> ▷ Have you used the signals you worked out for stopping all movement, moving into spoon position, and letting your partner know how much you adore him or her? If not, incorporate the signals in your snuggling.

— YIN DELIGHT —

Who was guardian last time? The other partner chooses a favorite bonding behavior, and acts as guardian.

— YANG EXPLORATION —

UNFOLDING

Partner A lies on the floor on a blanket in the position he or she usually curls into when feeling abandoned, unloved, or betrayed. Partner B kneels by his or her head and gently holds it for a moment, eyes closed.

Then, with lots of kisses, Partner B slowly takes at least five minutes to untangle Partner A gently, limb by limb, until he or she is resting comfortably on his or her back, palms up, arms and legs straight, but relaxed. Partner B should make a conscious effort to send Partner A healing energy to dissolve all old programming relating to defensive isolation.

When Partner B has finished, Partner A thanks Partner B by holding him or her for a while. Change roles.

QUESTIONS (INTERCOURSE)

After the Exchanges, you will probably want to return to conventional sex to complete your comparison. However, sometimes people ask, "If we want to stick to karezza after the Exchanges, how often do we have intercourse or orgasm?" We found it helpful *not* to have intercourse every day. We spend at least one day, and often several, in between intercourse occasions. However, on those other nights we're conscientious about engaging in bonding behaviors—at least for a few moments—such as kissing, holding each other, endeavoring to go to bed at the same time, and snuggling in the morning once both of us are awake. These behaviors help us to remain less goal-oriented.

If you and your partner return to sex with orgasm after the Exchanges, you'll get a clear picture of what the passion cycle looks like in both of you. That should help you determine how often you'd like to experience it.

You may also wish to take turns deciding which affectionate activity you would like to begin with on your *next* intimate occasion. That way, if anyone has a longing for a particular behavior, including intercourse, his or her desire can be granted with very little delay. Planned intercourse can be more soothing than spontaneity. It gives you both something to look forward to, and it helps prevent frustration. In contrast, wondering when you're going to make love next can easily trigger frustration, or cause you to misread your partner's intentions.

Taking turns has taken a lot of pressure off, and has had some surprising results. Possibly the most surprising are that I sometimes find myself choosing five-minute, fully clothed cuddles on the sofa—and my wife is inviting me for naked romps in the moonlight.
—Pierce

Before beginning, talk about what you experienced following the previous Exchange.

> ▷ Do you feel a larger purpose in what you are doing together? If so, how would you describe it?
> ▷ Have any happy coincidences or unexpected gifts flowed from your time together? If so, are you showing your gratitude by nurturing your partner?

— YIN DELIGHT —

Who was guardian last time? The other partner chooses a bonding behavior, and acts as guardian.

> ▷ Touching and sucking of nipples and/or breasts
> ▷ Several moments of chest-to-chest, skin-to-skin contact
> ▷ Gently placing your palm over your lover's genitals with intent to comfort
> ▷ Several moments of synchronized breathing
> ▷ Cradling, or gently rocking, your partner's head and torso (works well on a couch, or with lots of pillows) for at least five minutes
> ▷ Gazing into each other's eyes for several moments
> ▷ Holding, or spooning, each other in stillness for at least twenty minutes to a half-hour
> ▷ Several minutes of stroking with intent to comfort
> ▷ Several minutes of hugging with intent to comfort

— YANG EXPLORATION —

Choose either of the following activities, if you're both agreed. If not, do the first one.

SPINE TINGLES

Have your partner lie on his or her stomach on the bed. Gently, slowly stroke upward from the tailbone to the neck, using hand-over-hand motions. Do it at least three times, and more if you like. Then place one hand on the sacrum (tailbone) and the other hand at the top of the spine, and rest your hands there for several moments. Can you feel energy flowing between your hands? What does your partner feel? Change roles.

INTERCOURSE

The pilot uses kisses, touches, and the gentle movements of his body next to her to make her feel loved. Limit direct genital stimulation to the most fleeting and affectionate of gestures, focusing instead on the rest of her body. Allow genital responses to arise naturally as part of the relaxation response that promotes sexual arousal. Avoid oral sex (of course). Her sole responsibility is to relax and enjoy his creative touches and affectionate generosity. She should not try to arouse herself or him in any way, although she is welcome to offer nurturing, affectionate touch.

If either partner grows overly aroused, lie still next to each other, synchronize breathing, and gently rest your hands on each other's genitals until you are both calm.

Keep your touch gentle and reverent. Communicate your adoration.

This is an intercourse Exchange so, if you are both ready, connect genitals and lie still. Choose scissors, bridge, or some other side-lying position, yab-yum (woman seated in man's lap, facing him), or woman-on-top position (if she's willing to remain still).

Have intercourse as often as you like, but keep the movements gentle and avoid deep or vigorous thrusting. *Pause frequently* to savor the stillness and more subtle energy flows. Stop when the energy stops flowing for either of you. Make no effort to heat yourselves up. Relax instead.

Regardless of who is guardian, should either of you sense your partner becoming too hot, tensing up, or constricting breathing, listen to your intuition! Stop and suggest deep breaths. Do some Energy Circulation (page 310) together until things calm down. You would do well to ignore your partner's sincere and convincing assurances that she or he has it all under control. Your intuition is likely to be more reliable under such circumstances than your partner's assessment.

Avoid intercourse until after the next two Exchanges, though you may always end your snuggling with some comfortable, intimate position, like scissors, without intercourse.

SELF-OBSERVATION

When I was climaxing all the time, I suffered from so many mood swings (euphoria, anxiety, resentment, wishful thinking, demands) and related self-doubts that my perception was unreliable. I also found it hard to pick out the key feelings that revealed the destructive and self-destructive patterns I needed to release.

The fewer passion cycles I trigger, the easier it is to spot the self-sabotaging thoughts—and the easier it is to see that they are as groundless as bad dreams that dissipate in the morning. Why? Because the rest of the time I feel balanced and loved, not anxious. Waves of intense feelings after an orgasm stick out as exceptions; they are not the rule. They can be helpful, pointing to anything holding me back from deeper intimacy. They show me what false beliefs are still in my way. This clearing process is natural, but therapists and energetic healing approaches can facilitate it.

You may soon be returning to conventional sex. When you do, keep track of your feelings for the first two weeks. Here are notes from two couples who made similar experiments. (Not to spoil your fun....)

> I have always been greatly bothered by knowing that my husband believes orgasm is natural and no problem, so recently I said, "Okay let's try it for a month *with* orgasms, just to see." I thought it would be good for me to let go of the fear of orgasm that the Samael Aun Weor classes had started by demonizing orgasms.
>
> So we did twice have orgasms intentionally, and after that he said, "That's enough. Can we please go back to what we have been doing?" He said this even though I was happy to continue experimenting. Our sex-without-orgasm practice is "making love" for him, whereas what just happened was "only sex."
>
> For me the experiment was also a reminder that orgasms let out the lovely magical feeling you have built up during intercourse. Plus

they are such an addictive thing; the next day annoying feelings of being in the mood for more kept interrupting my thoughts. Sex without orgasm leaves such a long-lasting satisfaction as compared to sex with orgasm that it is almost ironic.

My wife and I have been trying to get pregnant, so we keep going back and forth. Every hangover is worse than the last. Actually, I'm not sure if that is as much true as the fact that every period between hangovers, we get so much deeper, so much clearer and closer, that the hangover just seems worse than before. I do not know how I got along previously without this understanding.

Before beginning, talk about what you experienced following the previous Exchange.

> ▷ What did you like best about what your partner did while making love? Did anything surprise you?
> ▷ Did you feel adored? Did you feel satisfied today? How would you describe your feelings?
> ▷ Did you allow yourselves any periods of stillness to see if you could feel subtle or joyful energy moving?
> ▷ Did you stop making love when the energy stopped flowing, or try to stimulate each other back to another high? Try stopping when the energy stops.

— YIN DELIGHT —

Who was guardian last time? The other partner chooses a favorite bonding behavior, and acts as guardian.

— YANG EXPLORATION —

Experiment with various intercourse positions *without intercourse*. Tell each other what's good, or not so good, for you in each one. Put the emphasis on comfort so you will be able to make love for long periods of time with intervals of stillness. You may wish to try lying on your sides with the woman's legs wrapped around the man (and supportive pillow arrangements). Be creative.

Choose the most comfortable position you find and be still in it for at least fifteen minutes. Let yourselves relax completely. *Focus on what you feel where your skin meets your lover's skin.*

Between now and the next Exchange, confine your intimacy to gentle kisses and touches, without intercourse.

BRAVO!

This Exchange is the last one. Whether or not you decide to return to orgasmic sex after the Exchanges, you will probably find you have an orgasm from time to time anyway. This will give you the opportunity to compare the effects of fertilization-driven sex with bonding-based sex.

Orgasm can be an educational gift—especially after you've experienced the benefits of bonding-based lovemaking. Be a scientist for the two weeks after an orgasm. Make notes on a calendar, if possible.

Do you notice flashes of friction or resentment in your relationship with your kids or co-workers? Fluctuations in your energy level? In your degree of optimism? Confidence? Clarity? Depth of spiritual practice? Love for your partner?

Does your partner seem different? Does your desire to engage in bonding behaviors change? Do these behaviors feel different to either of you? How about your level of sexual frustration? Don't be surprised if both of you notice effects, even if only one of you climaxes. And don't be surprised if the effects are often so subtle that you doubt your perception. Track them anyway, so you can see if there's a pattern.

Be as gentle as you can with each other's feelings, and try not to take any mood swings too seriously. (Chapter Nine has some useful suggestions for coping with a passion cycle starting on page 257.)

Before beginning, talk about what you experienced following the previous Exchange.

> ▷ What did you feel where your skin met your lover's skin?
> ▷ Do you feel grateful to your partner? Why?
> ▷ Tell your partner what you think of bonding-based lovemaking, as honestly as you can. (You may want to

discuss this question again two weeks after your return to fertilization-driven sex. Hindsight is sometimes sharper.)
▷ Are there other questions you want to ask each other about the experience?

— YIN DELIGHT —

Who was guardian last time? The other partner chooses a bonding behavior, and acts as guardian.
▷ Touching and sucking of nipples and/or breasts
▷ Several moments of chest-to-chest, skin-to-skin contact
▷ Gently placing your palm over your lover's genitals with intent to comfort
▷ Several moments of synchronized breathing
▷ Cradling, or gently rocking, your partner's head and torso (works well on a couch, or with lots of pillows) for at least five minutes
▷ Gazing into each other's eyes for several moments
▷ Holding, or spooning, each other in stillness for at least twenty minutes to a half-hour
▷ Several minutes of stroking with intent to comfort
▷ Several minutes of hugging with intent to comfort

— YANG EXPLORATION —

Just for fun, check your state of mind after three weeks of Exchanges. The Harmony Index provides a way to measure your progress.

HARMONY INDEX

Which of the following are true for you?

He   She

——— ——— I'm sleeping better.

——— ——— I'm able to relax, and allow myself to be nurtured.

——— ——— I've cut back on, or dropped, the use of a stimulant.

——— ——— My health has noticeably improved in some way.

——— ——— I'm thinking more clearly.

——— ——— I'm in less pain.

——— ——— I have a sense of being "in the flow."

——— ——— I'm smiling or laughing more.

——— ——— I'm less anxious.

——— ——— I'm more productive and deal with tough problems more effectively.

——— ——— The kids are behaving better.

——— ——— I'm bickering less with my partner, in-laws, or bothersome bureaucrats.

——— ——— I feel more loved.

——— ——— I'm wasting less time.

——— ——— I feel like we'll always be friends whatever happens.

——— ——— Aspects of our relationship have healed.

——— ——— I'm feeling less broke, exhausted, and/or rushed.

——— ——— I'm making more progress with a project.

——— ——— My fear of intimacy has decreased.

——— ——— My partner is nagging me less.

——— ——— I feel more supported.

——— ——— I'm more willing to ask for help when I need it.

——— ——— I'm more sociable.

——— ——— I'm more generous.

——— ——— I have fewer hassles at work, or I'm better able to deal with work stress.

——— ——— I'm more easygoing.

——— ——— I've lightened up—depressions are less frequent.

——— ——— I feel more youthful.

——— ——— I feel like my intuition has improved.

——— ——— I have a sense of optimism about the future.

What would your relationship look like if you chose to use bonding-based lovemaking except when you intend to procreate? Would it increase your genuine desire to remain together?

Thank your partner for trying the Exchanges. Enjoy your future explorations!*

*You may also enjoy the suggested activities at this Web page: http://www.reuniting.info/resources/exchange_of_the_day.

NOTES

PREFACE

1. Sam Roberts, "The Shelf Life of Bliss," *New York Times,* July 1, 2007.

1a. Bianca P. Acevedo and Arthur Aron, "Does a Long-Term Relationship Kill Romantic Love?" *Review of General Psychology,* 13(1), 2009: 59–65.

CHAPTER ONE: BIOLOGY HAS PLANS FOR YOUR LOVE LIFE

2. Fisher, Helen, *Anatomy of Love: A Natural History of Mating, Marriage, and Why We Stray* (New York: Ballantine Books, 1995).

3. Jody Van Laningham, David R. Johnson, and Paul R. Amato, "Marital Happiness, Marital Duration, and the U-Shaped Curve: Evidence from a Five-Wave Panel Study," *Social Forces,* 79(4), June 2001: 1313–1341.

4. K. S. Birditt and T. C. Antonucci, "Relationship Quality Profiles and Well-Being Among Married Adults," *J. Fam. Psychol.,* 21(4), Dec. 2007: 595–604.

5. D. F. Fiorino, A. Coury, and A. G. Phillips, "Dynamic Changes in Nucleus Accumbens Dopamine Efflux During the Coolidge Effect in Male Rats," *J. Neurosci.,* 17(12), June 1997: 4849–4855.

6. "Promiscuity Breeds Better Babies, Study Shows" *Mercury,* Nov. 2, 2006, http://www.news.com.au/mercury/story/0,22884,20687497-921,00.html.

7. G. L. Lester and B. B. Gorzalka, "Effect of Novel and Familiar Mating Partners on the Duration of Sexual Receptivity in the Female Hamster," *Behav. Neural. Biol.,* 49(3), May 1988: 398–405.

8. R. P. Michael and D. Zumpe, "Potency in Male Rhesus Monkeys: Effects of Continuously Receptive Females," *Science,* 28, 200(4340), April 1978: 451–453.

9. D. Klusmann, "Sexual Motivation and the Duration of Partnership," *Arch. Sex Behav.,* 31(3), June 2002: 275–287.

10. James N. Powell, *Energy and Eros: Teachings on the Art of Love,* (New York: William Morrow and Company, Inc., 1985): 182.

11. A. B. Emiliano, et al., "The Interface of Oxytocin-Labeled Cells and Serotonin Transporter-Containing Fibers in the Primate Hypothalamus: A Substrate for SSRIs' Therapeutic Effects?" *Neuropsychopharmacology,* 32(5), May 2007: 977–988.

12. G. L. Kovács, Z. Sarnyai, and G. Szabó, "Oxytocin and Addiction: A Review," *Psychoneuroendocrinology,* 23(8), Nov. 1998: 945–962.

13. Jim Young, et al., "Stable Partnership and Progression to AIDS or Death in HIV Infected Patients Receiving Highly Active Antiretroviral Therapy: Swiss HIV Cohort Study," *BMJ,* 328(7430), Jan. 2004: 15.

14. C. E. Detilliona, et al., "Social Facilitation of Wound Healing," *Psychoneuroendocrinology,* 29(8), Sep. 2004: 1004–1011.

15. "Parent that Takes Care of Offspring Tends to Outlive the Other Parent, Study Shows," CalTech Press Releases (Monday, June 8, 1998), http://mr.caltech.edu/media/lead/060898JA.html.

16. G. Holstege, et al., "Brain Activation During Human Male Ejaculation," *J. Neurosci.,* 23(27), Oct. 2003: 9185–9193.

17. "The Orgasmic Brain," Saturday, July 9, 2005, *All in the Mind*, Radio National (Australia), http://www.abc.net.au/rn/science/mind/stories/s1407052.htm.

18. Julian Savulescu and Anders Sandberg, "Neuroenhancement of Love and Marriage: The Chemicals Between Us," *Neuroethics*, 1(1), March 2008: 31–44.

19. VanLaningham, Johnson, and Amato, "Marital Happiness": 1335.

20. Alexei Barrionuevo, "In Tangle of Young Lips, a Sex Rebellion in Chile," *New York Times*, Sep. 12, 2008, http://www.nytimes.com/2008/09/13/world/americas/13chile.html.

WISDOM OF THE AGES: TAOISM

21. Brian Walker, trans., *Hua Hu Ching: The Unknown Teachings of Lao Tzu* (San Francisco: HarperSanFrancisco, 1992).

22. Ibid.: 83.

23. Ibid.

24. Ibid.: 84.

25. Ibid.

26. Ibid.: 85.

27. Ibid.

28. Douglas Wile, *Art of the Bedchamber: The Chinese Sexual Classics Including Women's Solo Meditation Texts* (New York: State University of New York Press, 1992): 45, 48.

29. Ibid.: 8, 50.

30. Ibid.: 70.

CHAPTER TWO: ELEPHANTS IN THE LIVING ROOM

31. Mantak Chia and Michael Winn, *Taoist Secrets of Love: Cultivating Male Sexual Energy* (New York: Aurora Press, 1984).

32. Mantak Chia and Manewan Chia, *Healing Love Through the Tao* (Huntington, NY: Healing Tao Books, 1986): 291.

33. Wile, *Bedchamber*: 10.

34. John Lee, *The Flying Boy* (Deerfield Beach, FL: Health Communications, Inc., 1989): 10.

35. John Humphrey Noyes, *Male Continence* (Oneida, NY: Oneida Community, 1872), http://www.sacred-texts.com/sex/mc/index.htm.

36. Publius Ovidius Naso, *Remedia Amoris (The Cure for Love)*, published 5 BCE, part IX, (adapted from A. S. Kline's translation: http://www.tonykline.co.uk/PITBR/Latin/CuresforLove.htm#_Toc523020782).

37. Louis Untermeyer, ed., *A Treasury of Ribaldry* (Garden City, NY: Hanover House, 1956): 7.

38. Chia, *Taoist Secrets*: 44.

39. Herb Goldberg, *What Men Really Want* (New York: New American Library, 1991): 112.

40. Ibid.: 77.

41. Swami Satyananda Saraswati, *Kundalini Tantra* (Bihar: Bihar School of Yoga, 1992).

42. Nicole Christine, *Temple of the Living Earth* (Sedona, AZ: Earth Song Publications, 1995): 18, 19.

43. Leonard Shlain, *Sex, Time and Power* (New York: Penguin Group, 2003): 158.

44. Chia, *Taoist Secrets:* 3.

45. Keith Dowman, *Sky Dancer: The Secret Life and Songs of the Lady Yeshe Tsogyel* (London: Routledge and Kegan Paul, 1984): 248.

WISDOM OF THE AGES: CHRISTIANITY

46. Elaine Pagels, *Beyond Belief: The Secret Gospel of Thomas* (New York: Random House, 2003): 174.

47. Except as otherwise noted, I have used the following translation: Jean-Yves Leloup, *The Gospel of Philip: Jesus, Mary Magdalene, and the Gnosis of Sacred Union* (Rochester, VT: Inner Traditions, 2004): 157.

48. Ibid.: 87.

49. R. McL. Wilson, *The Gospel of Philip* (New York: Harper & Row, 1962).

50. James M. Robinson, ed., *The Nag Hammadi Library,* revised edition (San Francisco: HarperCollins, 1990).

51. Leloup, *Gospel of Philip:* 109.

52. Leloup, *Gospel of Philip:* 107.

53. Leloup, *Gospel of Philip:* 111.

54. Leloup, *Gospel of Philip:* 105.

55. Leloup, *Gospel of Philip:* 109.

56. Leloup, *Gospel of Philip:* 91.

57. James M. Robinson, ed., "The Exegesis on the Soul," *The Nag Hammadi Library in English,* third edition (New York: Harper & Row, 1988): 195.

58. Wile, *Bedchamber:* 8, 50.

59. Robert J. Miller, ed., "Gospel of Thomas," *The Complete Gospels: Annotated Scholars Version* (Santa Rosa, CA: Polebridge Press, 1992, 1994).

60. Leloup, *Gospel of Philip:* 83. The fragment is damaged, but scholars generally translate it this way.

61. Dennis Ronald MacDonald, *There Is No Male and Female: The Fate of a Dominical Saying in Paul and Gnosticism* (Philadelphia: Fortress Press, 1987).

62. Elaine Pagels, *The Gnostic Gospels* (New York: Vintage, 1989): xvii.

63. Elaine Pagels, *Beyond Belief: The Secret Gospel of Thomas* (London: Pan Macmillan, 2005): 34.

64. Michael A. Williams, *Rethinking "Gnosticism"* (Princeton, NJ: Princeton University Press, 1999): 174–175.

65. Margaret Farley, *Just Love: A Framework for Christian Sexual Ethics* (New York: The Continuum International Publishing Group, Inc., 2006): 254–255.

66. Peter Brown, *The Body and Society: Men, Women, and Sexual Renunciation in Early Christianity* (New York: Columbia University Press, 1988).

67. Elizabeth A. Clark, vol. ed., *Jerome, Chrysostom and Friends,* Studies in Women and Religion, vol. 2, (Lewiston, NY: The Edwin Mellen Press, 1979): 165–166.

68. Charles Williams, *Descent of the Dove: A Short History of the Holy Spirit in the Church* (Grand Rapids, MI: William B. Eerdmans, 1939): 13–14.

69. Farley, *Just Love:* 257.

CHAPTER THREE: A WHALE'S TAIL

70. Also see Christina Ferrare, *OK, So I Don't Have a Headache* (New York: St. Martin's Press, 1999); and Judith Reichman, *I'm Not in the Mood* (New York: Harper Paperbacks, 1999).

71. Jennifer Berman and Laura Berman, *For Women Only: What You Need to Know about the Inner Lives of Men* (New York: Henry Holt and Company, LLC, 2001).

72. Rose M. Kreider and Jason M. Fields, "Number, Timing, and Duration of Marriages and Divorces: 1996," *Current Populations Reports,* Feb. 2002, http://www.census.gov/prod/2002pubs/p70–80.pdf.

73. Willard F. Harley, Jr., *Love Busters* (Grand Rapids, MI: Baker Book House Company, 2002): 35, 37.

74. Janice Kiecolt-Glaser, et al., "Marital Stress: Immunological, Endocrinological, and Health Consequences," The Psychoneuroimmunology (PNI) Research Program in the Institute for Behavioral Medicine Research at The Ohio State University, 2001, http://pni.psychiatry.ohio-state.edu/jkg/marital.html.

75. Wile, *Bedchamber:* 7.

76. Walker, *Hua Hu Ching:* 85.

77. Wile, *Bedchamber:* 6.

78. Lisa Diamond, *Sexual Fluidity* (Cambridge, MA: Harvard University Press, 2008).

79. Ibid.: 11.

80. Ibid.: 218–227.

WISDOM OF THE AGES: HINDUISM

81. Powell, *Energy and Eros:* 109.

82. Ibid.: 108–109.

83. Paramhansa Yogananda, *Autobiography of a Yogi* (Los Angeles: Self-Realization Fellowship, 1979).

84. Georg Feuerstein, "Traditional Tantra and Contemporary Neo-Tantrism," http://www.traditionalyogastudies.com/articles_tantra-kundalini_neo.html.

85. Georg Feuerstein, *Sacred Sexuality* (Los Angeles: J. P. Tarcher, 1992).

CHAPTER FOUR: AT THE HEART OF THE SEPARATION VIRUS

86. Richard Dawkins, *The Selfish Gene* (Oxford: Oxford University Press, 1976): 22.

87. Alison Motluk, "Scent of a Man," *New Scientist,* Feb. 10, 2001, http://www.skyaid.org/Skyaid%20Org/Medical/scent_of_a_man.htm; and Christine E. Garver-Apgar, et al., "Major Histocompatibility Complex Alleles, Sexual Responsivity, and Unfaithfulness in Romantic Couples," *Psychological Science,* 17(10), Nov. 2006: 830–835.

88. Paul MacLean, cited in "The Triune Brain," http://www.kheper.net/topics/intelligence/MacLean.htm

89. Geoffrey Miller, *The Mating Mind: How Sexual Choice Shaped the Evolution of Human Nature* (London: William Heinemann, 2000).

90. M. Daly and M. Wilson, "Evolutionary Social Psychology and Family Homicide," *Science,* 242(4878), Oct. 1988: 519–524.

91. Marjorie Shostak and Nisa, *Nisa: The Life and Words of a !Kung Woman* (Cambridge, MA: Harvard University Press, 2000): 243.

92. Meryl Hyman Harris, "Designer Genes: Women May Stray When Ovulation Peaks," SexualHealth.com, http://sexualhealth.e-healthsource.com/?p=news1&id=530053.

93. G. K. Mak, "Male Pheromone-Stimulated Neurogenesis in the Adult Female Brain: Possible Role In Mating Behavior," *Nat. Neurosci.*, 10(8), Aug. 2007: 1003–1011.

94. Robin Baker, *Sperm Wars: Infidelity, Sexual Conflict and Other Bedroom Battles* (New York: Basic Books/HarperCollins, 1996).

95. Geoffrey Miller, Joshua M. Tybur, and Brent D. Jordan, "Ovulatory Cycle Effects on Tip Earnings by Lap Dancers: Economic Evidence for Human Estrus?" *Evolution and Human Behavior,* 28 (6), Nov. 2007: 375–381.

96. Jeffrey Kluger, "The Science of Romance: Why We Love," *Time,* Jan. 17, 2008; and M. G. Haselton and S. W. Gangestad, "Conditional Expression of Women's Desires and Men's Mate Guarding Across the Ovulatory Cycle," *Horm. Behav.,* 49(4), April 2006: 509–518.

97. Leo Tolstoy, *The Kreutzer Sonata,* http://etext.lib.virginia.edu/toc/modeng/public/TolKreu.html: Chapter 2.

98. V. Griskevicius, et al., "Blatant Benevolence and Conspicuous Consumption: When Romantic Motives Elicit Strategic Costly Signals," *J. Pers. Soc. Psychol.,* 93(1), July 2007: 85–102.

99. Doron and Sarah Tikvah Kornbluth, *Jewish Women Speak about Jewish Matters* (Southfield, MI: Targum Press, Inc., 2000): 69–71.

100. D. Marazziti and G. B. Cassano, "The Neurobiology of Attraction," *J. Endocrinol. Invest.,* 26(3 Suppl.), 2003: 58–60, http://www.ncbi.nlm.nih.gov/pubmed/12834023?dopt=Abstract.

101. D. Marazziti, et al., "Alteration of the Platelet Serotonin Transporter in Romantic Love," *Psychol. Med.,* 29(3), May 1999: 741–745.

102. E. Emanuele, et al., "Raised Plasma Nerve Growth Factor Levels Associated with Early-Stage Romantic Love," *Psychoneuroendocrinology,* 31(3), April 2006: 288–294.

103. Van Laningham, Johnson, and Amato, "Marital Happiness;" and Birditt and Antonucci, "Relationship Quality Profiles."

104. Roberts, "The Shelf Life of Bliss."

105. Robert Lee Hotz, "Get Out of Your Own Way: Studies Show the Value of Not Over-thinking a Decision," *Wall Street Journal,* June 27, 2008: A9.

106. J. Olds and P. Milner, "Positive Reinforcement Produced by Electrical Stimulation of the Septal Area and Other Regions of Rat Brain," *J. Comp. Physiol. Psychol.,* 47(6), Dec. 1954: 419–427.

107. Kent Berridge, "Simple Pleasures," *APA Online,* 18(11), Nov. 2004, http://www.apa.org/science/psa/sb-berridge.html.

108. B. R. Komisaruk, B. Whipple, and C. Beyer, "Orgasm," *The Psychologist,* 21(2), Feb. 2008: 100–103; and Fiorino, Coury, and Phillips, "Coolidge Effect in Male Rats."

109. H. Fisher, A. Aron, and L. L. Brown, "Romantic Love: An FMRI Study of a Neural Mechanism for Mate Choice," *J. Comp. Neurol.,* 493(1), Dec. 2005: 58–62.

110. Andreas Bartels and Semir Zeki, "The Neural Correlates of Maternal and Romantic Love," *Neuroimage,* 21(3), March 2004: 1155–1166.

WISDOM OF THE AGES: CORTEZIA

111. Denis de Rougemont, *Love in the Western World* (Princeton, NJ: Princeton University Press, 1983).

112. Victoria LePage, *Mysteries of the Bridechamber* (Rochester, VT.: Inner Traditions, 2007): 244.

113. Tobias Churton, *The Gnostics* (London: Weidenfeld and Nicolson, 1987): 75.

114. Jean-Luc Aubarbier and Michel Binet, *Le Pays Cathare* (Luçon: Editions Ouest-France, 2001): 31.

115. Jean Markale, *Courtly Love: The Path of Sexual Initiation*, trans. Jon Graham, (Rochester, VT: Inner Traditions, 2001): 100.

116. Tobias Churton, *Gnostic Philosophy* (Rochester, VT: Inner Traditions, 2005): 185–186.

117. Ibid.: 184.

118. Markale, *Courtly Love:* 209–210.

119. Ibid.: 100.

120. Ibid.: 27–28.

121. Moshe Idel, "Sexual Metaphors and Practice in the Kabbalah," in *The Jewish Family: Metaphor and Memory* (Oxford: Oxford University Press, l989): 205–206.

122. Marsha Keith Schuchard, *Why Mrs. Blake Cried: Swedenborg, Blake, and the Sexual Basis of Spiritual Vision* (London: Century, 2006).

CHAPTER FIVE: THE PASSION CYCLE

123. See this "post orgasmic illness syndrome" (POIS) thread on the Naked Scientist Forum: http://www.thenakedscientists.com/forum/index.php?topic=6576.0.

124. Holstege, et al., "Brain Activation."

125. W. J. Jenkins and J. B. Becker, "Dynamic Increases in Dopamine During Paced Copulation in the Female Rat," *Eur. J. Neurosci.*, 18(7), Oct. 2003: 1997–2001.

126. Komisaruk, Whipple, and Beyer, "Orgasm."

127. "Parkinson's Medication Appears to Trigger Excessive Gambling: Mayo Clinic Findings Strengthen Uncommon But Reversible Link Between Dopamine Agonist Drugs and Pathological Gambling," Mayo Clinic, July 11, 2005, http://www.mayoclinic.org/news2005-rst/2925.html.

128. Vicki Brower, "Loosening Addiction's Deadly Grip: Recent Research Paints a Picture of Addiction as a Progressive, Chronic Neurological Disease that Wreaks Havoc with Brain Chemistry," *EMBO reports*, 7(2), 2006: 140–142, http://www.nature.com/embor/journal/v7/n2/full/7400635.html.

129. S. Hood, et al., "Dopaminergic Challenges in Social Anxiety Disorder: Evidence for Dopamine D3 Desensitisation Following Successful Treatment with Serotonergic Antidepressants," *J. Psychopharmacol.*, Oct. 8, 2008, [Epub ahead of print] http://www.ncbi.nlm.nih.gov/pubmed/18838500.

130. L. de Haan, et al., "Subjective Experiences During Dopamine Depletion," *Am. J. Psychiatry*, 162(9), Sep. 2005: 1755.

131. P. Willner, A. S. Hale, and S. Argyropoulos, "Dopaminergic Mechanism of Antidepressant Action in Depressed Patients," *J. Affect. Disord.*, 86(1), May 2005: 37–45.

132. "Suicide risk dims hope for anti-addiction pills," Associated Press, April 23, 2008, http://www.msnbc.msn.com/id/24277263/.

133. Serge Sevy, et al., "Emotion-Based Decision-Making in Healthy Subjects: Short-Term Effects of Reducing Dopamine Levels," *Psychopharmacology* (Berl), 188(2), Oct. 2006: 228–235.

134. Constance Holden, "'Behavioral' Addictions: Do They Exist?," *Science,* 294(5544), Nov. 2001: 981.

135. John J. Medina, "Of Stress and Alcoholism, Of Mice and Men," *Psychiatric Times,* (25)8, July 1, 2008, http://www.psychiatrictimes.com/display/article/10168/1167009.

135a. Kyle K. Pitchers, et al., "Endogenous Opioid-Induced Neuroplasticity of Dopaminergic Neurons in the Ventral Tegmental Area Influences Natural and Opiate Reward," *Journal of Neuroscience,* 34(26), June, 2014: 8825–8836.

136. T. Kruger, et al., "Specificity of the Neuroendocrine Response to Orgasm During Sexual Arousal in Men," *Psychoneuroendocrinology,* 23(4), May 1998: 401–411; and M. S. Exton, et al., "Cardiovascular and Endocrine Alterations After Masturbation-Induced Orgasm in Women," *Psychosom. Med.,* 61(3), May–June 1999: 280–289.

137. S. Brody and T. H. Krüger, "The Post-Orgasmic Prolactin Increase Following Intercourse Is Greater Than Following Masturbation and Suggests Greater Satiety," *Biol. Psychol.,* 71(3), March 2006: 312–315.

138. Simon W. Townsend, Tobias Deschner, and Klaus Zuberbühler, "Female Chimpanzees Use Copulation Calls Flexibly to Prevent Social Competition," *PLoS One,* 3(6), 2008, e2431 DOI: 10.1371/journal.pone.0002431.

139. A. H. Harcourt, A. Purvis, and L. Liles, "Sperm Competition: Mating System, Not Breeding Season, Affects Testes Size of Primates," *Functional Ecology,* 9(3), 1995: 468–476.

140. P. Haake, et al., "Absence of Orgasm-Induced Prolactin Secretion in a Healthy Multi-Orgasmic Male Subject," *Int. J. Impot. Res.,* 14(2), April 2002: 133–135.

141. M. S. Erskine, "Prolactin Release After Mating and Genitosensory Stimulation in Females," *Endocrine Reviews,* vol. 16, 1995: 508–528, http://edrv.endojournals.org/cgi/content/abstract/16/4/508.

141a. T. H. Kruger, et al., "Prolactin secretory rhythm in women: immediate and long-term alterations after sexual contact," *Hum Reprod.* 27(4), April, 2012: 1139–43. doi: 10.1093/humrep/des003.

142. Brian S. Bird, Robert D. Schweitzer, and Donald S. Strassberg, "The Prevalence and Correlates of Postcoital Dysphoria in Women," *International Journal of Sexual Health,* 23(1), 2011: 14–25, doi: 10.1080/19317611.2010.509689. And A.V. Burri and T.D. Spector, "An epidemiological survey of post-coital psychological symptoms in a UK population sample of female twins," *Twin Res Hum Genet.* 14(3), June, 2011: 240–8, doi: 0.1375/twin.14.3.240.

143. Jill Cyranowski, "Lifetime Depression History and Sexual Function in Women at Midlife," *Archives of Sexual Behavior,* 33(6), Dec. 2004: 539–548.

144. A. Reavley, et al., "Psychological Distress in Patients with Hyperprolactinaemia," *Clin. Endocrinol.* (Oxf), 47(3), Sep. 1997: 343–348.

145. Mbaruk A. Suleman, et al., "Physiologic Manifestations of Stress from Capture and Restraint of Free-Ranging Male African Green Monkeys *(Cercopithecus Aethiops),*" *J. of Zoo and Wildlife Medicine,* 35(1), March 2004: 20–24.

146. J. Bancroft, "The Endocrinology of Sexual Arousal," *J. of Endocrinology,* vol. 186, 2005: 411–427, http://joe.endocrinology-journals.org/cgi/content/full/186/3/411.

147. S. K. Putnam, et al., "Testosterone Restoration of Copulatory Behavior Correlates with Medial Preoptic Dopamine Release in Castrated Male Rats," *Horm. Behav.,* 39(3), May 2001: 216–224.

148. B. E. King, M. G. Packard, and G. M. Alexander, "Affective Properties of Intra-Medial Preoptic Area Injections of Testosterone in Male Rats," *Neurosci. Lett.,* 269(3), July 1999: 149–152.

149. Ray Moynihan, "FDA Panel Rejects Testosterone Patch for Women on Safety Grounds," *BMJ,* 329(7479), Dec. 2004: 1363.

150. A. Fernández-Guasti and G. Rodríguez-Manzo, "Pharmacological and Physiological Aspects of Sexual Exhaustion in Male Rats," *Scand. J. Psychol.,* 44(3), July 2003: 257–263.

151. G. Rodríguez-Manzo, M. Asai, and A. Fernández-Guasti, "Evidence for Changes in Brain Enkephalin Contents Associated to Male Rat Sexual Activity," *Behavioural Brain Research,* 131(1), April 2002: 47–55.

152. S. P. Yang, Y. Lee and J. L. Voogt, "Involvement of Endogenous Opioidergic Neurons in Modulation of Prolactin Secretion in Response to Mating in the Female Rat," *Neuroendocrinology,* 72(1), July 2000: 20–28.

153. Richard A. Friedman, "Sex and Depression: In the Brain, if Not the Mind," *New York Times,* Jan. 20, 2009, http://www.nytimes.com/2009/01/20/health/views/20mind.html.

154. M. Jiang, et al., "A Research on the Relationship Between Ejaculation and Serum Testosterone Level in Men," *J. Zhejiang Univ. Sci.,* 4(2), March–April 2003: 236–240.

155. Helena C. Kraemer, et al., "Orgasmic Frequency and Plasma Testosterone Levels in Normal Human Males," *Archives of Sexual Behavior,* 5(2), March 1976: 125–132; and M. S. Exton, et al., "Endocrine Response to Masturbation-Induced Orgasm in Healthy Men Following a 3-Week Sexual Abstinence," *World J. Urol.,* 19(5), Nov. 2001: 377–382.

156. Daniel Goleman, *Emotional Intelligence* (New York: Bantam Books, 1995): 17.

WISDOM OF THE AGES: MALE CONTINENCE

157. Noyes, *Male Continence.*

CHAPTER SIX: THE ROAD TO EXCESS

158. Fernández-Guasti and Rodríguez-Manzo, "Sexual Exhaustion in Male Rats."

159. "Romeo Guinea Pig Causes Baby Boom," *BBC News,* 30 Nov. 2000, http://news.bbc.co.uk/2/hi/uk_news/wales/1048327.stm.

160. Terry Burnham and Jay Phelan, *Mean Genes: From Sex to Money to Food—Taming Our Primal Instincts* (New York: Penguin Putnam Inc., 2000): 35–36.

161. Jennifer Viegas, "Brain Study: Why Desire Drives Us Wild," *Discovery News,* March 9, 2007, http://dsc.discovery.com/news/2007/03/09/desire_hum.html?category= human& guid=20070309133000.

162. Robert M. Sapolsky, *Why Zebras Don't Get Ulcers,* third edition (New York: Henry Holt and Company, 2004): 133.

163. "The Misfits: The Genetic Legacy of Nomadism May Be an Inability to Settle," Economist.com, June 12, 2008, http://www.economist.com/science/displaystory.cfm?story_id=11529402.

164. J. G. de Jong, et al., "A Single Social Defeat Induces Short Lasting Behavioral Sensitization to Amphetamine," *Physiol. Behav.*, 83(5), Jan. 2005: 805–811; M. Kabbaj and C. Isgor, "Effects of Chronic Environmental and Social Stimuli during Adolescence on Mesolimbic Dopaminergic Circuitry Markers," *Neurosci. Lett.*, 422(1), July 2007: 7–12; and I. Weiss, "Early Social Isolation, But Not Maternal Separation, Affects Behavioral Sensitization to Amphetamine in Male and Female Adult Rats," *Pharmacology, Biochemistry and Behavior*, 70(2–3), Oct.–Nov. 2001: 397–409.

165. G. L. Wang, N. D. Volkow, and J. S Fowler, "The Role of Dopamine in Motivation for Food in Humans: Implications for Obesity," *Expert. Opin. Ther. Targets*, 6(5), Oct. 2002: 601–609.

166. "Sugar Can Be Addictive: Animal Studies Show Sugar Dependence," *ScienceDaily*, Dec. 11, 2008, http://www.sciencedaily.com/releases/2008/12/081210090819.htm.

167. C. Colantuoni, et al., "Evidence that Intermittent, Excessive Sugar Intake Causes Endogenous Opioid Dependence," *Obes. Res.*, 10(6), June 2002: 478–488.

168. Angela Pirisi, "A Real Sugar High," *Psychology Today*, Jan./Feb. 2003, http://www.psychologytoday.com/articles/index.php?term=pto-2556.html&fromMod=popular_addiction.

169. Sandy Chase, "Diet Food Backfire," *ScienCentralNews*, July 4, 2008, http://www.sciencentral.com/articles/view.php3?type=article&article_id=218393129.

170. Robert Roy Britt, "Monkeys Pay to See Female Monkey Bottoms," *LiveScience*, 28 Jan. 2005.

171. D. Martindale, "Fast Food May Be Addictive," *The Canadian*, 2006, http://www.agoracosmopolitan.com/home/Health/2006/03/06/01123.html.

172. Freund, M., "Effect of Frequency of Emission on Semen Output and an Estimate of Daily Sperm Production in Man," *J. Reprod. Fertil.*, vol. 6, Oct. 1963: 269–285.

173. Sapolsky, *Zebras*: 351–352.

174. Cynthia Kuhn and Scott Swartzwelder, *Buzzed: The Straight Facts About the Most Used and Abused Drugs from Alcohol to Ecstasy* (New York: W. W. Norton & Company, 1998).

175. Hugh Garavan, et al., "Cue-Induced Cocaine Craving: Neuroanatomical Specificity for Drug Users and Drug Stimuli," *Am. J. Psychiatry*, vol. 157, Nov. 2000: 1789–1798.

176. Jennifer Viegas, "Sexy Strangers Sway How Men See Mates," *Discovery News*, March 12, 2007, http://dsc.discovery.com/news/2007/03/12/mateselection_hum.html?category=human&guid=20070312140030. Incidentally, women evaluated their relationships lower after exposure to highly (exciting?) dominant males. Douglas T. Kenrick, et al., "Evolution and Social Cognition: Contrast Effects as a Function of Sex, Dominance, and Physical Attractiveness," *Personality and Social Psychology Bulletin*, 20(2), April 1994: 210–217, http://psp.sagepub.com/cgi/content/abstract/20/2/210.

177. For an informative, entertaining, fast-paced look at how porn affects men's perceptions, watch the documentary *Adult Entertainment: Disrobing an American Idol* by Lance Tracy, http://www.1726entertainment.com/.

178. Patrick Carnes, *Out of the Shadows: Understanding Sexual Addiction* (City Center, MN: Hazelden, 1992): 18–19.

179. "Sexually Active Friends and Dating Practices Can Signal Increase in a Teen's Substance Abuse Risk," Columbia National Center on Addiction and Substance Abuse at Columbia University, press release, Aug 19, 2004, http://www.casacolumbia.org/absolutenm/templates/PressReleases.aspx?articleid=366&zoneid=61.

180. K. C. Bradley and R. L. Meisel, "Sexual Behavior Induction of c-Fos in the Nucleus Accumbens and Amphetamine-Stimulated Locomotor Activity Are Sensitized by Previous Sexual Experience in Female Syrian Hamsters," *J. Neurosci.*, 21(6), March 2001: 2123–2130.

181. K. C. Bradley, et al., "Changes in Gene Expression Within the Nucleus Accumbens and Striatum Following Sexual Experience," *Genes Brain Behav.*, 4(1), 2005: 31–44.

182. K. C. Bradley, et al., "Sexual Experience Alters D1 Receptor-Mediated Cyclic AMP Production in the Nucleus Accumbens of Female Syrian Hamsters," *Synapse*, 53(1), 2004: 20–27.

183. J. G. Kohlert and R. L Meisel, "Sexual Experience Sensitizes Mating-Related Nucleus Accumbens Dopamine Responses of Female Syrian Hamsters," *Behav Brain Res.*, 99(1), 1999: 45–52.

184. K. E. d'Anci, R. B. Kanarek, and R. Marks-Kaufman, "Duration of Sucrose Availability Differentially Alters Morphine-Induced Analgesia in Rats," *Pharmacol. Biochem. Behav.*, 54(4), Aug. 1996: 693–697.

185. P. Radaa, N. M. Avena, and B. G. Hoebel, "Daily Bingeing on Sugar Repeatedly Releases Dopamine in the Accumbens Shell," *Neuroscience*, 134(3), 2005: 737–744; and "Sugar Can Be Addictive."

186. Sigmund Freud, Letter from Freud to Fliess, Dec. 22, 1897, http://www.pep-web.org/document.php?id=ZBK.042.0287A.

187. "Addiction Largely Determined By Our Genes—Annual Meeting of the Royal College of Psychiatrists," *Medical News Today*, July 5, 2008, http://www.medicalnewstoday.com/articles/114044.php.

188. Alan I. Leshner, "Addiction Is a Brain Disease, and It Matters," *Science*, 278(5335), Oct. 1997: 45–47.

189. David Belin, et al., "High Impulsivity Predicts the Switch to Compulsive Cocaine-Taking," *Science*, 320(5881), June 2008: 1352–1355; Nanci Hellmich, "Obesity Linked to Fewer 'Pleasure' Receptors," *USA Today*, Oct. 17, 2007; Nora D. Volkow, et al., "Low Level of Brain Dopamine D2 Receptors in Methamphetamine Abusers: Association with Metabolism in the Orbitofrontal Cortex," *Am. J. Psychiatry.*, 158(12), Dec. 2001: 2015–2021; and Jens. C. Pruessner, et al., " Dopamine Release in Response to a Psychological Stress in Humans and Its Relationship to Early Life Maternal Care," *J. of Neuroscience*, 24(11), March 2004: 2825–2831.

190. "2014 Pornography Survey and Statistics," (2014) http://www.provenmen.org/2014pornsurvey/pornography-use-and-addiction.

191. Klaus Grawe, *Neuropsychotherapy: How the Neurosciences Inform Effective Psychotherapy* (Hillsdale, NJ: Lawrence Erlbaum Associates, 2006): 270.

191a. Valerie Voon, et al., "Neural Correlates of Sexual Cue Reactivity in Individuals with and without Compulsive Sexual Behaviours," PLOS One (2014): DOI: 10.1371/journal.pone.0102419.

192. Graham Tearse, "Parkinson's Drugs 'Made Me Gambler, Thief and Gay Sex Fiend,'" *The Observer*, Dec. 9, 2007.

193. David E. Riley, "Reversible Transvestic Fetishism in a Man with Parkinson's Disease Treated with Selegiline," *Clinical Neuropharmacology*, 25(4), 2002: 234–237; and Renato P. Munhoz, et al., "Increased Frequency and Range of Sexual Behavior in a Patient with Parkinson's Disease After Use of Pramipexole: A Case Report," *J. of Sexual Medicine*, May 6, 2008, http://www3.interscience.wiley.com/journal/120126347/abstract.

194. Susan Milius, "Courting Both Ways: Doped-Up Male Fruit Flies Fancy Other Males," *Science News*, May 20, 2008, http://www.sciencenews.org/view/generic/id/32367/title/Courting_both_ways.

195. James Hannaham, "Why Bathroom Sex Is Hot," *Salon.com*, Aug. 31, 2007, http://www.salon.com/mwt/feature/2007/08/31/bathroom_sex/.

196. "HIV Rates Rise in Gay New Yorkers under 30," *Gay.com*, Sep. 12, 2007, http://www.gay.com/news/article.html?2007/09/12/3.

197. Brian W. Vaszily, "Check Out All the Violence Here! Or How I Jolt You into Submission to Get Your Money," http://www.sixwise.com/newsletters/06/04/19/check_out_all_the_violence_here_or_how_i_jolt_you_into_submission_to_get_your_money.htm.

198. Daniela Fenker and Hartmut Schütze, "Learning by Surprise," *Scientific American Mind*, Dec.–Jan. 2008–2009: 47.

199. Gary Wilson, *Your Brain on Porn: Internet pornography and the emerging science of addiction*, (Margate: Commonwealth Publishing, 2014) and A.L. Roberts, M.M. Glymour, and K.C. Koenen, "Does maltreatment in childhood affect sexual orientation in adulthood?" *Archives of Sexual Behavior*, 42(2) 2013: 161–171, doi: 10.1007/s10508-012-0021-9.

200. Patrick Carnes, *Don't Call It Love* (New York: Bantam, 1992), as reported in Gail Johnson, "Sex Addiction Has Devastating Effects," *Georgia Straight*, Nov. 20, 2008.

201. "Dopamine May Play New Role in Depression," *WebMD*, July 28, 2005, http://www.webmd.com/depression/news/20050728/dopamine-may-play-new-role-in-depression.

202. N. M. Avena, et al., "After Daily Bingeing on a Sucrose Solution, Food Deprivation Induces Anxiety and Accumbens Dopamine Acetylcholine Imbalance," *Physiol. Behav.*, 94(3), June 2008: 309–315.

203. J. M. Bostwick and J. A. Bucci, "Internet Sex Addiction Treated with Naltrexone," *Mayo Clin. Proc.*, 83(2), Feb. 2008: 226–230.

204. Laura Helmuth, "Addiction. Beyond the Pleasure Principle," *Science*, 294(5544), Nov. 2001: 983–984.

205. Martin Werme, et al., "Delta FosB Regulates Wheel Running," *J. of Neuroscience*, 22(18), Sep. 2002: 8133–8138.

206. Jeffrey M. Schwartz, *The Mind and the Brain*, (New York: ReganBooks, 2002): 83–86.

207. Doidge, *The Brain that Changes Itself*: 107.

208. Richard Dawkins, *A Devil's Chaplain* (New York: Houghton Mifflin, 2003): 103.

209. "The Orgasmic Brain," *All In the Mind*, July 9, 2005.

210. Angela Pirisi, "A Real Sugar High," *Psychology Today*, Jan./Feb. 2003.

WISDOM OF THE AGES: KAREZZA—ALICE B. STOCKHAM, MD

211. Alice B. Stockham, *Tokology: A Book for Every Woman* (New York: R. F. Fenno & Company, 1893), http://www.archive.org/stream/tokologybookfore00stocrich.

212. Alice B. Stockham, *Karezza: Ethics of Marriage* (Chicago: Alice B. Stockham & Co., 1896).

213. Alice B. Stockham, *Karezza: Ethics of Marriage,* second edition (Chicago: Alice B. Stockham & Co., 1903): 23–24, 96, http://www.sacred-texts.com/sex/eom/index.htm.

214. Ibid: 13.

215. Ibid.: 23.

216. Ibid.: 25–26.

217. Ibid.: 49–50.

218. Ibid.: 30.

CHAPTER SEVEN: LEARNING TO STEER

219. Louis Cozolino, *The Neuroscience of Human Relationships* (New York: W. W. Norton & Company, 2006): 119.

220. Terry M. Levy and Michael Orlans, *Attachment, Trauma and Healing* (Washington, DC: CWLA Press, 1998): 14.

221. Laura Sanders, "Still Crazy (In Love) after All These Years," *ScienceNews,* Nov. 17, 2008.

222. Kerstin Uvnäs Moberg, *The Oxytocin Factor* (Cambridge, MA: Da Capo Press, 2003): 60–61.

223. Doidge, *The Brain that Changes Itself:* 113, 120.

224. Ashley Montagu, *Touching: The Human Significance of the Skin* (New York: Harper & Row, 1986): 174, 14.

225. Levy and Orlans, *Attachment, Trauma and Healing:* 1–2.

226. "Love Is a Battlefield," *This American Life,* Aug. 31, 2007, http://www.thisamerican life.org/Radio_Episode.aspx?episode=317.

227. David Derbyshire, "A Baby's Smile is Just the Tonic to Give Mothers a Natural High," *Mail Online,* July 7, 2008, http://www.dailymail.co.uk/health/article-1032599/A-babys-smile-just-tonic-mothers-natural-high.html.

228. G. A. Coria-Avila, et al., "Conditioned Preferences Induced by Sex and Drugs: A Comparison of the Neural Bases," *Rev. Neurol.,* 46(4), Feb. 2008: 213–218; and T. R. Insel, "Is Social Attachment an Addictive Disorder?" *Physiol. Behav.,* 79(3), Aug. 2003: 351–357.

229. Montagu, *Touching:* 198.

230. Doidge, *The Brain that Changes Itself:* 116.

231. Deborah Blum, *Love at Goon Park: Harry Harlow and the Science of Affection* (Cambridge, MA: Perseus Books Group, 2002).

232. Diamond, *Sexual Fluidity:* 208.

233. Herbert Benson, *The Relaxation Response* (New York: HarperTorch, 1976).

234. Rebecca Skloot, "Why Is It So Damn Hard to Change?" *O: The Oprah Magazine,* Jan. 2007.

235. Ibid.

236. Shmuley Boteach, *Kosher Adultery: Seduce and Sin with Your Spouse* (Cincinnati, OH: Adams Media Corporation, 2002).

236a. C.T. Snowden, et al., "Variation in oxytocin is related to variation in affiliative behavior in monogamous, pairbonded tamarins." *Hormones and Behavior,* June, 2010 http://bit.ly/b7NwJB; Pfefferle, Dana, et al., "Female Barbary macaque *(Macaca sylvanus)* copulation calls do not reveal the fertile phase but influence mating outcome," *Proceedings. Biological sciences / The Royal Society,* 275(1634) Mar. 2008: 517–578, Paul R. Abramson and Steven D. Pinkerton, *Sexual Nature/Sexual Culture* (University of Chicago Press, 1995): 48.

WISDOM OF THE AGES: KAREZZA—J. WILLIAM LLOYD, MD

237. "Woman and the Larger Love" (1933); "A Brief Definition of the Larger Love" (1929); and "New Ideals in Love" (1926), a lecture delivered before the Workers' Forum of Los Angeles, California. All available in the Labadie collection at the University of Michigan in Ann Arbor.

238. J. William Lloyd, *The Karezza Method, or Magnetation: The Art of Connubial Love* (Roscoe, CA: Lloyd, 1931), http://www.sacred-texts.com/sex/krz/index.htm: 60–61.

239. Ibid.: 60–64.

240. Ibid.: 13.

241. Ibid.: 52.

242. Ibid.: 31.

243. Ibid.: 39–40.

244. Ibid.: 48, 32.

CHAPTER EIGHT: SCIENCE THAT BINDS

245. Larry J. Young and Zuoxin Wang, "The Neurobiology of Pair Bonding," *Nature Neuroscience,* vol. 7, 2004: 1048–1054.

246. J. R. Williams, C. S. Carter, and T. Insel, "Partner Preference Development in Female Prairie Voles is Facilitated by Mating or the Central Infusion of Oxytocin," *Ann. NY Acad. Sci.,* vol. 652, June 1992: 487–489.

247. Marla V. Broadfoot, "High on Fidelity," *American Scientist,* May–June 2002.

248. O. J. Bosch, et al., "Brain Oxytocin Correlates with Maternal Aggression: Link to Anxiety," *J. Neurosci.,* 25(29), July 2005: 6807–6815.

249. K. L. Bales, et al., "Neural Correlates of Pairbonding in a Monogamous Primate," *Brain Res.,* vol. 1184, Dec. 2007: 245–253.

250. A. Bartels and S. Zeki, "The Neural Basis of Romantic Love," *Neuroreport.,* 11(17), Nov. 2000: 3829–3834; and Bartels and Zeki, "Correlates of Maternal and Romantic Love."

251. D. Marazziti and M. Catena Dell'osso, "The Role of Oxytocin in Neuropsychiatric Disorders," *Curr. Med. Chem.,* 15(7), 2008: 698–704.

252. M. R. Melis, et al., "Oxytocin Injected into the Ventral Tegmental Area Induces Penile Erection and Increases Extracellular Dopamine in the Nucleus Accumbens and Paraventricular Nucleus of the Hypothalamus of Male Rats," *Eur. J. Neurosci.,* 26(4), Aug. 2007: 1026–1035; and J. L. Cameron, et al., "Dopaminergic Stimulation of Oxytocin Concentrations in the Plasma of Male and Female Monkeys by Apomorphine and a D2 Receptor Agonist," *J. Clin. Endocrinol. Metab.,* 75(3), Sep. 1992: 855–860.

253. Fiorino, Coury, and Phillips, "Coolidge Effect in Male Rats."

254. Doidge, *The Brain that Changes Itself:* 114.

255. Lloyd, *Karezza Method:* 29.

256. J. J. Legros, "Oxytocin: A Natural Means of Treating Psychological Stress," *Bull. Mem. Acad. R. Med. Belg.,* 157(7–9), 2002: 383–389.

257. Joseph LeDoux, Center for Neural Science at NYU, quoted in Goleman, *Emotional Intelligence,* http://thinman.com/spiritual_darwinism/Emotional_Intelligen.html.

258. S. L. Brown, et al., "Providing Social Support May Be More Beneficial Than Receiving It: Results from a Prospective Study of Mortality," *Psychol. Sci.,* 14(4), July 2003: 320–327.

259. "Hormone Oxytocin Calms Arguing Couples," News-Medical.Net, Dec. 8, 2008, http://www.news-medical.net/?id=43843.

260. E. A. Murray, "The Amygdala, Reward and Emotion," *Trends Cogn. Sci.,* 11(11), Nov. 2007: 489–497; and comment in *Trends Cogn. Sci.,* 12(5), May 2008: 171–172.

261. I. D. Neumann, "Brain Oxytocin a Key Regulator of Emotional and Social Behaviours in Both Females and Males," *J. Neuroendocrinol.,* 20(6), June 2008: 858–865.

262. K. M. Grewen, "Effects of Partner Support on Resting Oxytocin, Cortisol, Norepinephrine, and Blood Pressure Before and After Warm Partner Contact," *Psychosom. Med.,* 67(4), July–Aug. 2005: 531–538.

263. J. Holt-Lunstad, W. A. Birmingham, and K. C. Light, "Influence of a 'Warm Touch' Support Enhancement Intervention Among Married Couples on Ambulatory Blood Pressure, Oxytocin, Alpha Amylase, and Cortisol," *Psychosom. Med.,* Oct 8, 2008, published online before print 10.1097/PSY.0b013e318187aef7.

264. K. M. Grewen, et al., "Warm Partner Contact Is Related to Lower Cardiovascular Reactivity," *Behav. Med.,* 29(3), Fall 2003: 123–130.

265. L. B. Billings, et al., "Oxytocin Null Mice Ingest Enhanced Amounts of Sweet Solutions During Light and Dark Cycles and During Repeated Shaker Stress," *Behav. Brain Res.,* 171(1), July 2006: 134–141.

266. G. L. Kovács, Z. Sarnyai, and G. Szabó, "Oxytocin and Addiction: A Review," *Psychoneuroendocrinology,* 23(8), Nov. 1998: 945–962.

267. M. Egli, "Prolactin Secretory Rhythm of Mated Rats Induced by a Single Injection of Oxytocin," *Am. J. Physiol. Endocrinol. Metab.,* 290(3), March 2006: E566–572, http://www.ncbi.nlm.nih.gov/pubmed/16467487?ordinalpos=&itool=EntrezSystem2.PEntrez.Pubmed.Pubmed_ResultsPanel.SmartSearch&log$=citationsensor

268. C. A. Pedersen and M. L. Boccia, "Oxytocin Maintains as Well as Initiates Female Sexual Behavior: Effects of a Highly Selective Oxytocin Antagonist," *Horm. Behav.,* 41(2), March 2002: 170–177.

269. C. Caquineau, "Effects of ··-Melanocyte-Stimulating Hormone on Magnocellular Oxytocin Neurones and their Activation at Intromission in Male Rats," *J. Neuroendocrinol.,* 18(9), Sep. 2006: 685–691.

270. Dean Ornish, *Love and Survival: The Scientific Basis for the Healing Power of Intimacy* (New York: HarperCollins Publishers, 1998): 2, 3.

271. James A. Coan, Hillary S. Schaefer, and Richard J. Davidson, "Lending a Hand: Social Regulation of the Neural Response to Threat," *Psych. Sci.,* 17(12), Dec. 2006: 1032–1039.

272. Detilliona, et al., "Wound Healing."

273. Young, et al., "Stable Partnership and Progression to AIDS."

274. "Caregiving May Lengthen Life," Forbes.com, Dec. 19, 2008, http://www.forbes.com/forbeslife/health/feeds/hscout/2008/12/19/hscout621946.html.

275. Mark D. Lange, "Giving Can Change Your Mind," *San Francisco Chronicle,* Dec. 25, 2008, http://sfgate.com/cgi-bin/article.cgi?f=/c/a/2008/12/25/EDS014SODB.DTL.

276. A. Sanbe, et al., "Alcohol Preference in Mice Lacking the Avpr1a Vasopressin Receptor," *Am. J. Physiol. Regul. Integr. Comp. Physiol.,* 294(5), May 2008: R1482–1490.

277. Bosch, et al., "Maternal Aggression."

278. M. Ansseau, et al., "Intranasal Oxytocin in Obsessive-Compulsive Disorder," *Psychoneuroendocrinology,* 12(3), 1987: 231–236.

279. G. Paolisso, et al., "Pharmacological Doses of Oxytocin Affect Plasma Hormone Levels Modulating Glucose Homeostasis in Normal Man," *Horm. Res.,* 30(1), 1988: 10–16, http://www.ncbi.nlm.nih.gov/pubmed/3065208.

280. M. Kosfeld, et al., "Oxytocin Increases Trust in Humans," *Nature,* 435(7042), June 2005: 673–676.

281. M. R. Delgado, "Fool Me Once, Shame on You; Fool Me Twice, Shame on Oxytocin," *Neuron.,* 58(4), May 2008: 470–471.

282. John Tierney, "Anti-Love Drug May Be Ticket to Bliss," *New York Times,* Jan. 13, 2009, http://www.nytimes.com/2009/01/13/science/13tier.html?_r=2&ref=science.

283. R. A. Turner, et al., "Preliminary Research on Plasma Oxytocin in Normal Cycling Women: Investigating Emotion and Interpersonal Distress," *Psychiatry,* 62(2), Summer 1999: 97–113.

284. C. Grape, et al., "Does Singing Promote Well-Being? An Empirical Study of Professional and Amateur Singers During a Singing Lesson," *Integr. Physiol. Behav. Sci.,* 38(1), Jan.–March 2003: 65–74.

285. Paul J. Zak, "The Oxytocin Cure," Nov. 10, 2008, The Moral Molecule (blog), http://blogs.psychologytoday.com/blog/the-moral-molecule/200811/the-oxytocin-cure.

286. S. Brody, "Blood Pressure Reactivity to Stress Is Better for People Who Recently Had Penile-Vaginal Intercourse than for People Who Had Other or No Sexual Activity," *Biol. Psychol.,* 71(2), Feb. 2006: 214–222; and S. Brody, "Penile-Vaginal Intercourse Is Better: Evidence Trumps Ideology," *Sexual and Relationship Therapy,* 21(4), Nov. 2006: 393–403.

287. E. A. Jannini, et al., "Lack of Sexual Activity from Erectile Dysfunction is Associated with a Reversible Reduction in Serum Testosterone," *Intl. J. Androl.,* 22(6), Dec. 1999: 385–392.

288. Gordon G. Gallup, Jr., Rebecca L. Burch, and Steven M. Platek, "Does Semen Have Antidepressant Properties?" *Archives of Sexual Behavior,* 31(3), June 2002: 289–293. Gallup puts this result down to the non-sperm ingredients of semen, many of which are probably still present with unprotected non-orgasmic sex. To date, no one actually knows what creates the benefit. Interestingly, some women are allergic to semen.

289. B. M. Kogan, et al., "Monoamine Metabolism in Different Forms of Paraphilia," *Zh. Nevrol. Psikhiatr. Im. S. S. Korsakova,* 95(6), 1995: 52–56.

290. "Doctor Discovers the 'Orgasmatron': Physician Working with Pain Relief Device Stumbles Upon Delightful Side Effect," *ABC News,* Nov. 9, 2004, http://abcnews.go.com/GMA/Living/story?id=235788&.

291. George Davey Smith, Stephen Frankel, and John Yarnell, "Sex and Death: Are They Related? Findings from the Caerphilly Cohort Study," *BMJ*, 315(7123), Dec. 1997: 1641–1644.

292. David Batty, "Are Sex and Death Related? Study Failed to Adjust for an Important Confounder," *BMJ*, 316(7145), May 1998: 1671.

293. Steven Reinberg, "Lots of Sex May Prevent Erectile Dysfunction: It's the 'Use It or Lose It' Principle at Work, One Expert Says," *US News & World Report,* July 3, 2008.

294. E. B. Palmore, "Predictors of the Longevity Difference: A 25-year Follow-Up," *Gerontologist,* 22(6), Dec. 1982: 513–518; and L. A. Abramov, "Sexual Life and Frigidity Among Women Developing Acute Myocardial Infarction," *Psychosom. Med.,* 38(6) Nov.–Dec. 1976: 418–425.

295. Winnifred B. Cutler, "Women's Responses to Genital Stimulation: Evidence for the Functional Role of Timing," Presented at INABIS '98—5th Internet World Congress on Biomedical Sciences at McMaster University, Canada (1998), http://www.athena institute.com/inabis98.html.

296. G. G. Giles, et al., "Sexual Factors and Prostate Cancer," *BJU International,* 92(3), July 2003: 211–216; and M. D. Leitzmann, "Ejaculation Frequency and Subsequent Risk of Prostate Cancer," *JAMA,* 291(13), April 2004: 1578–1586.

297. "Sex Drive Link to Prostate Cancer," Jan. 26, 2009, BBC News, http://news.bbc. co.uk/2/hi/health/7850666.stm. See also, S. J. Jacobsen, et al., "Frequency of Sexual Activity and Prostatic Health: Fact or Fairy Tale?" *Urology,* 61(2), Feb. 2003: 348–353.

298. Dean Ornish, "Changing Your Lifestyle Can Change Your Genes," *Newsweek,* June 17, 2008, http://www.newsweek.com/id/141984.

299. Charles Barber, "The Medicated Americans," *Scientific American MIND,* Feb.–March 2008: 49.

WISDOM OF THE AGES: BUDDHISM

300. Leslie Kaufman, "Making Their Own Limits in a Spiritual Partnership," *New York Times,* May 15, 2008, http://www.reuniting.info/download/pdf/Spiritual%20Partner ship.pdf.

301. Dowman, *Sky Dancer.*

302. His Holiness the Dalai Lama, *A Survey of the Paths of Tibetan Buddhism* (1988) http://lamayeshe.com/otherteachers/hhdl/survey.shtml.

303. H. H. the Dalai Lama, "The Good Heart," http://sacred-sex.org/buddhism/14th-dalai-lama-and-sex.

304. H. H. the Dalai Lama, *The Berzin Archives,* http://www.berzinarchives.com/web/en/archives/advanced/kalachakra/attending_kalachakra_initiation/question_sessions_hh/question_hh_initiation_04.html.

305. H. H. the Dalai Lama, "The Good Heart."

306. H. H. the Dalai Lama, *The Berzin Archives.*

307. H. H. the Dalai Lama, *How to Practice: The Way to a Meaningful Life,* trans. Jeffrey Hopkins (New York: Simon and Schuster, 2002).

308. June Campbell, *Traveler in Space: In Search of Female Identity in Tibetan Buddhism,* (New York: George Braziller, 1996).

309. "The Emperor's Tantric Robes," *Tricycle,* Winter 1996, http://www.anandainfo.com/tantric_robes.html.

309a. Jonn Mumford, *Ecstasy Through Tantra* (St. Paul, MN: Llewellyn Publications, 2002): 9.

310. Thich Nhat Hanh, *Being Peace* (Berkeley, CA: Parallax Press, 1987): 251.

311. The Legend of the Great Stupa Jarungkhasor, http://www.sacred-texts.com/bud/tib/stupa.htm.

312. Mircea Eliade, *The Two and the One,* trans. J. M. Cohen (London: Harrill Press, 1965): 43.

313. Glenn H. Mullin, *The Fourteen Dalai Lamas* (Santa Fe, NM: Clear Light, 2001): 373–374.

CHAPTER NINE: BRIDGING THE GAP

314. Thomas W. Laqueur, *Solitary Sex: A Cultural History of Masturbation* (New York: Zone Books, 2004): 277.

315. Frederick C. Crews, *Unauthorized Freud: Doubters Confront a Legend* (New York: Viking Press, 1998).

316. Simply Freud (website), http://www.simplyfreud.com/about-freud.htm.

317. James H. Jones, *Alfred C. Kinsey* (New York: W. W. Norton & Company, 1997): 511–522; and Judson Landis, "The Women Kinsey Studied," *Social Problems,* in Jerome Himelhoch and Sylvia F. Fava, eds., *Sexual Behavior in American Society* (New York: W. W. Norton & Co., 1955): 112.

318. Jones, *Alfred C. Kinsey:* 512.

319. James H. Jones, "Dr. Yes," *The New Yorker,* Aug. 25 and Sep. 11, 1997: 110.

320. James H. Jones, *Alfred C. Kinsey:* 511–522; and Judson Landis, "The Women Kinsey Studied": 112.

321. Landis, "The Women Kinsey Studied": 112.

322. Terry M. Levy and Michael Orlans, *Attachment, Trauma and Healing* (Washington, DC: CWLA Press, 1998): 163.

323. Laqueur, *Solitary Sex:* 281.

324. Ernest Crawley, *Studies of Savages and Sex,* ed. Theodore Besterman (New York: E. P. Dutton and Company Inc., 1960): 19–21.

325. Daniel Lord Smail, *On Deep History and the Brain* (Berkeley and Los Angeles: University of California Press, 2008).

326. Karen Kaplan, "The Evolution of Darwin's Theory," *Los Angeles Times,* February 8, 2009, https://www.latimes.com/archives/la-xpm-2009-feb-08-sci-evolution8-story.html.

327. Kabbaj and Isgor, "Effects of Chronic Environmental and Social Stimuli"; and Weiss, "Early Social Isolation."

328. Mark A. Smith and Megan A. Lyle, "Chronic Exercise Decreases Sensitivity to mu Opioids in Female Rats: Correlation with Exercise Output," *Pharmacology Biochemistry and Behavior,* 85(1), Sep. 2006: 12–22.

329. Savulescu and Sandberg, "Neuroenhancement of Love and Marriage."

330. Ornish, *Love and Survival:* 2, 3.

331. John Cacioppo and William Patrick, *Loneliness* (New York: W. W. Norton, 2008): 93, 105–108.

332. A. Campbell, "The Morning after the Night Before: Affective Reactions to One-Night Stands among Mated and Unmated Women and Men," *Human Nature,* 19, 2008: 157–173.

333. J. H. Medalie, et al., "Angina Pectoris among 10,000 Men," *Am. J. Med.,* 55(5), Nov. 1973: 583–594.

334. Dania Schiftan, "Sexual Behavior in German-Speaking Switzerland," University of Bern, Oct. 2006, http://www2.hu-berlin.de/sexology/BIB/sch/behswit.htm.

335. O. J. Bosch, et al., "The CRF System Mediates Increased Passive Stress-Coping Behavior Following the Loss of a Bonded Partner in a Monogamous Rodent," *Neuropsychopharmacology,* Oct. 2008, http://www.ncbi.nlm.nih.gov/pubmed/18923404?dopt=AbstractPlus.

336. J. Thomas Curtis and Zuoxin Wang, "Amphetamine Effects in Microtine Rodents: A Comparative Study Using Monogamous and Promiscuous Vole Species," *Neuroscience,* 148(4), Sep. 2007: 857–866.

337. Robert H. Coombs, "Marital Status and Personal Well-Being: A Literature Review," *Family Relations,* 40(1), Jan. 1991: 97–102.

338. Helene Raskin White, Allan V. Horwitz, and Sandra Howell-White, "Becoming Married and Mental Health: A Longitudinal Study of a Cohort of Young Adults," *J. of Marriage and the Family,* 58(4), 1996: 895–907, http://www.faqs.org/abstracts/Family-and-marriage/Becoming-married-and-mental-health-a-longitudinal-study-of-a-cohort-of-young-adults.html.

339. Catherine E. Ross, "Reconceptualizing Marital Status as a Continuum of Social Attachment," *J. of Marriage and the Family,* 57(1), 1995: 129–140.

339a. "Marriage and Committed Romance Reduce Stress-Related Hormone Production," *Science Daily,* Aug. 17, 2010.

340. David P. Barash and Judith Eve Lipton, *The Myth of Monogamy* (New York: W. H. Freeman and Company, 2001): 153–154, 190–191.

341. Ibid.: 161.

342. Lloyd's *The Karezza Method* is available for free online at http://www.reuniting.info/karezza_method_lloyd.

343. www.reuniting.info.

344. Moberg, *Oxytocin Factor.*

345. Ariadne von Schirach, "From Pornography to Withdrawal," *Spiegel Online International,* Oct. 28, 2005, http://www.spiegel.de/international/spiegel/0,1518,382078,00.html.

346. M. G. Welch, et al., "Outcomes of Prolonged Parent-Child Embrace Therapy among 102 Children with Behavioral Disorders," *Complement. Ther. Clin. Pract.,* 12(1), Feb. 2006: 3–12.

347. C. Propper, et al., "Gene-Environment Contributions to the Development of Infant Vagal Reactivity: The Interaction of Dopamine and Maternal Sensitivity," *Child Dev.,* 79(5), Sep.–Oct. 2008: 1377–1394.

348. Barbara Dafoe Whitehead and David Popenoe, "The State of Our Unions: The Social Health of Marriage in America 2001, Who Wants To Marry a Soul Mate?: New Survey Findings on Young Adults' Attitudes about Love and Marriage," The National Marriage Project, Rutgers University, 2001, http://marriage.rutgers.edu/Publications/Print/PrintSOOU2001.htm.

WISDOM OF THE AGES: RAINBOW SERPENT TRADITIONS

349. Merilyn Tunneshende, *Don Juan and the Art of Sexual Energy* (Rochester, VT: Bear & Company, 2001): 176.

350. Ibid.: xv.

351. Feuerstein, *Sacred Sexuality.*

CHAPTER TEN: THE PATH OF HARMONY

352. Marc Kaufman, "FDA Investigates Blindness in Viagra Users," *Washington Post,* May 28, 2005: A08, http://www.washingtonpost.com/wp-dyn/content/article/2005/05/27/AR2005052701246.html.

353. Apomorphine HCL, or Uprima.

354. Amanda Gardner, "Almost Half of Women Have Sexual Problems," *Washington Post,* Oct. 31, 2008, http://www.washingtonpost.com/wp-dyn/content/article/2008/10/31/AR2008103101138.html.

355. Curtis and Wang, "Monogamous and Promiscuous Vole Species."

356. Bremelanotide, or PT-141.

357. Sarah-Kate Templeton, "Viagra Plus Passion: The New Lust Drug," *Sunday Times,* Feb. 22, 2004, http://www.timesonline.co.uk/tol/news/uk/article1026381.ece.

358. Mary Roach, *Bonk: The Curious Coupling of Science and Sex* (New York: W. W. Norton, Inc., 2008): 250.

359. Meryn Callander, "Intact! Protecting Our Boys from Circumcision," *Kindred Magazine,* vol. 10, June–Aug. 2004: 16–25, http://www.kindredmedia.com.au/ library_page1/intact_protecting_our_boys_from_circumcision/84/1.

360. Gary Ruskin and Juliet Schor, *"Junk Food Nation,"* The Nation, Aug. 11, 2005, http://www.commondreams.org/views05/0812-25.htm.

361. Lloyd, *Karezza Method:* 62.

361a. This suggestion comes from the work of Diana and Michael Richardson. *Tantric Sex for Men: Making Love a Meditation* (Destiny Books, 2010).

362. Ibid.: 41.

363. Cozolino, *Neuroscience of Human Relationships:* 119.

364. Stockham, *Karezza.*

365. Cited in Stockham, *Karezza:* 104.

WISDOM OF THE AGES: TRANSORGASMIC SEX

366. For more, see Francisco Moreno Téllez, "Sexualidad Transorgásmica," two-part article in Spanish: Part 1—http://www.ecovisiones.cl/taller/stransorgasmica.htm; Part 2—http://www.ecovisiones.cl/taller/sex_transorgasmica_II.htm.

THE ECSTATIC EXCHANGES

367. If you're looking for ideas of activities to do with a sweetheart, browse through some of the activities at this Web page: http://www.reuniting.info/resources/exchange_of_the_day.

368. www.reuniting.info.

369. Doc Lew Childre and Howard Martin, *The Heartmath Solution* (San Francisco: HarperSanFrancisco, 1999): 267.

INDEX

immaculate conception, 45
   pre-papal, 97
   return of true, 98
Chrysostom, Archbishop John, 46, 53
circulation, of energy. *See* Energy
   Circulation
circumcision, 277
Clark, Elizabeth A., 46
Clinton, Bill, 111, 154
Clinton, Hillary, 81
Clitoral Truth, The, 40
cocaine, 90–91, 105–106, 146, 147, 151,
   241
co-dependency, 183
coitus reservatus, 24, 169
Comforter, 47
companionship (non-mate), 237–238.
   See bonding program *and* pair-
   bonding
   as "medicine," 86, 138, 220, 264
   benefits of, 148, 216–218, 261
   karezza, substitute for, 249–250
compulsivity, sexual. *See* orgasm *and*
   supranormal stimulation
congestion, genital, 200, 201, 226, 251,
   278, 280
Constantine, 43
continence, sexual, 11, 167. *See also* male
   continence
   and Buddhists, 231, 233
   and Christians, 46–47, 97–99
   and native peoples, 80, 243
   and risks of repression, 39, 157, 256
   and testosterone levels, 121
   and unrealistic goals, 268
Coolidge effect, 4–6, 93, 115, 121, 134
cortezia, 97–100
cortisol, 210–215, 223, 245, 248
counseling, usefulness of, 169
Council of Nicaea, 47
courtly love. *See* cortezia
Graig, Larry, 155
Crawley, A. Ernest, 243
cross-dressing, 154
cross-tolerance, 147–148

Crowe, Simon, 222
Crystal, Billy, 27
cues, passim. *See* dopamine, spikes
   addiction, 136–165, 235, 242, 264
   bonding, xviii, 10, 67, 104, 172–194,
      216
   list of bonding, 178
Cupid, passim
   poison defined, xvii, 1–2, 9, 28, 75

D

Dalai Lama, 231–234
Dangerfield, Rodney, 216
Dangers and Benefits of Intercourse, 19
Dawkins, Richard, 24, 165
de Laboulaye, René, 283
de Rougemont, Denis, 97, 98
delta-FosB [Δ-FosB], 161, 293
demiurge, 43
depletion, passim
   and perception, 28–38, 125, 127,
      208, 282
   experiment, 145
   feelings of, 7, 9, 24, 27, 34–9, 183,
      241, 261
depression, passim
   and brain activity, 106, 109, 159,
      206, 211, 215–216
   and infant bonding, 89
   and men's orgasm, 59, 103, 112, 144,
      258
   and women's orgasm, 34, 36, 51,
      118, 225
   improvement in, 112, 148, 216–218,
      223, 248
   in pair-bonders, 247
   medication risk, 110, 120
   rates, 34, 227
Diamond, Lisa, 62, 83
Ditzen, Beate, 215
divine feminine, role of, 98–100
   Feminine Principle, 70
   Lady Yeshe Tsogyel, 231, 234
   Mysterious Mother, 17
   Parvati, 69

libido *(continued)*
> questioned, 41, 57, 228, 240, 260, 277, 281
> relief from inflamed, 164, 228, 242, 250, 259–263
> sublimation of, 39, 99, 200, 241

limbic brain. *See* mammalian brain
Lloyd, J. William, 199–202, 208, 253, 260, 278, 280
loneliness, 238. *See* social anxiety *and* isolation
> and health, 244–250

Loneliness, 245, 250
Long, Barry, 274, 328
longevity, 8, 218, 224, 271. *See* immunity
Love and Survival, 217
Love Busters, 55
Love, Sex & Nutrition, 223, 285
"love vaccine," 220

M

MacDonald, Dennis R., 45
MacLean, Paul, 77–79
Mahayana, 233
Maher, Bill, 9
maithuna, 69
male continence, 129–132
Male Continence, 130–132
mammalian brain, passim
> and mate choice, 83, 96, 266
> cartoon, 122–123
> source of emotions, drives, impulses, 77, 87, 291
> defined, 6, 76–79
> primitive, 81, 133 et seq.
> serves genes, trumps rational brain, 78–83, 123, 166, 210, 249
> seeks pleasure, avoids stress, 126, 139, 150, 209 et seq.
> similar in all mammals, 2, 78–79

marijuana, 54, 301
marital satisfaction, decline in, 3, 12, 28, 50–56, 85, 241. *See* habituation
Markale, Jean, 99

marriage,
> erosion of, 11, 86, 134, 242. *See* divorce rates
> sexless, 2, 9, 51–55, 185
> spiritual, 46–47, 269

Mary Magdalene, 45, 97
Mason, Jackie, 84
massage. *See* oxytocin, and touch
Masters & Johnson, 288
masturbation, 39–41. *See* orgasm
> and mood swings. *See* mood swings
> and prolactin levels. *See* intercourse, compared
> as self-medication, 41, 142, 153, 160, 238 et seq.
> beliefs about. *See* orgasm, popular wisdom
> compulsive. *See* supranormal stimulation and orgasm
> evolutionary purpose, 41
> experiments with avoiding, 163–164, 254 et seq., 267–268. *See also* continence, risks
> frequency in human males, 38
> in history, 148, 239–243

mating program, xvi–xvii, 63, 73 et seq., 93–94, 105 et seq.,
> clash with bonding program, 124, 198
> not limitless, 228, 276

Mead, Margaret, 241
Mean Genes, 74, 135
meditation, 40, 111, 148, 162, 168, 226, 251, 258, 263
Mehinaku, 80
menstruation, 36, 38, 82, 121, 200, 243
menopause, 130, 339–340
merging experience, 23, 169, 194, 201, 279, 281. *See* duality, overcoming
methamphetamine, 106, 151, 157
Miller, Geoffrey, 79
Miller, Henry, 282
monkeys, 198, 228
> and habituation, 5
> and porn, 141,

ABOUT THE AUTHOR

Marnia Robinson (with degrees from Brown and Yale) is a former corporate lawyer who left her career to investigate how ancient sacred-sex prescriptions can heal disharmony in intimate relationships. She and her husband, Gary Wilson (Will), a human-sciences teacher, have given presentations worldwide on the unwelcome effects of evolutionary biology on intimate relationships and the striking parallels between recent scientific discoveries and traditional sacred-sex texts. They maintain the Web site Reuniting: Healing with Sexual Relationships (www. reuniting.info) and have contributed pieces to various books and magazines. They live in Ashland, Oregon.

About North Atlantic Books

North Atlantic Books (NAB) is a 501(c)(3) nonprofit publisher committed to a bold exploration of the relationships between mind, body, spirit, culture, and nature. Founded in 1974, NAB aims to nurture a holistic view of the arts, sciences, humanities, and healing. To make a donation or to learn more about our books, authors, events, and newsletter, please visit www.northatlanticbooks.com.